Ivan Antic

SÂMKHYA

An Ancient Science of Nature and the Human Soul

SAMKHYA PUBLISHING LTD
London, 2022

Translated by
Milica Breber

Proofreading & editing by
James Joshua Pennington, PhD

Cover image:
Shree Kapila Yantra
© Copyright: 2022 by Ivan Antic

The Templar Cross in the background represents
creative rationality and the West.
The form of the yantra and the lotus represents
the wholeness of the human soul and the East.
Nine circles represent the complete development of man
through the principle of eneagrams.

Dedicated to my mother Angelia,
My greatest teacher
And the greatest soul I know

TABLE OF CONTENTS

PREFACE

Sâmkhya is an ancient school of teaching that describes the relationship between nature and human essence. It is distinct in that, unlike all the other teachings which attempt to do the same while defining nature and human essence from the widest perspective possible, it is completely objective and devoid of any metaphysical speculation, be it symbolism or mythologization.

While other teachings deal with the type of nature we can perceive with our senses, where all higher dimensions are represented as being "divine" and "supernatural", *Sâmkhya* treats all the higher dimensions as component parts of natural causality. By doing so, *Sâmkhya* presents nature in all its glory, something that modern science has failed to achieve.

Together with the comprehensive depiction of nature, *Sâmkhya* also presents human nature in a unique way, offering a comprehensive in-depth analysis. Despite the prevalence of teachings that depict humans as sinful creatures alienated from the divine whole, such as modern-day science insisting that humankind originated as an accidental bioproduct that occurred during DNA division error, something akin to the human being an upgraded monkey. To *Sâmkhya*, human essence is nothing but the consciousness of the same Absolute that engenders the entirety of nature.

For the truth to be expressed so simply and deeply, *Sâmkhya* does not resort to complex teachings or explanations, but expresses the whole matter simply and clearly using 'systemic thinking'. The basic characteristic of 'systemic thinking' is an insight into the fact that the living whole is something more than the sum of all its factors where the fundamental properties of a living system come from the interactions and relationships between the factors, and these relationships tend to repeat themselves within certain configurations and schemes. The issue here is the dynamic process of relationships which reflect a certain quality best expressed in scheme mapping, the way it was done a long time ago in *Yi Ching* and *Cabala*.

1

In *Sâmkhya* mapping was arranged by formulating categories of nature (picture 1), the explanation of which comprises the substance of this book.

Finally, becoming acquainted with the relationships given in the scheme cannot be limited to the components of one system only, but they must also cover their environment, the context of the system which addresses the nature of the subject that experiences it. It all points to the vital role a subject plays as the outcome of all the scientific research. The issue of a conscious subject is the ultimate goal of science. It has been discovered that not only do humans act as conscious subjects, setting the conditions of the experiment with which the foundations of nature are revealed, but they alone decide on the outcome of the experiment, on the very nature of reality. The role a conscious subject plays on the nature of reality is not a contemporary issue regarding experimental physics, but was, as such, established by *Sâmkhya* thousands of years ago, in a more profound way than modern physics has managed to execute.

I will attempt here to show that *Sâmkhya* is the first, and to this day unsurpassed, science of human being as a conscious subject and the key factor of reality.

The book is the result of my transcendental experiences and an assay to ascertain and understand them, and not a need to philosophize on the subject. Even the writing itself proved to be a way of establishing my experiences more concretely. Over thirty years ago, I started to write the book to myself first, as a reminder, and only later, in this final edition, I adjusted the contents to modern-day readers. To avoid becoming too subjective, I placed my understanding of the experiences within a theoretical framework which is old enough, proven to be true, and objective. However, I was unable to find a system older than *Sâmkhya*. It later appeared as though *Sâmkhya* was much more comprehensive owing to the experiences I had gone through; as such, they were necessary for a better insight into the system, rendering this a more original and radical depiction than all the previous ones, avoiding subjectivity in *Sâmkhya* at all costs.

With my practice of Buddhist meditation (*zazen*, for about 40 years) and self-research, a scheme of *Prakriti* (nature) categories crystallized all by itself from theory of *Sâmkhya* (picture 1), as the universal map of existence. Not only did I recognize the ontological status of my altered states of consciousness across all the dimensions of astral in it, but the ontology of the religious, philosophical, mystical, scientific, artistic, and psychological experiences, the way they have been passed down to us through history and literature, and the way they manifest in the reality of life, here and now, to many of us. Years of impartial perception and learning have convinced me that the scheme of the categories of nature, in a manner shown in this book, is the universal map on which the ontological status of everything living can be ascertained flawlessly, and relying on this map a traveler on the spiritual path can never be lost trying to know themselves and everything they are.

All my efforts here can be reduced to an attempt to clarify all the details of this ontological map in the context of a holistic view on the world and 'systemic thinking' of the new science. I have explained the scheme in the light of religious, mystical, philosophical, and scientific experiences that are common knowledge, or at least, they have reached me through various writings and observations. In that sense, they are limited, and this depiction is merely an attempt to conduct further research regarding this topic.

The mainstay of *Sâmkhya* is in that the differentiation of human consciousness and human authenticity is realized in terms of nature's entirety (*Prakriti*) and the manifest world – in the transcendental soul (*Purusha*) – and not only within a narrow empirical sphere.

According to Sâmkhya the human soul is the consciousness that propels nature into existence. *Sâmkhya* names the very principle of transcendental, unconditioned consciousness as *Purusha*, i.e., the human. Not only does it speak of an intelligent design, but it also reveals human essence as the conscious subject of intelligence that engenders everything.

Sâmkhya, therefore, places both nature and human essence on the highest ontological level, while other religious and philosophical systems do not exceed specific categories within nature. Additionally, the scientific paradigms remain within empirical experience, as well.

Sâmkhya exceeds that because it is neither a religion nor a philosophy; it originated long before the onset of all the religious and philosophical systems, before all the projections into mythical, abstract, and symbolic interpretations. While other systems of thinking and belief separate the human soul from nature, or merge them in an awkward and unnatural way, *Sâmkhya* reveals their true relationship. It manages to do so because it boldly acts upon the insight into the human soul as being the same consciousness that engenders both nature and all the existence. *Sâmkhya* removes all the mediators between the human soul and existence. The truth is that throughout history such mediators, personified in theological, philosophical, and scientific institutions and paradigms, have proved to be a stumbling block in our attempt to have direct insight into our soul.

In this way, *Sâmkhya*, being a real science, deals with consciousness and how it is connected to the nature of existence. The science of consciousness, therefore, existed long before all the religions and was called *Sâmkhya*. It was not speculative but practical and led to the origin of the scientific practice of systematic human awareness, *yoga*, which is introduced to us in Patanjali's work *Yoga Sutras*. Religions and philosophies arose after the oblivion of this science of consciousness with the human's further decline into increasing conditioning of the mind.

Sâmkhya gives the highest status to human essence, this is the absolute divine consciousness, which engenders existence itself. *Sâmkhya* acknowledges the absolute divine consciousness as the essence of the human soul.

Nowhere else has the human soul been identified so clearly as in *Sâmkhya*.

Correspondingly, nowhere else has nature been revealed so clearly as in *Sâmkhya*.

Author

SCHEME
OF PRAKRITI CATEGORIES
The basic structure of the reality
of cosmic phenomena according to Samkhya

MAHAT = BUDDHI
The highest origin of being = wakefulness or unconditioned,
pure awareness of the outcome of beingness in general

AHAM - KĀRA
"I am a maker", personality, I-ness, will, the principle of individuation
a personification of shaping of everything that is

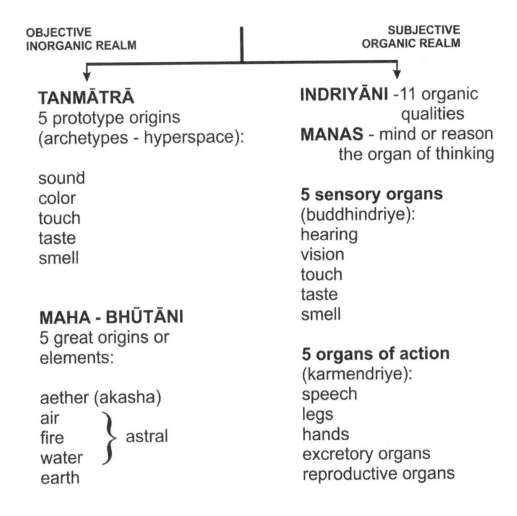

OBJECTIVE INORGANIC REALM	SUBJECTIVE ORGANIC REALM
TANMĀTRĀ 5 prototype origins (archetypes - hyperspace): sound color touch taste smell	**INDRIYĀNI** -11 organic qualities **MANAS** - mind or reason the organ of thinking **5 sensory organs** (buddhindriye): hearing vision touch taste smell
MAHA - BHŪTĀNI 5 great origins or elements: aether (akasha) air fire } astral water earth	**5 organs of action** (karmendriye): speech legs hands excretory organs reproductive organs

INTRODUCTION TO SAMKHYA

1. Basic notions of *Sâmkhya*

The basic structure of *Sâmkhya* system rests on the dualism of two principles: *Purusha* and *Prakriti*. *Purusha* is an abstract principle of consciousness, whereas *Prakriti* is the foundation of being and overall existence. *Purusha* is the transcendental, absolute, and unmanifested principle that engenders existence as such, while *Prakriti* is the whole manifested nature in all of its dimensions and proportions.

In a nutshell, there is no duality between these two principles, they are like two sides of the same coin. Still, it is important to differentiate between the two because the nature of our perception and mind is based on dualism, therefore, for practical purposes of our understanding. *Purusha* is the conscious one, it is the principle of individuation of a conscious subject; *Prakriti* is everything one can become aware of, the world of objects, as it were.

There is no existence without the awareness of existence. In their innermost essence, consciousness and existence are one, but they manifest as being different. Since we, too, are manifested individual beings, we know existence directly in this basic dualism. It is enough. Everything beyond this point becomes the mythology of our mind.

In this way, *Sâmkhya* explains the essence of transcendence (overcoming) which is the foundation of consciousness as such, and its spiritual and religious aspirations: *Purusha*, the human soul, as a principle of human consciousness, always overcomes *Prakriti*, the emergent nature, and the body, whereas a soul is always either above or independent, but we have the experience of existence because our consciousness is identified with the body of nature, with phenomena, like in a dream. Since it is always independent of the body, it can represent the principle of consciousness in the body and nature in general because consciousness itself is the ability of objective overcoming of what is being made conscious of, so that it may be viewed from several aspects and states as well as critical reconsideration, irrelevantly of space and time. Identification of consciousness with the object is invariably a characteristic of narrowed consciousness or unconsciousness. Therefore, awareness in itself is overcoming or transcending. In such a way, *Sâmkhya* reveals the objective consciousness per se. *Sâmkhya* differentiates between the objective awareness through the concept of *Prakriti* as everything that can be made aware of, hence, it can be overcome, too, and *Purusha* is the one who becomes aware and overcomes.

To put it briefly, the essence of consciousness is in transcendence; transcendence is in discrimination or differentiation of consciousness and objects (contents) of consciousness; consciousness of anything is not possible without the experience of transcendence; the experience of transcendence is the essence of the overall human experience and creativity in this world, all the culture and spirituality. To study in detail the differentiation between *Purusha* and *Prakriti* means to realize that *Sâmkhya* represents the science of transcendence, that is to say, consciousness.

The fact that consciousness is at the base of all phenomena we can simply acknowledge in our experience as such. Carefully observe everything you see before you. Everything we see, every form, living being, or thing, existed as an idea first, or the consciousness, principle, and intention, and only later it materialized in the form we see now. For example, the intention to write words created a pencil and stationery; a house originated from the idea of a dwelling; a car comes from the idea of transport; our body was created out of the idea and intention of our soul to express itself in this world. Everything we perceive as "matter" is only the building material, a means of expressing ideas. Matter itself creates nothing because if it were capable of creation, consciousness as such would no longer be required. Everything would be unconscious **because unconscious matter cannot create consciousness**. Every concrete shape that exists is a realization of an idea or consciousness, everything is the result of intelligent design. It all exists to make the human aware and through this act of awareness to be returned to their conscious outcome. Through human awareness existence gains meaning, it becomes finalized, whole, and complete. This is what *Sâmkhya* teaches us: not only how and what the initial point of consciousness is, but also why.

The system of *Sâmkhya* represents the first, the oldest, the purest, and the most objective principle of the differentiation of consciousness in people through discerning between natural and spiritual, unconscious and conscious – *Prakriti* and *Purusha*. *Sâmkhya* is the first fundamental ontology, the science of being and its cognition. All of the experience of the differentiation of consciousness we have become aware of so far, all the culture and science included, will have to be scrutinized by *Sâmkhya* and double-checked for objectivity.

In many other philosophies and religions, this same principle of dualism is contained, albeit conditioned and altered. The principle of *Purusha* has been degraded and modified mentally in a certain way, into the idea of God, representing everything that is good and spiritual, otherwordly, heavenly, whereas *Prakriti* has been made into notions of 'inferior nature', and everything negative and conditioning, 'this-worldly', and material. Esoteric Christianity has brought forth the idea of resurrection as the closest depiction of transcendence of the inferior nature into the divine spirit. Resurrection is nothing but a metaphor of transcendence or overcoming the unconscious and material (*Prakriti*) in the divine spirit of the human (*Purusha*). Only in the system of *Sâmkhya*, these two fundamental principles remained completely devoid of all the mental, ideological, mythological, religious, and symbolic modifications. That brings the importance of *Sâmkhya* to the fore in modern times when the ideas regarding reality have become liberated of mythical and symbolic thinking due to secularization and scientific development, but, at the same time, they are still tainted and abused more than ever before. This makes the purity of the original, objective perception of reality more important than ever.

Prakriti consists of 23 categories (according to the scheme in picture 1.) that compose the whole nature in all the dimensions. When the human becomes aware of all the categories and their functions, they then overcome them, transcend them, and attain perfect consciousness of the reality of existence, and ultimately, of the consciousness of themselves. To know oneself as the pure consciousness (soul or *Purusha*) is not possible without knowing the

9

object of consciousness (*Prakriti*). Therefore, self-knowledge (*Purusha*) is attained by the perfect cognition of the true nature of objects or contents of the consciousness (*Prakriti*). Humans, then, become authentic; they become *Purusha* because the notion itself also means *human*, or more accurately put *human essence*, as such. Namely, from *Purusha*, as the principle of transcendental cosmic consciousness that engenders everything, individual monads of consciousness known to us as souls are born. They further incarnate into the bodies and reside in nature, in *Prakriti*, transferring the principle of transcendental cosmic consciousness into the overall formed life. All the natural forms of life are the result of the intelligent design of the highest consciousness, and not some unconscious elements that are unsuccessfully explained through evolution, or myths, and God's creation. There is a certain evolution happening in life, but it, too, is a product of the intelligent design of the transcendental consciousness, rather than nature itself.

In *Sâmkhya*, through the notion of *Purusha*, for the first time in history, and nowhere else so clearly and directly, the highest cosmological and spiritual principle unites with human essence, with the soul or Self.

Nowhere else but in *Sâmkhya* through the polarization of *Purusha* and *Prakriti* is the relationship between the consciousness and existence revealed so clearly in all the aspects that point to their unity.

Sâmkhya shows us that human essence is the same as the essence of reality the whole cosmos rests on, that cognition of reality is not a possibility to humans without attaining self-knowledge, hence, they must seek for it within themselves first – and, consequently, they must be the reality they aspire toward. The same has been discovered by modern science after realizing the key role the subject plays in quantum physics experiments, with the slight difference that science is still in the dark as to the kind of practice which would connect the conscious subject with the reality on the most subtle quantum level and become its creative factor. Such a practice has been around for a long time, it comes from *Sâmkhya* and was presented in Patanjali's work *Yoga Sutras*.

In other systems and religions this truth is blurred and demonstrated by giving advice "know thyself" or in mystical depictions of God-knowledge as self-knowledge. Only in *Sâmkhya*, it is shown objectively and concretely with all the details.

The purpose of working on one's self and acquiring self-knowledge is only in achieving awareness or awakening. One does not have to become anything new because *Purusha* resides deep in the soul. All it takes is to stop identifying with what one is not, and one is nothing of the manifested, of *Prakriti*. As souls, humans are only a principle of consciousness in accordance with which *Prakriti* or nature shapes itself and creates everything that exists in the manifested cosmos. ***The very presence of human souls as witnesses is the creative factor which initiates the forming of nature and all life.***

Individual souls do nothing, and neither does their ultimate outcome *Purusha*, they are devoid of properties, they affect **with their mere presence** all the nature that forms and creates, the way the metal reacts to the proximity of a magnet. Without them, nature would be a completely unconscious field of causality and conditioning, without sense or purpose. All the negativity taking place is a direct reflection of the lack of soul's consciousness.

The measure of the presence of souls in nature is not the same. Consequently, their influence on forming nature is not the same. The weak presence of the soul is otherwise known as 'young souls' and their impact of consciousness is far weaker, nature predominates in them with its conditioning. A strong and much fuller presence of the soul in *Prakriti* is characterized by a greater presence of the consciousness of oneself, of one's true nature, and with it the overcoming of natural causation and bigger power to act on the forming of nature. The higher presence of the soul generates a higher presence of good, beautiful, constructive, and harmonious; the diminished presence of the soul paves the way for the ugly, destructive, inharmonious, and evil. A complete presence of the soul is characterized by complete independence of *Prakriti*, total human freedom or authenticity combined with the highest power to act. In other traditions, it is called human enlightenment, liberation of the soul, or resurrection.

The self-knowledge (*Purusha*) is attained through the perfect knowing of the true nature of objects or contents of the consciousness (*Prakriti*), therefore, in order for the soul to be realized or liberated it must ground itself to the maximum, it must make itself more present here and now for the existence and life itself, in *Prakriti*. In other words, for humans to know and realize their soul the *Prakriti* or nature must be known as accurately as possible, with scientific precision. Only then is *Prakriti* or nature, fully realized. ***This grounding signifies all the maturing of people and humankind.***

To be able to participate creatively in life and nature, souls incarnate into physical bodies with oblivion, insufficiently aware of their true, transcendental essence, *Purusha*, and end up identified with their body and nature, *Prakriti*. All of human development can be reduced to awakening the soul's consciousness by becoming alert to all the secrets of nature. Having known nature as such, it cognizes its true essence at the same time. The soul knows itself through the insight that it is nothing of the being and existence (*Prakriti*) as such, but it represents the consciousness (*Purusha*) which engenders being and existence itself – ***during its time in the body***. This is a long process and composes all the drama of life that humans experience. It also consists of multiple incarnations of souls into the body, and not just a single life.

By accelerating the process, by being able to discern the soul and consciousness, one becomes aware of the essence of all the "spiritual practices" and working on oneself that is present in all the spiritual and religious traditions, although many of them have lost their authenticity and degenerated into imitation and even abuse. The only tradition that has kept the original meaning and the practice of differentiation of the soul's consciousness (*Purusha*) as regards the being (*Prakriti*), is the practice of yoga, or meditation the way it has been recorded in Patanjali's *Yoga Sutras*, in the meditative practice of early Buddhism, and in Zen Buddhism (shikantaza).

Sâmkhya, Patanjali's yoga, and meditative practice of early, Pali Buddhism in their essence represent the same thing, like an equilateral triangle, no matter how they get presented, they lead to the same outcome, albeit from different angles. Although Buddhism does not make any references to *Sâmkhya*, it defines the practical realization of differentiation of consciousness as regards the existence itself, or the awakening as it is theoretically presented in *Sâmkhya*. Initially, this practice of the differentiation of consciousness was also present in the oldest religion in the world *Jainism*, as the ascetic purification of an individual soul (*jiva*) from all that is bodily (*Prakriti*), but this practice has gradually deteriorated over time and became religion reduced to imitation and materialism only.

Awakening of the human soul is directly linked to the relationship between Spirit and nature, i.e., *Purusha* and *Prakriti.* **Spirit and nature are connected through individual souls and their awareness, that is to say, the consciousness an individual soul brings along contributes to the whole nature**. Nature automatically forms under the attractive force of the consciousness. All phenomena in the world happen following the same pattern. The Absolute, as the source of consciousness, manifests itself through its individual souls. That is why it is often said that souls are emanations of the divine Absolute. This takes place to practically and effectively engender the Absolute, or the consciousness of the Divine, to experience all of the aspects of its existence, in all the details, all of the opposites and possibilities, even by (seemingly) alienated individuals using their free will and self-knowledge to achieve the purpose. For the same reason, the Absolute, who is indivisible by nature and nothing can be outside of it, creates an illusion of a separate individual (the human) to recognize itself in it. Only then is the awareness of existence present in absolute terms, in all the aspects of existence, from the highest to the lowest. The consciousness of the Absolute becomes realized only through humans in everything that is; in the whole of nature it manifests itself through all possible forms, but only to a certain degree, in some aspects and possibilities. However, in humans, it manifests through the human karmic drama, it encompasses all the meaning of all the aspects and possibilities of existence, that is to say, it attains the most subtle awareness of itself.

Manifestation or emanation of the consciousness of the Absolute (*Purusha*) in all of its aspects and possibilities (*Prakriti* or nature) has its gradation, proportions, and dimensions. They are shown in the scheme of the categories of nature or *Prakriti* (picture 1.). The dimensions of manifestation of the consciousness in nature we can also see in the versatility of all the natural forms that are about, most of all, in the general division into minerals, plants, animals, and people. All of these forms of existence conduce consciousness and perception of the existence of the Absolute consciousness into all of the forms of existence and experience ***and retrieve it enriched to the divine Absolute or Purusha as the awareness of itself***. This return may be understood as the circling of the whole, the way it is presented in Taoistic philosophy with the symbol of circling of *yin* and *yang* in the symbol of *tai chi*.

Man (*Purusha*) is a conscious subject of all the objective nature (*Prakriti*). In humans, the same consciousness that was only experiencing the simplest forms of existence finally contracts itself, through the very shaping and movement, in minerals, plants, and animals alike. Before the incarnation into a human body, the individual soul created all of the mineral, plant, and animal forms in higher dimensions. Due to this connectedness, there is a sense of energy union with the entirety of nature within humans which manifests as love toward existence. It is in those moments when humans are most aware of themselves and existence itself. In other words, this is precisely when humans correctly recognize consciousness of themselves as the consciousness of the very meaning of existence.

2. Transcendence is the ability to discern between the natural and spiritual in other traditions

To understand the basic principles of consciousness, which is transcendence, or *Sâmkhya* in its rudimentary form, without any impurities of symbolic and mythical distortion, the way they were shown to us in the scheme of categories (picture 1.), we must examine to what degree their principles survived in other ancient heritages with all the varying modifications. We are more accustomed to them because they are more familiar to us. To reach a diamond in the rough, we must clean it of all the layers covering and smearing it.

Since the beginning of our journey to survive in this world, we have made a serious effort to distinguish between what has been given to us naturally, and what is holy and exceeds natural causality and regeneration, and effort to discern eternal from the transient, immortal from mortal, and consequently good from evil.

In other words, our primeval aspiration has always been to be different from nature in spirit, to be aware because the fundamentals of consciousness invite discrimination, and the essence of nature is in causal connectedness of all its occurrences, in identification, or the conditionality of all phenomena. An objective awareness of nature is the only way to overcome conditionality.

A religious experience of this quality was expressed in the olden times in the form of emphasizing a sacred religious experience as opposed to that of the profane. From time immemorial, humans have made a conscious effort to distinguish conscious from the unconscious, to establish and expand knowledge as a precondition for their survival, to discriminate between the spiritual and bodily with equal clarity as the heaven from earth, or life from death. Everything spiritual they were able to acknowledge as being their authenticity and liberty, like that which is of heavenly or divine in character, that what gives a unique meaning to every phenomenon in the general unity of nature. Without freedom of this kind, life has no meaning and becomes an area of conflict of alienated parts and meaningless transience.

In all the old cultures a visible discontent with humans as is naturally given is present, and a profound aspiration for the "second birth" is imminent in the conscious and spiritual way of living. All the myths, rituals, and legends from the dawning of history show a longing to liberate the human body of unconscious natural elements and transform them into the embodiment of Spirit, the freedom to act, create, be responsible, and introduce culture into the civilization. Somebody may become a "true man" to the degree they cease to be a "natural humans". This metamorphosis is not a result of some natural process, like it is the case with all the other psychophysical activities, but solely a cultural and spiritual act of accepting the full responsibility for the eternal meaning of beingness which is a feat aimed at the very few, spiritually mature individuals – it is an act of free will of a complete person. Apart from the diverse natural connectedness of everything, the only truly new occurrence that takes place in the cosmos is a conscious personality and its free will. This transformation is brought about through the experience of transcendence of natural causality. It is something that has yet to happen. It happens only in the human personality once it becomes conscious and whole. Without a "second birth" in free will and consciousness, it was assumed, rightly so, that humans do not exist at all, and do not exist a "material beings", given that the birth of their physical body is in no way different from other processes of reproduction in nature – characterized by transience, perishability, and dying of everything that is born (John, 3:3-7).

A fundamental differentiation of this kind, that is to say, the experience of transcendence gave rise to all great religions and schools of ethics. Wherever there is a mention of the "second birth", resurrection, and a "new man" being born the issue is, in reality, about the awakening of human essence, soul, or *Purusha*.

Due to the necessity of the second birth religiousness and spirituality have come to exist, this insistence has also produced all the culture humans enjoy whose general meaning is in overcoming unconscious natural causality and time. A religious person's whole life is a process of awareness of their soul. The quality of every type of religiousness is in its longing for eternal values which proves that nowadays the state of natural birth is not authentic and can, therefore, often be painful even unbearable. It appears to be unbearable because one's physical birth has not begun to exist truly in its authentic state; it is still a spontaneous flow of natural happening which entails all the physical movement, emotional, and mental activities. Destiny or karmic drama of every human is a reflection of the process of awakening, following the measure to which our life is a part of spontaneous natural phenomena as opposed to the measure to which we remain free, making decisions and overpowering natural urges with our soul's consciousness.

Humans begin to exist in this world only when they raise awareness of their transcendental soul, only when they become conscious beings. By mere physical birth, humans received only the first true chance to do it consciously. When they were born, they were created beings. All the beings in nature come about in the same way, their survival depends on this. They are born of others and are, consequently, conditioned by others. Humans are different from all the beings in that their essence is not of this world. They begin to exist only when they initiate their essence (*Purusha*), and together with it their free will and the power to act. Secondly, a

16

true birth is their act of creation which can happen only when they acknowledge themselves as the personification of the Creator, i.e., the Spirit that engenders everything (*Purusha*). This second, true human birth is therefore nothing but acknowledging everything humans have always been. Hence, the only proper name for this can be awakening, the way it has already been done in Buddhism, or the liberation from illusion, as was presented in the tradition of *Advaita Vedanta* by Adi Shankara.

The fundamental importance of the 'second birth' is best expressed in the Gnostic vision of a bird breaking the eggshell representing the cosmos. For humans to be truly born, they must break the shell of the naturally given world the way a bird breaks the eggshell, begins to fly of its own will, and only then begins to exist truly. The natural, biological birth of the human is in many ways similar to the origin of the egg. Humans are 'born' but it is hardly the final act; their biological birth is only a possibility for the other, true spiritual birth, like the bird, a symbol of the spirit, which has yet to emerge forth from its eggshell.

The second adequate comparison could be with a seed and a tree. With the biological birth, the human is a seed that holds a tree within. It must fall apart for it to sprout into a tree that yields abundant fruit. If it does not change, it will only rot. If it wishes to keep itself, it will lose itself. If it surrenders, it will be granted eternal life. This describes the natural process of the human's origin, first closed off in bodily subjectivity, followed by spiritual growth that unlocks the potential of the soul; for a human to manifest that what objectively is – that is the whole idea of resurrection.

If the process of origin has been finalized, if we truly began to exist with mere natural birth, then we could never become aware of ourselves, nor would our existence become personal during the act of awakening. None of this would ever happen. Individuality would not be possible then. It would continue to be a process of natural determination and we would hardly be any different from animals.

The essential human aspect happens only with the transcendence of natural causation. Humans becomes truly human only when they cease to identify with the body and bodily mind, with becoming aware of themselves in a wider context, in the context of the whole, of the divine consciousness which engenders the body and mind. The bigger their identification with the body is, the lesser the human they are, hence, the bigger the suffering. The less identified one is with the body, the greater the human one must be; the nobler, and spiritual, more one's own, and more objective toward everything. There is not a single example of an ideal of humanity, spirituality, and nobility that is not comprised of overcoming the egocentric identification with the body and ego.

The experience of sacred as opposed to that of the profane not only represents the essence of religiosity, but also the consciousness itself whose foundation is in discriminating between the subject and object, or the world known from the unknown one.

The earliest philosophical thought expresses the same differentiation as the foundation of the awareness of being in the question: "What is Being?" "Why are there beings at all, instead of Nothing?"[1] This question is possible only in the context of differentiation between *Purusha* and *Prakriti* which is "beings at all", in the context provided by *Sâmkhya*.

Nature exists with a simple purpose of acquiring the full meaning of its existence, its outcome or essence, only in regards to the consciousness of the human soul (*Purusha*). Up until that point, it appears as unrealized, pointless, and destructive. Only a spiritually resurrected human (as a result of the experience of transcendence) sees the world for what it is: as the holiness of the divine creation. In such true seeing of things, as they are, their spiritual authenticity and freedom are encountered. It is immanent to being.

The more the human soul is unaware of itself, the more nature seems destructive and conditioning. The soul's consciousness and nature are mutual and polarized, rather than dualistic and exclusive. Without manifested nature, consciousness would be merely abstract and basically nothing, and without the soul's consciousness, nature would not have possibilities for a meaningful creation and, therefore, for the survival itself. It would have no reason to exist. It would be a dungeon for the being without the possibility of

---

[1] See more details on this in Martin Heideggers's work:"Introduction to Metaphysics" (Einfuhrung in die Metaphysik von Martin Heidegger, Max Niemeyer Verlag, Tubingen, 1966.)

escaping into the freedom, in short, lifeless. Nature is not possible without the soul's consciousness. In their essence they are one, when we know the essence of nature, we then see it as the divine consciousness and nothing but that; such cognition we can have only when we become aware of our soul. When we are unaware of reality, nature appears to us as dead matter and our enemy. However, nature is only a way of manifesting the divine consciousness. The consciousness gives meaning and an ideal according to which the natural phenomena keep perfecting themselves.

This lays the answer to the question at our feet as to in what context the 'second birth' and transcendence of natural causality can be considered a possibility at all. It is possible only in the context of understanding the polarization of the consciousness and nature (*Purusha* and *Prakriti*) – by cognizing their essence – which something that *Sâmkhya* presents us with.

3. Sâmkhya is an archaic model of transcendence through acknowledging the unity of consciousness and existence

If the purity and grandeur of the vision of humans were measured only in terms of liberating their spiritual authenticity from any natural causality of beingness, and a different or a fairer measure there is not in sight, then we would be right in saying that *Sâmkhya* aspires to be the purest vision of humans – liberated from any mythology or symbolics, even metaphysics, at that.

Coming to us from behind the horizon of measurable time, but becoming more familiar as one of the six medieval philosophical systems in India, *Sâmkhya* represents the oldest and the most direct attempt of humans at expressing the essence of their spirituality, origin, and purpose of their consciousness with which they exist in nature as unique and creative beings. That what the teaching of *Sâmkhya* fundamentally sets apart from all the other occurrences in a spiritual culture that originally set out with the same intentions is its clarity and wholeness. It encompasses the overall beingness without exceptions, it systematically reveals origin, purpose, and all the conditionality of not only the objective, physical world, but of the subjective psychological experience, as well, in a completely straightforward way, parsing all the components of experience and existence, without added fantasy, symbolism, or myth. It does not impose itself as a form of interpretation but only reveals what is. It achieves that only through a conscious insight and practical discerning of everything existing in time (defined in the notion of *Prakriti*) from the divine consciousness (defined as *Purusha*), whose unconditionality engenders the being to be, that is to say, to be aware of itself (which is marked by the *buddhi* category). Surgically and meticulously *Sâmkhya* dissects all the categories of existence as they are (scheme in picture 1.), and by doing so only discloses what existence facilitates and what it is.

The unique clarity of *Sâmkhya* is based on its polarization of the being (as *Prakriti*) and the freedom that engenders it (*Purusha*). This underlines *Sâmkhya* as the highest ideal of objectivity. This kind of polarization makes things more clearly, it crystallizes the consciousness of the being, its differentiation, and leads us to recognize the archaic prototype of the fundamental ontology in *Sâmkhya*, rather than sheer dualism, like the previous interpreters of this system have suggested. Advocating the classical metaphysical standpoint, they wrongly projected *Purusha* into a spiritual monad alienated from nature. We will perceive *Purusha* here as the pure unconditionality that engenders all the existence, and the awareness of it (*buddhi*) most of all.

Liberating the spiritual essence of humans from natural causality, from death, and transience is a fundamental aspiration of all the religious traditions and systems of self-development. It is aspiration toward the transcendence of the conditioned existence. This aspiration has crystalized everywhere as the differentiation between the spiritual and natural, real and false, divine and mundane, "salvation of the soul" in Christianity, or the overcoming of suffering in Buddhism. This aspiration has attained its most profound reach in Buddhism, especially in Nagarjuna's teaching where two kinds of realities are discernible: *samvrti* or the relative truth which is the product of reason that like a veil covers the absolute truth, and *paramartha* which is the ultimate purpose or transcendence in the widest sense. While the primeval aspiration for human authenticity in other systems and religions manifested itself in a more or less indirect way, through some myth, an idea of God and resurrection, in *Sâmkhya*, yoga, and Buddhism is expressed quite clearly as the urgency of transcendence within oneself, within one's own being. It was possible because Buddhism as such stems from (Patanjali's) yoga, and yoga is a practical experience of transcendence. This practice of yoga exists owing to its theoretical background: *Sâmkhya*. While in other religions gods and their followers kill and fight over some territory, shallow water, and supremacy threatening the disobedient with eternal fire and sulfur, *Sâmkhya* objectively, impartially, and clearly demonstrates the following:

(1) what is to be overcome or transcended (here *Prakriti* is the foundation of the being);

(2) what engenders this transcendence (*Purusha*, the human soul that overcomes and engenders the being);

(3) what the meaning of the whole process is (for human to acknowledge their authenticity in their soul, *Purusha*), and

(4) what the position of humans in the whole process is (for them to be makers, doers, a suitable place in which – *Prakriti* - and their meaning – *Purusha* – permeate one another and discern, thus becoming aware).

To put it briefly, there exists the only Absolute One that has two aspects: the active and the passive one. In the active aspect resides *Prakriti* or nature whereas in the passive or static one is *Purusha* or the consciousness. The active aspect actualizes the static or the potential one. Nature actualizes the consciousness that would be nothing in itself without the actualization in all the forms of the existence of nature. This actualization is followed by an outcome of its own, and its ending is in a self-conscious personality of humans where the consciousness acknowledges itself as its own essence or soul, but this time in its actualized and life-giving form.

Through the teaching of *Purusha* and *Prakriti, Sâmkhya* provides a context for understanding the meaning of transcendence. Transcendence is awakening. Awakening entails two facts that the being is unconscious and that it can become conscious. These two facts are: *Prakriti* as the unconscious being and *Purusha* that must overcome (transcend) the being if it is to engender the awareness of it.

* * *

In other systems, religions, and philosophies human essence and purpose were trying to find themselves in some modifications of the being itself, in *Prakriti*, in its sensory or supersensory forms of existence (that were proclaimed to be "divine" to suit the purpose), or in the oblivion of existence while only in *Sâmkhya* human essence boldly recognized itself in the transcendental consciousness that engenders the existence itself as such, in the divine soul it originates from and that the whole nature aspires toward, in *Purusha*. All the religions (apart from Buddhism), philosophies, and belief systems are mechanisms of the oblivion of the consciousness of soul or Self, projections into space and time, loss of presence in reality. Only in *Sâmkhya* does human authenticity differentiate itself in relation to existence in general, the way it is, through awareness, and not an ideological conviction while in other traditions it was sought after within the conditioned beingness (*Prakriti*). This is the reason why it can be said quite truthfully about *Sâmkhya* that it represents the first real fundamental ontology, the basis for knowing the world. The world we perceive largely depends on our focus, the point from which we observe it which caused the modern philosophy to adopt a view of questioning the fundamentals of cognition of that what is. A more fundamental view than the one *Sâmkhya* sets forth is impossible to find because it knows the subject for what it is, equaling it with unconditionality or the transcendental consciousness that engenders everything that is.

What does this fact mean in practical terms? Does it mean that the consciousness which engenders everything is human essence? It means that humans attain a conscious distinction of themselves as regards nature once they overcomes projecting its existence into space and time, and at the point when he, as the conscious subject, becomes aware of the fact that they are the very outcome of the overall existence. Up until that point, they did not begin to exist in an authentic sense, only nature existed before then spontaneously governing 'his' body, feelings, and thoughts. By projecting themselves into nature humans give it all the power over themselves. This state entails two things at least: firstly, not even nature itself, while impacting the body like this, is realized in its sense and is therefore out of balance and destructive; and secondly, the chief reason why humans are while being in this state, completely identified with the natural phenomena, has no peace in their realization, and suffers as a consequence of it. By discriminating the consciousness of their soul from the elements of nature, they within themselves lead to authenticity both nature and the soul that engenders all of this. This is the whole point of transcendence.

Discrimination which is the issue here entails neither dualism nor renunciation from anything, only enlightenment. Existence in its essence is the consciousness itself. Existence appears to us as something coming from the outside that is dominantly unconscious (*Prakriti*) only because our standpoint is like that – because we are unaware of ourselves as the pure consciousness itself (*Purusha*). The problem is only in us. The dualism of conscious – unconscious, *Purusha - Prakriti* exists only in our observation, and not as some objective outer reality.

Human consciousness is engendered by the very forces that engender existence itself, both the conscious subject and the world as such – this has always been true for existence itself and for the human, in its essence. Our consciousness is only a spark of the same consciousness that induces the entirety of existence. There is no multitude of consciousnesses. It is one and the same in everything; it only manifests itself individually in the individual human. Therefore, nothing gets divided, and by our submission or transcendence, we abandon nothing, but become what we are meant to be. Also, even though it appears like a paradox, through the transcendence of existence, we affirm the realization of the meaning of existence.

* * *

The whole of *Sâmkhya* could be reduced to the following: to the being and the consciousness that invites the being into existence. The being is everything that exists in any way possible. Only that what engenders everything can engender the awareness of everything. That is why consciousness is present in the most conscious being – in humans – as their essence. It is present to a lesser degree in everything else and that facilitates human perception of the meaning of everything else. Therefore, for humans to realize their essence all they need to do is to divert their attention and all of the life energy away from bondage to the objective beingness and turn it (with the practice of meditation) toward themselves, toward their Self or the source of their consciousness. This turning toward themselves is transcendence at the same time because, with it, humans overcome the manifested being, and become all of that which generates existence.

Transcendence and turning exist only for the mind which is attached to its objects, to the outside; only because of identification does it appear to humans that they must divert themselves from this world to 'realize' immortal spiritual essence; they must abandon 'something' in order to gain 'something'. It is nothing but a mind game. *Purusha* is transcendental only to the conditioned mind; to the being it is immanent.

The secret of transcendence and turning toward oneself is in the following paradox: when subjects become completely aware of themselves without any objectivization, as the pure 'I am', ***they, then, ceases to be a subject (I), and become pure objectivity, pure existence, and, at that moment, existence reveals itself as the consciousness that engenders everything.***

The subject (I) seems like a detached and separate entity, something 'subjective' only when we experience ourselves through objectivization, as one of the objects amongst the numerous other objects. When we do not see ourselves and our true nature, we think we are separate individuals. The mistake is in that the measure of outer objects we tend to apply to the nature of the subject, to ourselves, and based on that mistake we project all the objects. When we turn toward ourselves and see ourselves, 'I' as it truly is, we see that our essence is the consciousness that engenders everything, that our true 'I' is its individual expression, and there is nothing objective, nothing else out there.

Sâmkhya bases its spirituality on the discrimination of the being in general (*Prakriti*) and the one who is aware (*Purusha*). Nature is basically our relationships, as humans, toward ourselves; its existence depends on our state of consciousness. It is not objectivistic – something that is objective and external. The illusion that nature is an objective outer world exists only because of the illusion of subjectivity. ***The more we are convinced that we are a separate, independent subject, the more we see the world as an object. The objective***

24

world is only a reflection of our subjectivity. That is why space and time in nature are relative occurrences that are entirely dependent on the human's state of mind. It is a mutual process: **when humans are insufficiently aware of themselves, of their soul, automatically as a consequence of that the world of objects is created, namely as the materialization of their unconsciousness**. The whole physical universe is a materialization of human unconsciousness. In that sense, it is often said that the world is an illusion, *maya*, that life is nothing but a dream, but it also means that humans create their reality, even when they are not aware of it. The only way to become aware of ourselves is through work and karma; we learn our true nature in contrast to outer reality. They already do so through culture and science. They are still far away from the goal. To accomplish it successfully only one more step is needed: to become aware of the true nature of the very consciousness. That is where the science of Sâmkhya steps in. **Without the awareness of the true nature of consciousness as our own essence and the essence of the existence itself, we cannot do anything right or proper with our consciousness**.

* * *

The whole schematic structure of the *Sâmkhya* category represents consistency in enabling direct and clear disclosure of the being as it is. The categories of *Sâmkhya* are the guiding light for the culture of the objective designing of the being, awareness, and affirmation of the soul's consciousness in this world. However, the former depictions of the *Sâmkhya* systems have been somewhat different than ours.

In modern depictions of Indian philosophy, *Sâmkhya* invariably gets portrayed as a dualistic school that deals with the relationship of the transcendental Spirit (*Purusha*) on one side, and independently functioning nature (*Prakriti*) on the other side, which consists of 23 categories in total. It is claimed that it, by means of paradox, ties and deceives the Spirit away from its authenticity, freedom, unconditionality, and perfection. They all mostly end with a conclusion that the system emphasizes insurmountable essentialism and paradox where the perfect and timeless Spirit, which is human essence, somehow gets caught and enthralled by time creations and activities of nature, that it inexplicably identifies with its unconditionality, causing humans to experience all the trivial dramas caused by the imposed and inauthentic beingness of the world (*samsara*) as though it were their fate. Humans endure pain, suffering, and endangerment, and consequently the struggle for liberation from suffering.[2]

We will show here that such gross misunderstanding of *Sâmkhya* stems from misunderstanding the very categories of *Prakriti*. They bridge over the gap between the transcendental being (*Purusha*) and the experiential world (*Prakriti*) by demonstrating all of the relativity of spacetime manifestation of the world. Therefore, *Sâmkhya* neither falls under the category of naive essentialist views, nor the dualist systems. Misunderstanding of the categories was inevitable because the basic condition for understanding them is not only personal but the cultural maturity of the society on the whole. Two prime categories are personality (*aham-kâra*) and intellect (*buddhi*), and they define maturing or contraction of time. The system which discloses the true nature of the being cannot be understood in any other way than in the maturation of time which engenders the authenticity of the being itself. We will see that the notion of *Prakriti* was impossible to understand in the right way before understanding quantum nature as the universal field of reality. The same applies to the other categories *Sâmkhya* teaches about. Modern physics has yet to grasp their understanding. By relying on *Sâmkhya*, one may understand the fundamental facts of nature in a far better way.

A typical misunderstanding of *Sâmkhya* can also occur due to the lack of meditative practice as a necessary precondition for understanding some of its interpreters. Namely, the basic paradox, the way unconditioned *Purusha* ends up being conditioned by *Prakriti*, signals the wrong approach to things, i.e., failing to take into account the seer of the problem. An individual soul, *jiva*, is the one that identifies *Purusha* with *Prakriti*, and not *Purusha* itself. Humans are the one who should, in their individual experience, actualize the unconditionality of *Purusha*, and not *Purusha* itself – it is always unconditioned.

---

[2] On such a classical depiction of *Sâmkhya* see: Sarvepalli Radhakrishnan: *Indian Philosophy*, and Mircea Eliade: *Yoga, Immortality, and Freedom*.

Sâmkhya is not some dualistic teaching but only expresses itself in terms of dualism due to the very nature of an unrealized individual soul that this teaching is intended for, a person is the only one who sees things subjectively in dualism. Why does *Sâmkhya* use the terms of dualism is perhaps best explained by Lao Tzu at the beginning of his *Tao Te Ching*: 'The nameless is the beginning of Heaven and Earth; the named is the mother of all things... These two have the same origin but differ in name. That is the secret of secrets, the gate to all mysteries.' Of the pure being as One nothing can be said, even that it is. If we intend to utter a few words on the subject and thing in the most straightforward manner, we must do so by discerning One into the existing one, what is in every way possible, and into what the existent engenders, brings into awareness, what invites a being into existence; into a material foundation and the idea which turns matter into form. That is why *Sâmkhya* speaks of *Prakriti* as the being, and of *Purusha* as the one that causes the being to come into existence. It works by guiding the ordinary human understanding to enlightenment or self-knowledge, and moves standard human understanding along the lines of relative dimensions of subject and object; hence – dualism. ***Dualistic conceptualization is the necessity of thinking and not the state of the reality itself***. *Sâmkhya* has achieved the understanding of unity through dualism for an average human because their experience of the world is dualistic due to subjectivity, and it did not proclaim duality as the highest reality. Apart from this, dualistic conceptualization is the most direct and also the purest. Without it, thinking declines into a myth or symbolism. As it has been illustrated in Tao Te Ching (42): 'The Way gave birth to one; One gave birth to two; Two gave birth to three. Three gave birth to all things.' This 'two' refers to dualism, right next to One. From 'three" a myriad of concepts and myths are created.

Purusha causes the presence of consciousness in *Prakriti*, through the human consciousness organizes *Prakriti* through humans into a higher, purposeful order, into technology, civilization, and culture.

Sâmkhya is unique in that it presents nature in all of its categories: from the highest intuitive and conscious cognition (*mahat-buddhi*), its implementation and reflection in the personality (*aham-kâra*), to all the sensory and organic abilities (*indriyâni*) in all the dimensions, from the physical to the superphysical (*tanmâtrâ* and *maha-bhŭtâni*).[3]

The division into organic and inorganic worlds set forth here does not correspond with the scientific division, at least the one found in chemistry and biology. It simply refers to the symbolic designation of the mode of beingness.

It is as though this scheme represents a distant prototype of the modern division of reality into **psychic** (*res cogitans*) - *indriyâni*; **physical** (*res extensa*) - *tanmâtrâ* and *maha-bhŭtâni*, and **cultural** - *aham-kâra* and *mahat-buddhi*.

A more accurate depiction in the spirit of *Sâmkhya*, **the categories of mahat-buddhi, aham-kâra, and manas represent the ontological or cognitive area of Prakriti, and all the other categories represent the ontic or the area of objective existence, the existence itself.** We should do well to remember this for understanding well all the future explanations.

The scheme of *Prakriti* categories encompasses all the possible experiences: sensory, psychological, scientific, artistic, religious, and mystical. In *Sâmkhya* all the natural laws find their place, from evolution and mechanics to quantum physics without discrepancies because they deal with its various dimensions and proportions. For example, quantum laws are applied in *akasha* and the laws of mechanics in the element of earth. This unites the microcosm and macrocosm without discrepancies.

It is the only one amongst a plethora of systems that successfully unites philosophy with nature because it never set them apart in the first place, as it is not one-sided. The highest mystical states are equally close to it as is the harshest reality because it delves into the relationship between consciousness and nature from their experiences, and not by their division or emphasizing one at the expense of the other – which is always the case when interpretation is put ahead of experience. It interprets nothing but ascertains everything the way it is.

Since it presents the whole nature, in all of its dimensions, as one big field of causality, *Sâmkhya* represents the supreme prin-

---

[3] See the scheme of the *Prakriti* categories, picture number 1.

ciple of tolerance. It justifies the existence of everything: everything that exists in any way possible has its cause for existence. It is, therefore, above good and evil. Nothing is unnatural to it since *Prakriti* is comprehensive.

Apart from this whole area of causal but purposeful time phenomena (*Prakriti*), *Sâmkhya* indicates the unconditioned principle of consciousness (*Purusha*) as the fundamental reason for the existence of everything, our awareness of phenomena (*buddhi*) first and foremost. It is neither separate from nature nor in dualism with it, although it is independent of its activities. In nature it directly manifests only through the human's self-knowledge; it is the only opening of nature through which the spirit of absolute freedom seeps through directly and lights up entirely. Through human likeness, nature directly opens and discloses its outcome. In all other forms, it does so in an indirect way, as the attractor of the evolution of nature in overcoming conditionality for the sake of survival which is the purpose of forming all living beings. In a nutshell, it manifests as life itself.

The spirituality of *Sâmkhya* presents the crucial problem of every culture and civilization, and that is the relationship between natural necessity (social restrictions included) and freedom. It demonstrates how freedom manifests in nature: although it is immanent to the being itself because there would be nothing were it not for freedom, it does not manifest itself equally and diffusely everywhere because it would be disintegrated then, but it manifests completely only through the human soul, as the peak of human culture. In such a way, *Sâmkhya* gives meaning to humans in such a way that is not reflected in any other spiritual tradition. Everywhere humans look up from the shadow of gods and higher forces. Here and there the divine essence of humans is expressed ever so slightly, only to be superseded by their sinful, problematic, and conditioned nature. *Sâmkhya* is quite adamant in that respect, as well: *Purusha* is the human; both in the absolute and the relative sense.

Having established *Purusha* as the original freedom which is immanent to existence, to human essence (*Purusha*, from which the human soul stems), one denies the reality and authenticity of suffering, as well as, conditionality because **what is conditioned by**

time cannot attain eternal freedom. For something like that to hap-
pen, the soul (Purusha) must be primevally free. That what is by its
nature, in its essence, bound, can never be free, whereas the experience of liberated and enlightened people testifies to the fact that
the human soul can be free. *It can be so because its freedom is imma-*
nent, essential. Something cannot come out of nothing. Everything
is merely an actualization of what was already present in the form
of potentiality. That explains why freedom can exist only because
we are fundamentally free already. The issue is only whether we
manifest it or not, whether we reside in our essence or not. If the
experience of suffering and inauthenticity exists, it is only a sign
that humans are not integrated within themselves and with their
essence, that they are not awake because they forget themselves,
their soul, that they have been cast out of the heavenly state of
their Self, from the reality in which they reside only when they are
awakened, and that they function on the lower categories of bigger
conditionality of beingness as if through a dream, using minimal
abilities of their mind (*manas*) and body (*indriyâni*). Since humans
cannot exist without their Self or soul, having abandoned, forgotten, or negated it for the sake of something else (an idea or some
authority) or somebody else, in the long run, must cause pain. Everything that is not authentic and inherent is painful in itself.

All the suffering has only one foundation; the loss of oneself.
Since we cannot lose ourselves in either space or time, but only forget ourselves, awakening is the salvation of all the suffering, i.e.,
oblivion.

Such a simple solution to the biggest problem of human existence (suffering) was not acceptable to academic interpreters of
Sâmkhya who based their findings solely on classical texts. Texts
which originated under archaic circumstances had to be perfectly
precise, hence, quite scarce to the taste of modern reader, and consequently, vague and unconvincing. Precise in their information
for those who work on themselves and do not seek explanations
from the outside, in ready-made interpretations. Most of the old
texts are informative codes which realize their meaning only upon
proper usage, that is to say, during a person's perseverance on the
path to awakening. They are, therefore, incomprehensible to anyone who does not implement them in such a fashion. The best illu-

stration for this is lacking to understand *Purusha* adequately. They are by definition above the body and mind, above everything existing, and cannot, therefore, be understood with the relative mind which is tied to the body and thought contents. A strong attachment of the mind to problematic experiences, and passive participation of the consciousness in it, leads to the wrong conclusion that the vision of classical *Sâmkhya* on the primeval predetermination of humans for the absolute freedom is nothing but a big rationalization, rather than the solution to the problem. What *Purusha* is can only be realized with the transcendental consciousness which is free from the body and mind. *Sâmkhya* has been interpreted most dominantly by those who lacked this experience. Apart from that, interpreters approached *Sâmkhya* mostly from the Vedantic or Judeo-Christian standpoint which is based on metaphysical speculations on the dichotomy of the being and essence.

As an exception to this rule, we should mention here one of the first presenters of *Sâmkhya* into western languages, Richard Garbe who in his study *Philosophy of Ancient India* boldly states that "In Kapila's doctrine, for the first time in the history of the world, the complete independence and freedom of the human mind, its full confidence in its powers were exhibited. It is the most significant system of philosophy that India has produced."[4] However, these words remained only in the form of a bold personal view and were not accepted further. We will try to set it right here.

Academic interpretations always protect the collective interests, and they are set against individuality and personal freedom. All institutionalized religions and political principles are based on collective interests and exploitation of an individual. Hence, for them, the teaching of *Sâmkhya* is unacceptable because it shows that human essence is the same freedom which engenders the world.

4. Religions and the system of *Sâmkhya*

It is necessary to distinguish between the systems, such as *Sâmkhya*, and various religious practices. Once this distinction be-

---

[4] A minor correction is needed here to clarify that *Sâmkhya* is older than India and all of its philosophical and religious traditions.

comes clear, it will be self-evident that the issue of theism and atheism is wrong to put before *Sâmkhya* because religions often deal with it, and partly philosophies, and not systems, as such.

Before all else, it should be said here that *Sâmkhya* is the essence of true religiousness and there is no difference between those two, however, true religiousness in its original and authentic form is the transcendence of ostensible individuality or the resurrection of the human into the divine consciousness which engenders everything. Therefore, *the essence of any notion of God and religiousness itself is based on the idea of transcendence. Sâmkhya is the only system that objectively and thoroughly shows what has transcended and how.* Institutionalized religions and religiousness known to us today are lacking this essence. Modern religions and religiousness have been reduced to myths and rituals as means of mass mind control by those that rule over people. Furthermore, institutionalized religions were created by the rulers who made it their task to govern over people with the intention of making the transcendental human essence, the divine consciousness that engenders everything or *Purusha*, suppressed out of human and into the dogma, myth, or eschatology. Religion is a method of mind control that constantly projects human essence outside of the human, and by doing so it becomes unconscious ("the human's unconscious"), as well as alienated. The little religious experience and practice that acts as the principle of true human salvation and understanding the divine, such as apophatic theology, for example, is the one that describes the transcendental nature of the divine most accurately, and is preserved in very rare esoteric works aimed at individual users, such as monks.

The system is a school of awareness of the mind and overall existence which leads to the direct human awakening by practicing or, the way it is expressed in religious terms, as a liberation, that is to say, a salvation. The system does not require any previously established beliefs, uncritical acceptance, or collective devotion of anything, the only thing which is required is a personal effort to become liberated by disclosing the being as it is. The only authority the system relies upon is the experience of those "who traveled the same road" (*tathagata*) who can be guides through the existence, as such (*tirthankara*).

32

Two kinds of roads can be found leading toward spiritual realization. One is the road of collective worship and submission to a religious ideal which is the dominant type of religious practice in the modern world. The other one is the road of quest and direct, personal knowledge of the existence. It is typical for the systems of individual growth of which *Sâmkhya* is one. The former road relies on the support from the outside in the form of some religious authority and is, therefore, very suitable for the majority of people whose mind is naturally turned toward the outside without a possibility of internal control. The latter road only requires dedicated effort and work on oneself, as well as an objective attitude of alert questioning of the whole body and mind, something which is a characteristic of the limited number of people. What the former, collective road, projects into an idea of God, the same thing the latter, the individual road, identifies as the spiritual self-knowledge or the reality of the being. Hence, both the religion and the system of *Sâmkhya* deal with the same problem, but on a different ontological level.

Four different kinds of consciousnesses or thoughts should also be differentiated. They are: religious, philosophical, theoretical, and practical. They can all refer to the practice of liberation or human salvation, but with more or less deviation which is necessary for the various types of human characters and their ability to comprehend.

There is the most deviation in religious thinking (hence, the number of conflicts that follow it), it is the most general and, consequently, the most acceptable for the masses. It is received as a ready-made package from the outside which never changes, instilling a false sense of certitude to those who are unable to change, and most people fall under that category.

In philosophical thinking, the idea of existence and essence is within reach to a smaller group of people, generally to those who are capable of consistent and critical thinking, at least for a while and are more inclined to use their intelligence instead of feelings. Their own "philosophy of life" is something that very few people are able to have since the majority are quite happy to be members of some religion simply by being born into some family, society, or country.

Theoretical thinking is much closer to the fundamental idea of awareness because it is based on direct insight and perception. Although theory used to be identified with philosophy in the olden days, it is very different from it nowadays in its connectedness to the practical application. Theoretical thinking gives a reliable framework and system one can work with. Theory is a system according to which practice is applied. *Sâmkhya* is an example of such a theory.

Finally, the practice represents the most concrete effort of a person in his/her struggle for attaining consciousness. The best example by far is the practice of yoga.

Theoretical and practical thinking are the most narrow and seldom used area because they are the hardest to accept and realize. It is easier to stay in the religious and philosophical spheres that deal with general issues and problems, rather than analyze these matters within oneself through practical implementation, and dedicate one's whole life to an arduous endeavor and personal transformation. It may practically refer to the individual experience in accordance with the given circumstances, but philosophical and religious also when referred to general states. For this reason, it may be deliberated on in general terms during public debates, while the practice is open for discussion only eye to eye with the master who has gone down this road before us and is of great help to those who are intent on taking it, in accordance with time and circumstances in question.

This division is a reflection of dimensions humans are made of: the physical body, feelings, intellect, and the soul. The majority tends to identify with the physical body and, as a consequence, with the religion they were born into. A fewer number of people grow emotionally attached to their convictions and beliefs. Even fewer than them engage in intellectual research for the deeper meaning of religiousness, and the fewest of all discover it through practice completely individually, as their own soul, or the Self. The higher the dimension, the higher the principle of individuation in spiritual knowing.

All four ways of thinking have their value and reality within the order, they have their dimension and proportion, their reason for existence and none of them is wrong; the only thing wrong thing is to mix or impose them onto others. Each way of thinking contains within, in an elementary form at least, the remaining ones. It is hard to be a practitioner without a philosophical or religious vision, nor could religions survive were it not for theory and practice. It is of vital importance to realize that the only thing which keeps an opinion right and healthy is practice. Through practice, philosophy, too, receives its original meaning which draws it one step closer to theory.

The fundamental difference between *Sâmkhya* and religion is in that *Sâmkhya* is a system with which humans change and awaken themselves and by doing so reaches the state of authenticity. The same process religion turns into a myth and projects outwardly for collective and symbolic processing. In that way, religion represents the simulation of real work on oneself. Simulation can be useful as an introduction to the problem of working on oneself but can be a very successful means of deception and diverting oneself away from the real work on oneself and creating an illusion about the work. Unfortunately, the latter is the case in most religions.

Sâmkhya is a process of individuation which liberates – religion is always a process of collectivization which conditions.

Sâmkhya is a system which speaks of the necessity of perfecting the consciousness and primeval freedom because the consciousness that was given naturally to humans for survival fills only a minimum of their requirements, often it is lost and deformed due to various influences and does not play the leading role in the experience of existence. To start playing the leading role, it must be empowered through practical work on oneself. *Sâmkhya* provides the necessary theory and plan (the scheme of categories) as valuable assistance. Its practicality makes it contain the essence of both philosophy and religion, although it does not address it in a mundane way the way priests and philosophers do, to make sure they gain the acceptance of the masses. Unaware people deal with this essence only by projecting it into space (temple, idol, symbol) and time (cosmogony, myth, eschatology). The practice is an act of awareness where space and time of all the projections contract in the human's personality and direct responsibility for spiritual freedom. *Sâmkhya* speaks of a singularity of spirituality in human essence.

As we will later see, *Sâmkhya*, although it is a system, defines the essence of true religiousness because it considers the overall existence by carefully examining all of its categories, not putting a fixture on anything until the authenticity of consciousness is actualized through the human's personality, the one that engenders the very existence. By becoming aware of all the experience of existence it affirms life because no other consciousness or religiousness is a possibility other than the affirmative one. It is different from mundane religious practices as a system because the norms of an authentic spirituality of this kind are on a higher level than the widely accepted religious traditions (not the esoteric ones), especially Judeo-Christian, above the identification with the psycho-mental experience of personality. The realms religions often describe as 'heavenly' and 'divine', in *Sâmkhya* are a part of *Prakriti* and its categories, the one's immaterial nature, and its higher dimensions belong to (*tanmâtrâ* and *maha-bhûtâni*), which are merely out of reach of the physical senses (*indriyâni*). Although it is not presented in such a way, the basic characteristic of mass religious practices is their closedness into the empirical experience, so that by constantly stressing it a contrast would be created and an illusion of contact with the 'divine' and 'heavenly' (according to the scheme of categories it is a relationship between the organic, subjective, and inorganic, objective realm). It results in psycho-mental conditioning and achieving certain compromises with them, most commonly in some symbols and "strong faith" we choose to place in a myth. There is no doubt that it is of great benefit to the conditioned human, but on the road to the full affirmation of the human soul, this must be overcome. *Sâmkhya* creates the basic facts of existence on a higher level. It reveals them for what they are, primordially and directly through the human personality (*aham-kâra*) and the pure awareness of oneself (*buddhi*).

***

In *Sâmkhya* there are only two facts:

1. Everything that exists and composes the universe in all the dimensions. It is called *Prakriti*.

2. The principle of consciousness on the existence of everything, that what invites the being into existence; the transcendental consciousness that draws every form of existence toward its
outcome and meaning, one step closer to the awareness of oneself.
It is called *Purusha*.

On a somewhat lower level of understanding the same facts
of nature and consciousness are modified by psycho-mental conditioning.[5] That is why they get projected as myths of the creation of
the world (their sheer versatility and vastness in number proves
the effect of psychological conditioning at the point of their origin),
the dramas of divine beings, and saviors and an abundance of fa-
bulous odysseys which through imagination demonstrate the
processes in nature and human psyche as their component part.
Understanding the being and the consciousness is intuitive but vague, it existed in all the religious ideas, through the differentiation
between the heavenly and earthly, the Creator and the created,
eternal souls and mortal bodies. The nearest idea to that of *Purusha*
was the experience of the Holy Spirit in Mazdaism. However, only
in *Sâmkhya* the consciousness and existence are established as they
are, without the peace-making function of the mind, psycho-
mental distortions, and traditional conditioning.

5. Name and origin

The name of the founder of *Sâmkhya*, the "red wizard" Kapila,
was legendary during the age of *Rg Vedic* hymns, at the beginning
of the first millennium B.C. In *Mahabharata*, several successors of

---

[5] This problem, which *Sâmkhya* solves, was depicted in Plato's "allegory of the
cave" (The Republic, VII, 514a2 - 517a7). It remained without explication until
Heidegger, who in his Deconstruction of "Plato's Doctrine of Truth", made an
effort to discern unconcealment of beingness (which in *Sâmkhya* is engenderd by
the unconditionality of *Purusha*) from an idea which imposes unconcealment
aiming to fully illuminate it (the category of *buddhi* best correlates with it), and
the interpretations of reality as self-evidently true statements (lat. adaequatio),
which in *Sâmkhya* is the category of *manas*. On further information one would
do well to acquaint themselves with Heidegger's lectures "What Is
Metaphysics?", and "On the Essence of Truth" (Vom Wesen der Wahrheit,
Vittorio Klostermann, 1967) in which the essence of truth is disclosed as the
freedom (*Purusha*) of the being (*Prakriti*).

his work are also mentioned. It is said that the knowledge of Kapila is undisturbed. *Svetasvatara Upanishad* (V, 2) mentions Kapila: "He, the non-dual Brahman, who rules over every position; who controls all forms and all sources; who, in the beginning, filled with knowledge omniscient Kapila, His own creation, whom He beheld when he was produced – He is other than both knowledge and ignorance." There had been previous attempts to look for the sources of *Sâmkhya* in either the *Vedas* or *Upanishads*, but, judging by the reputation of its legendary founder and, even in those days, renowned ancient teachings, it is clear that all of it makes very little sense. Jainism, Buddhism, and *Sâmkhya* all belong to an ancient cult of heroes or winners (of the human soul over nature), the cult of spiritual awakening, while the *Vedas* are remnants of the cult of gods that developed much later. These two cults should clearly be distinguished. Due to this difference, Kapila was certainly not one of those Aryans who were sticking to *Vedas*. Although the time of his life is almost impossible to ascertain, it is known he lived before sixth century B.C.

There are legends from recent times that suggest that he passed on the knowledge of Sâmkhya to his mother Devahuti.

The name Kapila means "redhead", and the question remains what a redhead was doing amongst the dark-skinned Asiatic people, and a first-born sage (*rsi*), at that. The answer to this is provided by the Hindus themselves who, even to this day, teach that they received *Vedas* from "white sages in the north". In those ancient times, Grand Tartaria was located north of the Indian subcontinent, a Slav-Aryan empire that spanned Western Europe and China, Siberia and Pakistan, as well as the Indus Valley. After the last ice age, they withdrew from history and did not maintain their culture, but left it for the safekeeping with other nations to preserve it for some future times to come. For the same reason, they left the science of *Vedas* in the hands of Hindu people. *Vedas* underwent a major transformation there and unfortunate degradation. We can only assume that prior to this they left the science of *Sâmkhya* in the Indus Valley.

On the other hand, the Vedantic philosophers may have a point when they interpret the name of Kapila as an epithet of the 'golden egg" (*hiranyagarbhah*) the whole universe came out of.

Regardless of the fact that Kapila was a redhead Aryan, or maybe even the incarnation of the very Absolute, the system got its name from identifying and defining all the categories that compose a being (*Prakriti*), so that the Absolute as such could be revealed, the one that facilitates and gives meaning to the wholeness of natural phenomena, and which is the only true human identity (*Purusha*).

The word *Samkhyă* (with the final 'a' stressed) means number or counting (it is a specific area of *Sâmkhya* that deals with maths and physics), while *Sămkhya* (with the initial 'a' stressed) loses its purpose of numerical calculus and relates to discernment, classification, the type of weighing out and objective measuring which is performed when something is being decided.[6] The root of the verb *khya-*, "pronouncing", gives *Sâmkhya* its terminological meaning of categorization.

We can, therefore, say that the word *Sâmkhya* means **logical association to discern and establish the relevant**, as a form of **teaching** or **awareness**, hence, the **differentiation of the consciousness itself**.

The notions that compose *Sâmkhya* as such appear at the very beginning of Indian spirituality and have been presented in various ways in many works. In the Rig Veda, which is even older than this, it is said that the sun is the visible eye of the universe in which the human resides, *Purusha*, and it is the same human as in the physical human, the inner essence, the soul which facilitates becoming aware of overall nature as a witness (*sakshin*). There, also, we find some vague and initial indication of theory of *Sâmkhya* on the divine spirit and nature (*Purusha* and *Prakriti*). *Upanishads* bristle with main comprehensions which can be found in theory of *Sâmkhya* but bring them forth in a unique, versatile way with pronounced theistic tendencies. What they have in common with *Sâmkhya* is dissatisfaction with the inauthentic beingness of in this world; the basic principle that a correct cognition is the only

---

[6] It should be emphasized here that the letter *m* is not a labial nasal but a sign for nasalizing the preceding vocal, similarly to the letter 'n' in the name of Ana. In Sanskrit, it is *anusvara* n which is stressed with a dot above the vocal. In the internationally standardized Latin transcription we use here, it is a line above the first 'a' in the word. Hence, *Sămkhya* is transcribed and pronounced as *Sânkhya*.

39

means of salvation where the deciding role is played by the human. The great epic *Mahabharata* (originated from 4 century B.C. to 4 century A.D.) has in itself almost all the notions from theory of *Sâmkhya* and deals with them quite exhaustively, mostly in the parts *Anugita, Bhagavadgita,* and *Moksha dharma.* The issue here is about *Sâmkhya* which is monistic and theistic where *Purusha* is equaled with *atman* (Self) from *Upanishads.* At around that time, *The Laws of Manu* were written which similarly base their cosmological conundrums on the basic notions that can easily be found in *Sâmkhya.* Up until this point, the epic *Sâmkhya* was developing itself in a variety of ways.

During the scholastic period of Indian philosophy, a brave but failed attempt happened to found and separate an independent philosophical system of *Sâmkhya.* The oldest classical work testifying to this attempt that has reached us over the centuries is *Sâmkhya-kârikâ* by Ishvara Krishna from the third century A.D. This work with its 69 verses is among the most beautiful pieces of writing of old Indian literature. It is the most significant reduction of a system toward pure spirituality which inspired many commentators. The second in line is *Sâmkhya-pravachana-sûtrâ* or *Sâmkhya-sûtrâ,* which are ascribed to the founder of the system, Kapila. It originated later, in the fourteenth century, although many of its parts are much older. His most significant commentary work, *Sâmkhyapravachana-bhashya* by Vijnanabhikshu, originated in the sixteenth century, that ties *Sâmkhya* even more to the basics of *Vedanta,* whose influence at the time signed the death penalty for the development of *Sâmkhya* as an authentic system. *Sâmkhya tattva kaumudi* by Vachaspati is one more work that commands attention from the ninth century.

Owing to works like these, a classical system by the name of *Sâmkhya* was acknowledged to be one of the six orthodox scholastic systems (*darshana,* the others are: *nyaya, vaisheshika, yoga, purvamimamsa,* and *vedanta*) in Indian philosophy, which themselves are the traditionally acknowledged heritage of *Brahmanical* science and constitute a group of teachings that confirm the authority of the Vedas (*astika*). Although confirmation of this kind proved to be undoubtedly beneficial for *Sâmkhya* mainly to survive a myriad of schools of India back in the day, it is clear that it has nothing in common with the systems that acknowledge the authority of Vedas because it is older than them, since Vedas themselves refer their notions to *Sâmkhya* and its founder Kapila.

The exact provenance and date of origin of *Sâmkhya* are almost impossible to determine, but it bears little significance since it has managed to survive only owing to its eternal value. The true origin of *Sâmkhya* is in the primordial and fundamental aspiration of humans to discern within themselves their consciousness from all the unconscious and spontaneous natural phenomena. However, delving deeper into the roots of spirituality defined by *Sâmkhya*, the protoculture of indigenous people is impossible to overlook, the one that thrived in the valley of the Sindhu River (Indus) with elaborately executed city-states such as Mohenjo Daro, Harappa, and Kalibangan. Although reliable material evidence is still lacking that would confirm the origin of *Sâmkhya* in these parts, we have reasons that lead us to such a conclusion.[7]

The first reason is that the spirit of *Sâmkhya* with its, for that day and age unparalleled atheism, and existentialism, worldliness, and rationality in the material culture particularly, seems to deviate from the metaphysical and religious notions of all the other cultures.

Secondly, this territory has the oldest religion in the world *Jainism* which apart from having certain similarities with *Sâmkhya* (liberating the soul from the binding matter), with its pronounced principle of non-violence toward all the living beings, clearly sets it apart from the Brahmanical practice of sacrifice at a Vedic ritual. Afterward, all the yogic and ascetic practices of spiritual purification originated from Siddhattho Gotamo or Buddha, the founder of Buddhism (5. century B.C.); god Vishnu, the central figure of Indian epic mythology, who initially represented the solar deity of the indigenous population; then Shiva, the destroyer and at the same the

---

[7] In the nineteenth century, the prevalent thought was that Indian logic has been brought to Greece. W. Jones was of the opinion that Callisthenes, who accompanied Alexander The Great on his invasion of India, found completed logics and brought it to his uncle Aristotle, Greek philosopher. C. B. Schluter published a book titled "Aristotle's metaphysics – the daughter of Kapila's science of *Sâmkhya*" (C.B.Schluter: Aristotles' Metaphysik eine Tochter der Samkhya - Lehre des Kapila. Munster 1874). To these associations, we can only add that Aristotle's metaphysics proved to be a prodigal daughter.

creator of the world with his phallic symbol found throughout India, lingam – the symbol of the power of creation and life energy. The affection of the indigenous people toward the cults of nature, depicted in the innumerable figurines of fertility goddesses, had a vital influence over the "softening" of an abstract attitude toward spirituality. Not in philosophy only, but in art, as well. Appreciation for the movement of natural energy had its most spiritual expression in tantrism. All of this blend constitutes the recognizable and unique fiber of Indian culture time has very little influence on, except for leaving open wounds after such attempts.

Finally, the most important reason we wish to emphasize here is the similarity and closeness between *Sâmkhya* and yoga. They rely on completely identical assumptions and are different only in that one represents a theory and the other one practice. *Sâmkhya* as its most significant characteristic emphasizes establishing and discerning the structure of the category of the being (*viveka-marga*) with such precision unparalleled anywhere else in the world, discrimination that gives the necessary clarity and orientation for liberating humans from ignorance and conditionality. Yoga is, apart from all this, dedicated to psychophysical exercises of mastering and subjugating (the radix "yuj" means coupling, summation) the unbridled passions of an unconscious being for the sake of freedom and authenticity of the human soul because, most commonly, a clear insight into the problem is not enough for people to find an existential solution. A certain discipline is required for the soul to be unbound.

Patanjali's *Yoga-sŭtras* (*Yogasŭtrâni*, recorded around 2. century A.D.) may be considered the best depiction of *Sâmkhya* in practice, they demonstrate in detail the discipline required for the whole of *Sâmkhya* to be understood and all of its principles to be realized in one's own experience.

It is evident that some elements of yoga originate from the ancient shamanistic tradition which is essentially in common to all the peoples in the world. However, only in the Indus valley, this primeval aspiration of humans to overcome the natural causality received its crystal clarity in the unique and unsurpassed spiritual culture of yoga. Spirituality was further perfected as science within it. In other parts of the world, it either remained an archaic technique of ecstasy, or lost itself in the folklore and religious mythology.

At that time in the whole of the Middle East, there was no culture as developed as the one found in the Indus valley. According to the research, it is more original and older than Sumerian and ancient Egyptian and represents the true focal point of cultural influences of the great cosmopolitan whole of the ancient world, from India to Egypt. The remains of the cities in question, known to us as Harappan culture, show a very high degree of social organization and way of life the ancient communities managed to maintain for over a millennium, disrupted only by the frequent flooding of the Indus River. The cities were meticulously planned urban units of non-pastoral peoples with about 30,000 inhabitants, and streets that intersect at perpendicular angles in the direction of east-west and north-south, multistory houses with flat roofs built from uniform baked bricks of the exact size – never before seen in history. Most houses had built-in bathrooms and drainage systems connected via clay pipes to the street canals. The main area of the house was an indoor yard, and obviously, great care was given to bathrooms (it seems that ritual baths have their origin in India). No traces of guns or combat vehicles were found, not even in figurines and seals that are abundant in number.[8] There are many handmade toys which would be practical for children even today, carts with mobile wheels, and so on.[9] Likewise, a very precise system of measurements was found, the rolling dice with sides numbered from one to six, the same one that is much abused today. Interestingly enough, not a single building was found that could serve the purpose of being a shrine or a temple. The central building was a large bath, next to the grain storage with an intricately executed ventilation system. Taking into account the fact that settlements of this kind everywhere in the world at that time, but much later also,

---

[8] We may observe here that throughout the entire Slav-Aryan and Sumerian cultural heritage we find no traces of wars or human fighting, but only motifs from nature and peace-minded socializing of people who voluntarily follow their rulers and gods. Only much later, in the Greco-Roman period, we find mostly scenes of wars and destruction.

[9] The identical votive cart figurines were also found in the Balkans in Vincan culture, dating approximately from the same period.

were characterized by cosmological and religious symbolics woven into the architectural design, all of this gives the Harappan culture a unique worldliness in history unparalleled to this day. Their undeciphered alphabet may shed a little light on their secrets someday in the future.[10]

The official historiography considers this civilization, which maintained itself very conservatively on the same foundations, to have disappeared off the face of the earth as a result of great floods and climate changes that gradually devastated lush forests and arable land. However, their cities were later discovered to have been destroyed during a war against unknown adversaries.[11]

Harappan culture rebuilt itself several times over the millennia, but always on the same foundations. Such a level of conservativeness confused the explorers. A more thorough deliberating on this issue would indicate that they rebuilt an already perfected social policy and city culture for the simple reason that at that day and age a more perfect model was not in existence.

A recent discovery of the ancient city of Dwaraka situated below sea level and west of Gujarat whose age is estimated to be *at least* 12,000 years old based on geological changes in sea level, shows that the Indus valley civilization was not limited to the

---

[10] In all likelihood, the secret is more concealed than revealed today because the identical letter, the same one we find in the Indus valley, is found on the opposite side of the world, on Easter islands (the so-called Rongorongo script). This is yet another proof that adds to the falseness of the official history.

[11] Both the epic descriptions of nuclear blasts in *Mahabharata* and the archeological material evidence point to the fact that Harappan civilization was wiped off the face of the earth in a nuclear attack. Radiation was found that measured ten times higher than normal levels even today, signs of vitrification in the bones of victims (who found their death in homes or casual strolls in the streets - which proves their death was sudden), and remnants of green glass on the ground and in melted clay bricks (something that happens on nuclear testing grounds only) onset by sudden exposure to very high temperatures like during a nuclear explosion. For further understanding as to what nuclear weapons of mass destruction were doing in ancient history - see the book: Forbidden history - Prehistoric Technologies, Extraterrestrial Intervention, and the Suppressed Origins of Civilization Edited by J. Douglas Kenyon. The whole world has ample evidence of cutting-edge technology in the ancient past, in the form of megaliths and edifices that the human hand is still incapable of producing despite all the modern technology available to us today. The official history is a lie.

mainland part only which we are familiar with today, but it also covered a patch of land which is submerged underwater today due to the rise in sea levels. About 12,000 years ago, at the end of the last ice age, sea levels rose over 120 meters (400 feet). It flooded many ancient coastal cities belonging to very advanced civilizations. This places the origin of the system of *Sâmkhya* far more distantly into the past, older than all the attempts made by official historiography to tie it to Vedas, giving it only a few thousand years of age.

The mundanity of Harappan civilization could with its unison of material and spiritual culture act as a beacon to humanity via the spirituality of *Sâmkhya* which presupposes that the consciousness is the foundation of every existence that is manifested as human authenticity only, as the human's peak of the culture of beingness. With this, it contributes to the principle of tolerance and the freedom of personality on which it aspires to build a civil, i.e., city-state.

Cities are melting pots of assorted life experiences of existence, they accumulate, mature, and become crystallized in them. A civil culture is such a system of livelihood which with its organization from the *outside* induces humans to be well-bred as well as conscious. Religions aspire toward the same goal, but with ideological and mythological conditioning. Both the secular and the religious culture (the former more so in the material sense, and the latter more psychologically) with their *outside* arrangement cultivate people. *Sâmkhya* represents the *inner* accomplishment of the ideal of the culture of beingness which can be manifested completely only through individuality and personality. The perfection of a citizen culture (as of yet unaccomplished) represents only a far cry of the perfection of the Absolute which, according to *Sâmkhya*, is manifested in the human. A secular, civil culture in its most profound aspect is a necessary external support for the construction of the inner spiritual culture which, unlike the religious one, does not manipulate using psychological conditioning, nor is it one-sided, but provides a concept of general culture preparing the human for the true spiritual freedom and the maturity of existence. This further accumulates evidence that a system such as *Sâmkhya* could have originated only in an ideally organized civil society due to its interaction with it, in a society that Harappan civilization aimed to achieve. Hence, this is the only territory on which it may survive in the future.

PURUSHA

The word *Purusha* denotes the human quite literally. In the system of *Sâmkhya*, this word does not refer to the human's bodily being or sex, but to the human's spiritual essence which means a complete unconditionality that surpasses all the conditionality of the being (*Prakriti*). It represents the outcome or essence of the existence of entire nature. The human body is nothing but a suitable natural shape for manifesting this essence which overcomes (transcends) all the conditionality of existence. *Sâmkhya* names *Purusha* as the only suitable and the only possible place in the whole of nature for such a manifestation to take place.

According to *Brihadaranyaka Upanishad* (1.4.1) the etymological origin of the notion *Purusha* has to do with "the one who before this whole (*pûrva*) burned all evils (*ush*)" – therefore: pure, primordial, and absolute good.

This defines the essence of *Sâmkhya*.

We will stress it once again: what engenders the overall nature and the existence itself is called *Purusha* in *Sâmkhya* and is at the same time human essence.

There is not a single system of knowledge and spirituality in the world that reveals human essence as clearly and as directly as this one does. This renders *Sâmkhya* unique.[12]

Purusha cannot be reduced only to the human Self, but more likely to what the Self engenders, and in that sense, *Purusha* represents the source of human Self or soul. Likewise, *Purusha* can-

---

[12] Although human essence is like this, the human still has to become aware of it and actualize it individually, since it was not revealed at birth. In other systems of development and knowledge, human essence is at best linked with the Divine, briefly mentioned that the origin of the human soul is in God, and therefore, it should somehow find its way back to God which is all projected into religious mythology and dogma to prevent a further actualization of the truth. The way it can best be actualized is found in Sri Nisargadatta Maharaj's teaching. Additionally, *Yoga Vasistha* is one of the classical texts that best conveys this truth.

not be reduced to the presence of the consciousness itself either, but to what engenders the consciousness as such.

Purusha is the unconditionality itself which engenders both nature and the awareness of its existence in the Self.

Purusha has no properties, but for the sake of understanding it, it may be designated as the divine absolute.

Purusha is expressed in the human as the soul.

We have already stated that *Sâmkhya* is the most primeval spirituality because it has been liberated from all the layers of mythology and symbolism. It addresses the matter directly. Therefore, we have two fundamental notions: *Purusha* and *Prakriti*. *Prakriti* is everything that exists and *Purusha* is what engenders everything; it is manifested in the human as the awareness of everything that exists. *Prakriti* is everything that objectively exists, and *Purusha* engenders the conscious subject of all the objective existence, but a subject who is not limited to their psychophysical individuality, that is to say, ego, but is a subject in the absolute sense, as a place where the objective existence acknowledges itself, where it finds its outcome or meaning; as opposed to which the objective existence as such is not even a possibility.

Only owing to the fact that the source of the conscious subject is transcendental as regards the whole nature or the objective world, can the human as the conscious subject become acquainted with absolutely everything that exists in nature. If the essence of human consciousness is within humans, they would not be able to do so. They would forever be conditioned by themselves, the same way they are for as long as they keep identifying themselves with their psychophysical being. Their ability to overcome this identification makes them open to cognizing the objective reality and the whole nature as well as its meaning. The consciousness of our soul is equivalent to space: in the identical manner in which space contains within itself everything else, all phenomena, and all the events, our soul, too, is the divine consciousness that holds within the universe itself. However, since the universe is the field of manifestation of *all* the possibilities, we can also be unaware of ourselves and our soul. Not permanently, but only temporarily while we dream that we are living.

Purusha is the first fundamental notion in *Sâmkhya*, and the other one is *Prakriti*. The overall existence of the universe is *Prakriti*, within it, there is everything that happens in any way at all. Everything that can exist has always existed in its latent form in *Prakriti*. *Sâmkhya* described *Prakriti* a long time ago as something we know today by the name of the Field, the Universal quantum field, the Quantum hologram, or Matrix in physics all the forms of existence come from, from subatomic to cosmic, together with all the laws of nature.[13]

The transcendental property of the essence of humans, *Purusha*, facilitates the objective awareness of the world in the human. Together with it every understanding is made possible, and every kind of goodness and love because goodness and love are nothing but the reflections of understanding the wholeness of the being and the true nature of phenomena.

It is enough to see a being for what it is in the objective reality to love it. To see the objective reality means to see the energetic nature of the holographic universe in which everything is interconnected by one divine consciousness which engenders everything. This energetic experience of reality or some being is the feeling of love. Love is the feeling in us when we become aware of the energy which creates and connects us with other beings and the whole. That is the reason why we enjoy nature spontaneously, why we always learn to love somebody that we first got to understand very deeply.

Any kind of evil or negativity is brought about only due to the identification with *Prakriti*, with the being and its phenomena, due to the failure to transcend them and become aware of their objective nature. Any constraint on human development can be associated with identifying with beingness and the inability to consciously discriminate one's self from beingness for the sake of objectiveness.

If there were nature only, *Prakriti*, but without *Purusha*, life as we know it could not happen. There is accumulated evidence

---

[13] On the universal quantum field in modern physics see Gregg Braden's book: *The Divine Matrix,* and Lynne McTaggart: *The Field – The Quest for the Secret Force of the Universe.* On the holographic paradigm see Michael Talbot's book: *The Holographic Universe.*

that suggests DNA is a result of conscious intervention and creation, rather than evolution. The foundation of DNA consists of the codes of light that receive information from the sun, from the stars, and which momentarily communicate with the whole. Consciousness is the foundation of all life.

The sphere of life of nature is the field of causality and purposefulness, rendering itself incapable of producing objective and creative consciousness. Nature itself is such that it clearly demonstrates that consciousness is not a product of nature, but its cause.

Purusha, as the foundation of the overall existence, is unconditionality which engenders the phenomena of everything, and the awareness of the phenomena (*buddhi*) first and foremost. This essence is resolved and disclosed only in the human being, identifying human essence with *Purusha* as a result. That is the essence of all the ancient lore on the divine origin of humans, their shared likeness with God, and the urgency to acknowledge themselves as God through self-knowledge.

This fateful solution is not created over time, it can happen only by the transcendence of the being and time as identification of freedom according to which everything already is, therefore, by consciously being present in it or acknowledging it. Specifically, it means that this can be realized with the human's awakening to what is, to the existence itself as well as the unconditionality which engenders it. It happens by contracting the time (into now) on the right spot (here), within one's self, in the Self.

Prakriti is time, *Purusha* is timelessness which is experienced as the eternal present. With the expression of *Purusha*, unconditionality as such is identified which engenders nature and the place from which the awareness of unconditionality springs up, and that is the human. The purpose of human survival is in enabling the manifestation of the essence which is achieved by our own awakening, by our awareness of who we are.

Since human essence is not in nature but in the consciousness which exceeds it (after realization of its sense), humans have never been able to find a sanctuary within it, nor will they ever find it – until the point they are able to contract and express the timeless essence of nature. For as long as they perpetuate in this endeavor relying on time and outer objects, they will suffer.

50

Purusha is not even that which is considered to be absolute but is the freedom the absolute facilitates, it is voidness devoid of any negative properties. It is the first condition for the existence of everything, a condition we cannot do without. Hence, the voidness in question has the most supreme creative power, although it does not engage in actions itself.

In the systems outside of *Sâmkhya,* early Buddhist teaching, Nagarjuna's teaching, and Zen, the essence of *Purusha* as voidness or *sunyata* is denoted properly.

Purusha is the freedom that engenders an insight into existence as it is. That explains why the insight or pure consciousness (*buddhi*) is the first category of existence, and at the same time, the outcome of *Prakriti*.

Unconditionality of *Purusha* is pure nothingness or, more accurately put, a nothingness that through its voidness disables any obstacles from standing in the way of existence being generated initially, and any potential obstacles that may occur on the path to cognition. This renders timelessness and independence of the human soul (*Purusha*) regarding to the phenomena of nature as the only guarantee for the human's liberation, consciousness, and creative transformation. An important characteristic of everything created in nature (*Prakriti*) is unconscious conditionality of causality and constant renewals (*samsara*). For the being that is by its nature under restraint, there is no way to set itself free. Testimonials of the liberated ones from time immemorial, however, tell a different story altogether. Suffering the natural causation and psychomental bondage to the bodily form, as well as the psychological experience of living in time are not important properties of the human soul. If they were, nobody would ever be liberated from ignorance and awakened from unconsciousness. If the human soul were of the same nature as what was conditioned by timeline and events, there would not be a conscious subject in the objective nature, humans could not be what they are; they would have a proper Self, the one that absorbs the flow of the experience of existence. Were it not for the contracting effect of the flow of life into the Self, the chronology of the experience of events would never reach its destination as the awareness of the phenomena, it would go on forever being blindingly conditioned by the time of its duration.

51

All the other beings live in unity with nature and experience no suffering as a result. Only humans conflict with it because their result is of a different kind, or until the point, they reach awareness of its result and their independence (*kaivalya*). Then they become the master of nature because they become open for manifesting the divine consciousness which engenders everything.

All the other beings are only aware of the objects, they do not have the awareness of themselves as being the subject, and are therefore incapable of changing themselves. Only humans, apart from the awareness of the objects, can have the objective awareness of themselves as also being subjects which ultimately engenders change within themselves. In this change and the ability to work on themselves all the culture and development are contained. Owing to their transcendental essence, Purusha, humans are capable of becoming aware both of the subjects and of themselves as the subject who experiences the objects because they receive their consciousness and essence from what surpasses both the subjects and the objects, the whole nature, and the very existence, Purusha. The consciousness cannot come from nature which is unconscious and conditioned by causality. The consciousness can only come from what is already conscious, from that what exceeds all causality, and which by definition is Purusha.

If the human soul were no different from the categories of nature's conditioning, we would not be able to differentiate the facts of its phenomena and ultimately have a will of our own. There would be neither memory nor consciousness in nature were it not for what facilitates the overcoming of time and all the individual events of nature. Human free will provides the choice between good and evil, or freedom and slavery. The more liberated one is it terms of realizing their own essence, the freer they are. Therefore, we are able to choose between freedom and slavery only because, being aware of our own essence, we are aware of the choice in the first place. Without such awareness, freedom could not be a possibility, at all.

Only owing to Purusha as our essence can we be both unconscious and conscious, and can unconsciously choose or create slavery for ourselves as well as use our consciousness to set ourselves free; we can be both in heaven and in hell. Owing to our transcendental es-

sence, Purusha, we can experience everything while at the same time be free from everything.

The primeval nature of *Purusha* engenders nature to be always and in everything different, new, and never the same, to be deadly, disgusting, and miraculously beautiful in its liveliness and vitality, to be paradoxical and logical, to be heaven and hell.

Owing to the quality of unconditioned *Purusha* the whole nature resides on the principle of liberty which engenders nature and all the living. However, liberty, as such, is a double-edged sword, it also entails the freedom to turn oneself into a slave as well as the oblivion of the freedom itself. It is all possible in the realm of free will which is natural.

Furthermore, the principle of freedom is always individual, it never manifests itself the same, and is never repetitive. This principle reflects itself in the whole nature where nothing is ever the same or replicated, absolutely everything within it is varied and unique, and that means everything is individual. Free will is also individual in the human personality, it is realized individually and always uniquely; invariably through self-knowledge only.

Due to the ontological difference between time and timelessness, or *Prakriti* and *Purusha*, the being and the essence, the consciousness, and its world of objects come into existence. It stands there in this place of no boundaries like the light of wakefulness with which this world as such can be closely observed. If the purpose of consciousness is in discrimination and overcoming, it is then always discriminating something from nothing and overcoming everything. Additionally, only nothing engenders an insight into something. If it were not for nothing, which surpasses everything, an objective insight into something would not be a possibility. Seers must, in their essence, be above the seen. If they are on a lower plane than what is observed, they are completely unaware of it. That explains why consciousness is the very act of overcoming the observed.

Psychic objectivity is generated by overcoming the objects and contents. The consciousness is nothing substantial, neither an activity nor a state for that matter, it is the *very act of overcoming the objects* or contents. The pure consciousness or wakefulness (*buddhi*) is the act of surpassing the beingness in general, and complete objectiveness towards it that engenders, in the most straightforward manner, the unconditionality of nothing that overcomes *everything* (*Purusha*). Finding oneself differentiated from the whole being and the overcoming of it engenders the appearance of the consciousness of the being (buddhi) and its total discernment, which is the self-knowledge and liberation of humans, made possible by the fact that their essence excels it because they are nothing of the overall being. If human essence (*Purusha*) were of the being, humans could never become aware of themselves since the being by its nature is unconscious and conditioned. The being is everything that exists as nature as opposed to the complete unconditionality from everything. Therefore, a conscious decision and establishing that the being can exist at all comes from the one who always excels it, from the unconditioned voidness that provides essence to the being, enabling them to be, here and now.

Purusha is, therefore, the unconditionality of beingness from everything, voidness (*sunyata*) that as such engenders the completeness of nature. Hence, it cannot be in any kind of a relationship and connection with its causally conditioned phenomena over the course of time. It is unconditionality in whose freedom all the nature floats about, all that exists owes its survival to it, although it remains unnoticed. With this invisibility, it is always separated from nature and logically irreducible to it because it is independent of the temporality of any process. This inconceivable voidness is not a result of discarding the being or some negation process. Quite the contrary, the very ability to discern negation for the sake of establishing, selecting, and consciously diverging (the being away from the non-being, or oneself away from everything that is not our essence) is possible only owing to this unconditionality which surpasses everything because it is our essence. It is, therefore, the complete affirmation of the being, but not at the end of the time process of affirmation, but before or beyond it, as that what engenders both the being and its affirmation.

By exceeding time *Purusha* engenders the objectivity of existence as such; timelessness of nothing draws the temporality of something toward the meaning of its beingness. It, similarly to vacuum, induces explosive expansion and the manifestation of the world, thus rendering it available to clear insight.[14]

The voidness of unconditionality of *Purusha* is, therefore, more original and thorough than the being and its negation than discernment and the light itself. It is a necessary requirement of everything, although it does not fall under the category of the being. As a result of the overcoming of everything, it must as a notion be determined only as "nothing", although it is not mere nothing but the addition of the meaning of everything and its overcoming in the freedom that engenders all, and which is adequate for humans only - as their essence. Hence, voidness is everything that exists, and more than everything. This voidness is also the fullness of everything that is.

Purusha is the freedom that is not jeopardized by the origin of the being nor will it be liberated by its disappearance because it is fundamentally independent of everything that exists, like the freedom that engenders it, together with all the changes. The consciousness crystallizes existence to the point it becomes transparent for the presence of unconditionality which engenders it. Then, it becomes clear that the existence itself is made possible owing to the fact that the emptiness of unconditionality is no different from existence; existence resides on emptiness; the contact of existence with the voidness generates the awareness of existence. The consciousness is a manifestation of unconditionality in contact with the being, the manifestation of freedom in existence.

Emptiness cannot exist all by itself because it would be mere nothingness then, and that is not possible. It must be expressed as something and this expressing of the unconditionality of voidness is the only one that exists as the universe of nature (*Prakriti*). Nature is in its organization of categories such that it contracts and directs itself toward the manifestation of the freedom that engenders everything. The evolution of all the forms of life demonstrates this direction.

---

[14] This position of *Purusha* in *Sâmkhya* can clarify the secret of the origin of matter in space: it is generated into existence by the very vacuum of cosmic space. Emptiness creates a form which manifests the creativity of the voidness. This is one of the cosmological theories of contemporary physics.

The unity of voidness and the created form does not entail the annulment of something which has been "created", but only a manifestation of the voidness through a form. Only voidness at the base of each form can engender the infinite freedom of the forming of everything always in a new and unique way.

The creation of the world out of nothing or the voidness (the Greek word for this is *chaos*), is the underlying theme of all the great cosmogonies. This fundamental principle often gets lost in them, although it was clearly presented in the beginning, such as, for example, in the Old Testament with the expression of free decision "let there be". Immediately after this, it gets lost in the coarser forms of expression. In Mazdaism, the principle of freedom is a lot more pronounced. However, only in Buddhism, especially in its essential interpretation by Nagarjuna, and in Taoism with Lao Tzu, the unity of emptiness and the form in time is clearly emphasized, the unity of nothing and something, the absolute and the relative (Tao and Te), as well as the principle of momentary creation in non-linear time. In their works, this unity is most directly guessed as the outcome of beingness which is manifested through human self-awareness.

Presented in this way, as the essence of the ancient heritage and religiousness, the emptiness of *Purusha* is the precondition for wakefulness (*buddhi*). *Purusha* is separated (*kaivalya*) from all the experiences and states of being (*guna*). The more the meaning of beingness gets contracted in the consciousness of the Self (*buddhi*), the more the emptiness of unconditionality opens up wider and proves itself to be the chief attractor of this contraction that heals humans. Only from the emptiness that outdoes it, the being becomes what it in its wholeness fundamentally is because nothing remains afterward that would deny this completeness. Only when the subject of this contraction, humans, do not find their stronghold regarding the awareness to any of the living shapes but instead finds it in the freedom of unconditionality, they are allowed to be fully awake. Likewise, only through the bliss of wakefulness, they are able to ascertain that existence is always whole, complete, and free, that nothing individual within it has a purpose unto itself, and is therefore never at risk. Like when the Earth is observed from the cosmos and it looks so whole and round, as one being, while at the same time, when observed from the surface, it appears that a multitude of people is in a perpetual conflict.

Only owing to *Purusha* which overcomes *Prakriti*, forgiveness, and mercy toward everything that happens is possible. The fact that the human soul is unconditioned (absolute) and transcendental, tolerance, mercy, and love can happen; *Purusha* overcomes any entanglement of the opposites of local (relative) phenomena of nature. From the perspective of the transcendental soul we see that all of the phenomena is one, that the whole *Prakriti* is one being, thus rendering all the individual beings only seemingly individual, even more so, they are all unconscious until they awaken to the reality of their divine soul. Hence, the love and lack of ability to resent anything, even the worst possible conduct of any living being.

Only because the human soul overcomes the world and time, humans are able to have grace, a kind heart, and love; they are even stronger if the transcendental soul in them is more aware of itself. Owing to *Purusha*, love is the only possible survival. Unconditionality from anything is, in reality, unconditional love and forgiveness. Freedom that engenders the world is the love that creates it because nothing can be created without love, the same way nothing can be without freedom and exist. All evil comes from the identification with the being, from the ignorance of the transcendental nature of the human soul.

Only based on its originality in the freedom of nothing which overcomes everything because it facilitates everything, humans can face nature and become aware of its meaning. The subject's relationship towards the world is made possible by their personal consciousness (*buddhi*) being engendered by the pure unconditionality of the emptiness which is not of this world, and which is beyond both the subject and the object.

Only with the stronghold in emptiness can humans see the meaning of all these natural phenomena and rid themselves of the time conditioning of specific contents. Without the insight into the shallowness of their survival in time, humans can neither establish a conscious relationship toward nature, nor themselves completely.

The unconditionality of the timeless voidness engenders the human soul which is the only realization that can awaken us from our unconscious state. Awakening is, in reality, overcoming the being which is unconscious by its nature, and, therefore, wakefulness brings revival to the soul which exceeds the being. It is an act when the consciousness which creates the world starts living through humans; through our personality, and deeds.

Voidness is manifested as wakefulness in our self-knowledge.

When voidness starts to live through us, when we awaken, things then remain as they are: free and devoid of any substantiality. The one who sees things in this way, as they are, as the pure unconditionality that exists, is said to be awakened. Such humans are authentic in their essence; they exist because they see things as they are as a result of their wakefulness.

If human essence was not an expression of the same unconditionality which manifests nature, a realization of human essence would not match recognizing nature for what it is, nor would this compatibility play out as the awakening of the human.

Due to the unconditionality of human essence, only in us, humans, does existence disclose itself fully in its divinity. We become the only ones endowed with the stillness and equanimity in the liberating acknowledgment of the meaning of everything. Humans (*Purusha*) can be authentic only when they have ascended to emptiness when they have been emptied out and liberated from the body which originated in time together with all of their personal and psychic conditionality (once they overcome *indriyâni, tanmâtrâ,* and *aham-kâra*). Once they have liberated themselves of the natural influences but managed to hold on to the full wakefulness (*buddhi*),[15] humans no longer see the material world of separate creations, but only the freedom to be everything that there is. Then, the existence itself is freedom. One does not exist without the other. Only owing to the fact that in human wakefulness existence acknowledges its freedom and authenticity, the whole objective nature creates a conscious subject, it is its fundamental aspiration and the reason for its existence.

The emptiness of *Purusha* in *Sâmkhya* is not a mere negation of the being or the act of something being emptied, but the blank-

---

[15] This is the key moment because the material world disappears to the human spontaneously as well, in deep sleep and a coma, therefore, without the presence of consciousness.

ness which engenders the unconcealed presence of the being, which reveals its fullness and reality. Without emptiness and wakefulness, humans would be non-existent, concealed, or unannounced (*avyakta*). Nothing, therefore, refers only to nothing between humans and the completeness of existence, their reality. To be in the reality of existence means to be fully awakened. People are, however, dominantly unaware and absent from the reality of the being, it remains undisclosed to them. That is why they suffer and commit evil acts. They fail to see that the voidness is the only condition for the being, and even less so, they are unaware of the fact that the being is in its essence empty (*sunyata*) which is the root cause as to why it can exist, at all. If it were not empty, it could not be.

***

The relationship between *Purusha* and *Prakriti* can be understood as the relationship between the conscious and unconscious.

The human being is the microcosm. It means the 'cosmos in miniature', and all the laws of nature are contracted within the human being. That makes the human in unity with the cosmos, which alone allow for an objective awareness of the cosmos. Since the human is a microcosm, the cosmos are revealed through self-awareness. Absolutely everything that a human does in these cosmos involves self-awareness.

The relationship between nature and spirit which engenders nature in its completeness can reflect itself fully in the human being only. *Purusha* and *Prakriti* unite completely only in humans – and for the same reason, they discern most fully within humans for making sense of it all. This discernment entails the following: once humans become authentic, that is, in their Self or soul, *Purusha* becomes completely actualized through them and *Prakriti* becomes translucent and disappears. It ceases to exist as the world of objects. At that point, humans are awake (*buddhi*) or enlightened. To the degree an individual soul does not reflect the consciousness of *Purusha*, its own source, but remains identified with the contents it keeps projecting outwardly, to that degree *Prakriti* exists as the solid world of objects, as the whole nature, at that. Therefore, ***Prakriti or nature exists only as objectivized oblivion of human es-***

sence, during the state when humans are unaware of themselves. The whole nature is merely materialization or actualization of the unconscious state. In this manner, it like a mirror assists human awareness, more accurately, it retrieves the consciousness back to *Purusha* itself. Nature (*Prakriti*) is the mirror in which the soul (*Purusha*) recognizes itself.

There is a myriad of conscious monads or souls, that incarnate into this oblivion, their collective presence engenders the existence of this entire physical cosmos. Therefore, the physical cosmos is a collective impact of a plethora of incarnated souls.

It all happens spontaneously on the micro-plane as well, in the everyday life of humans: when they sleep and experience a deep state without dreams, they then reside in their Self, in their soul where the emergent world does not exist, and where *Prakriti* is no longer. When they re-enter themselves, they become once more identified with the body, and the emergent world comes back on, the whole nature, too. Naturally, the body and nature existed during sleep also, simply waiting for the human to wake up. However, it all happens because the whole nature is made possible by a great multitude of souls that have always been incarnating, and the laws of nature being the way they are, allow for inertia to a certain degree to take place, the physical nature does not come into existence instantly, nor does it dissolve in an instance, either, in the form of an illusion or a soap bubble. There are proportions of phenomena within it, only in higher and more subtle proportions where thoughts and notions can be generated at will instantly. On the lower proportions phenomena are slower and their inertia engenders forms to last longer. Such laws of nature should not trick us into believing that anybody other than the souls themselves creates the overall nature, that they contain the principle of consciousness in charge of directing energy to create everything, both material forms, and events alike.

Prakriti or nature exists only as oblivion of human essence when humans are not conscious of themselves. It means the world appears for that soul only when it becomes identified with the body.

Observed from the perspective of the bodily mind, it appears as though the soul falls into a state of self-oblivion while it gets incarnated into a body and identifies itself with the phenomena. Afterward, it seems that it awakens gradually by learning to discern itself from the body, and returns to its 'heavenly state' which it had prior to its birth.

However, it is not the same process from the perspective of the soul. It never experiences oblivion. It, with its 'decline into an incarnation', consciously materializes the emergent world, all of its notions, generating both our body and the whole nature, too.

Purusha can never be unconscious, it can never 'decline' in any 'lower state', therefore its individual emanation, a conscious monad which is our soul, cannot do so, either. For the soul what we see as the 'fall into the matter and self-oblivion' is, in reality, a conscious act of creation of the body, materialization of ideas, accomplishment of the potentiality of nature.

Therefore, our soul is not born in the body, instead, it creates the physical body through which it partly forgets itself, and from the perspective of the bodily mind, it appears as though the soul was born in nature. This is the perspective of the body. If observed from the perspective of the soul, the soul's consciousness is an immobile witness, body is only one of its thoughts, a projection that encapsulates it and nothing more than that. The soul does not move, only the projected body gives an illusion of motion and action. The overall existing life is only an illusion of motion. According to the teaching of *Sâmkhya*, *Purusha* is an immobile witness, and all the actions are performed by *Prakriti* in the form of an illusion. Our essence or soul is the highest reality, an immobile principle of consciousness around which all the worlds are created, and all phenomena, too.

The fact that the whole nature is a materialization of self-oblivion, lies at the base of experience where we, with objective awareness, see ourselves in everything and everything in ourselves, and vice versa: by knowing ourselves we become objectively consciously aware of the nature of reality as one being which is ourselves. In objective reality, there is no difference between our essence and the reality itself.

While human beings are identified with the body they cannot see the original voidness of the absolute who engenders everything. To enlightened or awakened humans, the world disappears and only then can they begin to live truly with the full awareness and meaning because the disappearance of the world is a realization of their essence or purpose of existence. It is the liberation of voidness that keeps creating them at any given moment. For enlightened humans, the disappearance of the world equals the *occurrence* of their essence.

The experience of awakening is such where humans see clearly that not a single moment of the phenomena of the world would exist were it not for the eternal unconditioned emptiness (*akasha*) which engenders it, and this unconditionality is their only stronghold and destiny. Nothing at all exists apart from (or without) this unconditionality which is, therefore, no different from everything that exists. Unconditioned emptiness is shaped by phenomena, every form actualizes it. Without the voidness, existence as such is impossible, the same way voidness is not possible without existence. Consequently, the world of objects is not real but acts as if it were real for as long as humans are unconscious of themselves and identified with it.

Therefore, the following paradox happens at the point of awakening: the existence we have been identified thus far disappears, and only with its disappearance we discover the reality of existence. That explains why people find it hard to awaken because they fear they will lose what is real (only to them), what they own, the being they are identified with, and the result will be losing it without which all they have to look forward to is 'dark nothingness' alone. It is, however, the consequence of being identified with the being, and not the loss of it which really happens only after enlightenment.[16] This is a way in which people mistake the cause for the consequence. All evil stems only from ignorance of the true nature of life and blind identification with it. Hell is described as a place where people rid themselves of the illusions and identification, and is, therefore, filled with pain and suffering of the body. Only illu-

---

[16] The physical experience of the emergent world (*indriyani*) disappears for man in two ways: (1) by a spontaneous crossover phase of his individuality from *indriyani* to the inorganic realm (during sleep or death of the body), and (2) by ascending to *aham-kâra* and *buddhi* categories - in this experience humans are awake, while at the same time liberated from the world of emergence. This liberation is what makes him awaken.

sions cause suffering. Those who failed to use the opportunity to liberate themselves of the identification with the being during life must be liberated of the same in hell by nature itself, albeit, in a hard way since *it does not accept the human soul which is identified with it*. The soul which is identified with the body even when it exists cannot make heads or tails of its authenticity. Therefore, the situation is quite the reverse: *nature must find its essence in the human soul (Purusha)*. Everything that is hellish, diabolical, and evil, represents the inside out state where the human soul perpetuates in being identified with nature. Everything that is evil rests on this identification. Everything that is good begins with the cessation of this identification.

Unconditionality of *Purusha* is openness which guarantees presence and co-belonging to existence and consciousness. The silence of emptiness in the human heart is the only place which facilitates the possibility of co-belonging and consciousness, their unity which engenders presence and discernment of the world. The issue of consciousness or unconsciousness is only a matter of openness of the presence in existence or its being closed-off. To be present in existence means to be aware. If the Self were not empty, if there were something else in it, there would be no room for existence, it could not encapsulate the world as it is. If it were not quiet and without a thought, consciousness would not be possible, at all, because wakefulness is born only in the silence of the mind. No other way exists.

Unconditionality of *Purusha* is not the "truth", but the openness which engenders every kind of truth, both the subject of cognition as well as the object. Truth as such can only be in the element of openness from which everything originates.

Although *Purusha* is separate and independent from everything that exists, from our body and all the emergent world, it is closer to humans than everything else, every thought and deed, and the being itself, too. It is closer because it is the necessary requirement of their Self and wakefulness. Consequently, to unconscious humans, which means passive, inactive, and irresponsible ones, what is the closest seems the furthest away. Most commonly they project it outwardly as far as possible, into an idea of God. Without putting the complete focus on consciousness (*samadhi*), humans can never reach what is theirs; they always grab at what does not belong to them or is alien to them. They always try to be something they are not, rather than make an effort to be themselves. They keep wandering about like homeless men in their own world. They are supported by a collective conviction that this other is themselves, in fact. This conviction is the collective unconsciousness.

Unawakened humans seek shelter in many things that are not suited for the Self, and nothing but the Self can be appropriate. Everything that is different from it is transient, illusory, and painful. Humans are hurt by what is not authentic. Unawakened humans seek to find comfort in things. Once they see the emptiness of all this, they awaken. That is how emptiness facilitates the awakening of humans – the same way their full presence in existence awakens them.

Unconditioned emptiness, *Purusha*, is always present in us as the condition of our Self, as the creator of our soul, and supersedes all the transient natural creations. That explains why everything that is born dies so easily, due to the transience of time it is dead already, but the essence of everything is timeless immortal unconditionality. Nothing that has ever lived in time was ever jeopardized or in vain. *Sâmkhya-kârikâ* in verse 62. says: "Verily, therefore, the Self is neither bounded nor emancipated, nor does it transmigrate; it is Nature alone, abiding in myriad. forms, that is bounded, released, and transmigrates." *Purusha* is always free and realized, only nature acts and suffers the consequences of its actions (*karma*). From the position of *Sâmkhya*, human essence is neither born nor does it engage in actions and die. They are all of nature's activities. Humans can dream of them or participate in them like in a dream, although they are not required to do so. Humans can choose freely. In the availability of the freedom of choice lies all the secret of liberation. For humans to choose freedom, all they must do is be consciously present at its source, in themselves. The only humans who are not free are the ones who do not know that they can be free, instead listening to other slaves and slavemasters, forgetting about themselves and their primeval will to be what they are. The knowledge of freedom and its always readily available choice cannot be acquired by following the natural causality, but by overcoming it, through transcendence.

***

The essence of distinguishing *Purusha* from *Prakriti*, and ultimately the essence of the discipline of liberating humans from unconsciousness, according to *Sâmkhya*, is in knowing *Purusha* as an immobile and timeless center in humans, and *Prakriti* as the always spontaneously active and conditioned living which is placed around that center, as the axis, that forms the world, the human psychophysical being, and destiny (*karma*). They are necessary as such to provide experience for the orientation of consciousness, for finding balance, and for centering the inactive hub (*Purusha*). Once this is achieved, it reveals itself as all-important for shaping everything around it.

This means that every life is, in a sense, an imbalance. Realizing what the meaning of life is, brings balance and liberation from the whirlpool.

Unconsciousness and suffering are tied to the overall beingness of *Prakriti*. That is, when humans forget its essence as well as their own essence they lose their grip on reality. *Prakriti* is not the created and emergent world, but is, instead, the very principle of focusing which engenders balance for motion and forming of everything that exists. Holding oneself tightly to the being creates imbalance in the spontaneous forming of life on the path to its outcome and curtails the manifestation of their unconditioned center causing humans to lose their presence in it, in themselves. By losing presence and balance in the center, which is in themselves, the forming of nature is also disturbed. This is similar to turning the potter's wheel, except what gets shaped here instead of clay and ceramics is nature and the destiny of all the individuals in it.

A human being should be the one who shapes, a propellent force, and the balance for shaping, and not the shaped object. It is a message from *Sâmkhya* to humans: to be who they are, the creator, and not some object or a slave to the creation and the created. Hence, the fundamental differentiation between *Purusha* and *Prakriti* we can denote as *Purusha* being the one who decides on the being, which entails the authentic consciousness of oneself and the being, whereas *Prakriti* is that what is, what presupposes conditionality and unconsciousness. This discernment makes *Sâmkhya* the clearest doctrine of awakening.

Similar to the emptiness (*sunyam*) in the dialectics of Nagarjuna or Tao with Lao Tzu, *Purusha*, too, is an invisible or unknowable principle of all the visible and knowable phenomena.[17] It is eternal without action, not because it is incapable of it, but, quite to the contrary, because it is the fundamental prerequisite that precedes any action. Although it is the source of everything, it is irreducible as such. That what is of fundamental value should not be accessible to peril or transience. The awareness of the fundamental is crystallized only through discrimination and maintaining the presence of the inactive soul within, as opposed to the active and conditioning nature without. Humans are conditioned and lulled by abandonment and oblivion of themselves through identification with the outside world, and liberated and alerted by the presence in their Self, without rejection of any kind of phenomena, whether inner or outer. Any form of rejection of anything upsets the original transcendental nature of the Self – to the same degree as the identification with something.

This state of affairs means that nothing further can be said about *Purusha* since it represents that what transcends every rational experience. The description provided here offers nothing of the described. Only the philosophical terminology can be used to express what has been said so far, that it is the freedom of unconditionality that is life-giving to all the forms, that it is the source of creation which always remains independent, but signifies unity with everything created, for otherwise, nothing could ever be. The secret of this unity makes the world a magical place, attractive, and ultimately free; because of it life is accepted fully, with hope and love as a path towards the liberation of the soul; nobody would ever accept life if they originally did not possess the intuitive consciousness of the primeval freedom of their soul; hence, a personality that is more creative, conscious, and more free is more appealing – which corresponds with the higher degree the soul's consciousness that is present; as a result, this unity makes all the beings want to live. Without conscious participation in this unity

---

[17] In *Tao Te Ching* the same principle of differentiation as in *Sâmkhya* is presented, where *Tao* is *Purusha*, and *Te* is *Prakriti*.

66

with the divine consciousness via our soul, existence is but a cruel struggle where nothingness of death is always a winner, and life itself is just a negative abstraction, a dream, an illusion (*maya*) in which an unawakened human tries to exist and live truly, but invariably fails. Independence of the unconditioned *Purusha* facilitates liberation and awakening from this dream, it gives meaning and a constructive approach to life, without it life would always be destructive. Without *Purusha* nature would be completely conditioned and lifeless, it would be a dungeon for all the beings, without the possibility of exit into the meaning of existence, or more accurately put, without the meaningful contraction into consciousness and freedom. Its existence would be absurd and impossible. Owing to *Purusha*, a way out of the whirlpool of the causation of existence is out there, relaxation and calmness in meaning are possible, being born and dying is not everything that exists because our essence exceeds them.

The fact that *Purusha* is our essence means that we always exist (without ego), out of time and untouched by all the changes: in this and the other world; while being awake, dreaming, but in deep sleep, as well, when the worldliness is no longer present; above all the worlds; above life, and death as it were. This feeling that we always exist, beyond all the states of consciousness and the body, is always present in us, although it appears blurred at times.

The body is only a place where our eternal soul abides temporarily. Psychodynamics of nature has a very attractive power, it drives us to forget our eternal presence and identify with the transience of bodily phenomena. That makes us suffer in a dream because of something that does not happen to us and does not concern us, at all. Unfortunately, this simple truth we become aware of only when we awaken.

All the physical bodies have their own gravity, and our body is also a kind of magnet that goes around the world involving itself in various actions gathering impressions (*vasanas*) in the process from everything that keeps happening to it. A collection of such impressions construct our image of the world and personal history. A body coated in impressions like that becomes an even stronger magnet. Maybe this is one of the explanations why *Purusha* is generally identified with the transient phenomena.

Apart from this, it is important to understand that *Purusha* does not create *Prakriti*, but is, instead, pure unconditionality that facilitates its existence. The act of creation must take place in time, and time cannot exist before creation, it happens only as a modification of *Prakriti*. Classical texts say that *Purusha* invites *Prakriti* to create the world with its sheer proximity, with its presence. The way a magnet attracts metal shavings. The relationship between *Prakriti* and *Purusha* is the same as between a phenomenon and its meaning. Texts concur that *Purusha* has no properties and is devoid of action. What is meant by that is that its nature is transcendental, beyond possessing or not possessing any characteristics, beyond the being and non-being. In other words, *Purusha* is in us as our essence here and now, and is therefore undefinable in words which are aimed at outer descriptions and time projections. For *Purusha*, it is irrelevant whether the characteristics exist or not, whether it exists as the transcendental soul which is nothing of the being, or it manifests as the being itself, as the world. There are no differences for it there. ***All the differences exist in an unawakened mind only, to whom the relative world of dualistic relationships is the only reality. Hence, everything that has been said about Purusha refers to the unawakened mind, and not Purusha itself.***

Since *Purusha*'s prime quality is being transcendental, it is ultimately the chief attractor – that what induces into existence. On the road to understanding *Purusha* and *Prakriti* notions such as 'everything' and 'nothing' lose their boundaries and meaning. They become one. However, this 'one' is not 'something', therefore it cannot be said that *Purusha* and *Prakriti* are one. The soul 'creates' nature by non-action, with its mere presence; nature acts because the inactive soul attracts it to do so. The primordial aspiration of all the beings towards liberation stems from this attraction.

The most accurate definition of the relationship between *Purusha* and *Prakriti* is that *Prakriti* transforms itself for the benefit of the immobile and inactive *Purusha* in a way which seems that *Purusha* itself manifests through *Prakriti*, that it is the creator of everything. Hence, we have a mirror effect here (*Prakriti*) which moves while the image that is looking at itself (*Purusha*) stands still, but appears as though it is moving.

***

The most concise that could be said about the relationship between *Purusha* and *Prakriti* is that **all of the emergent and material world of nature (Prakriti) is brought about automatically as a response to the unconsciousness of the the human soul (Purusha) of itself while it is incarnated in man. Outside of its incarnation in humans, without the modifications of the mind, Purusha can neither be unconscious nor identified with Prakriti.** *Prakriti* is the materialization of unconsciousness, their dream (or *karma*, as Jains claim). By making their unconsciousness concrete and material, it helps them become aware of it and awaken themselves. It is the *karma* with which humans are forced to face their unconsciousness, the one they work with on the path to their awareness. In that respect, it is said that *Prakriti* works for the benefit of *Purusha*.

***

The independence of *Purusha* from *Prakriti* is the key to understanding human survival. By seeking refuge in the unconscious existence, we can find only suffering because human essence (*Purusha*) is primevally independent of the being and its unconscious elements. On the other hand, existence itself aspires to find its outcome and sanctuary in the perfect, independent humans (*Purusha*), in conscious humans, to illuminate themselves through it. Humans, by overcoming the conditionality of the being, attain not only their purpose but nature's purpose, as well. Thus, by tying themselves to it like some slaves, they only inflict suffering on themselves and nature, too.

Without their perfection, awakening, and independence, humans are unworthy of living in nature, as the continually disrupt and desecrate it. There they can find only suffering because their behavior is unnatural while, at the same time, they are unaware of the fact that they are trying to find a sanctuary in the being without realizing that the situation is quite the reverse: the whole of nature made them in order to attain freedom through them, that they themselves have been shaped to represent the embodiment of the wholeness of nature's beingness (therefore nothing "different" or "new" can be found in the objectivistic sense in nature, i.e., outwardly). Nature through the human form always aspires toward its outcome, toward the freedom of the awakened human soul. That explains why humans disrupt this aspiration if they attach themselves to nature lowly, if they continue projecting themselves out-wardly, if they are going in the opposite direction. He must find sanctuary in themselves because they are the ultimate goal of eve-rything. It practically means that everything we see outside, all the mistakes and imperfections, we should not project outwardly into the state of the world or other people, and make an outer problem out of it, try to change people and the world by force, but to rather **acknowledge everything and correct it within ourselves** the moment it appears. We should crystallize ourselves through the awareness of ourselves.

***

A lack of understanding everything that has been said rein-troduced the old problem regarding *Purusha*: a question was raised of whether it is one and the absolute, like *atman* in *Advaita Vedan-ta*, or if there is a multitude of *Purushas*, as monads, meaning one for each man. The commentators of *Sâmkhya-sûtras* made an effort to prove that there are as many *Purushas* as there are people, to make sure they are in some way different from *Advaita Vedanta* which at the time (around the fourteenth century) was becoming dominant and threatened to suppress the teaching of *Sâmkhya*. For, if they admitted to the fact that *Purusha* is only one and absolute, they would in no way be different from Shankara's *Advaita Vedan-ta*. Their chief argument was a claim that if *Purusha* indeed were the only one, then the first human to experience the liberation of their soul from *Prakriti* would automatically, with this act, liberate all other people.[18] Additionally, if *Purusha* (as the source of a soul) were universal, there would be no differences in the destinies of people.

This misconception is the result of an inability to distinguish between relative and absolute reality. Relative reality is the one that is projected by the mind (*manas*) from the experience of *Prakri-ti*, while the absolute reality is the one that surpasses the relative, the one that transcends it. Only a relative mind is capable of pro-jecting *Purusha* into a collective property of all people or envisaging it as an alienated monad trapped within an individual being. *Puru-*

---

[18] However, this does happen, although not instantly but in the linear time of the dimension we live in (the element of earth). Enlightened people gradually libe-rate all the other people, as well.

sha is neither individual nor is it collective, but is transcendental, instead. The experience of transcendental consciousness is the only prerequisite for comprehending *Purusha*, and that is the consciousness that has surpassed both the body and mind, all the contents that constitute the world and attribute characteristics to everything. *Purusha* is without properties. They are all a reflection of *Prakriti*. It could vividly be described using the allegory of the vessels filled with water, and in each one, a reflection of the moon can be seen. By observing through a reflection of *Prakriti* it appears as though there is a multitude of *Purushas*, within each individual (vessel).

Instead of the metaphor with the vessels in the old texts, we will deal with that problem here by understanding higher dimensions. It will become self-evident in the later text, in the chapter on the dimensions of nature, that dimensions exist as a pyramidal Gestalt, they refract one and the same light into a myriad of colors. Therefore, ***in order to understand the issue of unity or a multitude of consciousnesses (Purusha), the dimensions of nature should be properly understood***.

If there were only one universal *Purusha*, it would mean the world would, then, truly disappear every time human consciousness turned towards itself, to the Self, whenever the human falls fast asleep without dreaming. This is exactly what happens: during the deep phase of sleeping without dreams the world, as such, disappears for that person. Additionally, the world would disappear even permanent liberation or self-knowledge of the soul is attained. The fact is that the world goes on living while a person is in deep sleep or has attained self-knowledge, and other people are also witnesses to this. The reason for this is our current dimension we reside in (the element of earth), from which we observe the phenomena and think there is a multitude, although everything has a common source in the highest dimension.

In the highest dimension (the element of air) everything is momentary in the perpetual present, all the possibilities of existence coexist timelessly and in parallel, while those in the lowest one, in the physical world (the element of earth), are objectively separated across space and time, only one of the possibilities can take place at a time. The nature of dimensions is such that they make the world both real and imaginary simultaneously, every-thing is connected into unity, although it, to an untrained eye, appears like a multitude.

Therefore, because of the dimensions, everything seems to contain a myriad of *Purushas* and it appears that the world exists objectively, and the same applies to all the incarnating souls, they experience the same illusion. For the world to exist there must be a conscious subject for whom the world begins to exist, the one who becomes aware of the world. There are always conscious subjects because there is a multitude of *Purushas*, and the multitude exists because of the very nature of dimensions and refraction of one consciousness into a multitude. Although a multitude is nothing but an illusion, it gives an objective reality to the world we live in, enabling individual souls to function in one world as though it were real per se. They can also attain liberation of their own because of the connectedness of everything with the highest dimension.

If nature were material only, if there were a multitude of souls and occurrences, and if that were the only reality, only one dimension of existence, liberation would be permanently out of reach.

***

Apart from the dilemma about a multitude or a unity of *Purusha*, there is an additional question of the relationship between *Purusha* and *Prakriti*. If *Purusha* were eternally free and independent, what is the effect of *Prakriti* on it then, and why does it get involved in *Prakriti*'s experience, at all? The relationship between *Purusha* and *Prakriti* in the system of *Sâmkhya* cannot be observed metaphysically, but practically and ontologically. Although *Purusha* is not conditioned, it to an individual soul (*jiva*) seems conditioned, this is its image of reality because the soul itself is conditioned. It projects its conditioned reality. Hence, only to unenlightened humans, the issue of *Purusha*'s and *Prakriti*'s relationship exists. The emergence of *Prakriti* is relative, although a the human soul experiences the conditionality of nature in real terms, and *Sâmkhya* informs us that absolute freedom exists and is within reach, in the form of authenticity. No other way exists. Then *Prakriti* exits the stage, and all its conditioning ceases.

72

The problem of understanding *Purusha* and *Prakriti* can be reduced to the problem of self-knowledge of the one who has to understand the problem. *Purusha* is human essence and it cannot be comprehended via accumulated knowledge or patterns that can be applied to all the people, but only as an individual personal knowing. In other words, *Sâmkhya* is not metaphysics. The freedom of the human soul must happen in a personal experience to be existential, whereas every experience must have its opposition point to be experienced. Thus, *Purusha* and *Prakriti* are debated in dualistic terms. It is done in such a manner to bring it closer to the human's experience. Transcendental and absolute are not good starting points, but only relative and experiential. The experience of all humans is conditionality and suffering; *Sâmkhya* points to a whole context of existence, it stresses that the realm of suffering can always be overcome by the transcendence of *Prakriti*, that the transcendence of suffering is always possible because human essence – *Purusha* – is already transcendental in relation to *Prakriti*. *If it were not like that already, it could never become so in our experience.*

Therefore, whenever the liberation of the soul from *Prakriti* is the issue, or attaining spiritual independence, it is referred to as mental maturity, to the objective consciousness, and not a change in the state of the soul itself.

Having spoken about the practical experience of *Purusha* we must emphasize here that it as a principle of consciousness provokes *Prakriti* into existing. Matter exists *for the sake of* a conscious subject, and not vice versa. *All the material world we see around ourselves (Prakriti), and all the events in us as well as outside of us, have been provoked into existing by our souls (Purushas) with their mere presence.*

The universe is a hologram, and we are its conscious subject, its projector. That explains why all the enlightened ones discover is that nothing is outside of us, our Self is the absolute who is aware of itself ("this *atman is brahman*" say Upanishads). However, this kind of an insight is a result of the objective examination of the being (*Prakriti*). It seems incredible now. It is not our starting point, it is rather something we achieve having been acquainted with *Prakriti* first.

73

There is nothing further that could be said about *Purusha*. Only the being of an objective world (*Prakriti*) is something we can add further introspection and opinion about, and we will bring it forth in the following chapters.

PRAKRITI

In its original or authentic state, *Prakriti* is an unmanifested foundation of everything that exists as nature, the universal field of the being. Everything originates from it, it never manifests on its own in the experience of an average understanding of beingness. We experience only its results and products, that what is in the form of something special, while we deduce on it based on an assumption that everything has its cause, whereas the root cause or antecedent of everything must be the unmanifested (*avyaktam*) absolute foundation of the whole universe. *Prakriti* is the hidden or the implicit order, the comprehensive unity of the being outside of space and time. *Sâmkhya* is a theory of emanation because it speaks of one eternal, uncaused, and indestructible foundation that manifests everything that exists in an indivisible interconnectedness and causality.

In the description of *Prakriti*, we can easily recognize the description of the universal quantum field.

The word *Prakriti* consists of two parts. The root *kr-* (to do, to act, to make) expresses a constant primal motive force that is the essential constituent for shaping the world with its vibrations. Prefix *pra-* corresponds with *pro-* in the word "produce" and Greek *proto-*, especially in the word "prototype". According to this, the world is procreated, constantly manifested from *Prakriti* which is the common causal foundation (*pradhana*) of everything that exists by means of constant transformation (*parinama*). *Pra-* also means before, ago, and if we know that *kriti* refers to creation, the meaning of the word *Prakriti* is that it represents that what precedes creation, what precedes manifestation, a universal and primal foundation which facilitates the overall phenomena. *Prakriti* is unmanifested (*avyaktam*) for the same reason the principle of indeterminacy exists in quantum physics.

Purusha does not create *Prakriti*, but it engenders the manifestation of *Prakriti*. The way it happens can be understood dually, as a metaphysical and physical process.

The metaphysical description may add a finer touch to it by saying that *Purusha* is the Absolute who manifests as everything that exists and has relative properties (*Prakriti*). Hence, in the form of its own opposition. Since the Absolute is outside of space and time, its manifestation must be like this, it cannot be any different from itself. For its manifestation to remain the same, and yet different at the same time, the only way to manifest is in the form of a point. The opposition of something infinitely big is something infinitely small. The infinite is usually depicted as a circle or zero. The infinitely small is depicted as a point. Euclid's description attributes identical properties to both the point and the Absolute, as well, it is out of space and time which means that it is manifested instantly as everything that exists. We may call it the "divine particle" just the same. It does everything instantly. With this single point, the Absolute manifests all of its potentiality, the entire cosmos. Such manifestation in *Sâmkhya* is called *Prakriti*.

Prakriti has multiple dimensions and proportions, it exists as the gross matter, as energy, but as thoughts, as well. It has unmanifested and manifested aspects, gross and subtle, too. Only in its finest aspect *Prakriti* is a quantum field which is in the scheme of categories depicted as ether or *akasha*. *Akasha* or ether is what is called the quantum field in modern physics, or the holographic universe. *Akasha* is the foundation of nature that encompassed and unites the overall existence.

We have got one step closer to the physical description of the manifestation of *Prakriti*.

Prakriti from its highest or the most subtle aspect, *akasha* or the quantum field, creates everything that exists, all the cosmos and life. *Akasha* means space in translation. It means that space creates mass, that is to say, matter. Nowadays, this fact is common knowledge in physics.[19]

Here we will briefly describe the following.

The original manifestation of the Absolute or *Purusha* is endless space, without properties. Its first manifestation, as its opposition, is the **vibration** in the form of a point or "divine particle". *Akasha* or the quantum field vibrates in all sorts of ways. Its most sub-

---

[19] On how space, that is to say, the quantum field, creates mass, or matter, see the works of a renowned physicists Nassim Haramein.

tle vibrations create the fundamental particles which in turn create atoms, that further create molecules, and so forth, all the way to gross forms we view as the world, cosmos, and life. They are all merely vibrations, nothing else. There is no matter, only vibration we see as energy also.

In the heart of each torus, the one that forms the atom as well as the one that forms the galaxy, there is an empty field of *akasha* or ether. This empty field of *akasha* is what is commonly known as the "black hole" nowadays. Hence, the center of each torus field is the "black hole".

The primal manifestation of the Absolute as its opposition, the point or "divine particle", constantly tends to go back to the Absolute. It is logical, the opposite magnetic poles tend to unite. As though it feels alienated from its true nature and therefore aspires to return to the Absolute. It happens in the following way. The most subtle vibration of the point or "divine particle" is the photon. That explains why the photon is the fastest moving phenomenon in whole nature, it moves at the speed of light, and in all directions, because it wishes to go back to its unmanifested Absolute the fastest. Consequently, all the mystical teachings say the light is the rudimentary property of the creation and the Divine itself. Photon is non-material, and yet it exists in the physical world because it is a wave and a particle at the same time. In what way? Simply, there are different-sized photons. When they collide in their constant movement they do so under different angles. Different angles of photon collisions originate based on their differing size. This is how colors come about. Colors are nothing but different angles of photon refraction. That is why the whole existence is in colors. However, when photons of the same size collide, gamma photons, they create a stable whirlpool of stationary waves or a field. A torus field. It creates mass. It has been proved experimentally that light creates the mass. This is how the whole of the material universe is created, and we can perceive it with our senses, visible in all the colors as well as in light. Light is also the basic property of the microworld, atoms glow on their own, and so do our cells. Our DNA is a light code.[20]

Varying torus sizes, the whirlpools of *akasha*, create objects of varying sizes. The smallest ones create atoms and bigger ones molecules and living beings. In the gravitational center of a human being, there is one such "black hole" of miniature proportions. Bigger ones create planets whereas the biggest "black holes" create galaxies. Even the astrophysicists concluded that black holes create all the matter of the universe. The truth is – they create everything. They are nothing but vibrations in their essence, but in a way where they behave coherently as solid objects. This is a way in which nature exists both as information and gross 'material' form, it exists both in time and timelessly – all at once. These differences are the basis for the dimensions of nature.

Hence, the manifestation of *Prakriti* happens owing to *Purusha* who does nothing.

***

To sum up, *Sâmkhya,* as the most ancient of sciences, speaks of nature in the same terms modern science does, albeit, in different terminology where the universal energy quantum Field comes into play, or the Quantum hologram, Divine matrix, and the like, which is the primal (to our senses unmanifested) field of all the individual occurrences (which we perceive with our senses as the world around us), and which connects all the individual occurrences into One.[21] Owing to this general connectedness of every-

---

[20] An image of the shape of wavefronts of a single photon has been made recently, and it looks identical to the templar cross, the way it has been shown on the covers of this book. It is a cross resembling a square with splayed feet, each akin to the foot. The cross and square are ancient symbols of materiality and realization of consciousness on the physical plane. The vibrational movement of photons creates a mass that is similar to the "flower of life". Hence, the "flower of life" is the symbol of our soul that is the creator of the overall life in nature.

[21] In 1982. at Paris University a team of scientists led by the physics professor, Alain Aspect, conducted one of the most significant experiments of the twentieth century that still shakes the foundations of modern science. Aspect and his colleagues discovered that under certain circumstances subatomic particles like electrons, for example, can momentarily convey a piece of information from one to another regardless of the distance between the two. It proved irrelevant whether the space apart was 10 meters or 10 billion kilometers. In a way, one particle knew exactly what the other one was doing.

thing, a feeling of unity and love toward everything is possible. Our feelings are, more than anything else, a direct link to this universal energy Field which engenders the use of consciousness and feelings to impact the Field creatively and, consequently, the reality itself.

Prakriti is the universal energy foundation of the cosmos. However, energy is neither the source of consciousness nor is it conscious by itself. Consciousness stems from the transcendental *Purusha*. The consciousness is the universal attractor and energy director. Energy always moves towards the consciousness, it always has an informative character. This connection and attraction pull of the consciousness (*Purusha*) makes energy (*Prakriti*) seem as though it were conscious itself, and consciously sets about engaging in various actions, the same way it appears to us that metal shavings move of their own accord, although they are merely drawn to a magnet, as it were.

Therefore, *Sâmkhya* teaches us that the very presence of the human, *Purusha*, transforms nature, *Prakriti*, that is to say, creates all the emergent life we view as the objective world. Modern physics has arrived at similar conclusions when it was experimentally proven that subatomic particles behave as the pure energy field when humans are absent during the experiment, and then they can be in two places at the same time, they are not dependent on space and time in any way – the Double-slit experiment 1909 – whereas when humans are present, they begin to act as material particles defined by space and time. Only people who conducted this experiment were aware of how a particle should look and act, and it did

---

The problem with this revolutionary find was that it eliminates Einstein's assumption based on the belief that nothing faster than the speed of light exists in the universe. As a result, most mainstream scientists found the experiment discovery false, but, David Bohm, a professor of physics at London University, offered a more radical explanation. He claims that Aspect's finds confirm that the objective world does not exist, i.e., that despite the fact this universe seems material to us, made from solid ground, fundamentally, it is nothing but a hologram of gigantic proportions. Within it, every piece is a reflection of the whole and the whole itself is contained within every single piece. This facilitates the momentary communication of all the "pieces", everything is connected to One, as the ancient sciences have been trying to teach us for centuries. Instant communication is yet another way to say that consciousness is at the base of everything.

so in an identical manner. The consciousness created the physical reality through people. (Hence, the issue of a subject originated in physics, it became apparent that they are not only observers but active participants, as well, who play the deciding role on the experiment results. It was not until recently that the new physics learned to associate ancient knowledge with these experimental results.[22])

The foundation of everything is the quantum field (*Prakriti*), and consciousness (*Purusha*) is at the base of it. The consciousness connects all the particles into one and engenders their communication. The foundation of all life is consciousness. Owing to momentary communication between the subatomic particles the perception of the world itself and the awareness of existence is made possible.

The recent finds made by experimental physics were expressed a long time ago in the ancient text of classical *Sâmkhya, Sâmkhya-kârika* by Ishvara Krishna: 57. "Just as insentient milk serves as nourishment for the calf, so too does Nature (*Prakriti*) act for the sake of the Self's emancipation (*Purusha*)." 59. "Just as a fair dancer having exhibited herself to the spectators, desists from the dance, so does *Prakriti* desist, having exhibited herself to *Purusha*." 61."My opinion is that nothing exists which is more delicate than *Prakriti* who, knowing that, "I have been seen", comes no more within the sight of *Purusha*."

1. Frequences of manifested and unmanifested *Prakriti*

Apart from the philosophical *Sâmkhya* that is a matter for the debate in this book, there is also *Samkhyă* (stress on the final a) which deals with mathematics and physics. It is considered to be at least 12,000 years old. It describes nature or *Prakriti* as a singular field based on the timeless oscillatory state of space (*akasha*), which is a unique form of all the forms of existence, both manifested and unmanifested ones. To use more technical terminology, ***unmanifested or basic nature, such as ether or akasha, is based on the stationary or non-Hertzian waves, whereas the manifested nature we ob-***

---

[22] See more on this in Fritjof Capra's book: Fritjof Capra: The Tao of Physics.

serve to be a myriad of objects and phenomena, is based on the vector, Hertzian waves.[23]

The nature of non-Hertzian electromagnetic waves is stationary, volumetric, resembling a breathing, vibrating sphere. It is different from the transversal vector form of the classical electromagnetic waves. All the celestial bodies, stars, and planets, all the torsion motion of energy in nature, are based on this spherical non-Hertzian principle, from galaxies to individual living beings. They all breathe, their heart vibrates because their energy aura is a torsion field of stationary frequencies. *Sankhyă* teaches that human consciousness, the soul or *Purusha*, generates torsion waves, it is the chief attractor of all phenomena of nature.

The speed of light is the borderline that divides Hertzian from the non-Hertzian state of *Prakriti*. The Hertzian is all phenomena slower than the speed of light. The non-Hertzian state of *Prakriti* goes beyond the speed of light, it is, in effect, momentary. Since it is momentary it is at the same time independent of the space and time which means that all the possibilities of manifested existence are contracted into a timeless One there, or more accurately, they exist in parallel. Therefore, the Hertzian state is manifested *Prakriti*, and the non-Hertzian is unmanifested.

Over 12,000 years the mathematicians of *Sankhyă* knew that values of the golden section connect all kinds of electromagnetic radiation, of both Hertzian and non-Hertzian nature, manifested and unmanifested, expansive, compressive, and resonant states. Based on this they knew about the Pi number, the base of the natural logarithm, natural constants, speed of light and

---

[23] Nikola Tesla, more than a century ago, discovered and utilized a new kind of electromagnetic waves in his experiments which he named the non-Hertzian or stationary. He did so to emphasize their different property as compared to the classical, so-called Hertzian electromagnetic waves. During one storm he happened to notice a phenomenon of ball lightning. He then realized that electric energy moves not only vector-like but spherically, stationary as well, it becomes a ball. He understood quickly that if everything were energy, then all the non-Hertzian motion as such is more fundamental than that of the vector and Hertzian type which explains why all the celestial bodies are spherical in shape since such is the property of the physics of ether. The problem is that the existing science fails to recognize either of the electromagnetic waves apart from those H.R. Hertz proved to exist in 1888.

speeds higher than that, the fundamental frequency of the quantum field of nature, *Prakriti* (they measured it at 299 792 458 oscillations per meter of wavelength per second which is the speed of light in vacuum), they knew about values of particles, electrons, protons, and neutrinos, they were aware of what is known as the Planck's constant today which explains the transfer of energy without friction, that is to say without any losses...[24] In short, everything modern theory of the universal quantum field is based on, and much more: the way it connects to the human and their consciousness, what it means to the human and how humans can realize it within themselves. Moreover, they knew that the outcome of the universe manifests and realizes itself through humans, through their Self or the soul. There is no other way.

***

Humans, *Purusha*, is a factor that merges the unmanifested and manifested because they overcome *Prakriti*. This is the difference between *Purusha* and *Prakriti*: *Prakriti* is either unmanifested or manifested in nature, and only in humans its wholeness and unity of the unmanifested and manifested aspect of existence take place – when the transcendental consciousness is attained that exceeds them both. Only humans can be aware of all the aspects of *Prakriti*.

Therefore, the space and time of the three-dimensional 'material' reality we can perceive with our senses, originates spontaneously based on the immaterial timeless unmanifested essence of nature we cannot perceive with our senses and the relative mind. The manifested and unmanifested nature are two sides of the same coin. One like in a mirror reflects the other.

Modern physics discovered these two aspects of physical reality when it was discovered that subatomic particles behave as energy i.e., a wave, and as particles.

Energy i.e., wave existence of nature is unmanifested, called a quantum, a pure potential, a 'package' of vibrations something can come out of. What is to come about, which atom and element, depends only on the frequencies, and frequencies are thoughts and

---

[24] See more research into the scientific aspect of *Sâmkhya* in the work by Srinivasan: Secret Of Sankhya - Acme Of Scientific Unification (http://www.kapillavastu.com)

ideas. Thoughts are the most subtle forms of frequencies, information, according to which nature manifests and shapes itself.

The manifested state of nature are particles, atoms, and molecules, this material reality we perceive with our senses and the mind.

Unmanifested and manifested nature can both be adequately compared with a cartwheel. The unmanifested foundation of nature is like the center of the wheel which is immobile (stationary); the manifested nature is like the outer rim of the wheel that is continuously (in a vector-like fashion) moving.

***

Unmanifested and manifested nature as such is known in other systems, but most commonly either in a distorted, mythologized, or in the esoteric form. Apart from *Sâmkhya*, only Taoism has this truth about nature clearly expressed. Unmanifested non-Hertzian nature is depicted as *Tao*, and manifested, Hertzian as *Te*. The relationship between the manifested and unmanifested nature, understanding of both, and proper actions in accordance with both of them, were perfectly described in *Tao Te Ching*. The non-Hertzian actions from the perspective of Hertzian are called *Wu Wei* in Taoism, or action through non-action. The symbol of *Tai chi* (☯) represents circling of both manifested and unmanifested nature, from *akasha* to *buddhi*, and from *buddhi* to *akasha*, from the consciousness to form and from the form to consciousness, through all the opposites. Manifested nature conduces the consciousness and perception of existence of the Absolute consciousness into all the forms of the existence and experiences *and retrieves it having been enriched first to the divine Absolute or Purusha through the awareness of oneself (buddhi) which is the consciousness of unity*. This return may be understood as the circling of the whole, the way it was presented in Tao philosophy with the symbol of the circling of *yin* and *yang* in the symbol of *Tai chi*. Thus, the whole universe breathes and pulsates like a sphere.

The manifested and manifested nature is the rudimentary cause for the existence of the poles in the motion of energy and in the beings, *yin* and *yang*, in all the processes and phenomena. Based on this polarization the Book of Change, *I Ching* has come to exist,

83

which maps out schemes for all the processes and events, both on the small and the large scale.

***

Further points should be made regarding the practical understanding of how the unmanifested non-Hertzian nature and manifested Hertzian nature function in everyday life.

The categories of *Prakriti, aham-kâra,* and *buddhi* are those that function on the non-Hertzian spectrum of nature, irrelevant of space and time, here and now, stationary and holistically. The category of *manas* or the mind connects this part of the non-Hertzian spectrum with manifested Hertzian, with the three-dimensional physical reality, and functioning in linear space and time, with all the categories on the scheme of *Prakriti* under *manas* level which are *indriyâni, maha-bhûtâni,* and *tanmâtrâ.*

In simpler terms, this means that the power to act is greater the deeper the levels of consciousness are invoked for our functioning (theta or alpha), which are the levels of *aham-kâra* and *buddhi* consciousness, the awareness of a single I-am and pure consciousness without thoughts, and consequently, we have less power if we are on the superficial (beta) frequencies on the *manas* level, or the relative thinking mind. On the deepest level, we are one with everything, centered in here and now, whereas in the superficial, everyday mind we are powerless individuals driven by the illusion of time and tied to individual phenomena.

On the deeper level of consciousness, in the consciousness of unity, *mahat-buddhi,* there is no time, the aim has already been achieved, and the same works for the fundamentals of nature, in *akasha.* There is not a causative process of attaining a goal. It seemingly exists only in the superficial, relative mind.

The mind unites the unmanifested and manifested (non-Hertzian and Hertzian) aspect of reality like a mirror. The mind is a mirror the whole of nature reflects in, both unmanifested and manifested.

If we think in a Hertzian way, or the way we have learned to do with our relative mind (beta waves, everyday, active or the relative mind – linear motion, first the cause then consequence), such motion tends to lose its power and direction over time and does not fulfill the plan entirely, or does not fulfill it at all if we do not make certain changes and introduce the added impulse, the way Gurd-jieff taught in the "Law of Seven". At best, what is realized is only what we physically implement ourselves, if the physical implementation is an option, at all.

If we transcend thoughts (*manas*) and function from one I (*aham-kâra*) and pure consciousness (*buddhi*), we then function via the non-Hertzian side, via higher dimensions of the universe, or astral and *akasha* that creates the future events on the physical plane, and then the plans come off and we see it from this dimension as the "law of attraction", irrelevant of time or causality. Non-Hertzian functioning is completely inverse to what we regard as real and only possible with our mind. In the objective non-Hertzian reality everything is in reverse, it is the mirror image of our 'here', therefore, everything 'there' functions conversely, **everything has already been attained there and exists irrelevant of causality**. We function in the non-Hertzian way when we act with our whole being, both consciously (beta), and unconsciously (alpha and theta waves) while being completely committed, without a doubt (without the mind), through a command or pure intent, **as though the goal had already been accomplished**. Then our success rate is at its highest.

***

Going back to the philosophical and theoretical aspect of *Sâmkhya,* we could say that the phenomena of the universe in *Prakriti* are bent (*a-vikrti*) into One, while the world of objective experience is known as development (*vikrti*) or the emanation of this One into a multitude that engenders the experience of being in a conscious subject. It is the basic drive of the whole nature. This practically means that *Prakriti* is an implicit field in which there is absolutely timelessly everything that can exist in any way possible. Everything that was in the universe, everything that there is, and everything that will ever be are already contained within *Prakriti*. **Nothing new ever originates**. Everything that can exist and happen at all, exists somewhere and unveils. Everything that could be will be, it is so already, however in its unmanifested form. We can perceive like an event in the world only what is currently being manifested in the illusion of the linear time in the frequency range of our perception. Our mind (*manas*) is a factor that decides when

and how it will manifest itself from the general potentiality of everything (the "quantum soup" of all the possibilities, a term coined
by physicists). *The mind (logos) is an instrument of the manifestation of everything. Hence, at the same time, it is the instrument of the
concealment of everything.*

We can only perceive and there is nothing else we could do
while we are passive and conditioned, while our mind is conditioned by the senses and body (*indriyâni*). Once we attain one complete personality, *aham-kâra*, the Self, *buddhi*, we then acquire the
power to act based on the pure consciousness (*Purusha*), and we are
able to make decisions about phenomena and create events, that is
to say, we decide what is manifested from *Prakriti*.

If we translate this ancient teaching into a modern language,
we can say that in the universal quantum Field there are two possibilities of existence timelessly present (if we are sick, we are also
healthy there, if we are poor, we are also rich there, if we have one I,
we have all the remaining I's, and the states of mind...) only the
principle of consciousness is the one that decides on the energy
shaping of reality, what is going to manifest of, it all. That is the
reason why our convictions and deep-seated beliefs, which means
consciousness united with feelings, have a deciding role in the manifested reality we are in. If we properly form and direct our consciousness and feelings, we can then create a reality in and outside
of ourselves, we can heal instantly from any disease we have and
change our existence. This is the definition of faith (we can perform miracles with): unison of consciousness and feelings. Using
consciousness we form, and with feelings, we give energy to this
form. Our feelings are our energy bond with the Field. All we are
lacking is the consciousness of ourselves.

From the universal quantum field (*Prakriti*) certain particles
and atoms are formed, and the entire physical world is made up of
them. Which atom is going to be made depends on its electric and
magnetic state. It means that for one atom to change into some
other one, it is necessary to alter its electric field (Stark effect) or
magnetic field (Zeeman effect). The strongest electromagnetic field
in the human body is that of the heart chakra, the center of our
feelings. The energy field of the heart is approximately 3 meters
(10 feet) in diameter. A somewhat smaller field is created by the

brain, the center of consciousness. Chakras in the human being are psycho-energetic transformers that create the physical reality. The first three chakras relate to the connection of the energy foundation of nature or the quantum Field, the upper three to the mental state and presence of consciousness. In between the three lower ones and three upper chakras, there is the central heart chakra which unites them.

Classical texts emphasize that *Prakriti* is unconscious, yet active due to the proximity of *Purusha*. *Purusha* attracts the unconscious *Prakriti* into action the way a magnet attracts metal shavings. It is also said that it spontaneously acts for somebody else's benefit (*Purusha*'s), the way a cow produces milk for the calf. Texts do not go beyond descriptions like these, but the actions of unconscious *Prakriti* look as though they were conscious, something we can see in the overall nature: in the metabolism of cells, all the physiological functions, even our brain's functioning (it works when we sleep), it all happens spontaneously, but purposefully; in the somnabulic state, when the body performs complex physical movements, although consciousness is not present; in the instinctive behavior of animals and people. Unlike animals which do not have their individuality, but differ according to species, the unconscious behavior of humans is modified by individuality resulting in their awareness that their (unconscious) behavior is 'I act', only because it is individualized, it appears as conscious actions, different from the unconscious behavior of nature. It is different from that of the animals, primarily in its individuation, but is (still) not conscious. It is only an illusion of ego. The feeling of individuality, 'I' or ego, is also a manifestation of unconscious nature – although they are vital for facilitating the presence of consciousness which comes only from *Purusha*.

Unconscious or mechanical functions of nature, which are necessary for living, become an obstacle for the functioning of the mind and consciousness. An immature human tends to interpret a natural determination where the survival of the species is imperative as their conscious action, as their own will. It gives them an illusion of being taken care of, even numinousness. Their conscious life is then formative, they live mechanically, following the patterns of natural urges, social, or religious dogmas, never acting freely and creatively. Therefore, one should always have in mind that the natural determination in lower dimensions of *Prakriti* is necessary (in *indriyâni, maha-bhûtâni* and *tanmâtrâ*), and in the higher ones (*aham-kâra,* and *buddhi*) it proves to be the main obstacle to the awareness of an unconditioned soul, an illusion which has yet to be conquered.

In *manas* or the physical mind, the discrimination happens together with separation into the lower and higher dimensions. That is why our mind is often contradictory, it can be both conditioned and creative intermittently.

***

Before we acquaint ourselves with *Prakriti* and all of its categories, it will be useful to present the entire structure in our imagination in two ways. The first way of the objective or cosmic depiction of *Prakriti* will be that its whole structure, according to the scheme presented, we visualize in the form of an equilateral quadrangular pyramid. The other way which corresponds with the depiction of a subject or microcosm is in the form of a splayed cross.

It will be useful for us for two reasons, namely. Firstly, it is to do with the path our understanding has never before been systematically directed toward, and such imagination will be necessary for us to find orientation on it. Furthermore, here we will not deal with ideas only (they all fall under one of the 23 categories, under *manas*), but with those natural conditions and regularities according to which everything comes into existence, even the ideas themselves. It is the road that overcomes all the rational and notional barriers because it is the only one that raises awareness of the overall existence, the one that leads to the whole.

The second reason is that the form of a pyramid matches the structure of nature's manifestation perfectly (*Prakriti*). Nature has many dimensions and they form the pyramidal structure, hence, we can say that nature is a pyramidal Gestalt. A square at the base is the universal symbol of physical realization, of the material world we can become aware of through our senses. Same as the cross, it symbolizes the realization of influence performed by all four elements, that is to say, dimensions: earth, water, fire, and air. The non-material principle of spaciousness in which everything

88

takes place is *akasha* and it gets its vision in the focal point at the top of the pyramid, or the center of the cross. Once a two-dimensional cross is projected into the three-dimensional space it becomes a pyramid, and its center is the top of the pyramid. In this way, a pyramid may be considered a three-dimensional cross whose juncture point is its top. The dynamic energy principle of *Prakriti* is expressed by the triangles whose trinity is constituted by *gunas* (*sattva*, *rajas*, and *tamas*), the triple principle of phenomena of everything that exists. The purpose of the whole structure is contracted through synthesis and purposeful overcoming in the point at the top, in *mahat*, the creative cosmic intelligence which in the human being (microcosm) unveils as the pure wakefulness or alertness (*buddhi*), the supreme intellect or objective understanding. The point at the top of the pyramid is the unity of the being, a universal, timeless quantum Field, all the emergent phenomena in humans come from. The same point on the microcosmic plane is the center of the cross which represents the Self.

This contraction from the base to the top, and the disappearance of the pyramid, or more accurately *Prakriti* in the consciously achieved unity of the being (*samadhi*), something with which its purpose has been achieved, is of vital importance for understanding *Prakriti* and the whole of *Sâmkhya* system. *Purusha* is unconditionality here that engenders the phenomena of nature in general. It liberates itself from the veil of *Prakriti* and is put to the foreground as the important one, to the degree the pyramid, or the realm of the conditionality of nature, narrows itself down to the point of its complete disappearance or cessation in the point at the top without dimensions, in the awareness of unconditionality as the result of the phenomena of nature. The more *Prakriti* becomes subtle in the higher dimensions, the more it disappears leaving the open ground for *Purusha*.

The structure of a pyramid clearly indicates fundamental constants of nature which says that each level, which progressively represents the density of its vibrations and the speed of time of its phenomena, overcomes through quality contraction the preceding, lower one. The base of the pyramid shows its vibrations to be the slowest on that spot which means the conditionality of the space-time phenomena is at its highest there. Ultimately, it is manifested as what we generally refer to as 'matter'. Nature is all the more inert if the vibrations of its manifestation are slower and arranging themselves to become space and time consequently. This concretization into the matter is depicted by the symbolics of the square and cross. As we progress towards the top, the body of the pyramid contracts more and becomes more subtle, while the vibratory phenomena become faster which means that material conditionality grows weaker, whereas the ability to survive, transform oneself, and make decisions in the overall occurrences grows stronger and bigger. In other words, the time of duration of events in the upper spheres is more contracted and quicker. The issue of space and time is the issue of speed of the phenomena and level of the pyramid. The greatest speed of events when a being moves toward its outcome or purpose is the light, and it illuminates the remainder, those slower and more conditioned events, offers proof that a being as such exists. The light is above the whole of the physical world. Light can shine because it represents the attainment of meaning. All life aspires toward the light because it aspires toward the meaning. The top of the pyramid is light owing to which existence as such becomes visible in its entirety.[25] What reveals meaning to this illuminated being is the consciousness (*buddhi*). The category of *buddhi* is therefore at the top of the entire *Prakriti* scheme. Light and consciousness are mutual in the same sense that occurrence and its meaning are. One without the other cannot exist, at all. Stars would not exist without humans (*Purusha*), and without the stars, the cosmos would not exist either.[26] According to the pyramidal model all the versatility of forms and ways of living in nature, from the inorganic matter to all the forms of organic life, and the emergence of intellectual ability to define as well as the memo-

---

[25] It represents the symbol of the all-seeing eye at the top of the pyramid.

[26] To the objection that there were stars before people on Earth, the response is as follows: there are conscious subjects on other planets, too. A further point that stars existed before them, in the early stages of the development of the cosmos, the response is provided by Rig-veda, where it is stated that *Purushas* reside within the stars. They existed, therefore, for the sole purpose of creating a man, the conscious subject. Irrelevant of the fact whether *Purusha* happened to be in a star or a man. Besides, the awakened one sees no differences there, for him, it is the same. The whole universe is projected from the conscious subject, *Purusha*, from the man.

ry of the human mind (*manas*), is a unique manifestation of an entire spectrum of varying speeds of the phenomena of nature that may be observed. The matter is, therefore, slowed down and conditioned phenomena and thought is somewhat freer and faster phenomena of the same nature, the higher octave of its differentiation. The matter is form and the thought is information about the form. These higher, faster, and more contracted levels (*manas, aham-kâra,* and *buddhi*) with their mere contraction crystallize and reflect grosser and more conditioned forms. This reflection is otherwise known as awareness. The mind has often been compared with the mirror. In the same way, a thought is not outside of nature, it only overcomes the time of its lower manifestation. In the same way, a mirror reflects an image, while the wall (the mirror is hanging on) does not because it is not sufficiently polished, the internal organs (*antahkarana*), too, *buddhi, aham-kâra,* and *manas* can reflect a thought (name) of the emergent shapes of the lower, grosser nature because their frequencies are faster and more subtle then them.

Higher realms of nature are closer to unconditionality (*Purusha*) which engenders the consciousness of itself. Nature is more intelligent in them, but those levels are increasingly more narrow because for the higher presence of the consciousness to be executed proportionately greater energy input is required. Very few individuals are capable of this, the ones that already possess all the organic ability and experience (of culture) in the beingness. Hence, the most widespread forms of life in nature are the unconscious ones, such as the inorganic nature with its elements and minerals. It is also alive, but it is characterized by a lesser presence of the consciousness, it manifests as the form itself there, the consciousness is identical with the shaping and completely conditioned by it. There is a considerably fewer number of living beings that use the potential of the consciousness to a larger degree. They are plants and animals, for example, who apart from the forming, also use consciousness for perception and motion. Complete self-consciousness is the rarest occurrence in nature. It can be found here and there in some humans – who meaningfully and creatively participate in the phenomena of the being, and not mere existence and perception per se.

On the lower realms of the pyramidal structure of *Prakriti,* we see that the prevalent forms are gross and inert ones belonging to the mineral, plant, and animal world. They do not take part in the creation and forming of nature, but are, instead, conditioned by it. In higher dimensions of the same pyramid the conscious subjects reside, human beings, who use more subtle forms of the beingness of the same nature, in the form of information, mental activities, and to a certain degree take part in the creation and re-shaping the nature from that foundation, and are partly also conditioned by nature. When human souls develop and gain sufficient consciousness of themselves (*Purusha*) they acquire a creator capacity for creation and freedom which they mostly demonstrate in the periods between incarnations. During these periods, before their birth in the physical body, souls rehearse in the higher dimensions of nature how to create in the lower dimensions. Most mineral, plant, and animal species came into existence as a result of the planned, intelligent design of our souls.

The pyramidal structure of nature shows the hierarchy of all the life forms, as well as people who are all members of a human society which has both the noble, conscious, and enlightened individuals, but also the unconscious who are more conditioned by natural urges. A wide foundation of the pyramid corresponds with multitudes of people, the inert, susceptible masses who can easily be (psychologically) conditioned and frequently exposed to manipulations (by the media). The more one climbs to the top of the pyramid, the number of conscious people is even smaller in number because the body of the pyramid is narrowed even more at that point. On the very top reside the completely awakened ones, and they are always individual, independent personalities; all enlightened humans are original and unique. The individuation is the only way to enlightenment because the top of the *Prakriti* pyramid is composed of *antahkarana,* the 'interior organ' – hence, it does not get realized outwardly, but only as self-consciousness or awakening (*buddhi*). **The peak of Prakriti is inside humans, and not outside.** Only unconscious masses of people can share common beliefs and collective behavior patterns. People from the top of the pyramidal hierarchy see things directly as they are. The lower humans are on the pyramidal-ontological level, the more mediators they need to be able to know how life functions, to become aware of various concepts, myths, and symbols, whereas the ones from the bottom of the pyramid partake in existence by imitating traditional patterns set forth by the social and religious institutions; their perception of existence is limited to the physical objects perceptible by senses (sacral objects and articles). They are completely conditioned by outer influences. The lower the level of the *Prakriti* pyramid is, the more binding the mechanicalness of natural phenomena are, as well as objectivization, i.e., the importance attributed to objects.

This view on human society is elitism, but it is not discriminative because the top would never exist without the wide pyramid foundations. The foundations provide the peak. (Besides, everyone can change their status within this structure by changing the state of their consciousness at any given moment.) This is why nobody can reach the stage of enlightenment unless they become aware of it, and unless they learn to respect every single person beneath themselves who has uplifted them to enlightenment with their energy. Hence, mercifulness and infinite love follow every true experience of enlightenment. Unfortunately, lower strata have little awareness of the role they play – because *Prakriti* works unconsciously for the benefit of the human soul – they usually feel the heavy burden of the whole pyramidal structure on their back. *Sâmkhya* prevents us from dividing people by making us aware of this structure of nature and points in the direction of tolerance toward every form of life, accepting absolutely everything that lives and exists – because the pyramid has no redundant forms, it is whole on each of its levels. Everything that exists, every being or phenomenon, is a form of identification of *Prakriti* with *Purusha*. In that respect, everything is equal – although hierarchy as such exists in nature. The enlightened ones never divide people because they see the entire structure – however they see their functioning within the structure of the world according to the state of their consciousness. Divisions among people happen as a result of the unconsciousness of those people from the bottom of the social pyramid because their vision is always impaired by their tradition and faith. Discrimination, conflicts, and wars are possible only amongst the unconscious people.

The pyramidal structure of nature shows us that although there is the whole, it, too, has a clear hierarchy within which every beingness corresponds with its ontological status.

The evolutionary overcoming of the conditionality of nature and contracting the pyramid toward the top is otherwise also known as ascending toward the idea of goodness, beauty, truth, and salvation, while the increase of conditionality and disintegration, expansion of the pyramid toward its base, is in general terms known as decline to evil, unconsciousness, and suffering, slavery, loss of oneself, and the authenticity of the being. *Purusha* is beyond good and evil, it is the unconditionality in whose liberty existence can happen with all of its opposites.

The pyramidal structure of *Prakriti* can simply present to us the purpose of good and evil. In its structure, each level has its ontology and mode of functioning which is right and proper for that specific level. However, there are no clear lines between the levels, between different forms of beingness, so they overflow onto the neighboring ones. Once a mode of beingness from the lower level overflows onto the higher, in this higher level it is experienced as evil at work, as imposing the limitations. When it overflows from the higher to the lower level, such beingness is experienced as love, mercy, and good, as liberation.

The pyramidal structure of *Prakriti*, in which the top and the foundation exist simultaneously, demonstrates the relative beingness of nature: while its spacetime contracts on certain places, in *buddhi*, into the self-consciousness of the Self, at the same time it spreads outs into the world of a myriad of objects and phenomena. Consequently, the integration and disintegration are interactive. In nature self-consciousness and oblivion, name and form, love and hate, good and evil exist side by side. It is all joined at the top of the pyramid and overcome in the unity of all differences. All of them disappear in pure wakefulness. Additionally, for them to be overcome, they all have to be experienced first.

The pyramidal structure reveals the significance of the present moment, the way in which timeless present exists with time in parallel. The top of the pyramid is the timeless present, and the square is the three-dimensional world in time. The past and future of everything exist in the pyramidal way of collecting and finalizing meaning in the present, at the top of the pyramid, always afresh and completely. Although the process of contracting space-time is happening as we speak in every single detail, everything is eternal because it belongs to the whole of the pyramidal scheme. Each phenomenon of nature represents the holistic contraction of everything bygone and a condition for all new things to come.

The pyramidal structure of nature reflects the holographic model of the universe. The point at the top is every single detail of the universe, and the square foundation represents the multitude, whole, everything that exists in the physical universe. Everything that is individual is connected to everything else, to the whole. The whole reflects in everything individual – because there would be no top of the pyramid without a wide foundation.

The other aspect of our imagination in depicting *Prakriti* is the vision of a cross. The center of the cross plays the same role as the top of the pyramid. The horizontal line represents the horizon of the being and time. It is all the experiential world of *Prakriti*. The vertical one is eternity which refracts at the present moment – which is the point of intersection. The center of the cross is the Self: the intersection of being in time and unconditioned eternity takes place here, the conditions of time and being are overcome because they are faced with eternal spiritual purpose. That is why, at the same time, it is the center which ties them to the universe. When beingness is based on the true center, the Self, then the universe is their home, the whole of nature is their body, it is simply a wider whole of their being. The center of the cross is the conscious sub-ject; the arms of the cross are the space and time of the cosmos. They contract in their center. This, like the cosmological theory of the strong anthropic principle (SAP), indicates that the cosmos ex-ists with one goal only which is forming the conscious subject. It means that the cosmos is our inner world or our Self. In such a uni-ty relaxation and bliss in harmony is the only way of living. For humans who are out of balance, the universe is their enemy. They fight nature and suffer. Suffering always happens when someone rejects their own being because they fail to see its reality and worth. If everything that is outward is our inward, in fact, then everything we do not like in the outside world, the characteristics of other people included, is something we have as of yet not become aware of and overcome, instead, we unconsciously project them outside. It is the core of wrongdoing and sin. Failing to see and accept the meaning of existence for what it is, as our Self, results in a feeling of loss and inauthenticity which naturally breeds suffering, alienation amongst people, and toward nature, as well.

Nature is not some blind linear framework rolling away from nowhere and into infinity. It has its purpose which is attained by shaping existence into one suitable form where the purpose will be attained, where the time of happening will be overcome. This suitable form of nature is the human being. His Self is the section point between the vertical and horizontal resulting in their destiny being the necessity for overcoming the natural causality and transience. This is the cross all humans are crucified on, the one they must carry: to stop identifying with the being using the eternal spiritual purpose in their heart. This way, by saving themselves, humans save all of nature, as well. There is no other point where it can be led to the liberating perfection, but only in the liberated and perfect human. In other words, a perfect human is one that has awakened, and as such is merely a reflection of the already existing perfection of nature.

According to the scheme, the cross center is *aham-kâra*, while *buddhi* is like a lotus flower which from such a center sprouts and opens up to the unconditionality of the human soul (*Purusha*).[27]

The pyramidal Gestalt is an objective way of depicting the process of natural phenomena (*Prakriti*), whereas the cross is subjective. It points to the crossing of time and eternity, the necessity of cessation or the overcoming of time as the only way to transcend the causation of beingness. Because conditionality is none other than us failing to see that time in the absolute sense does not exist. Since the intersection point is the Self, this represents a subjective way of presenting *Prakriti* which is the existential realization of a subjective process.

The pyramidal depiction is categorical, and the cross-like one is existential, and they both need to be properly understood.

---

[27] See the image on the cover of this book.

2. Causation

Nature is the realm of causal origin. Nothing in it has been created as new and special, but has, instead, been made or manifested from a unique and universal foundation, *Prakriti*. The creation of the universe is a mere manifestation or development of all the potentiality contained within *Prakriti*. Everything that is manifested, as an inevitable consequence of an impact of a certain cause, has already existed in its cause before it got manifested in the sensory experience, in the implicit or hidden form, but an equally real state. The cause is, therefore, the state in which the consequence already exists in a hidden form on the more subtle levels of creation, but outside the sensory experience. After acquiring favorable circumstances it can manifest itself in the spacetime of the psychophysical experience of a certain subject. Therefore, the notion of creation can be actualized in the subjective experience only (*indriyâni* and *manas*) which is prone to a linear flow of events within the three-dimensional space. Only from this perspective can things appear as new. There is nothing new in nature, only what is concealed and then revealed.

Its realism *Sâmkhya* demonstrates best by claiming that what does not exist can never and in no way become the objective of a certain activity or experience. Afterward, every product contains within itself the substance of its material cause and exists objectively in it in the form of potentiality. If it were not so, everything could come out of everything which would contradict causality which exists in nature. Furthermore, it is said that the causal impact belongs only to that what has the necessary capacity for generating the corresponding consequence, otherwise, everything could generate a wide versatility of things. The development of everything in this world is a mere manifestation of what is hidden away as an imminent potential leading to the higher, more subtle levels of reality than the one which through the physical senses is known to reason.

Therefore, the cause and consequence represent the undeveloped and developed state of the same being. The being itself is timeless and absolute. In such a way, although everything moves and transforms every single moment, although everything that

97

originated in time is transient and can suffer no ultimate destruction since the essence of every being cannot be jeopardized by anything. All the possible states of being which get manifested in time, are present in their timeless outcome, in the highest dimension, in *akasha* (aether, quantum field), far above the physical realm of reality (the element of earth) which is characterized by substantiality and deterministic inertia, on which using the limited mind (*manas*) one can witness the transience of everything created. In *akasha* absolutely all the possibilities of the being that are manifested in time, past, present, or future are present and united. Nothing is lost or under threat there, nor is it born and dies. Every single thought, every word, deed, all the experiences gathered are stored there. Due to the unity of nature, personified in *mahat-buddhi*, our Self, essence, or soul, have no place where to get lost. Facing them is an inevitable occurrence for anyone who is becoming aware of themselves. Hence, the awakened one can never be someone without a clear conscience.[28]

The logics itself we use to ascertain nature as such tells us that if all the consequences are already contained within their causes in the latent state, to avoid regressing into infinite, there must be one uncaused cause, a universal field of being in which all the physical laws are united. It is *Prakriti*. This can be verified in a number of ways. Firstly, all the individual things are limited and conditioned by something outside of themselves, by a wider whole or force majeure. Thus, nothing individual can be the cause of the cosmos or whole. Consequently, all the things are pervaded by a

---

[28] Each soul faces its earthly plain and deeds down to the last detail once it exits the body upon its physical death. It enters the domain of *akasha* or aether, which are synonymous for *mahat-buddhi* where all the possibilities of existence are contracted into One. The soul experiences this One as light. This makes the experience of dying similar to the experience of enlightenment during life where in both cases the whole life is recapitulated with all the events that had taken place and then they are overcome. Humans are released from them, but they do not reject them, instead, they creatively leaves them behind having become aware of their meaning. Any rejection would merely bounce everything back in the form of a *karmic* burden. Liberation from *karma* and the drama of existence, the most subtle aspects of *Prakriti* conditioning, can only be achieved by accepting and overcoming it in the sense of all the potential modes of the beingness of *Prakriti*.

similar structure, such as atomic structure, for example, which all indicates to one common source of their origin. There is an active principle which is best reflected in the development of everything, and which cannot be identified with any of the stages of that development. It is something far wider than its products, although it remains immanent within them. There are always multiple causes that play an active part in inducing a single consequence rendering all of the creation in nature different and complex. They are all, however, conditioned, and as such cannot be a cause unto themselves. The unity in the cosmos we are witnesses to points to a unique cause of everything which cannot be outside of *Prakriti*, as its creator, since no cause can ever create of itself a completely different and independent consequence. The cause must contain more reality than the consequence or at least as much as it does. Nothing can come out of nothing. *Prakriti* is therefore unmanifested as the foundation, but it is no different from everything that exists. The difference between these two states, between the manifested and unmanifested, is directly dependent on the clarity of the presence of the consciousness which establishes nature as such. The degree to which this existence manifests itself depends only on the degree of our awareness of this existence. The presence of the consciousness that is this pure depends on the openness to unconditionality which facilitates both nature and the awareness of it.

The holism of the pyramidal structure of nature and its causality point in the direction of the reason for its existence – to manifest all the forms that could be. Nature is the field of complete freedom manifesting absolutely everything that can be manifested, a big scrapbook, in other words. Absolutely everything that can exist and happen in any way possible is somewhere in nature waiting to happen. This definition, more than anything else, can provide us with the tolerance and understanding of unfavorable events.

The field of manifestation of all the possibilities can, as such, exist in free will only. It is yet another way to say that everything is free will, although it is conditioned. The principle of causality and freedom are not opposed, they exist mutually. This is the explanation of the paradox: everything in nature had its causal origin, but at the same time it is a result of free will for everything that could ever manifest, hence, free will already be integrated within. Unconditionality the whole of *Prakriti* rests on is what engenders free will. It entails the option of free beings without freedom, as well, in the same way, those without freedom can set themselves free at long last. This double nature of the principle of freedom should always be taken into account.

The question of coincidence or predestination also becomes crystal clear in the light of what has been said about the causality of *Prakriti*, and their discrepancy is a false dilemma. Causality must exist because without it there would be no consistency of the physical laws and biochemical processes. But if only causality were the rule, there would be no development since it would all end up in a closed circle. Apart from causality, there must be a coincidence, as well, to pave the way for the freedom of choice and new opportunities. There must be a balance between causality and the freedom of coincidence. This balance is determined by the importance of the phenomena in question. What is crucial for survival is connected with causality and determination. What is less important is a matter of free choice and coincidence. It is quite the same whether we turn left or right while searching for food, but it is not all the same whether we find it and survive. To find food and manage to survive, we must have the freedom to move and choose.

At the base of the relationship between determination and freedom lies the relationship between *Prakriti* and *Purusha*.

Due to a unique cause, the whole nature is unique and undivided, there is absolutely nothing in it that cannot be singled out by itself. This unity of nature is, however, free because *it rests on unconditionality* and serves it entirely as its final goal. That is why all the beingness in it is conditioned and inauthentic until humans mature enough to reach the stage of the completeness of being, and by doing so leads it to the end result in their life experience. It is a process of individuation, and not a collective one. Only the pure unconditionality can engender something so unique and whole, complete within itself, yet versatile, perfect, and miraculous like the life of nature is. Since it rests on the unconditionality of *Purusha*, nature can manifest itself freely in various ways, it may contract itself into a concrete three-dimensional form, or some temporary entity, an object, being, or process, and the most completely of all into a conscious subject – the same way it may spread itself out into objective and inorganic nature. One possibility guarantees another.

Freedom directly postulates individuation. It is the reason why everything is unique in nature, why nothing is the same. It is so because everything aspires toward a conscious subject, and the basic property of the conscious subject is self-sufficiency and originality in actions. In the gross outward form, the principle of freedom manifests itself in the versatility of forms – formatively, and on the most subtle level as an act of free will in the functioning of a conscious subject – existentially. Once a subject does something new and original it is evidence that they are aware of what they are doing, that they are able to do it, and has done something to manifest their own free will. (In accordance with this, it should be said that there are subjects that are devoid of original actions because they do not have a will of their own, they are conditioned by outer influences and are, therefore, unaware. They are aware to the point they are independent of the outer influences and act on their own accord.) The form and actions are both the gross and the subtle aspect of the manifestation of freedom nature is based upon.

To avoid a paradox that unconditionality (*Purusha*) engenders the conditioned nature, we must stress that conditionality, i.e., the causality of nature exists only for an unawakened man. The more aware humans are, the more nature is (only) *to them* free and less conditioned. Furthermore, it is not monotonous and always linear; it is relative, complex, and often to a seer who uses "common sense" (*manas*) contradictory, even invisible. This is due to the fact that causality stretches over multiple dimensions of nature (*tanmâtrâ* and *maha-bhŭtâni*) which cause the relativity of time of their phenomena, thus, overcome the sensory experience (*indriyâni*). The process of causality is present, therefore, in the whole nature, however, we see only those parts that go through the three-dimensional physical world of our sensory perception, while other parts of the same process which span the extrasensory dimensions are outside of our scope of perception. This flexibility of causality of nature and failing to see the entire process provides a rational observer with the illusion that they are not conditioned and that life and events in it are free, a product of coincidence or only partially conditioned, that injustice prevails, and miracles happen.

What looks like an unjust fate, evil without a cause, or a miracle, are the component parts of the same general causality that exists in the whole nature, the only problem is we are unable to see it with the physical senses because they come from other dimensions of nature. Things may appear as wonderous, incomprehensible, or illogical, unjust, or evil only because we do not see the entire process of causal origin in nature, but only a fragment which is accessible to our senses. Awakened humans see that in nature on the whole there is no such thing as evil, everything in it serves the benefit of the free human soul. (It is an open question whether modern humans understand what their true interests are, what their soul is.) Additionally, because of the transcendent and non-linear nature of the inorganic realm of causality, many feel that life is conditioned by the whims of some capricious God. The issue here is to do with the other dimensions of causal phenomena of one same nature.

To understand it better we will put forth briefly several modifications of causality that are available to the experience of reason, and which have been systematized in the classical texts of *Sâmkhya*.

1. Direct causality (like a tree relying on its roots for survival, and manages to survive as long as the root exists to keep it alive).

2. Causality through simultaneity (when after the first phenomenon manifested itself the second one follows suit immediately).

3. Causality through mutuality or compensation (when something happens as a result of the balance of opposites).

4. Conditionality through an object (when something is invited into existence owing to some objective influences: light for the creation of sight consciousness and the sense of sight, sound waves for the hearing consciousness and the sense of hearing, objects in the mind for the mind consciousness and thoughts; positions of the planets that affect a person's character and mentality, a physical presence, and movement of a certain object etc.).

5. Causality through support (when a certain phenomenon always precedes another one and presents its foundation).

6. Causality through contents (there are contents that promote evil and those that promote mercifulness and spirituality,

bad food, and climate that have a negative bearing on the body and health, sensuality and the bad company that leads to a bad life, whereas good friends invariably push us in the right direction, anything that can become contents of the state of consciousness and any type of contents that stimulates contents similar to itself, whether they are good or evil).

7. Causality from the previous birth.

8. Causality through action (*karma* – consequences that manifest only as a result of certain actions and deeds).

9. Causality that is manifested only as a result of the meditative deepening, *samadhi* (focus, insight, serenity, *siddhi*...) and which can never appear on their own without meditation.

10. Causality that originates once certain factors are grouped together.

11. Causality that originates only when certain factors are split apart.

12. Causality through imitation and repetition of customs, tradition, convictions, suggestion, or mind programming (implanting certain contents into the subconsciousness in order to control people easier).

Due to a singular cause of the overall phenomena, nothing in nature originates as new, nor does it disappear because everything is energy which means that forms by themselves are nothing. It is only energy that keeps transforming while moving (life) due to the functional loss of balance of natural constitutions (*gunas*). If it did not move, it would not be energy. Its imbalance sets its own energy into motion (*prâna*). Additionally, due to the imbalance within the very constitution of nature, its causality is such that no causal process repeats itself in an identical way. For that reason, everything is different within it although order exists. Therefore, causality exists because of the singular foundation of the general emergence of the world, and the constant versatility of all the causal processes exists because of unconditionality this singular foundation rests on while the wholeness serves its purpose. Simultaneous repetition of certain causal processes happens in humans only, in their neuroses, philosophy, science, and technology. That is why it is so dangerous for nature which prefers freestyle transformations and dedicating its causality to the purpose, the wholeness of beingness that rests on unconditionality. Unlike the logical and technological causality which divides and enslaves, natural causality is entirely dedicated to wholeness and unity.

General causality of nature on lower and more gross dimensions manifests itself in the form of physical and biological laws, while on its highest level, in the mind (*manas*), it assumes the form of hidden predispositions (*samskara*) that condition, but also organize the psycho-mental activities of a subject. This organization engenders humans with the memory and ability to recognize physical laws.

The causality of nature is necessary for a unity and wholeness to be preserved because only when the nature is whole it serves the interest of the human soul (unconditionality). That is why every being, which is not whole, suffers in conditionality.

If we look at the scheme (picture 1), causality is inevitable only up to *manas* stage. In *aham-kâra* it begins to be overcome by a person's discovering the unity of nature which is analog to an integrated personality resulting in human awakening (*buddhi*). The human personality overcomes causality, the conditionality is resolved within it. Rivers, plants, and animals do not have a personality and are endowed with causality only. This makes the general conditionality through causality the most prevalent phenomenon in nature. Very few people are capable of being integrated personalities, to be the personification of the sense of beingness completely, thus rendering it spiritually present, at least on the plane of their own experience. Causality capsizes in existence, and anyone who fights for personal consciousness and freedom from the slavery of natural causality feels this weight in their heart. It is such that a multitude of beings must belong to it for the process of organic life that rests on causality to be maintained. Most people must serve this process, at best they are average people whose lives are dedicated to starting a family, working, and finding time for entertainment in their moments of leisure, and the worst-case scenario would be that they decline into an evil which represents only a tighter stronghold of causality over people's lives. (That is why evil often results in death or losing freedom.) They never become whole personalities (*aham-kâra*) because they fail to acknowledge the unity of nature. It is a feat very few individuals are able to pull off after a long and hard struggle against the gravity of a greater part of nature which serves the purpose of causality, and which is manifested in themselves as well as in the society that surrounds them. If they manage to resist the elements of natural causality which has its appeal since everything within it is predetermined and "natural", and achieve the process of individuation by means of transcendence, they know the unity of all the beingness, becoming complete beings themselves, awakened, and independent. They managed to escape the natural causality and suffering which its inconsistency always induces. By getting away from the natural causality they have ultimately attained the purpose of nature it serves fully because, by becoming complete nature in miniature, the microcosm, they in their experience attain the end result of *Prakriti* in general, and that is - it serves the manifestation of the divine consciousness through the human soul. By liberating the unconditioned divine consciousness within themselves, the one the whole nature rests upon, they become disinterested in its causality, they may remain as observers only, and not active participants that chain themselves to its causal phenomena. They are witnesses (*sakshin*) or those bearing testimony because they see the meaning of the whole existence and realize it through themselves. They have done everything that should have been done, so that nothing more remains, they attained clarity of vision regarding all phenomena of nature and not their own. This clarity is made possible by the unconditioned soul that is in them.

Nature always has a majority of people serving its purpose in maintaining organic life (particularly among women),[29] and it can,

---

[29] For the very reason of being the personification of *Prakriti*, some women who are mature enough can beautifully serve the interests of the divine consciousness (*Purusha*), and bear testimony of it, put its ideas into practice or be devoted to genuinely spiritual people better than most men can. On the other hand, men, despite being a personification of *Purusha* to a much higher degree, are far less aware of its nature than women, and in practice, they are often more distant from the divine consciousness than women. Both men and women will find it hard to agree with this because a person sees the hardest what is the closest to them and also innate. With this paradox, both men and women are in the same position as regards *Purusha*. It can be said that men and women alike have the same potential for the final awakening or enlightenment, however, they express it differently. Men are turned toward the world and society and

therefore, permit certain individuals to liberate themselves. They see their chance here, and those individuals are nature's ripest fruits that carry the seeds of its existence within, they are the personification of its purpose. Naturally, such accumulation of sense can happen to a very small number of people because it is the concentration of energy of the beingness in general. Very few people are capable of accepting all the power of life, the destiny of all beings, and the responsibility for their salvation. An ideal of life for the majority is to serve the interests of organic survival (*indriyâni*).

Nature has a teleological function, it is completely dedicated to liberating the presence of the consciousness that engenders it

---

consequently express their realization outwardly, they write about it, philosophize, give lectures, they are great teachers, bringers of light, gurus, founders of great religions, and the whole world can recognize them as such. Women are, however, closer to nature and they do not express their enlightenment outwardly as men do in the form of a spectacle, their enlightenment is more intimate and concrete, private, through their own being, through a quiet dedication serving life and consciousness to those that need them, their nearest and dearest, and anyone else they come in contact with. Unlike enlightened men who are known to the whole world, to recognize an enlightened woman one must come to her personally and find a way to her heart with full respect, and be worthy of her response. Often it is enough for them just to be mothers. There are so many enlightened mothers who do not attribute any importance to this but consider their enlightenment a natural state, never speak of it, but only show it through their acts of love toward all the living beings. *Mothers of this world with their unconditional love are the closest a person can get to the divine love that engenders all*. Men spread enlightenment all over the world, yet an enlightened woman is something one can see only when they get very close to her, and her enlightened deeds of love and understanding, and not the teachings of enlightenment. Both ways are necessary and complement each other. It is only that one is easily noticed in this world, and the other one is harder. Truth be told, it appears that judging by this, there are more enlightened women in the world than men. Men make more noise and make new religions, while women give birth to them in silence, feed, and clothem so that they could go on doing it. Since they are more attached to nature their vision of the divine consciousness of nature that engenders everything is much clearer, they are more religious than men. However, the suffering is also greater for them, due to the more intense experiencing all the details and opposites that are present in this world. Additionally, they often lack an objective understanding of what they are going through. The male mind is better at that – although it is harder for them to directly experience it, they do not find it difficult to objectively explain it. Men first explain and learn, and then they experience it. With women it is the other way round, they first experience everything.

entirely. This function is achieved through implementation which can only be accomplished through causality. Work is a practical application of consciousness, without work the consciousness is a mere abstract possibility. The whole nature transforms itself through work in accordance with the consciousness, and this transformation is orchestrated by all its beings, from bacteria to people and gods. Only with such participation in the life of nature through work, can humans crystalize the consciousness of their soul in this world because the consciousness of their soul facilitates the overall living of this world. That is why nature pushes humans to the highest limits to attain cognition and liberation through implementation.

On the lower levels of the *Prakriti* pyramid, work manifests itself in the form of physical activity. On higher, and that means interior levels (*manas, aham-kâra,* and *buddhi*), it becomes psychological and intellectual work as well as *karma.* Hence, *karma* is a comprehensive term that denotes work as such, some deed that yields results, and the consequences of this work or deed.

Karma is the basis for the meaning of existence.

In the domain below *aham-kâra* conditionality by the causality of natural phenomena rules where each destiny gets determined. However, only in a human being who has become the personification of unity and the meaning of beingness (*aham-kâra* and *buddhi*), which means the freedom from conditionality, only to them is it possible to overcome destiny, and liberate themselves from the law of causal actions (*karma*). Therefore, destiny does exist and happen below *aham-kâra,* where humans are still not their own, while they are still lacking their one and complete 'I'. By attaining *aham-kâra* it is overcome and they win. Destiny cannot be altered at will, only the level of its manifestation can be overcome, in a complete personality whose consciousness is always pure and unconditionally present with its free will.

Likewise, the pyramidal structure of *Prakriti* with its causality also inspires us to accept and tolerate every form of existence. If everything were susceptible to causality, then everything has a reason for its existence in the general order of things.

3. Emanation

The manifestation of *Prakriti* from non-manifestation (*avyaktam*) may be viewed from two angles: the macro and micro-cosmical ones. We have already established that the macrocosmic aspect would be an imagination of the pyramid. The microcosmic aspect would signify an objective turning toward the one who conditions the world, toward I-maker (*aham-kâra*), and the pure consciousness (*buddhi*).

The world does not exist without the subject who experiences it. This does not mean that the world is an illusion, but it only emphasizes the purpose and existential significance a subject has on the world. The truth of the matter is that ***the world exists in order to form the conscious subject***. The subject in the absolute sense is *Purusha*. On the realm of relative phenomena of nature, *Purusha* is the observer who through open eyes provides testimony of existence. The more awake and open those eyes are, the more present *Purusha* is. The whole nature exists for the observer. The observer exists for the whole nature. That is why there are not any fundamental differences between the macrocosmic and microcosmic manifestation. It is one and the same event. Their unity makes the subject and the world it resides in interactive.

It is a mistake to interpret the world as though it were an illusion, as something that exists in our perception or interpretation only. Not only is the world real, but it is the highest reality that there is. Together with the world, the conscious subject belongs to the same highest reality. There is no difference in magnitude and significance of the reality of the world and the conscious subject as such. The conscious subject is the primary cause of the world, but the world is not an illusion because of that. It is as real as the conscious subject itself. If we interpret the world as an illusion, it only to do with us not being aware of the true nature and importance of the conscious subject, of ourselves. It has always been the sole problem of humans, and their only task in this world is to know themselves.

Today in the Western world, with some delay, the same has been discovered in numerous results from the sphere of cosmology, astrophysics, and quantum theory, a whole series of amazing coincidences between the numerical values of certain fundamental constants of nature ("natural constants") such as, for example, the ratio between proton mass and electron mass. It has been determined that the fundamentals of the universe must be exactly as they are in order for the evolution of the life based on carbon to take place (according to many it is the only foundation for the origin of life) and its final result is humans as conscious observers. This prevailing fact eventually led to the origin of the cosmological theory of the *Strong Anthropic Principle* or SAP according to which all the visible properties of the universe, the way they are in everything, are not a product of coincidence or natural selection between a number of options, but are a consequence of quite a definite purpose: the creation of life for the origin of a conscious subject. This principle is as follows: "The Universe must have those properties which allow for life to develop within it at some stage in its history." A further claim based on this is that the universe was created with the sole purpose of origin and survival of the observers who are necessary for the existence of the universe.

While the *Strong Anthropic Principle* states that nature exists the way it is, and it cannot be any other way, to create the conscious subject, *Sâmkhya* takes it one step further and claims that no nature could ever exist without the conscious subject. **It is primary. It induces the whole nature into existence**. *Purusha* we can understand to be the absolute and transcendental subject. In classical texts of *Sâmkhya*, it is explained that *Prakriti* is an object, and *Purusha* a subject. This should be understood clearly because to *Purusha* an object could be the mind, as well. Therefore, it is said that it is transcendental (it surpasses the mind).

The purpose of the subject, and its fundamental importance for the existence of the object, could become a little clearer to us if we realize that the light of a single star, for example, could never be detected if it had not reached some observer, a subject. It would spread out indefinitely into the voidness and its existence would have no purpose. In nature, nothing could exist without a purpose. Hence, without a subject who is aware of their existence, stars would literally not exist, at all. Once a subject sees its light and becomes aware of it, the expansion of its light has achieved its purpose, it attained the actualization of the purpose of its existence in its consciousness. Only at that point has a star become what it is. Through a subject that observes it, this star has become aware of itself. All the objects seek and find the meaning of existence in a conscious subject. That is why it has been said that *Prakriti* serves *Purusha*.

The very word emanation (manifestation) testifies of the emergence of the objective world as though it were the loss of authenticity of the being (*Prakriti*). It is the same event, therefore, the basic characteristic of beingness-in-the-world is the oblivion of authenticity, failing to realize (*avidya*) and become aware of the true nature of existence, a reality that is always present as the outcome of everything. This outcome everything originates from is *mahat-buddhi*. It is the supreme initiation, the big wakefulness, it is the essence of beingness and, ultimately, human essence, as well. During an ordinary life, humans are completely unaware of it. Occasionally they become aware of their individuality and willpower (*aham-kâra*), even though they may become aware of some of their functions quite superficially (*indriyâni*) during their awaken state. That is also the only domain that humans perceive to be the manifested world: the organic world and those realms of inorganic phenomena accessible to their senses or those that come to them during extrasensory episodes. To an average human, nature manifests itself only in three-dimensional form due to the empirical conditionality of their perception. Organic life cannot exist without the three-dimensional causality. That is why it is used for the explanation of rudimentary regulations of *Prakriti* for an average understanding.

Emanation, or the manifestation of *Prakriti*, explains the meaning of the causality itself. The relevant one, the purpose or outcome of all phenomena of the manifested world the way it presents itself to the senses, is in the higher dimensions of nature, which **are not outward but are inward within the subject**. The perception of the world as such is entirely dependent on the maturity of the subject in question, on the presence of the consciousness in them. Higher categories, *buddhi*, *aham-kâra*, and *manas* constitute the "interior organ" (*antahkarana*) – while at the same time they represent the higher, more subtle levels where all the visible nature manifests from. Hence, the presence of those higher dimensions of nature within man. They are active in all three tenses (past, present, and future), while the sensory and action organs (*in-driyâni*) exist only in the present moment of linear time. That is why to understand emanation coming from the highest categories one needs to transcend time.

All of this is simply a problem of time: the highest reality is always here and now, in the existence itself, whereas our mind (*manas*) is never here and now, it is alienated from the existence because it always keeps projecting itself into something else, into time, always thinking what was and what will be, even when it makes an attempt to comprehend what is at the moment, the present moment escapes it. It is not possible to experience the present moment with an active mind. Human awakening really entails the return to the field of reality here and now which is achieved through the transcendence of the mind, and that means the cessation of the projection of time. It is possible only in a completely awakened (*buddhi*) person (*aham-kâra*). Humans cannot experience reality as the unity of everything until the moment they become its embodiment as a real and integrated personality (*aham-kâra*), nor will they be able to experience reality or the essence of everything any different than the awakened one (*buddhi*) who is always the one who is in the absolute sense, who is real, here and now. Because of this, the highest dimension of the being (*mahat-buddhi*) is the same as the human Self. Therefore, by knowing themselves, humans know the world around them and vice versa. It is a mutual relationship.

Emanation in *Sâmkhya* is not objectivistic but personalistic. It shows how the meaning of beingness of the universe receives its embodiment in the human personality only, and nowhere else. Nature manifests itself only to come to its purpose through humans, and to actualize it through their personality and creativity.

Personalism of emanation in *Sâmkhya* can be understood as the human who is awakening.

In its authentic state nature is the complete unity without any opposites, a timeless inviolable being. It is *mahat-buddhi*. Since human beings, during their average life, have no awareness of nature, in their experience it happens as the state of deep sleep without dreams (*sushupta-sthana*). It is the only phase of being during

111

which humans are completely oblivious of themselves and existence, although they reside in it in quite a relaxed fashion, in the essence of the existence itself which rejuvenates them. Their consciousness is in a dormant state here because it has not learned how to be one with the being, with existence itself, it has always been taught to project outside, to identify itself with its contents, with individual forms of phenomena, with thoughts and deeds, and they are all annulled in the presence of the being. Once they grow weary of wandering through events outside of themselves, humans completely relax from their thoughts and deeds, they falls in unity with themselves. However, at that point, they fall into complete oblivion and unconsciousness because they have always trained themselves to be aware of something else, never themselves, and the existence itself. We are unaware during deep sleep without dreams only because we are unaware of ourselves, of our true nature, and the true nature of existence. Awakened humans are characterized by constant wakefulness (*mahat-buddhi*) which lasts during this unity with the reality of the being which happens spontaneously in the form of deep sleep. It is simply due to the fact that the awareness of the awakened human is no different than existence itself.

Aham-kâra is the principle of individual forming. It is the subsequent phenomenon in emanation. After awakening and short-lived emergence of the primal and pure consciousness (*buddhi*), humans become aware of themselves (*aham*) and begins to move (*-kârah*) their body (*indriyâni*). Only at that point do they start to ascertain objects (*tanmâtrâ* and *maha-bhûtâni*), because they cannot feel themselves without the interaction with objects. From the cosmic point of view, *aham-kâra* is the principle according to which every creation and phenomenon is formed in nature. Everything is individually determined, otherwise, formlessness would produce no activity whatsoever, and *Prakriti* is always active. Matter and energy can exist only if they are formed in some way.

With the occurrence of *aham-kâra,* the development of the objective world is swung in motion. On the scheme we see that starting this category emanation branches outs into two parts. On the one hand, there is *indriyâni* which defines the physical body of all the living beings who are carriers of consciousness, and on the other hand, there are *tanmâtrâ* and *maha-bhûtâni* who constitute a subtle and gross primal state of the objective, inorganic world of nature. The basic characteristic of all of this is the ability to exist in multiple dimensions, or levels of vibration, the more subtle or grosser ones, indicated by the model of the pyramid where each higher level is more subtle than the preceding one. Becoming acquainted with the dimensions of nature is of vital importance for its understanding.

4. Teleology of *Prakriti*

Apart from causality, the fundamental teaching of *Sâmkhya* is that nature has a purpose for its actions. In the classical text *Sankhya-karika* it is said:

56. Thus, this effort in the activity of Nature, beginning from the highest mind (*Mahat*) down to the gross elements, is for the liberation of each soul; (and although) it is for another's benefit (yet) it seems as it were for itself.

57. Unconsciously, such as the milk flows out for the growth of the calf, so does Nature operate towards the emancipation of the human soul.

58. As people engage in acts to satisfy desires, so does the Unmanifested Principle (Nature) act for the emancipation of the soul; its ultimate goal is the abolition of suffering.

We have seen what impact the conscious subject has on the emanation or manifestation of nature. It is evident that the importance is not down to the subject itself, but the soul's consciousness which manifests through them in this world.

Nature forms and manifests so as to engender the manifestation of the soul's consciousness.

The soul's consciousness always manifests itself through all the forms of nature; the soul is behind the intelligent design in nature.

However, it is not enough. The ultimate purpose of manifestation is that *the manifested cosmos unites with the awareness of itself*. That is why, together with all the existing forms, humans were created, as well, as beings that will finally unite the soul's divine consciousness with all the outward manifestation of nature, with the existence itself, with understanding the purpose of manifestation. The moment of this unison is the *samadhi* state during meditative stillness, and it is demonstrated practically in action as *sahaja samadhi*.

Humans reach this summit of the meaning of existence individually within themselves using their karmic maturity, based on the experience of existence they have gained through all of their incarnations. This individual experience is still subjective and static, and their power of action is limited to one human only. Those are the states we see in some saints or enlightened people. They are very inspirational and beneficial for the world but are of very little practical value to humankind, their manifestation is often subjective and falls short of the global purpose nature aspires toward as a whole.

Humankind as a whole comes to the peak of manifesting the soul's consciousness and meaning of existence by building civilization, culture, and science.

The soul's consciousness is so vast that it requires scientific precision to manifest itself properly in this world.

We can see the manifestation of the soul's consciousness always and everywhere, especially in children, in good and soulful people, in their kindness, wit, and spirituality also, but the soul's consciousness is so powerful that it may act impractically unless it has been brought to awareness properly. Sometimes it can be destructive even, particularly when it is uncoordinated with space and time, and with the natural laws, too. All the destructiveness is, in reality, a misguided manifestation of the soul's consciousness, or rather the lack of it. There are such nations that are cordial and soulful in general, but quite impractical when practical work and development are the issues. The soul itself is such an overpowering force with a huge pull that even a tiny insight into it draws the human away from the manifested world, away from any identification with it. Once human witnesses the divine presence in everything, they lose the impulse to make corrections in the outward world. He begins to enjoy the wholeness of each moment, they see the divine presence in everything. However, that is merely the initial insight which induces a static approach to life and a naive relationship toward reality. It may even put a stop to the teleology of *Prakriti* toward *Purusha,* although it provides it with an insight that is of crucial importance.

For the soul's consciousness to manifest itself perfectly one should be well-acquainted with the true nature of the soul. The true nature of *Prakriti,* that is to say, nature and its laws can become clearer then. ***Knowing the natural laws is necessary for the soul's consciousness to manifest itself properly.*** Knowing the laws of nature is a science in itself. The development of science is automatically the development of civilization and culture. The development of all of that jointly falls under the teleology of *Prakriti* which is described in the above-mentioned citations from the classical texts.

In the times of old when *Sankhya-karika* originated a mere mention of the cow producing milk was more than enough. Today we are familiar with all the evolution of life and human development, therefore, the teleology of *Prakriti* we are able to understand in a far wider and complex context.

Once humans scientifically become aware of nature down to the last detail, they will consequently manage to overpower the influences of nature and manifest the consciousness of their soul as a result.

To overcome the influences of nature is possible only through the perfect knowledge of nature. Up until that moment, the human will function subjectively and imperfectly, constantly conflicting with the natural laws, and that practically means they will fall prey to natural influences.

The essence of the *Sankhya* teaching is that the human soul, *Purusha,* becomes identified with the body, with *Prakriti,* and by doing so experiences illusion and suffering. Once the true nature of the soul is cognized the illusion then disappears, and the soul attains its authenticity and unconditionality.

This process of knowing the true nature of the soul is the teleology of *Prakriti.* It begins with a human's becoming aware of the body and natural laws and goes on to expand to the overall development of civilization and culture. The human soul is so grand that all of this is the only thing that is happening in the world. The human body is not a physical body alone, there are no borders in nature, it is a hologram and one gigantic unity. ***The human body is the entirety of nature***. When a soul is born in the body it unites with the entirety of nature. ***Therefore, the teleology of Prakriti is a transformation of the entirety of nature, all of its evolution, all of human history and development – absolutely everything that transpires in this world***. That is a way in which nature improves itself in order to be more adequate for the manifestation of the soul's consciousness.

5. Gunas

One of the main characteristics of *Sâmkhya* is its teaching of *gunas*. The tripartite of conformation of nature is best preserved in the archaic physics of Jainism and *Sâmkhya*. It was used later in many philosophical and religious teachings with certain alterations.

In its original state, in the complete balance and holistic union of all the opposites and factors, *Prakriti* exists as the timeless and unmanifested being, as the only cause of everything created (*pradhana*). Its transformation (*parinama*) into an experiential world of the objective reality of a plethora of entities comes into being due to the dysfunction of the ideal balance of its constitutive states, *gunas*, and the disappearance of the unity of all the opposites. For this disruption and origin of the world, no outer cause is required in the form of a creator, it is spontaneously created through the play of the three constitutive attributes of *Prakriti* at every single moment. In other words, for any natural activity to take place a certain imbalance and inconsistency at its base is needed that will set things in motion. This explains why all the natural creations and occurrences are transient and volatile, and any attempt at attaching to them inevitably leads to loss and pain. Since the whole nature does not happen in time, but rather time happens within nature, the disruption of its balance, the "origin of the world", did not happen at a specific point in the past, instead, it happens spontaneously all the time as the immanent regularity of every form of life.

The three qualities, on whose functioning all phenomena of time and space come into being are called *gunas*, which literally means 'strings': *sattva*, *rajas*, and *tamas*. It is said that they weave the rope to bind the human soul (*Purusha*) to the objective world, making them lose their state of an independent witness in the process. By liberating themselves from the bondage, the drama of life experience and natural conditionality disappears, and *Purusha* remains authentic. The truth of the matter is that nature ties itself to various forms and shapes of renewable phenomena which, due to the necessary dynamics, is never fully balanced making it impossible to find any sanctuary within it. Nature restrains its permeability for the soul's consciousness and the very human soul (*Purusha*). Naturally, it does not do so entirely because it would not exist then. In the lower forms of life, such as mineral and plant worlds are, unconditionality is manifested to a smaller degree, whereas in the higher ones it is more markedly present, with the mind of humans as the most liberated form of natural phenomena. The full spectrum of life forms represents a varying degree of the conditionality of phenomena, but never the complete freedom.

Sattva literally means essence. Etymologically the word is derived from "sat" which means being. *Sattva* expresses everything that is well-balanced, noble, independent, and pure which is the consequence of victory over every form of imperfection, and its nature is good and luminous. It is therefore the most present in consciousness as the ability to discriminate. *Rajas* is driven to take part in activities and change, to fight to keep its place due to the attachment to all the previous actions. Discernment is its chief characteristic. *Tamas* is darkness, it opposes activity and maintains inertia of everything existing, it is the obscurity of identification which is a result of an inability to discriminate and take active participation in the ongoing change.

In the light of the manifested world *tamas guna* can be seen as "gross' matter, the mineral world, *rajas guna* as the realm of a painstaking endeavor of living beings in their struggle for survival, and *sattva guna* as the "heavenly world", i.e., the cosmic clarity of a conscious insight into the reality of nature, memory, and intelligence. To use the language of modern physics, *tamas guna* is the archaic personification of gravitational constant (G), *rajas guna* is the "quantum of electromagnetic action" or Planck constant (h), while *sattva guna* bears a clear analogy with the speed of light (C).

The image of the pyramid can also help us here. The square at the base is the symbol of materiality and inertia of *tamas*, triangles are symbols of the creative dynamics of *rajas*, whereas the top is individual self-consciousness as the attribute of *sattva*. The material foundation is given to everyone, free movement and development are given to a smaller number of beings, and self-consciousness is off-limits to most. *Guna* trinity that pervades the whole structure of *Prakriti* is also clearly depicted in the triangles of the pyramid.

Gunas are never apart, they are always present in everything, they support and cooperate with one another. The very emergence of the world is a result of *gunas* interacting, and the versatility of occurrences in the world happens as a consequence of one of the energies of *gunas* becoming more dominant. They can be viewed, like everything else in *Prakriti*, as a two-way process: as the objective cosmic manifestations and individual states. The cosmic aspect of *gunas*, their imbalance that generates everything into existence, is evidently present in everything. In nature, nothing is ever the same, nor is it completely determined. Nature is the perfect chaos, but it is not completely unstable. It is well-organized chaos, the perfection of a higher order that cannot be rationally envisaged. The chaos of nature happens when initial conditions of any of its processes have not been defined within the linear timeframe. The initial conditions of everything are in *Prakriti*, or more accurately put, in the disruption of the ideal balance of its *gunas*, and *Prakriti* is out of time. Therefore, a unit of time or moment (*ksana*) that contained the initial conditions for any process does not exist, and neither does the beginning of the world exist as such.[30] For the lack of a better word with which to describe the relativity of time, we can only say that the ideal initial conditions of everything are present at any given moment, the same way we can say that the

---

[30] Yoga-sūtras (III, 52) add to this by saying that *Purusha* gains his freedom when he sees the relativity of time. The illusion of the continuity of time is woven by *gunas* through intermittent bonding states. We are always involved in some existential content, we never seem to be able to relax. With the insight into the reality of the present moment (*ksana*) which helps us to realize that it is eternity, the creative activity of *Prakriti* disappears and returns to the original state in which *Purusha* is always free.

initial conditions are not within the time of our experience but in *Prakriti* as the timeless authenticity of nature. Although they are here and always present, they are as elusive as time itself.

It has been established without a doubt that no process in nature functions according to a system that could be foreseen; everything changes. Our ability to predict some deterministic processes depends on the accuracy of measurements of the initial conditions. This accuracy is never complete. Due to very tiny differences in the beginning, the system will become quite unpredictable over time, after development and repetition. What appeared to be slight alterations at the very start, will grow larger in proportion after a while. No matter how it appeared orderly and predictable in the beginning, it is bound to become chaotic and unpredictable. This kind of versatility and vagueness creates all the life and beauty we see around ourselves, a pattern in stone, a riverbank, bark of a tree, clouds soaring in the sky, birds flapping their wings. Everything is free to exist in its unique way, and this chaotic reality of nature is not an expression of its unsteadiness, it is instead, a dedication to pure unconditionality, to *Purusha*. Nature is always subdued to *Purusha* who is always present, therefore the meaning of its being is not associated with time. What appears as chaotic locally, shows the property of purposeful orderliness globally. In other words, constant dynamics of nature created by *tamas* and *rajas gunas*, as opposing poles, have their purpose in *sattva guna*. It is the attractor of downward phenomena of nature. Inconsistency in nature, is, therefore, present only locally, when a fragment of its happening is observed from an individual point of observation (*indriyâni*), something that gives an illusion of linear time flow. On a large scale, the universe as a whole is out of time and always perfect, nature is present here in its absolute sense, in the unconditionality that facilitates everything.

Owing to *gunas* the functioning of nature can't be understood using some system or concept, using the mind that is of time, which divides and synthesizes. It can be experienced in all the opposites and unity, through the bliss of unbridled passions and the suffering of knowing.

An additional point on the cosmic aspect of *gunas* would be that *sattva* denotes the purpose or idea of the form to be realized, *rajas* the power and practical work on implementing the shapes, and *tamas* obstacles or matter that are being worked on. Each phenomenon in the cosmos has its purpose it needs to realize (*sattva*) and the work on its realization (*rajas*) exists in relation to what opposes this activity and what should be overcome and refined (*tamas*). The purpose of *gunas* is to set (*rajas*) in motion toward achieving a goal (*sattva*) and establishing what has been carried out (*tamas*). *Sattva* corresponds with affirmation, *tamas* negation, and *rajas* is the struggle between the two. *Rajas* and *tamas* also represent a conflict of opposing principles, while *sattva* arises as the necessary overcoming of the previous state, otherwise, the dynamics of nature would not be of the creative kind, but absurd, as it were. Therefore, *sattva* is a quality of creative overcoming of opposites and discrepancies that block somebody's growth, a possibility for a new choice, making it a characteristic of consciousness.

The tradition picturesquely represents *gunas* in the form of a torch. *Tamas* is the burning fuel, *rajas* a flame, and *sattva* is light.

The psychological states of *gunas* are a subject of a detailed description in *Bhagavad-gita*. *Tamas* is a trait that prevails in everything that is unconscious, inactive, slavishly subjugated to urges and habits, the domination of anything without the desire for change. It signifies an inability to discriminate and transform, lack of activity that drives humans to all kinds of susceptibility, stupor, and laziness. It brings a lack of compassion for the pain of others and simple joys, too, failing to see what position to take, in other words, a complete lack of objectivity. In short, an extreme level of immaturity of a soul. *Rajas* prevails in all the activities that lead to success, through all the meanders of life, falling and rising again. It is a desire for satisfaction and fulfillment of physical needs mostly. It is the root cause of all the restless straining and use of energy, perpetual seeking, and perpetual failing to find anything permanent and constant in the world of eternal transformation. To put it briefly, it is the development of the soul in this world. *Sattva* is an insight into the purpose of activities and stillness after accomplishment. Its characteristics are knowledge, subtlety, and purification from all the layers that taint the purity of self-consciousness. These are the characteristics of all those who have been liberated from ignorance and passions (*tamas* and *rajas*), which is appeasement that liberates inauthenticity and full maturity of the human soul (*Purusha*).

Sattva is consciousness, *rajas* is the subject, and *tamas* is the object.

All the categories of Prakriti (the way they are in the scheme) have the property of all the three gunas. For example, *mahat-buddhi* in the aspect with *tamas* is the individual awareness of oneself, in the aspect with *rajas* it is the awareness of oneself that is simultaneously and occasionally connected with the objective consciousness or the soul which sees both the difference and all the illusions of individual consciousness, while in the aspect of *sattva* it represents the pure or objective consciousness of oneself as the soul's consciousness, or the consciousness of the divine Absolute, *Purusha*. The category of *aham-kâra* in the aspect of *tamas* is the lowest awareness of ego, limited to one's body and existence only. In the aspect with *rajas* it is the awareness during a dynamic interaction with other people which entails understanding and learning through conflicts with others while fighting for survival, whereas in the aspect of *sattva aham-kâra* is the pure or objective awareness of one's individuation, a single 'I' which is capable of conducting the soul's higher consciousness, and its ability to submit and abandon the ego. The category of *manas* in the *tamas* aspect represents the mind that is completely identified with the body and its contents, and which fails to distinguish between its contents and those imposed on it from the outside; it is a state of sleep and unconsciousness that can also be expressed in a waking state, and not during sleep only. In *rajas* aspect, we are dealing with an ordinary mind with its dynamics which takes it through all the temptations and opposites in an attempt to understand, the one that slowly begins to see the difference between the consciousness and unconsciousness, the one that introduces critical analysis into contents. In the *sattva* aspect, *rajas* is the pure reason that engenders objective understanding and discrimination of all the contents as well as the awareness of oneself, and the higher categories (*aham-kâra* and *mahat-buddhi*). It is similar to other categories of *Prakriti* that refer to the being and dimensions of existence. They are all expressed through the dynamics of *gunas*.

In connection with the spiritual purification, we can understand *gunas* better in the following way: *tamas* is the gross physical form whose states can be measured and ascertained objectively (the field of science); *rajas* is the domain of subjective experience of the interaction of personality with the environment through its psychodynamics, the subjective feelings, and thoughts exposed to change and inconsistency due to the functioning of opposites (the field of psychology, art, and philosophy); *sattva* is the state of unconditioned and always alert witness (*sakshin*), pure consciousness in whose light the experience of body and mind is made possible, but whose daily activities and changes of states do not apply on the witness and their independence (the realm of esoteric aspects of religions that express authentic spirituality).

Various spiritual practices also entail *gunas*. *Tamas* covers all those practices based on rituals, imitation, and crude control over the physical body (extreme dogmatism and asceticism typical for some monastic orders, fakirism, shamanism). *Rajas* covers all those techniques that are based on sheer reaction and experiencing certain effects, mediation of some astral forces, naturally or artificially created, or with the aid of psychedelic substances. These techniques are particularly popular today, as the 'spiritual technologies of New Age'. *Sattva guna*, however, involves the practices that permanently transform the whole being, the ones that act as guides for the spiritual growth (*bhavana*) and maturing to which one's whole life is dedicated to. The practices of yoga and Buddhism belong to this tradition. They contain not only the methods with which to achieve transcendental states of consciousness but their permanent attainment through ethics and understanding of their true nature.

Gunas also illuminate a complex issue regarding destiny and free will. According to them, the highest percentage of people in the world falls under the *tamas* category, those are the people who are completely conditioned by the law of destiny which cannot be changed, and who experience nothing but suffering if they make an attempt to do anything; *rajas* belongs to a somewhat smaller number of people who are able to seize their destiny by the horns, at least partly, and those who seek freedom, while the *sattva* quality belongs to the very few individuals who are free from a destiny that imposes natural conditioning.

Sattva is a personification of selfless mercy, *rajas* of passion that depicts an individual experience of being useful, and *tamas* is inert passivity that is unaware of the true nature of being. *Rajas* and *tamas* rule this world, while *sattva* is like god-sent, a characteristic of enlightened beings who have surpassed standard human existence domineered by two principles: passive indifference of natural selection (*tamas*) and active cruelty of relationships within society (*rajas*). Their gentleness takes no notice of the opposites all the individual things of this world are exposed to because they see those in the light of the whole. This results in their mercy and forgiveness. *Sattva* is expressed as kind-hearted goodness and love.

The world is set in motion by the force of the three immanent constitutive properties, and not some external stimuli.

Therefore, the very movement of energy is immanent to nature, while the goal or purpose of movement comes from the transcendental soul or *Purusha*, from the consciousness.

In *Sâmkhya*, nature is a holistic union, a big network of mutual relationships where each form of existence entails within itself all the remaining ones. Nothing exists in nature as a separate (according to the mechanistic-atomic model) entity but is in organic unity with everything else. This unity is what is generally referred to as life, and it is that what distinguishes the human from the machine. There is an inherent life force (*prâna*) in all the things which gives them vitality. In the teaching of *gunas* we have seen how the fundamental constitutive properties of a being generate living energy without being driven from the outside. Self-creation gives vitality to the being because only artificial contraptions require an outside creator. The secret of self-motion of the universe and its vitality lies in the relativity of time of creation which is engendered through a holistic pervasion between the absolute (eternal) and relative (local, regarding time). Absolute and individual, eternal and transient, permeate and support one another like breathing, for example, which is happening here and now. This is how everything in nature moves.

6. Prâna

This word denotes breath. It is the life force which Aristotle's term *energeia* in its literal translation denotes as the being in motion, being-at-work, a life-giving activity of the being, or its actuality. ***Nature represents the overall movement because it is fundamentally energy itself. The general motion is maintained by itself due to the dynamics of gunas.***

The general movement is what we see as energy. *Prâna* is, therefore, energy, the vital energy that facilitates life.

Energy is motion, and motion is none other than **connecting**. Energy is always the movement of something, bonding with something, whether it is opposing poles in electricity or magnetism, or an effort or power invested in a movement toward a certain goal, a realization of some plan. Once we **connect** with another human being we feel his/her energy.

Energy springs from *akasha* or aether, from the universal quantum field in which **everything is connected into one** outside the space and time, where the subatomic particles move and communicate instantly, irrelevant of space and time because they are already interconnected in a holographic unity. The same properties can be attributed to the consciousness or pure intellect, *mahat-buddhi*. The consciousness is when the meaning and sense of each phenomenon are joined together. For this reason, they are synonyms in *Sâmkhya* in the same way *mahat-buddhi* and *akasha* are synonymous in Patanjali's yoga, possessing identical quality. Once we fully become aware of the purpose and true meaning of phenomena (*mahat-buddhi*), we then see it as the energy phenomenon (*akasha* or aether). Due to the identical essence of consciousness and energy, the consciousness rules over the energy as its higher instance. Energy is an emergent substance regarding the being, and the consciousness is referring to the purpose of its motion and the meaning of this phenomenon, its ontology.

Prâna in *Sâmkhya* does not have an independent place like in the system of *vedanta* because, as a being in motion, it cannot exist independently of anything it generates with its motion. Similar to *gunas, prâna* is not objective or substantial, and we are able to deduce it based on consequences only.

This energy, which moves the autonomic nervous system, encapsulates the whole body and all of its finer levels. It circulates constantly throughout the body acting as the power which forms the organs in accordance with the required functions. According to the most evident circulation, breathing, can be divided into five different breaths: *prâna* is inhalation, reception, respiration; *vyâna* is distribution, expansion, circulation, the distribution of energy one has breathed in the body at the moment of cessation after breathing in; *apâna* is exhalation and elimination; *samâna* is assimilation and absorption of energy at the moment of cessation after breathing out; *udâna* is sublimation, the energy which acts independently, even opposed to other energies, like during excretion. There are several other divisions of *prâna* in Indian philosophies and yogic tradition, but they are all based on the fact that *prâna* manifests via some function, never on its own.

Prâna can be understood as Bergson's "vital spirit" (*elan vital*). This impulse (movement) is a purposeful transformation of forms in time, something we can be witnesses to in the whole nature, and we ascertain it to be the creation of life.

The full swing of life energy comes from the freedom that engenders a being into existence, the swing of *prâna* is a movement of manifestation of the being, its resistance to unmanifested unity, the same way inhaling resists exhaling. Fundamentally, *Prakriti* attracts living energy into motion for the sake of maturing the experiences of all the aspects and purpose of existence, that is to say, the maturing of consciousness. The purpose of any living creature is to mature. The peak of maturing is in the awareness of independence of the soul of an awakened human (*buddhi*). It is the focal point or axis which directs the movement of *prâna*, it is the goal of the whole nature that serves this purpose as the background for experience. Hence, the consciousness governs the movement of *prâna*.

All the life forms are movements toward the consciousness, toward the outcome. Any living form is, in reality, information by which consciousness is conveyed. Such movement, which is informative, gives life energy to everything.

Movement of all the living forms toward their timeless purpose, toward the outcome in consciousness, we perceive with our

125

mind as the life force that forms and creates everything. Old Indian tradition used the word *prâna* to describe it. Stars are the physical sources of *prâna*, or nature, the source of everything that exists, its starting point on the way to the unconditioned human soul (*Purusha*), toward the meaning of everything that exists. In this motion, from the physical source to the meaning, it forms all the living and objective world. The light of stars would be nothing were it not for the consciousness of the human soul which gives it meaning and goal in self-knowledge defining it as light. The soul's divine consciousness existed prior to the origin of the human body in other parts of the cosmos suitable for this, because it is the freedom that engenders stars to be and radiate light owing to such freedom. Hence, their bond with people. People and stars are like a river, its source, and estuary that belong to the same phenomenon, it is only the unconsciousness of the mind (*manas*), which is unaware of the fact that the divine consciousness resides in them, so they suffer from the illusion that it is created over time following a certain set of conditions. The proof that the consciousness is here and has been since time immemorial (searching for it is an empty illusion and an expression of unconsciousness), is the very presence of the sun in the sky and the overall nature, and the presence of the very subject and their awareness of the sun as a phenomenon.

Prâna is energy with which *Prakriti* manifests itself into everything existing, it is constant and indestructible, it only transforms itself from one shape into another, making every single phenomenon that exists in the universe a product of this energy modified under the influence of the *gunas*.

This energy field entails, apart from the sensory or physical level of reality, certain other, more subtle levels, higher dimensions, which are well-known to experimental physics but under different names and postulations. In the hermetic tradition of the west, they are best known as astral levels. (More on this can be found in chapter *Dimensions of nature*.)

Since energy is ubiquitous and exists in a timeless holistic union of everything individual with the whole, every form radiates and refracts it through itself. Visible forms are the consequence of the *prâna* movement. They are one, the movement of *prâna* shapes everything in nature, while the form has a rebound effect as information that directs *prâna*. Colors and shapes we see in nature are a spontaneous expression of its authentic transformation or movement, and consequently, their healing effect is the most potent, they fill us with joy, and natural remedies help us in the long run. Satisfaction and health are an expression of good *prâna* circulation. Artificial forms we encounter in urban areas, unnaturally flat surfaces and sharp angles, have a negative effect on us because they unnaturally direct the flows of *prâna*. Old architects knew this better than their modern colleagues and chose to construct buildings with many curves and details that are pleasing to the eye and spirit. On the other hand, as the opposition to the natural wilderness, refined and orderly shapes we find in urban areas help channel and organize the living energy, which is expressed in cultivating a finer lifestyle. Although they help, they are by no means sufficient. The Chinese tradition of *Feng Shui* has attained proficient levels of organizing the living space energetically.

The biggest proof that form modifies and directs the living energy, and vice versa, are pyramids as such. They are the only form with flat surfaces and sharp angles that positively centers the flows of *prâna*, both within and without itself. (Greek *piros* - fire and *amid* – in the center.)

The more complex a material is in its form and composition, the more complex its meaning is. The degree of complexity of living beings gives away the complexity and strength of *prâna* circulation. Humans are the most complex of beings and *prâna* flows in them the strongest, something which is evident in their impact on the Earth. The spectrum of this radiation can be divided according to the body parts and specific organs. The state and vitality of a body and organs are expressed in radiation. Apart from breathing, the most important *prâna* trigger throughout the body is food. Plants process solar energy in themselves only once making them and the honey the most beneficial food for the body. Herbivores eat plant-based food and process solar light twice, therefore, their meat is of inferior quality, whereas the meat of carnivores is of no dietary value for people. The eyes are one of the most important openings in the body through which life energy can flow. The health and character of the whole being can be seen in them. The speed of *prâna* circulation is visible in pupillary width and mobility of the eyes, the purpose of which is establishing contact with phenomena and absorbing experiences, that is to say, energy. The nature of every phenomenon is information aimed at the flow of energy, the likes of which a person can receive most directly through the eyes, but other senses, as well. Furthermore, *prâna* circulates very powerfully through the mouth, not solely for the purpose of nutrition, or life energy, but a kiss as the most significant in the whole energy exchange; a kiss is nothing but a tiny suction of another person's energy and giving away a little bit of one's own; further exchange takes place through the nerve endings or erogenous zones, and extremities of the body. Caressing is also a form of energy exchange, and that happens with every touch. Sexual union is the most complete energy exchange of two beings, through it we experience the ecstasy of the unity of all the existence by transcending ourselves (orgasm is a natural, albeit spontaneous and only short-lived experience of enlightenment – that is the reason why people find it so appealing); that explains why new life is born through it. For this reason, it is necessary that the unity is of different sexes because while uniting with the same sex, energy becomes overly one-sided and the completeness is lost, something only a unity of different sexes can provide, and without it, there is no conscious experience of the unity of being; everything becomes a simple imitation.

The quality of *karma* of the being a person unites with is of crucial importance because together with the exchange of energy, *prâna*, the information that acts as the carrier of *karma* is also exchanged. This explains why a promiscuous exchange of energy with simply anyone is highly detrimental. To avoid this, there are certain feelings a person should follow because feelings tell us who we should unite our energy with, and what individuals are harmful to our energy status. This is the reason why we fall in love, feel attraction, but repulsion, as well. When its aura is photographed it was scientifically proven that humans lose energy if they engage in sex without love, while they receive it when they make love with the person they are in love with. In the old times, people were aware of this when they strictly forbade promiscuity before marriage, especially in women because they tend to absorb energy more, whereas, men give it away more. Virginity, especially in women represents energetic, genetic, but also karmic, wholeness. By losing virginity energy is exchanged with the opposite sex.

The head with its round shape preserves a lot of energy since its function is to maintain the functioning of the central nervous system. However, the natural center of *prâna* in the body is not in the head but the center of the body (*solar plexus*). A well-balanced personality, aware of its whole being, with its looks and posture, testifies of the balance that gravitates to the stomach. Their movements are harmonious, a feeling of steadiness and proper upright position are the first indicators of *prâna* circulating as it should within the body. People who lack this balance and whose energy is without control, such as mental patients, drug addicts, or those who spend their entire lives in one extreme posture, with their conduct and movements give off their psychological imbalance and unstable presence of the consciousness. Each individual radiates their energy in the environment, and the physical movement is only a superficial aspect of this radiation. If we take a closer look at healthy, spiritually mature humans, for example, we will feel pleasure and attraction, while if we do the same with a mental patient, we will instinctively feel rejection and anxiety. A more conscious and mature individual has a more powerful and better aura of *prâna*. Its radiation is not invisible and does not take place in some finer levels only, but it encapsulates all the levels. Its impact, apart from the presence in the being that radiates it, can be conveyed by means of physical touch, bodily fluids, breath, and particularly voice, or sound. The effect of music on the mood is well-known, but also what effect humans may produce on their environment with their behavior and speech. Due to the unity of energy in nature, and the effect of the law of resonance, psychoenergetic states of other people we can experience within ourselves.

This is the reason why in Indian tradition, for instance, there are examples of teachers (*guru*) who with their mere presence in silence (*Satsang*) lead disciples toward enlightenment. A perfectly balanced *prâna* of the teacher balances out the *prâna* of the beings in their surroundings by means of resonance. A perfect *prâna* balance is nothing but a steady presence of the consciousness in existence. ***Unity of the consciousness with authenticity turns the prâna flows into a harmonious unison which is manifested as light. This***

ideal harmony can be seen in spiritual people as holiness. It is what we feel due to the powerful radiation of their aura.

All phenomena have their energy vibration. These vibrations we can feel in us the same way we feel colors. Each color is made up of certain vibrations. These vibrations we feel when we watch a specific color, and they provoke a definite sensation or mood in us. That is why we love some colors better than others. The so-called "aura reading" is nothing but the ability to recognize these feelings as clearly as when we watch colors. Aura can be seen only by people who are more sensitive and tuned in so that they are able to feel it so clearly like watching some color. They cannot see the physical color in somebody's aura, because aura cannot be detected with physical eyes like when watching a physical object, but with their feelings, they sense vibrations of a certain being to such a degree that they are able to interpret it as though it were a physical manifestation of colors. Therefore, if it is said that somebody has a red aura, it means that our sensation of the experience is identical to experiencing a red dye.

Although *prâna* is the only energy that creates everything in the cosmos, and the cosmos itself, too, it is not distributed evenly everywhere. If it were not for these differences, their refractions, movements, and transformations, there would be no organized life in space. Owing to the functioning of the *gunas*, this swing of nature toward reaching its ultimate purpose is expressed in the form of the life energy, a very versatile selection that generates a myriad of forms throughout the cosmos, making sure nothing is the same in two units of time.

Prâna in its purest form can be recognized in everything that is born, young, warm, and gentle. Humans, as the place of the highest presence of consciousness in nature, are also the most avid consumers of *prâna*. In its newly-born state, as a baby, the human body radiates the strongest. Hence, our feeling of sanctity toward every child, the very presence of its being rejuvenates and heals us, it dignifies the worst of men even. Its purity leads us to act responsibly and impeccably, to balance out manifesting our energy (although we are often inclined to "discipline" the child instead of disciplining ourselves with its sheer energetic perfection). A child is in possession of great vitality, the ability to grow, and general regeneration, both the physical and spiritual. Its unique and irresistible scent gives off the purity of *prâna*, and its powerful presence is best presented in the lively and unstoppable mobility as well as the un-provoked bliss of a child. What appears as a child's restlessness and playfulness, is, in reality, the *prâna* dance which gets expressed in constant movement always interacting with the wider whole, something we are able to recognize as the phenomenon of gathering experiences.

It is easy to recognize the effect of *gunas* in the movement of *prâna*. It is in the state of *tamas* where it flows away, where life ceases to exist by chilling, drying, or decay. The loss of *prâna*, the lack of its circulation, is easy to see in all humans who live a negative life. Its exchange with a wider whole is a way to know the intricacies of this whole and accomplish any goal; its complete opening and release of the flow is experienced as the bliss of the ultimate cognition. *Rajas* is a state of dynamic exchange and circulation with the purpose of healing or the standard rhythm of maintaining the status quo and preventing decay. *Sattva guna* is directly experienced in the shining smile of a healthy child that fills with bliss everyone around itself. The *sattvic* state of *prâna* comes to the fore in every positive and optimistic energy input toward a certain goal or some other humans, without any doubts or hesitation, therefore, with love. Only such actions are successful and many acts of healing power through a strong faith serve as the proof for that. The functioning of this kind demonstrates that no objective obstacles are in the path of achieving realistic goals, only the subjective ones. Crystallization of the *sattvic* energy input we can find in the "soft" school of Chinese art (*kung fu*) aimed at *chi* or *prâna* activation: Qi Gong and Tai Chi Chuan. The Chinese philosophical tradition shows in great detail how *prâna*, or *chi*, further moves along the polarities of *yin* and *yang*.

All the interpersonal relationships and the overall behavior of humans may be viewed in the light of *prâna* circulation, its movement, and exchange. The law of compensation and balance of the opposite states or poles (*yin* and *yang*) plays the key role together with the law of resonance. Thus, *prâna* activity we feel when we are emotionally and psychologically attached to a person, especially that of the opposite sex, and which is complete between parents and children because of the common physical background. When this relationship is on the rocks by one of the parties involved, even as a result of lies that drive a wedge between people more than a physical distance ever would, or is terminated for whichever cause, a sense of uneasiness fills the chest where *prâna* is centrally located, and anxiety follows suit. "Pain in one's heart" is not only a poetic metaphor. Mood swings of other people affect us via the law of resonance because they represent specific vibrations of *prâna*. Aware people tend to absorb them better and are able to experience them inside themselves ("in their heart"). For the same reason, they can give their energy to those in need. For the unfeeling people, it is often said that they are "heartless". On the other hand, in those rare moments of revelation of the truth about us, of our life, and the world, or the moments of sheer happiness when we are overwhelmed by bliss, we feel this sensation coming from the chest and from there it keeps radiating throughout our whole body, making it as light as feather. This happens frequently during meditative calmness.

The functioning of *prâna* in its most general sense represents the way of being of people in this world. It always happens in the form of some relationship, as an energy and impressions exchange between opposite states or sexes. This is why all the beings have such an inevitable and fateful impact on one another, they attract each other in love or destroy one another in hatred. The movement and life energy exchange has its varying degrees, as well. In the lower dimensions (bigger) of the pyramidal conditionality of nature, the unity of physical form and *prâna* movement as a way of information transfer is obvious in the looks and the overall behavior of plants and animals, where it is almost always at work. The moods of animals manifest directly in the way they look and their behavior always has an informative function on the environment. With more advanced abilities of the sensory organs, information gets transferred in a more articulate way, independent of the physical looks, and their contents become abstract. The ultimate reach of abstract communication of life energy takes place in the reason (*manas*), in the form of a thought. The opinion represents the naming of forms of beingness (*nama-rūpa*). It has been engenderd by sufficient concentration of experiences of naming or ascertaining in one spot, in the subject, in their attitude "I-maker", "I am the doer" (*aham-kâra*).

Energy cannot stay on the same level because it is not substantial but existential. If it does not move creatively upward, it will let itself decline spontaneously, and start spreading toward those beings where it would, in the long run, be able to transform itself into a conscious outcome. The expansion of life energy from the place where it can no longer keep to the place where it is needed happens everywhere, it is also known as entropy. It is the very act of dying that makes way for a new life. In cosmic proportions, it is what happens when stars explode when new celestial bodies are created from the dispersed elements, other stars, and living beings. In the microcosmic experience, the mistakes and tribulations of others serve as experience and warning to be good, or, in other words, a part of their scattered life energy has transferred onto us. It can get transmitted in a number of ways, from abstract symbols and written messages to very specific and fateful events. Anyone who has reached the level of spiritual awakening knows that they had at least one energy provider to back them up, a person whose destiny was to act as the energy supplier, at least through information, or even through complete actions. It is a rule that when a sufficient concentration of energy appears, like the experience that precedes awakening, the provider withdraws, and often dies. This regularity was described in the classical texts of *Sâmkhya* as the general aspiration of nature to serve the human soul which it does through certain individuals, after which it desists.

The greatest power to direct and transfer energy has such an individual who has attained a state of pure consciousness through maximum concentration, and that can only be the person fully aware of their soul. The consciousness is the essence of the energy of existence. Conveying or giving life energy, for the maturing of the fundamental qualities in humans, is love. Love is, therefore, nothing but the non-conceptual and direct experience of the general unity of life energy on higher planes of the being, where it turns conscious. It is said that the source of the being is God or love. The consciousness is a result of love, and love is the only gift of the authentic consciousness.[31] Awareness of the unique life energy works by means of sympathy toward everything that exists in its power. In the higher realms of existence where the consciousness is more present, the union of all of this is clearer.

The unity of love and consciousness in free will is the only true measure of spiritual maturity and creative endeavor. Only with a maturity of this kind can the functioning of *prâna* be properly understood.

Energy functioning (*prâna*) is always guided by consciousness where energy is only a somewhat cruder expression of consciousness that enlightens meaning to existence. If the energy phenomena were not guided by consciousness, it would be meaningless and absurd. However, this is not the case. Everywhere in nature, we find purposefulness, and that is a clear indicator that every form of natural phenomena, from that of a cell to cosmic proportions, is fully conscious of itself as such, at least on the elementary and most immediate level. All the things are aware of themselves as such, they know that they exist. Hence, they are perfectly able to serve the interests of the human soul, *Purusha*.

Our ancestors knew only too well that things are aware of their existence. Medieval craftsmen would kiss and salute their tools before getting down to business, as would a peasant do to their ox decorating them in wreaths before ploughing their field. Our modern conflict with nature, and all the ecological crises and issues regarding it simply show that we are still unaware of existence to the degree it is aware of itself.

The consciousness – energy – form (of "gross" matter) are the three aspects of *Prakriti* that can be understood as *gunas*, and are inseparable in every respect. The consciousness is *sattva*, energy is *rajas*, and the form is *tamas*. It is the trinity that facilitates nature's existence, the one which was merely anticipated in religious experiences. They only differ in the speed of vibrations of their phenomena. Since manifestations originate from the same being, the consciousness can direct energy and be aware of the form, the same way energy can affect the form and state of consciousness, and ultimately, even form can determine the contents of the conscious-

---

[31] The most renowned expression of this experience was given by Paul the apostle in his Hymn of Love. (1 COR. XIII).

ness and usage of energy. If they were apart, none of this would be possible. Therefore, the being, energy, and consciousness are the same, but in different vibrations and proportions. The being is the most gross of all, and the consciousness is the most subtle phenomena of one and the same. The being is a pure form, the consciousness its meaning, and energy the necessary mediator between the two, an expression of their interaction. To experience a being as pure energy means to be aware of it and experience it directly for what it is – which means to experience it with love. Love is the most direct experience of the being and consequently, the foundation for consciousness. Each experience is an energy process, hence, the three words being-energy-consciousness can denote only one thing: love.

***

Prâna we will understand the best if we are able to comprehend the physics of aether, the way it was proven experimentally by Nikola Tesla and Wilhelm Reich. Tesla went to great lengths to implement the physics of the aether through electric energy and wireless energy transfer, through all the inventions that marked the groundbreaking changes about to take place on our planet which improved our lives in every possible way. Wilhelm Reich discovered the same physics of aether in biology and organic life. His research into *bions* showed that cells and microorganisms that make life originate from aether, which is ubiquitous, and which is finer than organic and energetic phenomena, a universal foundation of all life, in which they dissolve only to be made up again under favorable circumstances. He then practically discovered the functioning of *prâna* which he named *orgon*, due to its link with the organic life he was researching.[32]

***

At the end of the *Prakriti* chapter (although the entire book is dedicated to its understanding), it must be emphasized that *Prakriti* is neither conscious nor does it exist by itself and for itself, but only

---

[32] On the research into orgons and bions see Wilhelm Reich: *The Bion Experiments on the Origins of Life*; Farrar, Straus and Giroux, 2013. and Wilhelm Reich: *Ether, God and Devil - Cosmic Superimposition*; Farrar, Straus and Giroux; First Printing edition, 1973.

as a pyramidal whole (Gestalt) that differentiates the presence of an unconditioned soul – that engenders it, but it does not create it. ***The emergence of nature is a spectrum of unveiling the human soul***; the bigger the disclosure, the clearer its emergence. *Purusha* facilitates the *Prakriti* experience, and the closer nature is to the principle of unconditionality, the more it acquires the awareness of itself. Nature is the closest to the divine consciousness at the top of the pyramid, in *aham-kâra* and *buddhi*, it flows into unconditionality there (into *Purusha*) and appears conscious although it cannot be, but seems that way due to the proximity of the consciousness that engenders it, which is *Purusha*. What engenders existence, engenders the awareness of existence because there is no existence without consciousness. Therefore, it is not wrong to say that *buddhi* is the pure consciousness although it is quite clear that the proximity of the unconditioned *Purusha* engenders its existence. *Buddhi* is also the highest intellect in man. As such, it is facilitated by the presence of the soul. The classical texts use a metaphor with the crystal which, although transparent, set against a colored surface seems to take on the color in question. In the same fashion, even the most crystal-like form of *Prakriti*, or the intellect (*buddhi*) appears to be conscious by itself, although it is only so due to the proximity of the soul's consciousness (*Purusha*).

Similarly, the crystal structure of the intellect (*buddhi*) is colored at the same time with the contents of the lower life forms (*Prakriti*). They prevent the leaking of the soul's consciousness through the intellect. This discrepancy between the soul's pure consciousness and lower forms of nature crystalizes the structure of the intellect. When it is crystalized enough, it will leak the soul's consciousness better.

On the consciousness in nature can therefore be spoken only provisionally for practical reasons of its teleology and energy motion. The only true consciousness or wakefulness is the absolute freedom from the emergent world and objectivation of nature itself. To come to this freedom "from", one should first acquire the freedom "for" the emergent world, and take it on in its entirety. As a result, only the complete understanding and the experience of existence as such leads to its transcendence. This is the whole point of becoming aware of *Prakriti*. All of its forms represent information only for human consciousness (*Purusha*). In nature, therefore, no consciousness as such exists in the substantial sense, nor is it stored somewhere, but the consciousness as such is mere disclosure of existence, being unveiled to an independent soul. And only to it. The degree of disclosure is the degree of consciousness of the human soul.

In Prakriti, everything is information that turns into matter and matter that turns into information. This constant transformation we see as energy or prâna. This transformation happens under the attractive influence of the consciousness in a conscious subject that comes as a reflection of the soul or Purusha.

The conscious subject is the factor that makes information transform into matter and matter into information, into consciousness. It does not 'transform', but rather show itself to the subject as matter, i.e., form, or as information, i.e., as a thought.

Material form and the thought of it is one and the same thing but split across different dimensions. Different dimensions within the same being are what differentiates a thought from a physical object.

All the dimensions are united in the being of man. That is why a human being as a conscious subject is perfectly able to manifest thought into a form, the same way they are capable of designing and understanding every single form that there is.

Whenever a conscious subject looks outside of themselves, they see material nature. When they look within themselves, in their soul that is a reflection of the Absolute consciousness, the material nature as such disappears. Nature fakes materiality only in front of the conscious subject who looks outwardly. Classical texts use a metaphor of the dancer that dances before the eyes of a spectator. Dance serves to attract the attention of the spectator. The attention of the spectator gives the purpose for this dance. Once the spectator becomes aware of themselves, their attention is no longer connected to the origin of the dance at which point the dancer desists, in other words, nature disappears in its form of the alienated world of objects.

Nature is nothing but a mirror in which the Absolute is knowing all possibilities.

The human soul is a small individual expression of the Absolute.

That is why nature treats the human in the same way.

That is why all the enlightened ones speak of the fact that the cosmos is in us, and that we are no different from the divine that facilitates everything.

This is the ultimate reach of *Prakriti's* depiction. The remainder is nothing but a personal account that will be inspired by the depiction of its categories, with the added suggestion that the description is never that what is being described.

CATEGORIES OF PRAKRITI

MAHA - BHŰTÂNI
OR
THE DIMENSIONS OF NATURE

1. The structure of spacetime

Nature is composed of multiple dimensions. All the dimensions are present in nature together, they are not transcendent or "otherworldly", nor are they abstract facts for mystics, philosophers, and physicists to speculate with. The presence of different dimensions in our physical surroundings is by no means hidden away, and we can recognize them in everything because everything that exists is the way it is owing to all of the dimensions of nature and interconnectedness of their regularities happening within the being of man.

Humans are made up of all the dimensions that make up the universe, they are their innermost essence. Until the point they become fully aware of their essence, they view the outside world as though it were outward and fails to see all the dimensions of it. To average humans, they are nothing but some abstract facts. To enlightened humans, the world disappears and all the dimensions of nature become one with them.

All the dimensions, or all the modes of spacetime in which nature resides, are shown in the scheme (picture 1) under the objective, inorganic realm *tanmâtrâ*, and *maha-bhûtâni*. Upon their gradual merging the three-dimensional organic world is formed, *indriyâni*, which expresses "outer" and (or) "more gross" manifestations of their subtle vibrations.

The highest and the most subtle dimension is aether or *akasha*, which corresponds with the universal quantum field in modern physics. It also corresponds with the pure human consciousness. We can understand it as space itself that is the universal outcome of everything else.

Next in line is the dimension that is represented by the element of air. It is manifested externally as well as in the gaseous state of elements. It is the world of ideas or thoughts in man.

All of that is followed by the element of fire which represents energy, and all the radiations happening in the outside world. In humans, it is an intention to make all ideas come true, our will-power that drives us every moment together with our thoughts.

Then comes imagination which, in detail and with all the aspects, forms a clear picture of an idea having been fully realized. It is sustained by emotions. Nothing can keep or be realized without emotions. The more we want something the more we are likely to achieve it. It is represented by the element of water. In the outer world, they are all liquid and plasmoid states.

Finally, there is the element of earth that represents the ultimate, physical realization of an idea. Externally, it is the gross or what we know in our experience to be the material reality.

All of this is the same process which is split across dimensions represented by elements. It is all in us, we are made up of all the dimensions of nature. That is why humans can think (air), entertain their willpower (fire), also imagination and feelings (water), and all of that in a physical body (earth). Only in a human being the power to think, have willpower, feel, and physically realize one's ideas are combined.

All of these dimensions the divine manifests through, have a pyramidal structure. The point at the top is *akasha* or aether. Afterward, there are elements that represent varying degrees of the contraction of ideas until they reach such a stage that we are able to see the gross physical reality on earth.

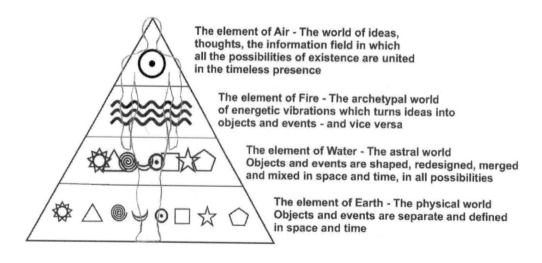

The element of Air - The world of ideas, thoughts, the information field in which all the possibilities of existence are united in the timeless presence

The element of Fire - The archetypal world of energetic vibrations which turns ideas into objects and events - and vice versa

The element of Water - The astral world Objects and events are shaped, redesigned, merged and mixed in space and time, in all possibilities

The element of Earth - The physical world Objects and events are separate and defined in space and time

This pyramidal structure contracts and splits simultaneously the manifestation of everything through dimensions, similarly to a prism refracting sunlight into all the colors of the rainbow. From an idea in the element of air to a concrete physical reality, there is no difference but the refraction of the same process into different aspects. When we hold an object in our hand, and a thought of that object in our mind, it is the same, *it is the same phenomenon, only split across different dimensions;* in the element of air it exists in the form of a thought in us, and in the physical reality (in the element of earth) as the gross form of the object in question. It is all due to the difference in time. In our thoughts the idea of the object is only temporary, it is the timeless present, whereas outwardly, this object is permanent in linear time to the degree laws of physics allow for it to be, or we choose to break it up with a new idea or form it into something else.

A material object is a form that exists in linear time, and a thought is an instant form of the same thing. The thought is in us because the higher dimensions are in us, and objects are outside in space and time.

Dimensions create a difference between thoughts and material objects. The divine Absolute uses dimensions to project linear time. The truth is, nothing new has ever been created, nothing objective by itself, only time has been created with the help of dimensions. Only in linear time (the element of earth) everything that is momentary and timeless and in unity with the Absolute (aether) looks like an object in space which exists over a period of time, it first appears and then disappears.

Therefore, when we create a reality we discover the relativity of time, we discover that the true reality is eternal, or timeless present, while simultaneously there is linear time we live in. We see both. Those of us who are unaware of the true nature of higher dimensions and pyramidal structure of space-time, tend to confuse objects and realities, they think that everything is momentary in all the dimensions, that everything is an illusion. This is not the truth. Reality is momentary only in the highest dimension, that is why we can go over all the realities instantly in our thoughts, in the downward dimensions where reality grows more conditioned over time.

Humans have the power to change reality to the degree they are able to conduct the consciousness from the highest dimensions onto the lower ones, all the way to the element of earth.

2. Nature as a mirror

In the scheme (picture 1) there is the following depiction: objective reality, shown on the left-hand side is composed of *tanmâtrâ* and *maha-bhŭtâni*, which also represents the inorganic nature; on the other hand, there is the organic realm of nature, *indriyâni*, which constitutes conscious subjects with all the sensory and activity organs.

Those two domains act as mirrors facing each other in parallel. The objective inorganic realm is becoming known in the subjective or organic realm, and vice versa, the subjective is known in the objective. The subjective consciousness receives objective value upon experience with the inorganic realm. In other words, this scheme goes to show a conscious subject in the objective world and the ways in which it acquires experiences.

It is the same existence, it is the same being, our being. Our physical body we use individually is not all we have, our true being is the whole existence, the entire universe.

However, the mind (*manas*) is a factor that twists the whole thing like a small mirror: it only identifies the body as our being, and that is why *manas* is positioned at the top of *indriyâni*. That is how the mind divides us from the whole. It represents a large portion of existence, everything outside *indriyâni*, as though it were outside of us, as though it were only the outside world, even alienated from us, and also in conflict with us. Then, we do not see our essence, what we are is being represented as though it were not us, at all. The whole of the outer world together with all the beings are us, and we experience them only as external objects we are trying to establish some kind of a relationship with. The same happens in sleep when we project the contents of our consciousness and subconsciousness outwardly into various objects and situations of the dream. Therefore, even in an awakened state, we live like in a dream. That is why it is said that humans are ignorant (*avidya*), and in need of awakening, enlightenment, and self-knowledge.

There is not a single mistake in that function. *It is the only way for the mind to capture the consciousness of Purusha and trap it into a physical body*.

This very structure of *Prakriti* or nature is the root cause for the consciousness to turn subjective, so that we begin to experience our inward as outward, and fail to be conscious of our true nature for as long as we keep identifying with the body and senses, with *indriyâni, but, instead, we can work practically with all the possibilities of the consciousness and existence as if they were objective creations.* It is the purpose of this whole creation. *It cannot be done in higher dimensions where everything is interconnected in unity, where everything is momentary and timeless.* The absolute consciousness wishes to manifest itself as everything that can be, to experience all of its potentials as a conscious subject. A three-dimensional world and conscious subjects in it are, therefore, required to work with all the potentiality of existence. This is the purpose of existence.

Through the activity of the body and sensory experience (*indriyâni*) we are able to see only one narrow bandwidth of nature's vibrations known to us as the three-dimensional physical world. It is the element of earth (in the scheme). Ten sensory and action organs (*buddhindriye* and *karmendriye*) belong to it, and are, therefore, called gross or outer organs.

Manas, aham-kâra, and *buddhi* belong to entities of subtle structure that surpass the three-dimensional and time conditionality of the physical body and compose our interior organ (*antahkarana*) which engenders the soul's consciousness to perform its function of the individual consciousness in the body (*jiva*), that is to say, to facilitate all the versatility of psychological and spiritual activities.

Those dimensions in *Sâmkhya* are called *tanmâtrâ* and *mahabhŭtâni*. Dimensions do not occupy some space and time, instead, space and time are in them.

Both space and time are relative. It is best reflected in the fact that they exist simultaneously and alternatively: when they are projected outwardly, they are manifested as the objective world, and when they are contracted into their outcome and purpose, they become the conscious subject then. Therefore, a conscious subject is nothing but the contraction of space and time into one spot, into

'I', into the contraction of existence into consciousness. The objective world is nothing but a projection of existence into a multitude, abandoning 'I am', and losing oneself and the consciousness of oneself. Hence, when the subject is fully awake and conscious, space and time disappear to them.

All the aspects of existence, although widely different and often led to a paradox, exist in nature, freely and equally, in a way that they form a harmonious whole. The whole can, however, not be understood from the perspective of the physical experience. It is a product of the element of earth, the last in *maha-bhũtâni* sequence, resulting in the whole of the physical universe being a mere consequence of the functioning of higher dimensions expressed in the prototype set up (*tanmâtrâ*) that contract in various vibrations and, depending on the mutual combinations, form the major elements (*maha-bhũtâni*).

This progressive contraction happens in the following way:

- a prototype element of the sound is produced by the element **aether** (*akasha*);

- *tanmâtrâ* of touch and sound together make the element of **air** (which as a consequence has these two properties);

- *tanmâtrâ* of touch and sound with color produce the element of **fire** (which has these three properties);

- once the taste is joined, the element of **water** is produced (which has these four properties needed for the sensory experience);

- when all the elements are joined with the smell, the **earth** comes into being, which is a total of all the other origins and elements (it has sound, color, touch, taste, and smell).

The earth is a product of all the dimensions and influences, thus, undergoing manifestation for all the reality of the beingness. Physical reality possesses the highest ontological value. That is why souls incarnate in the physical reality, creation is finalized there, all the dimensions of existence get actualized here, and souls as such with their act of embodiment implement this actualization.[33]

---

[33] This purpose of the incarnations of souls is expressed in esoteric Christianity in 'Our Father' prayer. It describes the implementation of all the laws from the divine Absolute to Earth, and all of them through man.

This ancient certitude of *Sâmkhya* we can explain better today using the terminology of modern physics. The highest dimension of the objectively manifested nature is aether or *akasha*. The same was claimed in *Sâmkhya*, and various other teachings, all the way to alchemy and the beginning of the twentieth century when aether was banned from science. In this highest or most subtle state nature possesses properties of spaceless and timeless holographic union. It is the quantum Field as the pure source and potential of all the possibilities. The nature of electromagnetic frequencies in this Field is Scalar or stationary, non-Hertzian because it is ruled by the unity of all the opposites. *Such Scalar field is the foundation of all life, it is the source of the overall energy or prana.* Today it is being discovered in experimental physics, but due to the prohibition on the term aether, it is given various other names: vacuum energy, zero-point energy, dark matter, quantum Field, matrix...

By progressive contraction of the prototype origins, the non-Hertzian Scalar frequency of akasha grows more Hertzian, the frequencies of energy movement become more transversal in nature, until such point when they acquire mechanical, vector, and three-dimensional movement in the element of earth.

***

Elements that constitute physical reality also represent dimensions of its phenomena. *Tanmâtrâ* means a prototype or "subtle rudiment of elementary matter", or literally "appropriate to that", subtle matrix. *Maha* means great, cosmic, or universal, and *bhuta* comes from the root *bhu* (grow, flourish, be, originate) and may denote a dimension of being, a way in which something happens, but also the element which is in question. It bears resemblance to the Greek *physis* which indicates the growing process, a material foundation, but also an intrinsic principle, the structure of the phenomena or being.

Indriyâni produces the full impact of *tanmâtrâ* and *mahabhûtâni*, together with *aham-kâra* and *buddhi* that conduct the consciousness of *Purusha* in nature. Organic life stems from inorganic.

On the scheme, we see the vertical division of categories to the left, non-organic, and to the right which is the organic side. The left, non-organic is the macrocosm, and the right, organic is the microcosm. One reflects the other like in a mirror. It is the holographic principle of *Sâmkhya*. Once humans acknowledge this reflection of the cosmos (the left-hand side) in the microcosm (the right-hand side), they acknowledge themselves as a unique personality, which is *aham-kâra* which overcomes this division.

Tanmâtras are objective but also partially subjective, because they produce only sensory organs in the subject (*buddhindriye*), while the big elements (*maha-bhûtâni*) are pure objective categories of nature since they engender all the other phenomena in space. Only with the big elements *maha-bhûtâni* and *tanmâtras* together the action organs (*karmendriye*) are possible, and together with them *karma*, as well, or the overall life drama which receives its outcome in the consciousness of 'I am' (*aham-kâra*).

The left, non-organic side of the scheme is of vibratory or wave nature until it condenses like the earth or physical reality, and then vibrations acquire substantial character, they act as matter creating organic world in the process (*indriyâni*). The organic world is not, therefore, substantial (material), but only acts that way due to the three-dimensional conditions in which it resides. **The foundation of the whole organic world and life are the electromagnetic frequencies**.

Schematic division of categories into the left-hand and the right-hand side gives us insight into why the natural phenomena happen dually, both as a wave (vibration) and as substantiality (particle), which is something that appears to perplex the physicists. *Tanmâtra* and *maha-bhûtâni* are manifestations of the vibratory phenomena of energy in higher (implicit) dimensions, while the substantiality of *indriyâni* is the realm where experiences of phenomena are acquired in the most concrete fashion (explicitly). *Akasha* is what is known as the quantum hologram in modern times, the universal Field, or divine matrix.

Outside the mind and in higher dimensions the potentials of all phenomena exist timelessly as nature or *Prakriti*. It has been said that everything that exists manifests from *Prakriti* (emanation) because it had already existed in it in the form of a possibility. Therefore, anything that could happen at all, the potentiality of anything, already exists in the unity of *Prakriti*. The mind merely focuses on individual possibilities causing them to get actualized. The sum of all the possibilities and phenomena are to be found in the highest dimension, in *akasha*. Access to it can only be made from *buddhi*, from the pure consciousness. The past and future of everything existing are located there. On the lower, material, three-dimensional plane, the mind only successively actualizes the possibilities, from everything that already exists it selects one by one, and to us, from our subjective point of view, it appears as though something new was taking place.

Due to the timelessness of all the potentials, *Prakriti* has vibratory or wave property, that is to say, momentariness.

The vibratory or wave organization of *Prakriti* was shown in all the five sections of the scheme as the highest and most subtle state of those sections. Those are sound or aether in the non-organic and the mind, hearing, and tongue in the organic part, in *buddhi*, as the most subtle creation of *Prakriti*. Let's observe *tanmâtra* of sound, as a primary manifestation of vibrations. It is possible only through space (*akasha*) because the sound is not possible without expansion. The vibrations of space form all the other elements and all the other phenomena. From an objective point of view, one can see only space (*akasha*) in which all the dimensions and phenomena are possible. It is particularized by certain forms that restrict our sensory perception and action. Only to curtailed subjects, closed off into their own egos, which observes phenomena from a certain reference point, forms seem like they are independent in space and in between each other. ***All the forms represent the modified space itself (akasha). Space creates mass. The first emergence in space, as its opposition, is the photon.***[34] When photons of equal size collide they create a vortex which becomes stable and this is how mass comes into being. There are many experiments to prove this.[35] This is a way in which all phenomena are interconnected into a unity. All the mystical experiences of the unity of the universe are possible only based on this.

Buddhi and *akasha* are synonyms in *Sâmkhya*: *akasha* in terms of the category and *buddhi* as the existential aspect of being-

---

[34] Many myths on the creation of the world say that in the beginning was the darkness, and then God created the light.

[35] See footnote no. 19.

ness. With them, *Prakriti* is the nearest to the idea of unconditionality (*Purusha*).

In what way are *mahat-buddhi* and *akasha* synonyms?

In the universal quantum Field (aether or *akasha*) everything is contracted into a timeless one, **everything is interconnected**, and the subatomic (quantum) particles communicate non-locally, they are connected irrelevantly of the space or time. Their communication is instant no matter how far apart they were. The consciousness has the same properties, it is nothing but the very connectedness of occurrences and things in their most subtle form, **the connectedness of information and meaning in purpose. The consciousness is making sense of each phenomenon the same way the quantum field connects all phenomena into a unity.**

This is the way in which consciousness, *mahat-buddhi,* and *akasha* (aether) are synonyms. *Mahat-buddhi* is mere openness for the presence of *Purusha* which is the true source of consciousness, and not the consciousness itself. All the categories of *Prakriti* are mere degrees of openness for the presence of the consciousness of *Purusha*. **Varying degrees or modifications of the presence of consciousness in nature create different dimensions and proportions.**

This fact that *buddhi* and *akasha* are synonymous we experience the most directly in meditation. By attaining the pure consciousness or awareness (*buddhi*) in the meditative discipline we realize we are neither our body nor our mind, but space (*akasha*) itself, in which the body and mind reside and take place. True meditation is all about becoming aware of the space as the source of being and consciousness. In the same way in which the body is in space, all the mind is in consciousness, too. That is why we can be objectively aware of the mind as well as the body. [36]

Space (akasha) is conscious (buddhi) – not because of itself, but because of the proximity to Purusha.

3. The nature of time

Space is the very form of phenomena, while time is a subjective experience of movement, or phenomena of this form toward

---

[36] More on this see in my book "Meditation – First and Last Step – From Understanding to Practice".

its purpose, or consciousness. Hence, the consciousness is the peak amount of the contraction of time, it is pure present, the presence itself. We are the most conscious when we are aware of the present moment. Always when we are identified with thoughts we are outside of ourselves, like in a schizoid state, outside the reality of the present moment, trapped in time. The more identification with time is overcome the more present the consciousness is. Time is a way in which something is formed and exists in experience. Time does not exist by itself, but only as a form of phenomena. Therefore, only the being exists, but not the time. The being is timeless because it is not substantial. However, since it is hard to perceive its timeless essence, we experience it as being something substantial, we project its happening through time. Such time becomes the oblivion of beingness, it becomes a way of avoiding the responsibility for accepting the purpose of existing here and now. Time is most commonly a mere substitute for the conscious presence in being, it is the space between knowing and being.

However, time is the necessary evil tool using which we gradually in a by-pass manner ('by the sweat of thy brow') arrive at the reality of existence. Our mind (*manas*) is designed to perceive matters one by one, never all at once. That is why our consciousness matures over time. Only by maturing over time do we become familiarized with the reality, even though its essence is always present here and now.

Time is a product of the subjective experience in space. When space is viewed from one reference point (the body, *indriyâni*), which is imperative in three-dimensionality which is the only one capable of sustaining the coherence of perception, something is experienced as nearer, while something else as further. This experience is interpreted in the psyche (*manas*) as something "former" (it had reached us sooner), and something as "latter". In that way, time becomes only a psychic interpretation of what goes on in space. The psyche spontaneously harmonizes itself with the physical reality of space which surrounds it by creating the perspective of time. The three-dimensional perspective of phenomena of subject-in-space, like in a mirror, in psyche, turns into the illusion of time. It means if only an eternal being exists, and if time is nothing but a mere projection of the mind, then the passage of time is also an illusion – the mind moves, but not the time. The mind must be in motion to gather information for the accumulation of consciousness in *indriyâni*, but there is no need for it to be enslaved by this illusion, as it usually is.

Time is a way in which the mind functions. The being does not move through time toward its purpose; it already exists within it, otherwise, it could not exist since its existence would be meaningless, and that means impossible. Only the mind moves while envisaging, and the whole of the objective world exists only for it. Only the mind attains the meaning, and its subjective experience (*indriyâni*) is enlightened with the objective cognition when it transcends time, and that means when it stops imagining the world as something else other than what it is when it discovers what truly is here and now. Only when the mind halts its wandering, wavering thoughts, the world for what it is reveals itself to the human. Then, they realize that nothing exists by itself and for itself, everything is one in *akasha*, while a myriad of independent occurrences and beings are ostensible for the subject that perceives them from a single reference point. ***They see that the illusion of subjectivity is the only cause for the illusion of an objective multitude***. Beings as such are not shaped in space nor do they move through it, but ***the very space shapes itself from one point to another, creating an illusion of the being in motion***. Like a wave that appears to travel along the surface from one point to another, while the reality is that the water itself moves periodically up and down in one wave. When we move our arm through space from left to right, it is not one same hand that does the moving, but the form of the hand successively and momentarily turns from one moment to another into a new position, something we experience as the movement of the same hand. This recalls an illuminated advertising sign where the light bulbs go on and off in a controlled manner, so that it appears as though the light form moves, integrates, and disintegrates, is born and dies, albeit nothing new is happening but an intricate light display. This whole flashlight circus of forming the space happens, naturally, only for immature observers, and for them only. They are the only ones who project the phenomena in space as if they were substantial.

The issue here is, therefore, a momentary creation of the world. Nothing in it is the same in two different moments, but the subsequent one has already been created as new and slightly altered due to the *gunas* playing. This is a way in which everything moves. The momentariness of creation engenders the overall movement of the universe. No other movement exists out there. This law of shaping the space we could name the **Wave Model of Quantum Fluctuation**.

[The idea of momentariness of phenomena is the foundation of Buddhist outlook on the world. The teaching that stems from such views involves an idea that objects and beings have no reality per se (*anata*), they are not born, that is to say, they never originate. This idea was particularly precisely detailed by the most illustrious restorer of Buddha's teaching, Nagarjuna, and further interpreted by Gausapada, one of Nagarjuna's followers, with the classical example of a torch. In his work *Karika* (in *Mandukya Upanishad*) Gaudapada explains how everything is, including itself, unborn. In *karika* (verse) IV 47-50., where he states that in the same way that a torch, once swung fiercely about, appears to create a ring of fire, the consciousness once swung about, and set in motion appears to be divided into a subject and object, the knower and the known, resulting in the illusion of continuity and the objective world. When the consciousness (torch) is still, there is no illusion of the world (a ring of fire). When the torch is in motion, its circular form is not outwardly imposed, nor did it abandon it during the moments of stillness, the same way the ring of fire is in no way different from being the same flame. In IV 91. he states that all the creations are mere modifications of space, *akasha* (aether), and there is no versatility among them. There is no such thing as the individual creations (of the being) that move through space, but the space itself, on its most subtle, subatomic level, that successively forms itself into everything that exists from one moment to another. The same was discovered by experimental physics when subatomic particles are apart, they remain and act as though they were still joined, irrelevant of space. What keeps them constantly tied to one another is the energy of the space itself. In this way nothing is born, nor does it originate in any way, but it already is everything as the modification of the whole, and the whole in question is nothing by itself.

Because if it were something by itself, it would contradict its nature, and everything said would fall through. If the whole were something by itself, the beings within it would also have to be 'something' by themselves, and the whole, then, would be unable to provide them with life. Everything would be separate and individual. In other words, individual beings and the whole are not different in any way.

Our being does not exist as an individual being, at all, the same way a drop is only water of the ocean. Our body does not breathe, nature breathes through our body; our body does not act, the wholeness acts through it; our mind, *manas*, does not think, the wholeness designs itself through *manas*. Our being is always in the wholeness of nature like a baby in her mother's womb. We have yet to be born. This birth is awakening (*buddhi*) which comes about when we become aware of this state, that nothing was born in the general natural causality, that nature itself (*Prakriti*) acts and designs everything. Only an awakened soul (*Purusha*) transcends nature. If it were not already like this, it could never be 'liberated'. Soul's 'liberation' is a realization of one's true nature. Our true nature is an unborn and unconditioned soul. Only owing to this fact (our true nature being the freedom that engenders everything) can a human being give life, forgiveness, grace, love, consciousness, and appeasement (*sunyata*).]

4. The vibratory characteristics of nature

Buddhi, tanmâtrâ of sound, aether, and *manas* with the abilities of hearing and speech are the highest and most subtle properties of the five groups of *Prakriti* categories. Their connectedness is easy to recognize in all the mystical and religious traditions where the creation of the world happens with a sound, or word (*logos, aum*), it is the primal vibration that created all the space of the world (*akasha*, its property is light also). Word as the modification of the sound plays the deciding role in the utter modification of phenomena. This law is evident in Hindu *mantra-yoga* as the vibratory formula that with mere vibrations produces certain effects, in Jewish *tetragrammaton*, devotional Buddhism, *philokalia* in Greek Orthodox church, and *dhikr* in Sufism. The same role is attributed to the assorted "names of gods" that reflect the creation process. Hence the name, as a vibratory formula, the key to the identity of the being. Many centuries ago, in ancient Egyptian mysteries knowing the names of gods engenderd a passage through all the dimensions and being born in the light of pure wakefulness, personified in Osiris as the sun. In other cultures, the knowledge of the names gave insight, even control over the essence of what was being named – which caused it to be hidden from people. A word uttered in higher dimensions, in the astral realm, is directly executed, it becomes instantly materialized. Hence, the efficacy of all the rituals of magic that contain within an inevitable part of the vibratory pronunciation of the word as a central point, be it liturgy or mass, sorcery or curse. All of the above-mentioned categories are at work. The awareness of the activity (*buddhi*) and its mental preplanning (*manas*), followed by speech, which is connected with hearing from the *indriyâni* realm that implements *tanmâtra* of the sound for vibratory shaping of phenomena through *akasha* descending onto the lower dimensions, because the shaping process moves in the downward direction, from the higher to the lower elements. All the way to the realization of everything on the level of the earth.

The shaping of everything happens under the influence of *aham-kâra* category. Because of it, space bends into a form of everything that exists, it contracts mass and energy centripetally into specific forms.

The five grand or "gross" elements, *maha-bhŭtâni*, result from subtle causes, *tanmâtrâs*, and their combinations. **Tanmâtras are informative fields for shaping the emergent world.** *Tanmâtras* are *hyperspace*, or that what is beyond the sensory and astral space – which are *maha-bhŭtâni*.

Within the space, the elements water, fire, and air encapsulate astral realms, with the element of water representing the most familiar experience of astral known to many people, because it is the closest to the earth, it is the astral we reside in while sleeping and during astral projection, while the fire and air are higher and more subtle astral realms. *Tanmâtras* are far more subtle realms of prototypes (or archetypes) of everything formed. When humans project themselves outside the body, they find themselves in the blessed light full of unbelievable colors in all the geometric and abstract shapes possible that move fast in unimaginable combinations all around. The truth is, they do not move around them because a reference point does not exist there, but they see them from all the aspects all at once.[37] Astral still reflects forms of the physical world, something that is quite apparent in the world of dreams, there are buildings, people, trees, landscape... but when we exit astral and move on to the hyperspace, which can be achieved by simple uplifting while still being consciously present in the astral realm, it all disappears, only amazing geometric shapes and other abstract figures begin to appear in very bright colors moving in all the possible and impossible ways around us, set against a dark background. After we gather some experience with this, we can notice that they move as fast as our thoughts do. *They are the archetypal patterns of our thoughts we see there as if they were on the outside of us*. It lasts for a very brief moment because a higher level of consciousness is required for a person to stay there longer. If they know how to create the archetypal patterns there consciously, they are in the position to control the events on the physical plane completely.

Since *tanmâtras* are at the same time prototypes for the senses (*indriyâni*), perception of the world as such is made possible. *Tanmâtras* are interior, subtle senses that facilitate the existence of the exterior, physical ones. For this reason, they are used for perceiving that what escapes the physical senses, the energetic and astral reality.

Tanmâtras **engender all the dimensions of the emergent world** (*maha-bhûtâni*) **and its perception at the same time** (five senses in *indriyâni*). **Tanmâtras are a link between the subject and the objective world (the bond of indriyâni with maha-bhûtâni).** This dual role of *tanmâtrâ*, facilitates subjects to experience the world, and their perception is analog with the dimensions the world manifests in. It will never be complete until the subjects familiarize themselves with *tanmâtrâ* realm – because humans will become acquainted with the objective world to the degree that they acknowledge the dimensions of existence within themselves.

---

[37] On the nature of hyperspace see Stewart Swerdlow's books.

5. All the dimensions of nature form our physical body

It is a well-known fact that the organic world comes from the inorganic with no clear lines between the two, but very little is known about how the supreme embodiment of the organic world, humans, is formed by the inorganic realm, how the cosmos forms the subject and humans' awareness of themselves, and the cosmos, too. This forming happens in accordance with the dimensions of nature (*maha-bhûtâni*) that produce *tanmâtras*. They all in their own way form one aspect of the being of the human. ***The human is a microcosm. Since the dimensions of nature are multiple, humans accordingly have several bodies that correlate with those dimensions.*** This makes humans capable of moving physically (earth), also feeling their movement (water), thinking where they are going (air) and always being awake and aware of all of it within themselves (*akasha*). If they did not have these faculties, they would never be able to know all the dimensions of nature, nature itself, nor would they be human, at all. This explains why they do not behave like humans while being unaware of nature for what it is until they become acquainted with the higher bodies and worlds. They had esoteric teachings that attempted to convince them of their existence. Although their intrinsic nature is such that they naturally possesses them (essentially), they must affirm their existence in their own experience to make them conscious (existentially).

The human being is a mechanism for transformation higher vibrations into lower ones, higher states of consciousness into those that are lower, and vice versa. The human being is a mechanism with which the divine consciousness acts in nature. That is the real reason why souls incarnate into human bodies. That is why the human being acts in all the dimensions because they are made up of all of them.

Higher or subtle bodies are the matrix for forming the physical body and together they are called *linga-sharira*. It is the astral body or the body of stars, the cosmos. It is composed of the subtle principles that form the objective world. The same principles form the physical body, as well (*indriyâni*), therefore, when humans exit it and find themselves with their consciousness in a copy of the physical body, the astral body, they are able to move across all the dimensions (*maha-bhûtâni*) of the objective world and have the perception of the subtle, interior senses (*tanmâtras*) in them. When they become aware of their higher bodies when they actualize them, humans become aware of the higher dimensions of nature, they see them for what they are in their entirety, they get one step closer to their outcome, and by doing so achieves the psychic objectivity and maturity. There is no other way.

For as long as they remain trapped in *indriyâni*, humans experience objective nature (*tanmâtrâ* and *maha-bhûtâni*) indirectly, through psychic projections and myths, through knowledge and religious convictions. Only when they leave the organic world and enter the inorganic realm and experiences it directly with their astral body, the peacemaking function of the mind disappears in complete cognition. That is the only way for humans to become realistic and objective. Without this experience, they are always subjective and conditioned by various convictions and knowledge, or in the worst case by psychosis and schizoid split as a result of closing themselves off into their subjectivity.

Humans experience higher inorganic dimensions most directly when they find themselves in their subtle body between two physical incarnations, or during the so-called "death". The human soul partakes in the creation of organic life from inorganic by means of intelligent design. It learns important lessons in a creative endeavor by forming the mineral, plant, and animal world. Many plant and animal species came into being this way, they were designed and projected by some soul, or several of them combined. Such ones are usually with exceptionally pretty shapes and colors, which nature itself does not need for the sake of survival, and it is apparent that "somebody made" them. The shapes of many plants have been harmonized with the health benefits they provide through intelligent design. Their shape becomes indicative of their purpose (celery for the bones, carrots for the eyes because cut crosswise it resembles the pupil of the eye, nuts for brains, grapes for the hearth, etc.).

Souls form their future physical body, as well.
That is why DNA does not contain within itself any information or plan on how to form the body, instead, DNA is nothing but a list of proteins, contents on the body build, albeit, without the specific plan for forming it.

156

The inorganic realm has the prototypes (*tanmâtrâs*) for forming everything organic (*indriyâni*) as well as all the dimensions (*maha-bhûtâni*). Therefore, the inorganic as such stands as an inner and to physical senses invisible principle according to which the organic forms as the "outer", sensory, and physically visible world. Humans, being the complete embodiment of the organic world, have *tanmâtras* and *maha-bhûtâni* as their **interior dimensions** that provide all the spiritual life, all the dreams, myths, and archetypes. This analogy caused the ancient heritage to acknowledge the cosmos in human form, and the human form as the microcosm.

The body is nothing substantial, nothing by and for itself, it is merely a three-dimensionally coherent form of existence. The body is action (*karma*), and the same applies to the whole physical universe. Nothing else. The body is the way in which the consciousness forms and matures, grows, and expands towards complete unconditionality. The consciousness, as the presence of meaning, cannot be diffuse and impersonal, it must obtain a concrete expression and embodiment to actualize its presence. The human body is the most beautiful, the most concrete, and the most complete embodiment of a place in nature where the consciousness can attain the actualization of the meaning of existence. Since the way in which nature exists is not monotonous but multidimensional, humans, too, are made up of many bodies, many ways with which they can exist. A way of living determines and shapes the consciousness of existence and vice versa. This, in turn, makes existence and consciousness mutual.

Becoming familiar with all the ways of existence, including those in the astral body, outside *indriyâni*, is of vital importance for expanding one's consciousness. ***Humans cannot expand their consciousness, nor make it objective if they do not surpass their identification with the body, but concretely, through out-of-body experience entering higher dimensions.*** The way to exist is to learn to direct one's energy, no consciousness can be without it. It has already been said that the being, energy, and consciousness are the same thing, the being is the grossest, and the consciousness the most subtle of manifestation. Being is the pure form, the consciousness is its meaning, and energy its irreplaceable mediator. We should keep this in mind with the brief description of higher dimensions

157

that follow because it will explain how this realm participates in the permeating and forming of the being, energy, and consciousness into the body of the subject, into a human being.

Of the higher, implicit dimensions of nature, we have been convinced and told about in various ways in all the religious and mystical traditions of the East and West alike. All the mythologies point a finger in that direction. In the esoteric tradition of the West, the more subtle vibrations and dimensions that those of the physical kind, are called the plane of astral light, or astral, also the Great Magical Agent, Magnetic fluid, The Soul of the Earth, Tetragram, Inri, Nitrogen, Ether, Od, etc. We will use the expression astral here whenever we refer to the more subtle and insubstantial vibrations of nature that are represented on the scheme as the elements of water, fire, and air. The astral realm is, therefore, a realm that encapsulates the earth to approximately 14 kilometers (8.7 miles) above and below the surface of the earth and helps with forming physical shapes and processes, it is the imagination with which nature forms the physical world and its perception. It is the world where dreams take place, images of our visualization appear, and out-of-body experiences become actualized. This world is as real as the physical one because if it were unreal like immature people think, there would be neither the dreams nor imagination as such – yet they exist. We forget our dreams easily because they play out in different, more subtle vibrations than those of the physical domain. Our attention easily loses focus in all the vibrations, other than the physical ones because it is the only place where it could be inert, albeit, not entirely there either. In the higher dimensions, one must be an aware participant in all of the phenomena which is something yet to be accomplished. Day and night switch is where the natural transition of the presence of individuality from the organic (*indriyâni*) to inorganic (*maha-bhŭtâni*) plane happens, and vice versa. In our experience, it is known as shifting from the dreaming phase to the waking phase, and the reverse. Astral is an objective realm by itself, consequently, individuality within is passive since it is subjugated by the objective laws of nature. This passivity psychology incorrectly interprets as unconsciousness. Humans are just as conscious in the dreams, as well, but only on the level of perception, they are not fully active participants. They be-

158

come so only when they are realized as a complete personality (*aham-kâra*), only when they reach that stage they are capable of acting on their own will in their sleep, without being a mere observer of what is going on. It is achieved through a persevering practice (described in *Aham-kâra* chapter). Higher realms of astral, fire and air, have patterns from higher categories, *tanmâtrâ*, which are the result of collective or objective experiences, archetypes, but it is also the domain into which subjective experiences from *indriyâni* are introduced, together with the dreams without archetypal contents. Something similar happens after the death of the physical body, as well, only then objectivity of this plane completely overpowers subjectivity connected to the physical body.

During the process of sleep, a spontaneous detachment of the astral body from the physical one arises when it moves on to the astral realm. It goes through the so far gathered experiences intensely and trains for the upcoming ones. Discharge of accumulated energy of impressions is the standard recurring theme in dreams, while training for all the eventualities in the drama of life is the main purpose of dreams. In dreams, we try out all the parallel realities that we were unable to realize on the material plane. Additionally, dreams represent a bond between the embodied mind and soul. That is the reason why we get so many important messages and inspiration while dreaming. The mind is too inhibited and conditioned in the body. In the astral realm it is a lot more liberated and open for the higher, more subtle influences, therefore, it absorbs them more easily.

In the astral realm, humans can be present in two ways: passively ("unconsciously") in a dream, or actively and consciously in an out-of-body experience of astral projection or, alternatively, during death. A conscious stay can be achieved through training, the practice of meditation, or it can also occur spontaneously, during a sudden disruption in the functioning of the cerebrum as a result of a blow, intense shock, pain, or using some drugs, and often while being administered anesthesia during an operation. The meditative practice provides constant alertness through cultivation (*bhavana*) and preservation of energy, it is the result of spiritual culture and brings knowledge of the objective world. Spontaneous experiences, one of which is "lucid dreaming", are mere fun outings that can act as incentives for a smooth crossover phase into the spiritual culture, and often those events are so eye-opening that a life is changed forever because they provide an insight into the higher worlds, if only briefly, where it becomes apparent that humans are independent of the physical body. Without an experience of this kind, there is no spirituality, and no developed system of beliefs or accumulated knowledge may replace it.

Aham-kâra is the principle of individuality that intermittently draws attention to either the physical phenomena (*indriyâni*) or the astral realm. *Aham-kâra* is individualized while the consciousness is still in the body, which explains why individuality in the body is not what it should be: unity, a single 'I', an expression of the wholeness of the being, instead, it is split and therefore changeable. Instead of illuminating their whole being with the light of the consciousness, they are limited to one ray of attention which intermittently moves from the subject to object, from the organic to inorganic field through different dimensions. Once placed in *indriyâni* it ties us to the physical reality and we do not remember our dreams, and when it shifts to astral we dream and do not remember the physical reality, at all. This movement is educational, so that humans move through dreams in interaction with the physical experience where they learn about all the aspects of existence, until, step by step, they illuminate their whole being across all the dimensions and realizes that it is all one, it is all energy that is conscious and that is in no way different from their being.

We can think both during awareness or in sleep; during awakeness actively, and in sleep passively. This is due to *manas* gathering impressions from the organic and inorganic domain alike. When we are dreaming and thinking we are doing the same thing: we are reconsidering possibilities for future actions. In thoughts, we reconsider all the possibilities abstractly, and in dreams, we do it more concretely, like in a drama.

The lower astral plane, represented by the element of water, is close to the physical world and its neutral vibrations more or less realistically reflect its shapes. It is a kind of a mirror of physical phenomena. Hence, the lower astral reflects the lowest physical drives, passions, and urges. They manifest here without any restrictions that are imposed on them in the physical world. Therefore, lower astral entities are the most negative demons that there are. They are unable to produce life energy and, as a result, feed off the energy of organic beings that produce it. Their nourishment is subtle, it consists of pure energy vibrations. The frequencies of fear and anguish are the densest and have the highest energy value for these beings who thrive on them. Consequently, demons appear to generate such states of fear and anguish in organic beings to be able to use them as a good food source.

Each form on the physical plane has its energetic expression that is visible in the astral plane which is the area of pure energy. Apart from the above mentioned low drives, there are exalted aspirations that the higher levels of astral reflects, the elements of fire and air. In the astral realm, the causes for inducing the consequences on the physical plane are created. Since they are more subtle, this area of higher astral has more creative energy which is felt strongly in it, so much so that humans do not wish to go back to their physical body.

Due to the energetic nature of astral, there are no static, inert states, but everything exists as the activity only. Everything happens here objectively without any delays. Therefore, for humans to maintain their presence in the astral realm during a projection, they must participate in its activity, or they will be instantly returned to their body. Due to a higher degree of reality, humans in the astral realm are "unconscious" because they have been taught to be only subjectively conscious (in *indriyâni*). They remain the same way when they interpret their dreams, they project them onto their subjectivity and "unconsciousness". They interpret dreams as unconscious processes because their fundamental state of mind during daily activities is generally unconscious. Dreams are completely objective and open events, and only to an average human being they may seem unclear and unconscious.

The ontological status of an average human is the same in *indriyâni* as it is in higher dimensions, in the awakened state and dream alike. The only difference is in the vibrations that give an illusion of different status. The awakened state gives a public characteristic to phenomena because of the nature of physical three-dimensionality which facilitates general agreement of several individuals regarding the reality, while they reside only individually in the dreams, where each individual faces existence personally and directly. The only reason for the "unconsciousness" of dreams is, therefore, non-compliance with public opinion. For the same reason, humans are unconscious of the overall reality of the being because the cognition of reality is always straightforward which means individual or personal. Until they become a personality, humans fail to perceive reality, they think reality is what other people tell them. Only a complete personality (*aham-kâra*) has a higher ontological status in the knowledge of the world.

An average human is a split personality and their state of wakefulness is only a slightly more coherent state of unconsciousness than the one they have during the sleeping phase. Their 'wakefulness' is, therefore, a dream in the dream, a 'lucid dream'. They are never truly awake because if they were, they would never have dreams. Dreams are possible only for a person who is sleeping, for the one who is unconscious, whether they are so during the day or at night. Humans dream during the night only because they dream all day long, as well. The difference is in intensity only.

What is experienced in the physical or subjective world as inward contents, the state and mood, in the objective realm, during sleep in the astral realm, happens as the outward phenomena, our states of mind and soul create a suitable atmosphere, setting, or plot for themselves during the drama of sleep, contents of our mind that are currently unconscious assume different identities there (persona, shadow, anima, animus), while the sensory organs may assume animal forms or indulge in unbridled passions. One should know that the expressive possibilities of astral are virtually limitless, same as imagination (this is what astral is: the imagination of nature), and no final interpretation of its symbolics and ways of functioning are possible – although certain patterns exist for the understanding of it, such as the description given above on how to function through the dimensions (elements), and archetypes. The energy of astral is neutral by itself, it, like water, assumes the form that existence and consciousness impose on it.

There is not a single source of light in the astral realm, it is diffusely illuminated with its own light in accordance with its shape because everything is energy. It gives light directly to each form, and the colors are much brighter than in the physical world.

All the sensory experiences are clearer because they are more subtle than the material ones; the sound spreads quite clearly here. There is no gravity here, one may walk like on the earth, but they may fly, as well. The acquired habits on the physical plane will decide on this, and also on many other things happening in the astral realm. For example, we have learned that we cannot put a hand through the wall, but we can do so in the astral realm, and once we try to do this we will feel as much resistance coming from the wall as our disbelief convinces us until we realize it is possible, and at that point, the wall will turn elastic or plasmatic. The same works for flying or any other aptitude considered "supernatural powers" (*siddhi*). The one who possesses extraordinary abilities on the physical plane, such as levitation or telekinesis, did a lot of rehearsal and reassuring of that on the astral plane.

While the lower layer of astral is closer to the physical world and mimics its lower passions to a large degree with its shaping, the middle one is filled with all sorts of activities, and the upper one reflects the highest aspirations possible on the physical plane and is therefore characterized by unspeakable beauty, vivid colors, and divine peace. In religions, this area is known to us as heaven. To unenlightened mortals, this is their ultimate reach before the next incarnation. Since the working force in the astral realm is emotion, their concentration in the form of strong faith engenders dedicated believers of some confessions to attain it. The most important contents of religions are various convictions of higher dimensions and ways of attaining them.

While the esoteric symbol of the element of earth is a square, the symbol of the element of water or astral is a crescent moon.

The next higher dimension of astral is the mental level, it belongs to the element of fire and its symbol is a triangle. The vibrations of this level are even more subtle than on the lower level of the astral realm It is characterized by having even fewer stable forms in it. They are as permanent and stable here as the thought in the mind of the one who resides here. The same way one who can find themselves in lower astral and maintain their presence is the one who has managed to distance themselves from debasing instincts, in the same way, only humans who have mastered objectively their thoughts can reside here, that is to say, those who are able to discern between themselves, their essence, and their thoughts. When we are objectively aware of them, they show themselves before us in a completely new, objective way so that we begin to see the cause of our every thought. There are often incidences of archetypal episodes here or "hearing god's voice". Staying here is an extremely important event for all humans, it also serves an educational purpose, often it represents a turning point in life, because on such a high level of objective domain subjective experiences have been left long behind, and humans as such are much closer to the insight into the collective experience of the whole humankind.

The next higher level belongs to the element of air and its symbol is a circle. This is the realm in which no forms exist, but staying in bliss here directly depends on one's ability to be awake and without thoughts. There is nothing subjective here due to the completeness of the being that with its totality outside of space-time disables divisions and appearance of any kind of a special object. The consciousness itself has become an objective factor, and only here a pure light that is the outcome of the being, energy, and consciousness can be experienced.

When in the astral realm humans ascend to the wakefulness of this kind, to the dimension represented by air, they are instantly thrown back into their body. Since the pure wakefulness is mere existence as such, it is in no way different from the human being, from any existing shape that happens from one moment to the next. This experience is expressed by *mahayana* Buddhists in the statement that "form does not differ from the void, and void does not differ from the form", more accurately, *samsara* and *nirvana* are the same.

Akasha engenders all the dimensions of the being as such, and is, therefore, irreducible to its emergent forms. All the dimensions are its mere modifications. Its symbol is an elongated circle, ellipse, germ, or egg (from which according to many cosmogonies the universe is born). Akasha is pure alertness which does not depend on the state of consciousness (air) or thoughts (fire) and feelings (water) but is present as the only outcome of the overall phenomena and shaping of the world. The being is no different to it from the energy and consciousness, from here and now. That is

164

why, one cannot reside in *akasha* because it is all that there is, it precedes everything. Unlike the individual, psychic wakefulness of the element of air, the wakefulness of *akasha* is an objective, primordial presence like the being itself, even more than that: it is the wakefulness humans had prior to their birth before the origin of the world took place.

In other words, we reside in *akasha* when here we cognize all the illusions of the thoughts, feelings, and body, as well as the world that they keep projecting, when it all disappears in our cognition and when only space itself remains, the one that facilitates all of this, as the only reality. ***When the reality of space which engenders everything we are able to recognize as our consciousness and essence.***

Tanmâtrâ domain is beyond all the dimensions of astral, which is lower and denser. This realm beyond astral is known as hyperspace. The lower astral encapsulates planet Earth to a certain height. Beyond that point is hyperspace, or *tanmâtrâ*. It is literally above the ground of the earth, in cosmic space. Humans can always during a conscious astral projection ascend using their astral body to reach this realm. This is where the original soul resides (oversoul), the one that does not get incarnated into the physical body but stays in the higher realm and is known to the human as 'Guardian Angel'. For the contact and working with hyperspace energy certain symbols are used, colors (royal blue) and imagination (the symbol of the original soul is the mathematical symbol for infinity ∞, of the silver color set against the blue background). With well-designed corruption of imagination, by deforming these symbols and faking colors magic was made of the kind that is now known to occultists.

It is important for humans to know that it is not particularly good for them to have extended stays in the astral realm because it is the area of manipulation with energies for very negative purposes and demonic beings. The human's place is in the higher dimensions, in *tanmâtrâ*, where the archetypal origins and true causes of astral and the physical world are located, it is the angelic dimension of our original soul.

To be whole means to have the perfect body, and it is perfect when it is actualized and exists across all the dimensions.

All the dimensions can, however, be actualized in the present moment only. Nothing exists outside of it. By the unconditional presence of the human soul here and now, human completeness has been accomplished. Once the mind is active to the point that it is identified with the body and starts projecting time, all of these dimensions become separate and 'transcendental', and to experience them one has to exit the body and get to know them objectively. The mind is the root cause of every objectivization, it splits all the dimensions, its state decides what dimension we will perceive and how. Once the mind is transcended we realize we have never been identical with the body, at all. That is why the act of exiting the body, in reality, is the experience of awakening and returning to the soul's higher, primal consciousness, and the return to oneself.

The presence of the consciousness in the form of a human soul is the human's embodiment or the act of enabling their body to be actualized in all the dimensions of existence. When they are in the past or future, they wander about in their dreams, their existence is unfounded and absurd, it can only cause sickness. Only in an awakened human personality (*aham-kâra*) the present has been scored, only in it *Purusha* and *Prakriti* intersect – as the consciousness and existence. Nowhere else can a cross be found with such correct proportions. In all the other forms of the existence of nature this intersection of consciousness and existence happens erratically and incompletely, they are all crosses with awkward angles, hence, they do not let in the awareness of existence completely, it is not crystal clear there. Deviations from proper intersections generate the whole spectrum of the world, all the elementary, mineral, plant, and animal life. However, this intersection of existence and the soul's transcendental consciousness does not happen perfectly regularly in every human's experience either, most people do not get hit by the vertical of eternity perpendicularly as compared to the horizontal of the experience of existence, instead, it slips into time, either past or future. This deviation from the presence in the present, from complete crystallization of the awareness of reality, is expressed as the mental projection of time. There are smaller or bigger deviations from the proper point of perspective, from the crystal clear view on eternity that shines through the transparent being. The biggest deviation muddies the being and makes it opaque, it, then looks like the gross physical body. It is the wrong perspective that does not stray far from the animal world. When crystallization sets in, the awareness, the angle rises toward the vertical, and only at that point the being becomes more fluid and meaningful, its higher, astral dimension is revealed. When it advances and reaches the mental world, the angle is almost perpendicular, and the perfect angle is in *akasha*, where the being grows completely transparent and disappears, to allow pure unconditionality that engenders everything. We can use our imagination to compare the four arms of this cross with the four elements, and the center with the fifth, *akasha*.

Setting the angle straight is overcoming the time and strengthening the presence of personality in the present, i.e., the embodiment of the present time in man. Only in cognition of this kind personality can mature. The awareness of what they are, of the reality, cannot be impersonal, it must have its embodiment which is the body. That is why a clearer presence of the consciousness induces a proportionately clearer crystalization of higher bodies, their higher and richer ways of existence. Differentiation of their awareness of existence automatically differentiates their body and personality from the impersonality of existence.

Whatever the current dimension they occupy, humans must be individually persistent and self-sufficient within it, they must be a personality. Such individuality forms their body from the vibrations of the dimensions they are in. It happens automatically under the influence of *aham-kâra* which is the principle of the individual forming of everything. Whatever dimension humans reside in, they are composed of the vibrations belonging to this particular dimension. The more they become an individual and conscious factor in the higher realms of the being, in feelings (astral) and thoughts, the more they develop the body of those levels. Embodiment is a way to actualize thoughts and feelings functionally. It means that humans become consciously present and independent in those levels, that the thoughts and feelings are just as objectively present and known to them as their body, and that they are their master, and not a servant. Humans are embodied and present to the degree that they are objective regarding the given phenomena and also awake. To be functionally and actively present in the higher dimensions means to be the master of the body, feelings, and thoughts, as well.

Exiting the body and becoming familiarized with the higher dimensions equals exiting unconscious passivity and mastering one's own faculties in all the dimensions of a person's life, in thoughts, words, and deeds alike. If we are not our own masters, we experience these higher dimensions only as a dream.

Without a conscious presence such as this, without the body to govern, a human's behavior is rather bland in the dimensions in question, they are passive and unaware of the true nature of their phenomena and also susceptible to their spontaneous influences. That is why, whenever they find themselves outside of the boundaries of their own body, they faint.

By becoming aware of the higher dimensions, humans crystallize higher bodies and uses them to survive the disintegration of the physical body. This is the key moment of all religious and mystical experiences of initiations into death and resurrection which is present all over the globe from time immemorial and personified in the most wonderful way in the character of Jesus Christ. The goal of this experience is to overcome death, decay, and unconsciousness.

Each higher body or state rules over the lower one because their capabilities are greater. Each higher body is more subtle, less inert, limited, conditioned, and unpleasant than the previous one. Here, too, we can recognize the form of the pyramid where each level is narrower and more subtle than the previous one. The crystalization of the higher level happens through the conscious and willing mastering the conditioning nature of the lower.

Similarly, everything that is 'higher' relates to our inner world, and this entails mastering the higher bodies which means the abandonment of attachment to objects, finding solace in turning to our inner 'I', toward oneself, toward our soul. The more we are in our Self in the way described, the more we are able to actualize our higher bodies.

The dimensions of nature are not one on top of the other, like a multi-tiered structure, but are, instead, states of existence. The grosser ones are 'lower' states by nature, closer to our coarser experience of perception, whereas the 'higher' states are detectable only when our perception becomes more refined. This is why the dimensions of nature correspond with states of consciousness, and the cognition of higher dimensions is nothing but mastering finer states of consciousness and ways of existence in accordance with them, within humans themselves. Since all the dimensions permeate one another within the same space, the greater presence of the reality of all the dimensions means the higher presence in the present moment. The obvious conclusion is that the higher presence in the present moment is the same as the ability to perceive all the dimensions, something which depends on the correctness of perception and actions in thoughts, feelings, and body. It can all be achieved through cultivating higher objectivity toward the thoughts, feelings, and actions, and the consciousness is objective only when it is not identified with the thoughts, feelings, and body when it surpasses or transcends them.

Only a permanent cessation of identification or the permanent state of transcendental consciousness engenders the permanent, clear, and objective consciousness of the higher dimensions. These so-called 'higher states of consciousness' or the consciousness of the higher dimensions may be acquired in a number of ways, as well, but it is always a temporary excursion into higher states of consciousness, after which a decline into grosser states is inevitable. It happens because we have not perfected ourselves in accordance with the higher dimensions of existence, our thoughts, words, and deeds are not united and harmonized with reality because the consciousness is still identified with higher states. Only when humans find their sole stronghold in the permanent state of pure or transcendental consciousness of their unborn soul, only then all the dimensions of existence of nature or *Prakriti* become perfectly transparent and present in the here and now. The perfection of nature is available only to the perfect human, *Purusha*.

Without mastering the physical body there is no conscious awakening in higher astral dimensions represented with the elements of fire and air, the one that is the true salvation of being "born in the Spirit" in the "heavenly kingdom" or the experience of a "new birth". Crystallization of this kind is the key moment not only in the human's individual life, after which they are far more mature and ready for spiritual truths and more liberated than ever, but for the maturing of humankind on the whole. The teaching of Jesus and his work is completely dedicated to such maturing, he initiated the whole of humankind into it.

It is important to stress that unless we master the physical body but remain identified with it and dependent on its influence, we fall prey to the lower astral influence and its entities. Hence, mastering the body is necessary for overcoming the lower astral influences and all the misery that comes from it.

Without crystallizing the higher bodies we may become victims of spontaneous activities and overflowing influences coming from the higher dimensions. The astral body may be formed (conquered, actualized) with the wrong emotions for evil purposes, such as black magic is, for example. Also during the intense pathological experiences of emotional imprints and contents. That is why astral experiences are common occurrences in mental patients, whether they are out-of-body episodes, or "hearing and seeing ghosts", or visions so strong they are in no way different from real life experiences.

Different levels of astral pervade one another, but they also pervade the physical realm, so that a certain physical form may be seen or experienced as though it were something completely different. Awareness or realizing personal integrity is none other than crystallizing each dimension on its plane and being able to *distinguish it from the other ones*. Only by doing so, they can be known objectively. Without an objective *discernment* and knowing them in detail, their contents are confusing, subjective, and more often than not, dangerous for one's mental health. Due to the non-existence of the integrity of a personality (*aham-kâra*), as the deciding factor in *indriyâni* and *maha-bhûtâni*, all the levels of the being permeate one another so astral creations can be seen on the physical plane, too. Their influence may overflow to *indriyâni* and humans can, then, be possessed by an astral entity, religious, or psychotic contents, depending on whether they are more objective or subjective by nature.

Similarly, without an experience of higher dimensions, the power of *indriyâni* may prevail over *tanmâtrâs* and turn humans into hardened materialists and atheists who cannot remember their dreams even.

Another way to describe influences of lower states is to say that they are a product of the functioning of multiple "I's". Humans are unconscious and conditioned by lower states only because they are disintegrated into a multitude of I-states that successively and almost inconspicuously shift at all times. Therefore, the attainment of a pure subject or one 'I' corresponds with the element of air.

The whole process of forming and mastering higher bodies is, in effect, attainment of one's willpower (aham-kâra), of the united 'I', by overcoming the dependence on outer circumstances that dominate over lives of unconscious people. On the scheme of the categories of nature a united 'I' or aham-kâra is placed beyond the organic and inorganic realms alike, beyond the physical body, indriyâni, and all the dimensions of the astral realm

With unconscious people who do not have one 'I' (who have not actualized *aham-kâra* category on the scheme), the conditionality of the physical body is a lifelong and insurmountable barrier, they depend on the physical influences of the environment because they are unaware that there are other options. They are susceptible to the outside world and their activities are determined by the influences of their feelings, convictions, and mental patterns that seem to belong to them, but the circumstances in question conduce their own agenda through people, and all because of their passive use of the consciousness and failing to put some effort into it to maintain it in a more stable form, expand its presence, and implement it on all the states of the being, and the higher dimensions of nature, as well. Unconscious humans cannot see that everything they carry within and experiences and fights for as if it were their own – is an alien creation. Nothing is his. Failing to realize this, people create a circle of *samsara*, rebirths in the most limited of bodies, the physical body. Limitations of the physical body are a mere reflection of the limitations of perception.

In the process described above, we can recognize the usual flow of emotional, sensory, and mental maturation and attaining the psychic objectivity the analytical psychology speaks of. It, however, can never be completely and creatively functional, unless it is followed by a specific experience of discerning the higher bodies, and experiencing each dimension in the same way we experience

171

the movement of our physical body. The saying that one learns to swim by swimming must be applied here. Those that fail to enter objectively the world of their feelings and thoughts, will never learn what they are truly like and will remain forever conditioned by them. Without out-of-body experiences, there is neither psychic objectivity nor complete personality. The essence of man's freedom and authenticity lies in the complete objectivity toward nature, something which is achieved by thorough detachment (*kaivalya*) and discerning the important from unimportant, knowing what is inherent to the human and what is not.

To put it briefly, the above-described actualization of the upper bodies is none other than our ability to tell them apart since they already exist but in a confused and unconscious manner, and, therefore, cannot be relevant to us. On the other hand, their differentiation is nothing but becoming aware of those functions that compose them, and that means the awareness of the body, feelings, expressions of will, and thinking process. Since these two functions already exist, albeit in a confused and unconscious manner, learning to discern between them means to establish them as they are by themselves. It is the practice of Buddhist meditation *satipatthana*, and it has been detailed in the book "Meditation – First and Last step. From Understanding to Practice".

As we have already emphasized the difference between *Purusha* and *Prakriti*, the issue here is not about some objective segregation of one from the other, it is an illusion that is imposed on us by the sensory experience in the physical world, but *exiting time in which we are not what we truly are. It is that what is objectively experienced as exiting the physical body and going to higher dimensions. Subjective slavery to time and substantiality create an objective problem, so much so that becoming acquainted with one's timeless authenticity and spiritual reality seems to be an objective liberation from the body that exists in time only*. It appears so, but solely from an empirical point of view, not the spiritual, where the whole nature is in complete unity and there is nothing that can be extracted from anything. Humans live in an illusion if they have an empirical point of view without a spiritual counterpart. The power of illusion and slavery in time, make one's liberation inevitably seem like overcoming the physical bodies by crystalizing the higher and more permanent shapes. The power of an illusion gives objectivity to this experience.

This brings us to our next point that the purpose of forming the human body is only a higher or more subtle existential function of nature from its forming of space and time. The spacetime of the objective world spontaneously shapes the organic human body and nothing specific has been done unless humans personally encounter the objective realm of the world they resides in. It cannot be achieved by mere physical moving about, in the same physical world as animals do, but movement along the higher, inner dimensions of astral and mental worlds. The path of humans is vertical by nature, i.e., it goes inward, toward them. Horizontally, that is to say, outwardly all the beings who are incomplete in terms of their sensory and functional capacity move, which are all the beings except for humans – even many people who do not use their full potential. The horizontal movement is typical only for the beings who still have a long way to go toward developing their sensory and activity organs and various other abilities. Once these capabilities are instilled in the human being, *indriyâni*, and become affirmed in the creative interaction with *tanmâtrâ* and *maha-bhûtâni*, which can only happen in certain individuals, especially in mature people, the only thing which is left is the upward movement, toward *aham-kâra* and *buddhi*. It is the only destiny of mature humans, and they cannot become mature and psychically objective without a straightforward introduction into the objective realms. ***Aham-kâra becomes integrated only with the subjective and objective realm of beingness*** (it can be seen in the scheme).

The whole nature is created to transform the grosser vibrations of a being into the more subtle ones. Not only through food, but the assimilation and refinement of all the experiences of existence, the overall perception, and actions. Our physical body is only a seed which through the cultivation process needs to develop by growing upward, toward the spiritual world, and open up its blossoms completely yielding luscious fruit of knowledge of good and evil, truth and lies, human and inhuman, being and non-being. The only aim of maturing and growth of this kind, eating these fruits, is to separate *(kaivalya)* the unconditioned divine consciousness, personified in the human soul, in the human's presence from everything that restrains it from manifesting itself in this world.

The manifestation of the divine consciousness of our soul in this world is a process of purifying separation – *kaivalya* – because *Purusha* is detached and independent of all the opposites and characteristics of the whole *Prakriti*.

The way a ripe fruit, the carrier of the overall life, falls off a tree on which it ripened, and only this act gives final meaning to its existence because if it does not fall off, it will rot barren on the branch, the same way there is no maturing for humans without detachment and independence. Humans are aware of their higher dimensions to the level they are independent of them, and they cannot be independent of them by pure avoidance, but only through a mature, objective, and independent cognition. The same way fruit is ripe only when it is ready to fall off, to separate itself from the being that produced it, the same way humans are mature, having become aware of all the dimensions of nature, and having recognized their independence from all of it. Detachment and independence are possible only with the meditative experience of the pure or transcendental consciousness.

Humans will be ready for this only when they in their personality (*aham-kâra*) completely integrate and affirm both subjectively (*indriyâni*) and objectively (*tanmâtrâ* and *maha-bhũtâni*) the experience of beingness, when none of the dimensions and possibilities of life are alien to them, and when they become the personification of life because they have accepted it fully with love.

The human soul has been independent of nature from the beginning of time, and there is no need for it to conquer its independence. To actualize and affirm their authenticity, all humans need is to help and affirm the life of nature in all its forms. The very support for the whole existence can lead to that what engenders the existence itself. Only with an absolute and functional love like that toward everything that exists, they establish their primal state, superiority, independence, and unconditionality of the divine consciousness which (in this way through them, in the form of an individual soul) facilitates the overall existence. There is no other way.

SYÂDVÂDA
THE LOGIC OF PARALLEL REALITIES

Of all the spiritual traditions in the world, it is quite certain that not a single one has managed to attain such level of tolerance in presenting the truth of the world, or the truth itself the way Jain logics has managed to execute in the "teaching of maybe", or *syâdvâda*. The word of *syât* comes from the Sanskrit root *as*, "to be", which also means "may be", and *vâda* means "teaching", so the word *syâdvâda* can be translated as the "teaching of maybe". It is the purest form of the secret of creation or the reality itself because it completely negates any dogmatism and one-sidedness, it establishes that all the realities coexist in parallel.

Jainism is the practice of the highest strictness of ascetic purification of the soul from all the bonds that tie it to the conditioned beingness. *Syâdvâda* which originated from it points to the manifestation of the being, and together with it its cognition. It consists of seven aspects where each one is correct in its own way and necessary for facilitating a clear contrast in dialectics with all the others so as to provide a clear insight. The nature of reality never manifests entirely in one way only, its expression is always and in everything abundant in discrepancies expressed by the "seven-valued logic" (*sapta-bhangi*) which says:

1. Arguably, it exists.
2. Arguably, it does not exist.
3. Arguably, it exists; arguably, it does not exist.
4. Arguably, it is non-assertible.
5. Arguably, it exists; arguably, it is non-assertible.
6. Arguably, it does not exist; arguably, it is non-assertible.
7. Arguably, it exists; arguably, it does not exist; arguably, it is non-assertible.

Just as the seven colors make up sunlight, in the same way, these predicates, once joined together, give a correct insight into reality. Each one is one-sided and insufficient if separated from the whole.

These seven predicates represent the ontology of consciousness through all seven chakras.

The first predicate ('arguably, it exists'), points to the identification with something that is, which is the strongest in the first chakra.

The second predicate ('arguably, it does not exist') points to the opposition the consciousness that is identified with something is inevitably faced with. The second chakra is an expression of primary polarization of energy with the opposite sex.

The third predicate ('arguably, it exists; arguably, it does not exist') describes the third chakra and initial triumphs of understanding the opposites, overcoming them with the help of some higher goal.

The fourth predicate ('arguably, it is non-assertible') points to the experience of unity with the existence which is always lost for words because it overcomes the mind based on opposites of lower states, and those are first brief experiences of transcendental consciousness. It is the first insight into the whole with which everything is accepted through the feeling of love, i.e., union, it is the characteristic of the fourth chakra.

The fifth predicate ('arguably, it exists; arguably, it is non-assertible'), indicates features of the fifth chakra, placed in the throat area, which gives the ability to express in words and thoughts for the first time something that IS, a reality that has up to that point been ineffable.

The sixth predicate ('arguably, it does not exist; arguably, it is non-assertible'), points to the sixth chakra, the third eye, which sees that no other objects but itself exist (nothing exists), only the consciousness which is ineffable exists for the very reason that it is only the being and existence. One sees things here that are ineffable.

The seventh predicate ('arguably, it exists; arguably, it does not exist; arguably, it is non-assertible') points to the seventh chakra and unity with the transcendental divine reality of here and now, in which existence is voidness and voidness is existence, and

176

that cannot be expressed because it can only be – because nothing else exists but it.

The whole universe exists in this sevenfold way. Conditionally, this "seven-valued logic" may be called the dimensions of the existence of spacetime. Everything exists in these seven dimensions simultaneously and in parallel, although each dimension plays out separately. Ourselves included all our lives, and every single event, too. The truth is, not ourselves the way we are known to us now in this body, but our soul which splits itself up into the seven individual souls (*Jiva*) and we are only familiar with one of them until we attain our full awareness. Our physical mind always perceives only one of the realities in question. Only in extreme cases can a person have a taste of the other reality, albeit briefly, or to put an effort into swapping one for the other. The others remain on different dimensions of spacetime and do the same job from their aspect of cognition and existence. Once all the aspects of individual existences are experienced and joined together, the individual soul unites with its source, the oversoul, which is the first emanation and embodiment of the divine consciousness. Let's remind ourselves that the overall emanation of *Prakriti* happens for all the aspects of beingness to be experienced individually. Since in reality, *Prakriti* does not exist in time, all the aspects of its existence are simultaneously experienced by *Purusha*.

All the aspects of existence are manifested as do all the possible realities.

What do these parallel realities look like? They are simply all the possible logical variants of all the possible phenomena.

In the first, something happened.

In the second, it did not happen.

In the third, it did, but also did not happen (the dialectics of opposites).

In the fourth, none of the first three possibilities took place, and something completely different originated (the unity of opposites).

In the fifth, it happened, but something completely different originated.

In the sixth, nothing happened, but something completely different originated.

In the seventh, it did, and it did not happen, and something completely different originated (the transcendence of all the opposites of existence).

With this *syâdvâda* secured its supreme principle of tolerance in this divided and conflicted world on the path of knowledge and living, and with its magnificent "arguably", which it places at the foundation of all the aspects as the most important, is potentially an unattainable ideal for all the mortal men.

TANMÂTRÂ

Under the influence of the principle of individuation and the forming of everything (*aham-kâra*) – which gives form to all the actions and phenomena – the fields of causal actions, *tanmâtras*, are formed in the higher levels, and from there, they form the lower ones. *Tanmâtras* are the matrix that produces forms on the lower, grosser domains. The literal meaning of the word *tanmâtrâ* is "prototype". Hence, *tanmâtrâ* is that what is the standard for the manifestation of the forms of all the entities or units that exist in the spaces of nature. According to the scheme it is above *maha-bhŭtâni*, the spatial forming of dimensions, adequately named hyperspace, containing all the archetypes for forming everything in space in all the dimensions.

Classical *Sâmkhya* establishes only five *tanmâtrâs*. They are the prototype origins of sound, touch, color, taste, and smell. The reason why only five have been cited lies in the fact that they are necessary and sufficient for forming the sensory organs (hearing, sight, touch, taste, and smell) which are, as such, irreplaceable organic conditions for the origin or occurrence of the subject of perception in the three-dimensional nature. This is consistent with the underlying and crucial teleological standpoint of *Sâmkhya* that the whole nature exists the way it is only for the purpose of creating of all the necessary conditions for the appearance of a conscious subject, which is the only suitable place in nature where the principle of consciousness (*Purusha*) is able to manifest.

Tanmâtras are more than anything the prototypes of sensory organs, or in other words, they are **interior sensory organs**. Apart from the physical organs we use in everyday functioning for perceiving the outer physical world, we also possess subtle interior organs which are used during sleep and our visits to the astral realm. With the subtle interior senses, *tanmâtras*, we can perceive everything that overcomes the physical world. If we are aware of the fact that the three-dimensional world is a mere final conse-

179

quence of the sum of higher dimensions, then it will be clearer to us that with the interior senses we can perceive higher and finer reality than the one available to us in the waking state through the physical senses. Owing to *tanmâtras* we are in the position to experience perception in the reality as well as in dreams, in the physical, but in the astral body, too, with which we exit the physical body during astral projection, and during the sleeping phase, and finally, everything that happens after the death of the physical body. Therefore, *tanmâtras* engender the broadening of the perception and consciousness we have in the physical body. *Tanmâtras* provide us with the insight into the overall objective world, but not only the one perceivable to us by senses but in all the dimensions as well, even beyond the element of the earth where we can no longer continue to perceive with our physical senses. Physical senses are mere extensions of the interior senses, *tanmâtras;* the reality of *tanmâtras* belongs to higher dimensions, the whole physical body, and all the physical reality are only the consequence of the functioning of higher dimensions, and all the life force and creativity come from the higher dimensions in question. Therefore, *tanmâtras* represent the bond that exists between the bodily mind (*manas*) with all the higher dimensions and the soul. This bond is frequently utilized unconsciously during sleeping, or intuitively because each intuitive insight, inspiration, and creative afflatus is connecting the mind via interior senses with the soul, with higher dimensions where everything that is created will eventually be manifested on the physical plane.

According to the scheme (picture 1), on the macrocosmic plane   *tanmâtras* originate from *aham-kâra* as the fields of causal actions for the forming of everything on lower or grosser planes using the principle previously mentioned in the symbolics of *ma-ha-bhŭtâni*. This is an objective realm of inorganic or "dead" nature dominated by creative principles of sound and space (*akasha*). On the microcosmic or subjective domain, *tanmâtras* shape the sensory organs in the form of matrix, and the action organs as a result of them, as the organic condition for the creation of all the living beings who are conscious subjects in nature.

Although we can make do, for practical reasons, with perception and action using these five *tanmâtrâs*, we must, for the sake of

180

complete objectivity, become familiar with the way these five have been singled out from the field of so much causal, informative impact, with the plethora of the created forms in the overall cosmos.

This multitude of fields can be reduced to, as we have stated before, to the five prototype elements of sensory perception due to the teleological purpose of nature to in-form (in-formatio) the necessary sensory and organic frameworks (*indriyâni*), as the receivers of information about phenomena, the receivers of news that crystallize the consciousness of the subject. It is clear that in nature the overall phenomena always revolve around something or someone. Due to the contracting effect, while entering the conscious subject, phenomena-information always move towards the soul, and via the soul to *Purusha*. That is the only place where the movement of nature reaches its outcome. While in the conscious subject nature contracts and crystallizes toward its outcome (via *manas* or the reason to *aham-kâra* and *buddhi*), in the remaining realm it manifests objectively in the form of both the grosser and more subtle shapes and processes (*tanmâtrâ* and *maha-bhûtâni*) that we can perceive with our senses (*indriyâni*). That is the reason why, because of the underlying significance of the subject, all the *tanmâtras* can be reduced to the five origins of sensory perception.

However, each form in nature is one active (formed) information, news for the consciousness; the whole nature, everything that has been created and formed within it, is one big holistic informative system which by shaping the organic constructions (*indriyâni*) engenders the presence of the absolute consciousness that facilitates all (*Purusha*) on one place, in the conscious, integrated personality (*aham-kâra*). On the one hand, the presence of the absolute consciousness is the driving force for the forming of nature as such, but on the other hand, its purposeful activity in the development of organic life engenders the conscious presence of the absolute consciousness. In that way, the two fundamental principles attract and stimulate one another: the essentiality of the absolute consciousness and the forming of nature.

A conscious subject is the user of all the information in nature. The information represents a manifestation of all the potentiality of nature contracted in time and space. That is why with the subject's focusing all their attention on the Self or soul, and that means by careful receiving and purifying the consciousness from all the entanglements and needless repetition of phenomena in thoughts (*cittavrtti*), the spacetime of manifestation of nature contracts (*samadhi*) to the complete primeval equanimity (*nirodha*) of the human soul (*Purusha*) in its authenticity (*svarūpa*).

Therefore, the purpose of developing organic life is to create an opportunity for receiving information (news) about the phenomena. As the pinnacle of this development a human being occurs in nature, it is the place where objectively information of phenomena contracts and where, as a result of the sufficient level of contraction or reaching a certain "critical mass" (concentration), the news about its purpose finally shines through. In this way, the overall creation of nature is, in effect, its awareness of the presence of the unconditioned human soul (*Purusha*).

There is no such thing as dead nature. What we consider to be matter is photon energy, in reality. When the observer is present, it demonstrates itself as "matter", a wave becomes the particle, and without it, energy remains nothing but pure energy.

That is why the pure consciousness (*buddhi*), as the result of all the information, has the highest creative power. Accordingly, nothing exists in nature as a separate material entity by itself and for itself, but every shaped phenomenon is mere purpose and meaning which informs the energy to create specific sensory and perceptual structures and forms. The essence of any physical beingness is to do with the meaning. Beingness is meaning, one becomes the other, and vice versa. As the meaning changes (information), the essence (form) changes, as well. Reciprocity between the effect of consciousness and form is expressed as the general movement of life energy or *prâna*. It is used as the carrier of information between the cells. Their shape and function is information, a form of consciousness that is accepted and recognized holistically in the entire organism. As a medium for the transfer of information certain bodies are used that are more subtle than the physical ones, and those are ethereal and astral. They transfer information simply by belonging to higher dimensions where the time is more contracted than the one on the physical level. The multitude of forms in nature exists only to engender permeation of different dimensions which, like a broken mirror, show the same informative process in various aspects and phases.

In this way, the dualism of the body and psyche, the physical and mental phenomena is overcome, and the manifestation of all the potential higher planes on the earthly one is explained. Only lack of awareness and inability to see nature in all of its dimensions gives an illusory impression of it being a multitude of separate, unconnected, and alienated individuals that endanger the subject with their chaotic functioning. There is a vague impression that the objectively existing nature has done its best to curtail the free human soul, that it harms the soul with unfortunate accidents or evil destiny.

The meaning and beingness mutually support one another according to the law of cause and consequence, but due to the relativity of time of different dimensions, causality is not always obvious to the subject from their three-dimensional point of view. Information and form make the essence of the process of manifestation of the objective world and, in the holistic union of the whole nature, between existence, consciousness, and information there is no difference or separation. Every artist has a personal experience of this. This unity is the essence of any true religious experience.

In Upanishads it was noted that the astral or subtle body (*sukshma*), which survives for a period of time after the physical form (*rūpa*) has died, and carries latent information for the future incarnation, called *nama*, and which means the name. It is also called *lingadeha*, *linga* meaning the sign, or the mark. Perception of the experiential world refers to name-and-form exclusively, *nama-rūpa*, or the meaning (information) of the form of phenomena and designing of shapes.

1. Informative fields

Let's take a brief look at how the fields causal or informative effect (*tanmâtrâ*) with the principle of individuality (*aham-kâra*) form entities of the physical world via astral, without restricting themselves to the sensory organs whose bond with forming the subject is evident.

Today we can speak more freely and clearly about this based on a recent discovery by the biologist Rupert Sheldrake on the morphogenetic fields (gr. *morphe*-form and lat. *genesis*-origin). Using this find partly for the depiction of *tanmâtrâ* effect in the much older system of *Sâmkhya*, we will name these fields, according to the tradition, **T-fields**, and T is short for *tanmâtrâ*.

The universe is permeated by various fields entirely. Their nature is sometimes so complex that it cannot be explained using the terms of physical laws because they extend beyond the dimensions of a material universe. Only their consequences are visible here. The only thing that can be said is that fields are manifestations of mathematical magnitudes in the regions of space. In the case of the gravitational field, it is geometric property or the bending of space. The field is always a way of producing the space itself, an immanent tendency toward wholeness and formation. For example, a magnetic rod underneath a piece of paper sprinkled with magnetic shavings using an electromagnetic field creates the lines of forces that circle from one end of the magnetic field to the other. However, if the magnet is divided into two, metal shavings will not divide themselves but will form two completely new fields. Similarly, the effect of these fields, as a real but invisible force of shaping, is the only explanation to the problem biology was faced with till Sheldrake's revival of morphogenetic field theory, which firstly marginally appeared at the turn of the twentieth century. The problem facing morphogenesis is: in what way do all the living beings get their specific form? Genes do not pass down this kind of information, whereas DNA stores only an extensive list of all the materials that constitute a cell composition, fundamentally, information for the creation of proteins. In its basic contents, it is identical (97%) in all living beings. It is an open question of how and according to which model proteins merge within the body? The basic cells are undifferentiated and, as the cell mass increases with division, an embryo is created. Some cells become brain cells and some heart cells. The old mechanistic view was unable to provide us with an answer to the question of how a cell knows what to develop into and where the model is according to which a being gets its unique physical form. This kind of information is neither stored in the DNA nor RNA.[38]

The second morphogenesis problem is regulation, or the ability of an organism to change or adjust to plan, should something unexpected happen during its development. If an egg of a seahorse, for example, while the mass still consists of undifferentiated cells, is divided into two, it will not halve the future embryo, but the remaining mass will develop into a smaller, but whole seahorse. The

---

[38] Only the very recent research into quantum genetics has managed to reveal true possibilities and dimensions of informative contents of DNA. However, they still fail to explain morphogenesis. The truth is that quantum genetics confirms the existence of T-fields on the genetic level because it has been established that DNA molecule information can exist as the biofield as well, therefore, non-physically, and can be transferred acausally, in the form of a T-field, and that the standard laws of quantum physics no longer apply to it, but the laws of biology instead. A DNA sample reacts instantly to the emotional states of its owner no matter how far apart they were. DNA communication is based on the same principles as grammar, syntax, and semantics, basically like a language and the exchange of information, or a way in which the consciousness operates. Our language is the way it is because of the identical properties of DNA. If information is converted to the frequency and as such using laser or radio waves focused on DNA, this information will affect DNA in such a way as to alter itself in accordance with the new pieces of information. Russian scientists have succeeded in turning a frog embryo into a salamander, by a simple transfer of the informational pattern from one DNA onto the other using laser. This explains why words and thoughts may have such a strong impact on the body of man.

Biologist Pyotr Garyayev proved experimentally that the development of the embryo requires external electromagnetic radiation. When the developing embryo is isolated from external cosmic radiation, it cannot develop normally, the body becomes completely deformed. This experiment proves theory of morphogenetic fields. Quantum genetics proves that our DNA is just an antenna that receives information from the stars and the cosmos, the wider whole to which all beings belong.

Apart from these two DNA spirals, there are many additional sequences of DNA that are not connected into spirals and the official science admits they have no idea what they are for, or a further claim is that they do not have any purpose (junk DNA). However, some independent research from Russia claims that this scattered DNA has the highest value for man and his higher abilities and true potentials, while the two famous spirals that are officially identified as DNA represent only information for the protein composition, or the material for cell composition.

same happens in humans when the cell mass divides during some stage of growth, identical twins will be born. This cell property is similar to the characteristics of a hologram where each piece of the big picture contains within the complete version of the entire picture. Each half of the growing cell composition contains the complete blueprint of the entire organism. The mechanistic view fails to explain this phenomenon, as well.

The third problem is regeneration or the amazing ability of some organisms to regrow lost body parts. The fourth one is symbiosis, an inexplicable phenomenon where microorganisms join in a union which, once it reaches critical mass, behaves like a completely new organism. There is no objective obstacle in the path of an assumption that our physical body is a result of a gigantic symbiotic colony of bacteria, and our nervous system the expression of the highest bacterial evolution in the symbiosis. With the correct understanding of T-fields, this assumption is no longer daring but is a logical response to this and many other phenomena that the classical mechanistic view has difficulty coping with.

By working via the higher, astral realms in the form of prototypes, T-fields form, as the invisible extended structures, every organism attracting it to its special shape or purpose in space and time. Therefore, every living form is shaped under the outer influences. Its genetic structure merely contains information on the material for building the body; its form and movement (destiny) originate under the influence of external patterns, or fields of influence.

T-fields act as reflections of consciousness, and not mechanically or accidentally, either. Materialistic and mechanistic understanding which rejects consciousness as the foundation of nature is unsustainable on all counts. For example, if cells moved about randomly and accidentally following a pattern of evolution and natural selection, for the cells to form a single fetus it would take several billion years and not nine months as it is the case now, because each cell knows exactly where to go and what to do.

It is important to observe the correlation of fields with the dimensions of nature, more precisely, their subordination. A bigger field (body) always acts as the principle of concordance and synthesis as regards the smaller fields (cells). It can be seen in the relationship between society and individual, ecological equilibrium in nature and biological units, as well as the higher states of consciousness regarding the individual experiences. Since all the planes permeate one another, and information is not separate from the form, the domain of the T-field effect via the higher astral levels is not separated from the physical form, and the effect in question goes both ways. Each individual organism is connected to its T-field and its behavior has a feedback effect on the structure of T-fields. Additionally, each biological species has its own collective T-field. In Japan in the 1950's the "hundredth monkey effect" was discovered. If a member of a certain species, such as a monkey, for example, discovers a new way of eating and shows it to the group it lives in, once a critical mass of individuals who have mastered a new craft is reached, this ability is suddenly automatically spread throughout the entire community, and globally as well, by means of some invisible effect. The same effect was ascertained at Harvard in the 1920's, in lab experimentation with rats. After the original idea to prove Lamarck's thesis that hereditary characteristics are passed down genetically, a group of rats was trained to find a way out of the labyrinth. The tenth generation learned to find exit immediately, but it took the first generation over a hundred attempts to do the same. However, both the control group, which was not trained and never mated with the others, showed the same aptitude in finding the exit instantly. Several years later, as a result of disbelief over the original results, the same experiment was conducted in Australia. Their rats found a way out during their first attempt – thanks to T-fields the previous experiments facilitated.

Sheldrake called this interaction *morphic resonance*. Independence of the functioning of informative fields from space and time is possible because the area of T-fields is more subtle or higher than the physical one. This subtlety is an expression of the contraction of spacetime in higher dimensions. Based on *morphic resonance* it was concluded that memory is inherent to nature. All the created natural systems on the physical plane inherit collective properties from earlier systems of the same species, regardless of space and time. This is how the behavior of microorganisms can be explained, ant colonies, plants, animals, even the formation of new crystal forms. Humans, too, are involved in the collective memory of their species. According to Karl Pribram's research into neurology, who

together with David Bohm formulated holistic ontological interpretation of modern scientific results within the framework of the
holographic paradigm, our memory is not placed somewhere in the
brain, but the brain is the perfect instrument for holistic communication with the whole or the holographic universe.

T-fields exist everywhere and always, on all the levels: from
the elementary particles, molecules, crystals, chemical reactions,
weather conditions, movement of the planets, and galaxies. Their
impact on the psyche, on making complexes, and neurotic patterns
that keep repeating (they function unconsciously because astral is
the realm of the unconscious). They are also effective in creating
patterns of everyday physical behavior. Most movements we make
are done spontaneously, in accordance with an acquired model.
The consciousness is present no more than a decoration there, like
a lamp that lights something in a very narrow circle, while the self-
consciousness almost has no bearing on the decisions that are being made.

On the scheme (picture 1), it is recognizable how the personality (*aham-kâra*) suffers the schizoid split into everyday consciousness of the bodily experience (*indriyâni*) and unconscious
prototypes of behavior (*tanmâtrâ*) in various dimensions of the
beingness (*maha-bhûtâni*).

Apart from the pattern of unconscious behavior of the body
and mind, the T-field effect is easily noticeable on large-scale phenomena such as egregore or archetypes of the collective unconscious, even the metaphysical patterns of evaluating reality. They
also have their impact on the society and culture on the whole as T-
fields of races, social groups, and cultural patterns.

Owing to morphic resonance, i.e., the feedback between the
physical phenomena and T-fields, the experience of beingness accele-
rates, learning and a way of life grow more efficient over time, and
many processes in the modern world can be executed much faster and
better than was the case before.

T-fields with their subtle informative influence attract or
navigate the movement of life energy (*prâna*), thus forming the
overall created harmony and purposefulness visible in nature. Everything that exists in any way possible, acquires the exact shape
needed for a certain purpose through the impact of the T-fields. It

does not relate to the internal organs of an organism only, but all the beings in the grand organism of the world.

Everything that exists on the material plane has its more subtle form of phenomena on the higher or astral plane. Everything has its track of time, radiation through space whose form is, at the same time, the meaning, as well. This does not apply to living beings only, but places, too. Those edifices that have for centuries been filled with supreme religious values and activities, radiate of their own, their frequency is felt by anyone who visits them, a very strikingly different sensation from other places filled with different activities. Sensitive people can "see" an event that took place in some location, or is about to happen. However, without some special psychic powers, everyone is familiar with the fact that when on a certain place something happened, even several decades ago, that event will fill our memory down to the last detail, no matter how insignificant it was. Traces and meaning of some memorable events we already carry in us. This mechanism always plays out in the same way. While we are walking down the street with nothing better to do, our mind acts as the resonance box for various T-fields to interweave and become repetitive within, T-fields that were generated by the environment or ourselves even.

All the "psychic phenomena" find their explanation in the functioning of T-fields, in permeating the higher dimensions with the lower. Such phenomena, as well as the miraculous harmony and purposefulness that exists in nature, inspire people to believe in some divinity or the "supernatural" powers. Their limitation to the material consequences only while failing to see the functioning of higher immaterial planes of the same (divine) nature, is the main reason for a phenomenon of this kind. Their vision is limited by their sensory and mental conditioning.

We cannot ascertain a supreme T-field that could be cast in the role of God because the idea of God in its most intelligent expression, and that is apophatic theology, corresponds with the unconditionality of *Purusha*. However, we can, which is always the case, make a contact with an already formed T-field through a religious ritual. Rituals have always been nothing but methods for making contact with specific T-fields. We can also connect to a certain T-field through meditative imagination and visualization of an already established divinity, like in Tantrism. This shows us that all the dogmatic religious practices based on rituals belong to the T-field effect and not some true religiousness that leads to the unconditionality of the soul. This is the reason why there are so many different religious practices. If there were only one prime or 'divine' T-field, communication with it (ritual practice) would be the same everywhere. Finally, it would override all the other fields and there would be no versatility of natural forms, or nature the way it is now.

(We speak of rituals here in this way, as a function for making contacts i.e., serving the non-organic astral beings in T-fields, because the true nature of rituals has long been forgotten by constant mechanical repetition. The purpose of the ritual was intended to act as a help for unconscious people to strengthen their 'magnetic center', that is to say, to maintain in the consciousness the purpose for their aspiration toward spiritual awakening. Additionally, to store certain information from the spiritual science through specific symbolics that has a deep impact on the unconsciousness when performed ritually. A proper ritual is a mechanism of temporary establishing contact with the informative field of higher states of consciousness. Rituals are needed for those people who are still not fully conscious, who do not have one stable 'I' operating within themselves, making their goals and intentions shift with shifting of the various outer influences, and with the shifting of their I's – although humans never experience it as such, they always interpret it as the result of "their will". Therefore, such people need one in common mechanism of conduct that will keep them glued to their will and desire to work on themselves, because without support like that they would easily wander off the spiritual path and lose themselves.)

Being caught in the radiation of various T-fields is often the root cause of certain ritual behavior of people. This knowledge has always been available to a smaller number of people who used it very craftily for the manipulation over masses. They were members of the secret societies, clergy, and politicians.[39] Very rarely can people be exempt from these influences, most commonly they fall

---

[39] Their knowledge of the power of informative fields is best reflected in their everlasting aspiration to own and control all the informative media.

prey to them too easily. Our thoughts are to a large extent an expression of the influence of various fields, either individual memory or collective heritage, or events that happen around us. Notions
are the most subtle forms of T-fields.

All these phenomena can be viewed in the light of T-field
functioning. Deeper analysis would drag us away from the underlying theme of *Sâmkhya*, that the timeless Absolute is the creator of
the overall cosmic phenomena and our true essence. In the macrocosm T-fields as such form laws, in the same way, the collective
experiences of people form T-fields of archetypes, whereas in the
subjective or microcosmic world they act as the role model for
forming thoughts and feelings that constitute our personality, habits, character, and destiny.

Having crystallized one's conscious presence on the more
subtle levels of phenomena, the presence which can be defined
with "I-maker, I am doer" (*aham-kâra*), is crucial for the human's
mastery over all the levels of the being that appeared to be disintegrated, autonomous, and conditioning prior to this moment. Under
the influence of the forming (*aham-kâra*), every phenomenon
forms itself as a separate entity, and the same applies to the activity
of the consciousness. In its functioning, it is not monotonous, but
oscillates continually, so humans experience versatile states of
consciousness. These oscillations can be such that they induce separation of some parts (states) from the main stream, which then
become relatively autonomous entities that behave like conscious
beings, although they are not of organic origin.

2. Non-organic beings

The teaching of *Sâmkhya* gives us a clear explanation as to
how and why the non-organic beings have come into existence.

Under the influence of *aham-kâra* category, the principle of
individuation, everything that exists gets some kind of a form, both
in the organic and inorganic world. In the organic domain, we are
familiar with all the living beings. In the inorganic domain there
are living and conscious entities but as non-organic, energetic entities. Since they are energetic they 'feed off" the energy they get

from the organic beings. Organic beings forward and produce energy, while the non-organic ones can only forward and exploit it.

It is important to understand two facts in connection with the functioning of the T-fields. First: it is the realm of a certain model of vibratory impact on the life energy to form phenomena, the ones that will act as an integral living entity that consciously yearns for survival. And the second: this field is accessed by specific conduct, such as ritual, for example, although every form of habitual psychophysical repetition is a reflection of enslavement to these entities.

Everything that constitutes *Prakriti*, due to the relativity of spacetime, can be both subjective and "objective" because the true objectivity is achieved only from the viewpoint of *Purusha* and then it relates to the overall *Prakriti*, and not its individual phenomena. That is why psychic creations are just as "objective" by nature as they are subjective: they can by a repetition of subjective states and investment of energy form a T-field that will in turn as the "objective force" have a feedback effect on humans, making them input more of their energy into this field by constant mechanical repetition.

Aham-kâra is the principle of shaping everything that exists, both the organic and inorganic, and that what constitutes the objective world (*tanmâtrâ* and *maha-bhûtâni*) and carriers of subjectivity (*indriyâni*). Since they are all from the same source (from *aham-kâra*), any shaped beingness can be either organic or non-organic, subjective or "objective", alternately one or the other, or both at the same time. Every living being is a result of the pervasion of organic and non-organic realms. Sensory experience is thus enriched with the imaginary, and imaginary is realized through the sensory. Since they are one in their origin, they have equal value and reality. That is why from the perspective of an awakened personality (*aham-kâra* and *buddhi*), the sensory reality (*indriyâni*) is on the same level with imagination and dream (*tanmâtrâ*), and abilities of imagination are the senses of a higher order for direct knowledge, **which are the senses of higher bodies.**

Were it not for interaction of this kind the organic beings would be common biological machines without inspiration and development, which is in opposition with the teleology of *Prakriti*

192

towards *Purusha.* The dialectics in question (*indriyâni* with *tanmâtrâ* and *maha-bhûtâni*) represents the psychic life of a personality (*aham-kâra*) as well as the guarantee for the miraculous unity of all the opposites and everything individually shaped when in the complete personality subject and object unite. This unity as immanent is already present, therefore the cognition of it has been made possible. From the human's personality (*aham-kâra*) the world projects itself and splits into the subjective and objective, imaginary and sensory existing world. That is why, in return, these versatilities are joined in the human's 'I' (*aham-kâra*) to be known, for the objective nature to be subjectively, personally experienced and for the subject, on the other hand, to be experienced in the non-organic realm and in doing so, became objectively aware of their own state and existence.

On the scheme, we can see that nature below *aham-kâra* divides itself into organic and inorganic worlds. It means, for the personality to be whole and free, the presence of the consciousness must be integrated not only on the entire realm of the organic experience but on all the levels of the inorganic world (*tanmâtrâ*), in all of its dimensions (*maha-bhûtâni*). This integration is otherwise known as the "astral body projection" or the art of dreaming, creation of the energy body or the 'salvation body' which resurrects upon one's physical death.

Under the influence of the individuation principle not only the living entities in the organic, three-dimensional world are formed in nature, but in the non-organic, as well. ***In the process of creation, the non-organic beings were created first, then the organic beings followed suit***. T-fields form the non-organic entities that exist in the astral realm in parallel with the organic, placing them in higher dimensions than that of the physical one, resulting in their consumption of energy of organic beings which get used as their food. Everything in nature that is in higher dimensions feeds off and uses whatever is in the lower.[40] The chain of food does not ex-

---

[40] When a specific living entity absorbs the lower one for its nourishment, it transforms it through the alchemical process into its own higher state. All the living beings are instruments for the transformation of *Prakriti*, from the lower and grosser to the higher and more subtle levels, to the highest outcome in the consciousness. One of the grossest aspects of such transformation is food. Man as

ist, therefore, only on the organic plane, but in the whole nature, too, in all dimensions.

Additionally, these fields are the factors that affect and engender organic beings (particularly man) to act in a way that does not concern their sole biological survival. In these inorganic fields, all the psychic life is played out (but not the spiritual one – it is important to differentiate between the two). These fields are the prototypes for forming all the illusions, images, imagination, desires, ideals, and inspiration. *Tanmâtras* are in charge of the psychological life, especially psychopathological, they form the events of dreams in the astral realm, they are the medium for participation in all the dimensions of life (*maha-bhŭtâni*). They contain everything that ordinary, mortal people can experience as an illusion of the "spiritual life" due to their inability to resurrect into the true spirituality that surpasses the whole of *Prakriti*.

It can be said that *tanmâtras* exist as a psychological alternative, or obstacle placed before the personality (*aham-kâra*) in its mission of cognizing the meaning of organic life (*indriyâni*) in all the dimensions (*maha-bhŭtâni*), as the area of illusions that must be overcome with the maturity of a steadfast consciousness.

On the other hand, T-fields are necessary because under the influence of *aham-kâra*, which is the creator of forms, cohesion is provided and meaning to every existence is given. Without them, the energy of organically formed beings would be an amorphous and meaningless flow in which not even the consciousness would manage to have any cohesion.

T-fields are a medium we use to become acquainted with all the secrets of nature. Many ground-breaking discoveries for humans and humankind alike came through inspiration, through a dream or imagination when the logical deduction was not of much use.[41] Without higher forces ("heavenly") humans would remain a

---

the peak of the transformation of *Prakriti* has the most versatile diet. He eats everything that can be eaten, even those things that should not be consumed!

[41] The creative aptitude of man directly depends on his openness for the contacts with T-fields because *Prakriti* forms the physical world via them. The best example for this is one of the greatest architects of humankind, Nikola Tesla, with his capabilities of imagination, out-of-body experiences, and wonderful friendships with beings from the other worlds. From the inorganic realm, the so-called "heavenly worlds' the most profound music often comes ('the music of

sheer biological individual, incapable of true growth. T-fields generate all the drama, contradiction, danger, but also the ability of salvation that are, fundamentally, inevitable parts of every form of development. This is the realm of all the challenges humans must overcome after becoming familiar with them in detail beforehand, in order to become complete personalities (*aham-kâra*) and always conscious, awake (*buddhi*).

Carriers of a great number of challenges for humans are these non-organic beings.

3. Why non-organic beings exist

Apart from everything that has been said about T-fields, the most important thing to know is that under their influence non-organic but intelligent beings can be formed, either naturally or artificially created, the ones that have their life, longer or shorter, and in the dimensions of their own equally real like the organic life forms on the physical plane.

This is possible because the principle of consciousness (coming from *Purusha*) pervades the whole nature, in a number of ways, not its organic forming only, but in its inorganic creations, too. They are all energy phenomena, and energy is merely a grosser aspect of consciousness.

The whole nature is (on the part of *Purusha*) an aware living being that manifests its functioning in various ways, according to the categories. That is why there are conscious non-organic beings on the astral realm, the same way that there are elements of the gross world (*maha-bhŭtâni*) and conscious beings on the organic realm (*indriyâni*), such as plants, animals, and people, as well (or at least most people belong to this category).

While on the physical plane all the things are aware of themselves as such, and their consciousness is conditioned by a concrete form of existence, on the higher dimensions the non-organic entities of conscious existence behave in a more fluid manner; their

---

spheres'). Paul McCartney, for example, heard the tune for his song 'Yesterday' in his sleep, and J. S. Bach, according to the testimony of his wife Anna Magdalena, had a habit of getting up in the middle of the night to play heavenly music on the harpsichord.

consciousness is in unity with the whole inorganic realm. Although they may have their permanent shape, they can also change it at will. Hence, the "spiritual creations" or "Force Majeure" known in folklore as gods, spirits, demons, fairies and elves, dragons and boogeymen, as well as various elementals of nature that by their character may belong to different dimensions, or the elements of earth, water, fire, air, and aether. They can form T-fields to define the form of physical phenomena and direct energy towards them. When these fields establish direct contact with humans, they become personified as the above mentioned "supernatural beings". In their fight for survival, they have to take energy, much like all the other entities in nature. They take energy from the organic beings who, due to their bigger coherence, produce sufficient energy, and are able to dispense with it needlessly, especially individuals who have a history of wasting their lives away. It is one of the main characteristics of humans, to burn through their energy in a needless and imbalanced way, to stunt the natural growth within themselves. If they did not do so, nature would without hindrance, easily and quickly, attain its spiritual goal. All humans would be enlightened.

Since they exist in higher dimensions, their power to act is superior to the one on the three-dimensional plane which is conditioned by space and time. Their most common decoy for attracting people into their net was the one Goethe's Faust was introduced to: the power of supernatural acts, mystical experiences, and extrasensory cognizance. T-fields represent the matrix for all the "supernatural" events. Such effects may be perpetrated by non-organic beings. Their doing is then, reduced to visions, voices, and apparitions that, like a three-dimensional movie, seduce humans to serve their goals. Many spiritual practices alert us to the dangers of going astray from the only goal which is the unconditionality of our soul.

It is very important, apart from all of this, to discern the nature of the impact of inorganic fields of influences (beings) according to the dimension they belong to (*maha-bhūtâni*). The ones that belong to the element of the earth affect instinctive and physical movement making habits in them. The ones that belong to the element of water affect us through emotional bondage of any kind. By leaving an imprint on us from the higher dimensions, the "supernatural" phenomena give an impression of numinousness or divine intervention which provokes strong emotions and increases the "faith" of humans to make them even more identified with these fields. The influence of the element of fire is expressed through the additional incentives for actions and activities, the need for change, as well as aggressiveness. The impact of non-organic beings from the element of air is characterized by the intellectual interpretations of odds and ends, they can be useful if they are not used too often. Beings from aether are the purest and highest, their influence is the most noble and beneficial for humans, that is why it is the least common in practice, and the most difficult to obtain. They convey pure inspiration for spiritual growth.

The effect of non-organic beings of the element of earth is directly manifested through the physical conduct and habits, most commonly associated with the habits of hoarding, accumulating material objects, abiding by the religious dogmas very strictly, as well as those that concern dietary habits and reproduction, and entertainment during leisure time. The beings of the element of water use a higher dimension for their influence, which is astral. Since it is like water that takes on the shape of any dish it is poured into, in the astral realm it is possible to project any image. They are always packed full with emotions that are the main factor of the element of water, of this dimension in question, so much so that the astral visions never leave humans indifferent, like standard witnessing of some outside phenomena, but they experience them with their whole being and complete obsession regarding what they have seen. That is why these beings affect us the easiest in our dreams, they enter our dreaming process making paradoxical and unbelievable situations and appearances. This is one of the ways how we can recognize them in dreams: the absurdity they use to attract the human's attention. When we see something in our dream that is totally illogical or something that simply does not belong there (a horse in our room, for example) it is a sign that some non-organic being is seeking our attention. Humans have always been more attracted to something absurd rather than something real. Finally, the beings of this element are responsible for all the hallucinogenic visions in the "awake" state of consciousness. They may appear in the physical world and provoke some events.

They must use the astral substance as a projector for their movies to attract the attention of people because, fundamentally, they are as helpless as plants. Their impact is not direct, they usually work in conjunction with instincts. *Non-organic beings have no power by themselves, their influence is always indirect via their element (astral) as a medium. They are unable to entrap humans nor do some (mis)deed to them, instead, they can only make them trap themselves and commit some atrocious act under their influence. There is no other way. It is very important to understand this.*

To understand why the non-organic beings have an effect on us, we must remind ourselves of our true essence. The human essence is the soul, and the soul is an individual emanation of the divine consciousness or the Absolute, *Purusha*. As such, it is the reflection of pure good and perfection (the way Plato described it). It is incarnated into a limited human body and self-oblivion to conduct the principle of consciousness through the whole range of experiences of existence, and by doing so, it retrieves the information on all the aspects of existence to the source, to the Absolute. *In this way, the consciousness of the Absolute pervades the overall existence: it does so through all human souls. The souls carry through the Divine consciousness of the Absolute across the overall existence. The truth is that the physical universe itself exists solely for the purpose of being a direct reflection of the existence of souls.* However, existence in the lowest proportions, one of which life in the physical world is, as well, is based on opposites and their dialectics. For the souls to be able to go through all of the opposites, even the opposite of their own essence which is pure good, they must experience oblivion of themselves, all the evil and negativity, and the remainder which is the exact opposite of good. They have the opportunity to experience so in this world. They cannot do that themselves. *They require assistance from the outside, something that will make them experience what is opposite to their essence. This help they receive comes from the non-organic beings.* They are conscious, functional, but, unlike humans, they are without a soul. They have an impact from higher dimensions onto the lower ones. It is experienced as a possession. Naturally, non-organic beings can act as both negative and positive, also there are the neutral ones, various elementals, and "spirits of nature", but their key educational purpose lies in experiencing the negative states. More accurately, experiencing all of those states that humans would never put themselves through.

It is the main reason for their existence.[42]

The beings from astral are negative, they possess and enslave humans using emotional conditioning and manipulation with their attention. They go so far as to awaken kundalini energy in an inexperienced man. They do that to make humans a good source of food for them; they are bursting with energy but knows nothing of the nature of their state, instead, they are obsessed with some religious and mystical contents planted by the non-organic beings. In that sense, it can be said that their role is fundamentally positive because they show weaknesses in action. That is the reason why it is often said that the devil tempts us.

The beings of the element of fire could use the lower effects of earth and water domain, of physical movement and emotions, to exert an influence that resembles willpower for action and specific "creation". This influence is easily recognizable in humans with the mission, when objectively, even though it is not in their best interest, they are fanatical and aggressive about achieving the goal. The results of human actions are abundant around us, some are constructive and others are destructive, depending on the influence of a higher element, air, which is creative thinking. Unlike lower non-organic beings that act through our bodily habits, feelings, astral

---

[42] This function of non-organic beings where they would be of use to the souls on their mission of conducting the consciousness throughout the entire existence and all the opposites is best depicted in myths and esoteric teachings all across the globe, but most accurately in Gnosticism in the teaching of Archons who enslave human souls, but also in Mazdaism in the depiction of balance between good and evil. One of the most illustrative architectural examples can be seen in Angkor Thom in Cambodia, a temple whose foundations are 10,000 years old, with 54 statues of *devas* or good spirits, and 54 statues of *asuras* or the negative demons, who play tug of war, and from the "Milky Way", that is to say from the Universal Field, they draw out a potion of immortality, kundalini, symbolized by the Naga snake, the principle of movement of all the processes in nature. Their number on five bridges (540) points to the precession of 26,000 years that represents the cycles of all phenomena on Earth (one precession is the sum of 12 eons symbolized by the astrological signs). All the temples of Angkor reflect Draco constellation, built about 10,000 years ago when the negative non-organic beings took control over the Earth, playing a key role in influencing people and human history.

visions, and willpower, the ones belonging to the element of air manifest themselves in the form of thoughts. Humans are seldom aware when they have their own thoughts, that they themselves create, and when the thoughts in their head are a manifestation of the inorganic field of influence in the element of air. They are all those thoughts that bring new and unexpected content into our lives, often unacceptable content, for that matter. The impact they have on the brain makes it hard for us to have the appropriate objective reaction to them.[43]

Once humans, due to their spiritual maturity, learn to distinguish themselves as the pure consciousness without thoughts, from the thought contents and activities of the beingness of the body and mind, and when they know all of these dimensions personified with the above-mentioned elements as a part of *Prakriti* and realizes they are not their own, then the non-organic beings of the element of air, even aether, turn into allies (emissaries), who can be of big use with their talking. Humans can hear them as a fine voice by their left, or even better, by their right ear, both in the astral realm and in their physical body. It is quite possible to have a dialogue with them and learn many things hidden from us in past, present, and future.

Aethereal emissaries act as pure intuition and cognition which surpasses cognitive abilities. With their help, humans experience sudden and unforgettable "flashes of enlightenment" which are life-changing. With their grace, humans sometimes becomes introduced to the highest truths until they grow strong and mature enough themselves, so that they can be worthy of them, recognize

---

[43] The whole of the inorganic realm is alive and intelligent. That is why its entities do not have a permanent shape but utilize astral energy for their versatile actions and manifestations. Some non-organic beings have a permanent shape, although they can change it, while the shape of others is determined by the pattern and frequency of their functioning as an archetype. In the writings of the early Christian church, there are detailed descriptions of such influences of non-organic beings of all the dimensions and methods of self-defense against them. By all means, similar experiences can be found in other spiritual traditions that cultivate the contemplative practice. Yoga and Buddhist meditations are two prominent practices that are the most efficient at liberating man of all the natural influences that disrupt the authenticity and unconditionality of the soul.

them in their own experience and take active and everlasting participation in them. Humans receive the mercy of such cognizance as an inspiration and invitation for their spiritual growth. In its highest element, aether, nature as such is the purest and the closest to its outcome, *mahat-buddhi*, hence the influences of this kind.

Let us once more emphasize the equality of the macro and microcosm; the already mentioned dimensions of the macrocosm embodied in the elements (earth, water, fire, air, and aether) compose the microcosm of the human being' as well, and that is why humans have a body (earth), feelings (water), desires (fire), thoughts (air), and receives inspiration (aether-*akasha*) – they are all their sheaths and nature's abilities that they utilize, but they are not their fundamental property. They identify with them: the more they identify with them the more they enslave themselves; the more they become aware of them by becoming acquainted with them, the more they differentiate from them and liberate themselves.

The versatility of the influences of '"celestial beings"' is just as familiar to us from religious tradition as it is equally present in folk tales with all of their peculiarities. Evil and demonic forces that entrap and deceive humans are differentiated from the positive forces that inspire ascensions, such as angels and archangels are, for example.

Entities from the air and aethereal realms have the most positive impact which comes to us in the form of a pure voice that reveals the truth about everything. With the help of this voice from the deepest silence within themselves, humans are able to see the energy substance of any phenomenon or event.

All of these elements permeate and interweave with one another, and a solitary influence of only one of the elements is very rare. A common case is that when some of them become stronger they begin to steal energy off the power of influence of others. Amongst them, there is an ongoing struggle to domineer over humans, their confusion leads to further instigation of this conflict, and invariably the result may be quite chaotic: humans with pure intuition and psychic thoughts, but deranged behavior (the so-called '"masti"'); or, the other way round, humans of impeccable behavior, but without a shred of spirit or creative thoughts (such as a banker, or a politician).

The fight for supremacy among the inorganic influences of higher and lower dimensions we recognize as something that tempts us. When the higher dimensions exert influence and manage to pull humans upward, the lower beings launch a counter-attack and strengthen their influence to try to win over humans and put them under their wing, which is now intensified more than ever before, to make sure humans do not escape. Therefore, to use the words of Friedrich Holderling: "'But where the danger is also grows the saving power'", and only in this way, but also by wandering between the rise and fall, good and evil, do humans finally find their real path. There is no other way. Only a pressure of this intensity can strengthen and crystallize man's personality and consciousness. The dialectics is the law of growth, something which is very important to know for all those who plan to grow alone. These influences are everything but benign and subjective in nature, they may also impact events and actions of everyday life, the non-organic beings may influence not only the situations but man's whole environment and all the people in their life. They may be the cause of serious accidents as well as very beguiling and fortunate circumstances. Non-organic beings can also appear on the physical plane in the form of some animals or some other living forms known to the human. However, this kind of event is unlikely to take place in urban settlements of modern civilization that houses humans with minds so blocked and mechanized that not even the higher forces may draw their attention any more. The truth of the matter is, that nowadays they are entrapped to the point that no additional slavery is needed, at all. These events are more likely to happen in rural areas, somewhere in the country.

Their strongest influence is manifested when they come to us in human form in either astral or the physical plane, especially if they are somebody dear and close to us, parents or relations, a loved one, or somebody like that. One of their most potent tools is the ability to materialize and dematerialize, making things cross over from one dimension to another, disappear from the physical reality and end up on astral, and vice versa. This process keeps happening all the time: we get thoughts, visions, and feelings from the higher dimensions that further have physical consequences on our life. This all is not so much a product of their power as it is their ability of intelligent beings to influence the processes of lower phenomena of nature which happen on their own anyway. These are all the abilities and powers of nature in general, and not specifically of non-organic beings, at all. As intelligent beings, they can only redirect some series of events and use our ignorance and limited perception.

It is of key importance for humans through contemplative empowering of the consciousness (*buddhi*) to learn to recognize the difference between such influences of the non-organic beings, or T-fields, phenomena within and without themselves, from the functioning of the soul's consciousness. Its functioning was firstly described in Mazdaism (in Zaratustra's teaching), and later in the sermons of Jesus and Orthodoxy, proclaimed as the announcement of the Holy Spirit. The consciousness of our soul is the greatest power in accordance with which everything (*Prakriti*) exists. It can manifest at will in all the possible ways: through the consciousness, or self-consciousness (*buddhi*), which is the most common, or as a specific person (*aham-kâra*), unless it embodies together with it in the physical body (*indriyâni*), not only on the physical plane but in all the other dimensions (*tanmâtrâ* and *maha-bhûtâni*), like an *avatar*. *Purusha* is the ultimate attractor of the overall phenomena, even though most of the events belong to natural causality, and only some of them, those particularly important ones, are created by the soul's consciousness itself. They can be recognized by spiritual people according to their signs, or directly.

Additionally, it is very important to discern various influences of the space-time phenomena of nature on our character, destiny, and contents of astral experiences, which depends on the position and movement of the Earth in relation to the Sun and all the planets of the Solar system. These astrological influences should be clearly distinguished from the influence of the non-organic beings, although, more often than not, they are in perfect alignment with them, especially the positions and movements of the Moon, Neptune, and Lilith (the mythological mother of all the demons). Astrological influences determine the wholeness of organic phenomena, while the influences of the non-organic beings are periodical and partial; they do not have the prevalent role on people's destiny.

* * *

This is the general depiction of the non-organic beings and their functioning according to the lower or higher dimensions. We can now enter their main classification.

There are four kinds of non-organic beings:
1. Natural.
2. Artificially created, elementals.
3. Divine beings.
4. Extraterrestrial beings.

There are also hybrids between people and one of the above-mentioned non-organic beings.

Natural non-organic beings

Natural non-organic beings live in the higher dimensions of nature, in the astral realm. They are known as the '"spirits of nature"' or natural elementals. According to the karmic evolution they are behind the human, which means that the human is closer to the divine consciousness than they are because of *karma*, which matures through human labor, creation, and conscious transformation. Natural non-organic beings have not taken that step yet. That is why they can be of use to the human or a magician who knows what to do with them, but they also take life energy from all those who do not seem to be making much progress in karmic evolution, who lead a passive life, or are prone to being negative. They may be viewed as little astral animals. Some are small and big, tame and useful, as well as wild and dangerous. Generally, their influence is neutral, it depends on humans only if they will be of help, or not. '"The spirits of nature"' do not possess people nor do they lead them to psychoses.[44] The possession is perpetrated by a special

---

[44] Psychotic patients are often described as 'split personalities' (often they are exactly that), but not all their parts are human. They make this absolutely clear to every psychotherapist they go to, but professionals have been educated not to listen to them, at all. Only recently have psychotherapists begun to listen to what

kind of natural non-organic beings known as demons. Their influence is extremely negative, but with a purpose. They exist because of people, to lead them to temptation and crystallization of their consciousness.

Artificially created beings

Artificially created non-organic beings are various kinds of elementals. They were generated by human activities, both conscious and unconscious, deliberate and spontaneous, individual, or collective (archetypes). Any activity on the physical plane which is repeated forms its field of impact in the higher dimensions that becomes crystallized in the form of an elemental. By constant repetition, this field receives more and more energy until it grows independent enough to start having the reverse effect on the physical plane. Their effect on the physical world and humans are solely negative by nature because all they seek is to receive increasingly more energy. Their functioning is also present in some cases of possession and psychoses.

Divine beings

Divine beings are those that finalized the karmic evolution on the physical plane, overcame the physical form of existence, and now function fully consciously in the highest dimensions of nature. We may view them as our older relatives. There are those of them who are higher, but also lower. The lower ones belong to the souls of deceased people from planet Earth who have become so enlightened that even after they die they continue to act for the well-being of humankind (such as *bodhisattvas*, for example). Higher divine beings are those that are far more powerful, they

their patients are saying, and they have started to accept the fact that there is some alien influence at work there, the way their patients have been telling them all along, but the way the whole of spiritual and indigenous tradition has been testifying of across the globe since ancient times. The pioneering work into this research field has been done by Dr. William J. Baldwin: "Spirit Releasement Therapy: A Technique Manual" and "CE-VI: Close Encounters of the Possession Kind" which are the books that illustrate the kind of possession we are describing here.

create planetary systems (they created our solar system, as well), and who also finalized their karmic evolution, but in a much more distant past than the earthly individuals which makes them ultimately more powerful because they are older. They are older not because their origin is from planet Earth, but from other stellar systems which existed in the universe long before the Earth was born. They manifest themselves to people as God(s), Archangels, and Angels. Some of the lower ones come in the form of extraterrestrials in human shape. Their influence is mostly positive, but to a large degree, it is neutral because they put humans to the test to choose their own path.

While on the macro plane the artificial non-organic creations (elementals) can, owing to the human's deceit, take on a form of divine influences and other bigger powers to the degree that they impact the whole tribes, peoples, social and historical epochs, alternatively, on the micro-plane, in man's intimate world, they take forms of their subconscious contents, and in doing so they take part in their psychological experience through dreams and everyday psychodynamics. The objection that the characters and phenomena in dreams are the sole property and projection of the sleeper falls through entirely because both natural and artificial non-organic beings act only psychologically and use astral amply (which is the domain of man's unconscious) for shaping their activities in our dreams. They govern the astral realm more skillfully than people govern the physical world. In effect, they achieve all their psychological influences for the very reason that humans are unaware of them as being alien, objective, and conscious non-organic entities in their dreams, and the remaining psychodynamics, instead they are convinced that all of it is either '"unreal"', or their own contents because they assume that they are the only conscious beings in the universe. That is the exact reason why they are the only ones who are unconscious in the cosmos. The whole cosmos is awaiting the awaken of humankind, in the same way an expecting mother is waiting for her child to be born.

The effect of the T-fields can be both positive and negative which largely depends on the state of man's consciousness and the dimension they come from. People must distinguish between the two: the former can save us, the latter enslave us.

Positive and negative properties of higher forces only a mature person can discern, but here we can give general guidelines for their initial, but unmistakable difference. Good and beneficial influences come once in a blue moon in man's life, maybe only once, in a vision, voice, or an event, very distinctly and clearly. Their message is always an inspiration for humans to start working on themselves. Bad influences, however, are very recurrent, act as parasites, they are very tempting, they impose by trying to talk people into something, they are inviting, and can drive humans crazy. They always offer something and try to strike a good deal. Their messages can be double-natured: either they are unclear and vague, or they give instant and ready-made solutions, even by answering all the questions so that humans are under the illusion they have achieved or learned something through their own efforts, while the truth is they remain the same, they 'receive' an answer they should come to by working on themselves. This is one of the ways in which they hinder human growth.

Many famous historical figures were mere puppets of non-organic entities.

The organic world comes from the inorganic. Nature forms the organic life using T-fields to establish all the life as we know it. It means that the inorganic domain is a medium by which nature teaches humans and governs over their destiny for as long as they remains unconscious. Natural and divine beings from higher dimensions know everything about the objective world making them indispensable teachers to any man. We must not come in conflict with them under any circumstances. Mystics and saints were inspired by them, nobody overcame subjectivity (*indriyâni*) without their assistance. However, they also serve the Creator of everything that has been shaped (*aham-kâra*). Through the highest entities of the inorganic realm, nature manifests its highest wisdom and worth. More accurately put, nature is the closest to *Purusha* on that very spot from which it receives the highest values. Lower dimensions of nature have elementals that form minerals, plants, and animals and see to the energy for their survival. Everything from the inorganic world may be personified to the subject in one way or another. These natural elementals show themselves to people as gnomes, fairies, or elves.[45] They rule over the mineral, plant, and animal world. Human development is more complex and aimed at higher nature (*aham-kâra* and *buddhi*). That is why there are divine beings to nurture them as such. All the entities have their pyramidal Gestalt, minerals, plants, animals, and people. Everything has its underlying principle of shaping.

T-fields are, therefore, imagination which is necessary for man's organic or physical structure (*indriyâni*), as an inspiration with which the objective world in its entirety can only be known, and by doing so a person's position in the world can be ascertained objectively. This imagination was a point of interest of many religions, but their activity also involves many other forms of creativity.

The whole of the objective realm is phenomenological energetic happening, while in the subjective realm the energy is more solidly formed into organic abilities. That is why the non-organic forms surpass by far the number of the organic ones, they are created, sustained, and last more easily, and no culture or responsibility is required for that. However, this property engenders the non-organic beings to convey directly the primeval intelligence of nature (*buddhi*) received from *Purusha*. That is why 'raw nature' is cruel and divine at the same time. Due to this state of affairs, the natural, artificial, and extraterrestrial non-organic beings take the energy of consciousness from the organic ones because they have more of it as a result of accumulation. The issue here is not so much in taking energy as it is the natural division which is at work because of the need for balance. Humans consciously accumulate energy into *indriyâni* so as to crystallize it in the personality (*aham-kâra*) and full wakefulness (*buddhi*). To succeed at this they must cease to waste it needlessly and pour it over onto the inorganic realm, into myths, dreams, and fantasies. The non-organic beings and the whole objective realm of nature teach humans the important lesson of accepting the original intelligence of nature so that they can liberate themselves from psychological complications that are typical for subjectivity, by testing them objectively. The eyes of the whole nature and all its beings look towards humans

---

[45] In medical textbooks, these experiences are referred to as Charles Bonnet syndrome.

growing in consciousness because in their being a great deed of enlightenment is taking place, the ultimate purpose of its efforts.

Natural and artificial beings are, therefore, a problem to the degree human miss out on their purpose, when they forget themselves and their self-consciousness. The more they are outside of themselves and the meaning of their survival, the more they wander about the psychedelic projections of inorganic creations, and they dream by forgetting about themselves, their own place, and role in the beingness, their own body in which through resurrection the meaning of the cosmos is found.

An average human, a mediocrity, has no conscious contact (experience) with the non-organic beings (except during sleep). Most commonly, they allow them to perform their natural function: work and reproduction. Abiding by the ethics of some ruling religion will also help them at that. Non-organic beings usually target people who are everything but ordinary, of which there are two types.

The first kind entails weaker individuals with widened perception who are therefore not particularly suitable for performing natural functions, for work, reproduction, and the survival of the species (they are, technically speaking, rejects of nature). Non-organic beings attack them with ease, take their energy, and make them lose their mind and die before their time. The same law of survival, natural selection, and ecological balance applies to everything in nature. For example, savannah hunters (lions and cheetahs) unmistakably attack prey that from afar appears to have some physical anomaly.

The second kind belongs to people with widened perception also, but who are psychologically more stable than average individuals. (Perception may be more open as a result of lability, but stability, as well. To average people, however, it is stereotyped into a single image of the world.) They are aware of the '"supernatural powers"' who also drive them to various temptations that can sometimes be so overpowering that only the lucky few manage to survive owing to the integrity and willpower of their persona – unless they become stereotyped by some religious interpretation of these forces. The base of the correct attitude toward non-organic beings lies in showing personal integrity and willpower. Only then, from attackers and deceivers do they turn into helpers to people in their further integration of consciousness, conveying to them all the necessary information. By liberating themselves, they attribute to the liberation of the whole nature and all of its beings. Nature through its imagination, using the non-organic beings, provokes humans to demonstrate their strength, willpower, and complete personality. The same way a woman does to her man, only more cunningly.

Extraterrestrial beings

We must emphasize the difference between the natural non-organic beings from the influence of alien intelligence, i.e., the divine beings. Alien impact on humankind is very scarce in number as compared to that of the natural non-organic beings, but they far outweigh the influence in the contents they provide. Their influences were of vital importance for the forming of human races and the development of culture. Many ancient stories contain an abundance of true information about how they influenced the life of this planet, but these pieces of information have been deliberately distorted in recent centuries and turned into myths – despite the numerous UFO sightings, many of which have been caught on camera.

They are those 'gods' from ancient traditions which, in written or oral form, testify to extraterrestrials 'coming down from the sky', and theirs is the 'kingdom of heaven'. They were building temples and megalithic structures that were not worked on by human hand or even using cutting-edge technology. The gigantic stones (weighing 800 to 1,200 tons) were lifted and carried to remote locations, but the reality of it all was concealed in a myth, and not even ample material evidence proving that they knew about phenomena such as precession lasting 25,800 years, something that is impossible to come by using simple observation from the Earth with nothing to go by but the most primitive tools, although our modern science claims they were in possession of this knowledge – no civilization lasted long enough to be able to measure these vast eons of time, making the obvious conclusion that they received all that knowledge rather that acquired it. For such knowledge, cosmic technology is required. People have been programmed to believe in the reality of myths so much so that now it is hard for them to accept the simple truth that lies behind the myth. The more reality has been turned into a myth the more the myths and all the fiction people have begun to experience as reality. Simulacra and simulation.

Extraterrestrial beings act rarely on the physical plane, and much more often via the higher dimensions of nature (their movement was described as the sixth phase in *Aham-kâra* chapter). It invariably happens that the natural non-organic beings start to mimic the extraterrestrial ones, i.e., the divine ones, so convincingly that they are able to materialize at times. However, situations, where people fell under the influence of extraterrestrial beings, is an even more frequent occurrence, the beings that came from higher dimensions people saw as the manifestations of '"gods"', interpreting their messages without being able to tell them apart from various other astral creations, their own projections, elementals, archetypes, and T-fields.

The underlying differentiation of inorganic influence from that of the extraterrestrial kind lies in the fact that inorganic creations are natural creations (they belong to *Prakriti*). Their actions are in accordance with natural causality and conditioning. Although the teleological function of nature is to serve *Purusha* in its entirety, we should not lose sight of the fact that it is, fundamentally, an unconscious and conditioning force, making all of its creations the same way, and the non-organic beings are its most eminent creations. It could be said that their educational function is aimed at generating the greatest and the most perverse challenges for the self-consciousness and integrity of humans, where hell and devil play the supporting roles – the types of challenges without which there would be no human consciousness.

Unlike all of these natural influences, the extraterrestrial kind is somewhat more spiritual, cultural, and scientific by nature (although not all of them[46]). The true source of consciousness in the subject is *Purusha*. Some planets house organic life that are

---

[46] Robert Noyce the creator of the microchip admitted that he received help for the creation of the microchip from the alien technology which was in the hands of the American government he worked for at the time.

much older than planet Earth, many of which have ceased to exist by now. The conscious subjects realized themselves as *Purushas* on those planets long ago (we are still in the early stages). Kapila left us with enough information about this stating that the aware individuals who extended themselves to the boundaries of *Prakriti*, having become fully acquainted with it, have risen to be the most sublime beings in *Prakriti*, containing within themselves all of the possibilities of existence as potentials of their own will. In Sanskrit (*Devanagari*, 'the language of gods') such sublime being is called Ishvara, and it is usually translated as God. Their only way of living is spreading spiritual life on planets where certain organic possibilities already exist for the creation of a conscious subject because only through it can primeval unconditionality be expressed, the one that engenders the very existence as such – *Purusha*. Although the teleological function of *Prakriti* is to create the conscious subject, the interest of nature has been satisfied with the conscious life being on the level of primates who are hunters and gatherers. The cultural and spiritual function in a conscious subject must be initiated from 'above', by the beings who already possess the principle of consciousness. Unconscious *Prakriti* cannot of its own create a conscious being. Therefore, Ishvara is the personified *Purusha*. He has a human form because he made us in his image. This image is the way it is because it simply is the most suitable form for the awareness of *Purusha* in nature and all the aspirations leading to this goal, and not because some God feels like it.

4. The cessation of influence of the non-organic beings

The influence of the non-organic beings stops when humans become entire personalities to such a degree that they are able to recognize their own independence from both the inorganic realm as well as organic. Through out-of-body experiences, they gain independence from *indriyâni* and in doing so they learn of the true nature of *tanmâtrâ* and the astral realm, equipping themselves with tools to recognize their own independence from this plane, as well. According to the scheme, *aham-kâra* is above them both. It is affirmed by the conscious integration of both of these realms, through a direct experience.

212

Since the non-organic beings have achieved their purpose by training through the temptations of *indriyâni*, a conscious subject, and lead them to become aware of their being as energy, to preserve and enlighten it, at which point their role and power stop. Like all the other natural creations, these, too, serve the interests of the human soul, *Purusha*. Humans with such integrated personalities have a direct consciousness. They no longer need imagination of nature as the additional help for that. Through the life of the human, the spiritual outcome of nature is realized.

The above description is a mere general insight into the inorganic realm of the beingness as such. Its discernment in the life of an average human is susceptible to gross misconceptions because it is also an area where the dreams play out together with the contents of collective unconsciousness. Hence, this represents a humble attempt to briefly jot down its context. Since this realm is very abundant and complex, far more abundant and complex than the organic realm which is also mixing with it, it is almost impossible to represent it fully down to the last detail. Its abundance can best be seen in all the drama and versatility of man's life experience. It is hard to describe how some non-organic beings try to attract the attention of people and affect them, all of their tactical abilities, even the humor they display while doing it. Their appearance and influence depend on the level of man's unconsciousness. They are, therefore, the strongest in mental patients they find it easy to toy with in both dreams and awaken states. The psychotic episodes are not imaginary, the patients themselves see and hear what cannot be detected via normal senses. They are "'sick'" only because they lack a critical approach to a different kind of reality they experience with their open perception. The underlying reason for a great many psychoses lies in the perception which exceeds physical senses and ignorance of the perceived reality, making them fair game to such forces, creating a gap between 'this' and 'that' reality. While being overwhelmed by astral (*tanmâtrâ*) human lose their personality (*aham-kâra*) as well as the feeling for physical reality (*indriyâni*).

The influence of the non-organic beings is very pronounced in small children, due to a large concentration of vital energy which they are always drawn to, and the open perception of children who see them with ease (and parents never believe them when they start describing things). The same happens with humans who during their spiritual ascension accumulate all of their energy into the consciousness: they become a target when the non-organic beings test out their stability, maturity, and the power of the presence of consciousness. That is how the devil's temptations of Jesus and Buddha came about.

We must stress here once more than one should distinguish between the non-organic beings as such, small and big, near and far (the ones that come from remote areas of the universe and live on astral), from various T-fields that exist temporarily or permanently, and behave similarly to the non-organic beings, making them hard to recognize one from the other sometimes.

The same way that in the organic realm there are all kinds of beings, from the tiniest microorganisms with ephemeral lifespan, to those huge and long-lived ones (elephants, whales, redwood tree...), the same applies to the inorganic realm, in the astral realm, where various entities reside: from small and short-lived T-fields in the form of psychological impressions (*vasanas*) and complexes[47], to enormous and long-lived non-organic beings that function to a big degree (but never completely) independently.

Possible astral influences by the living or dead people should also be discerned. One of the most important influences to be acknowledged and fully distinguished from that of the non-organic beings is the influence of the Oversoul. It represents the bigger part of our soul that is not incarnated in the body but remains in the higher dimensions. Its nature is very different from the nature of

---

[47] Esoteric tradition speaks of astral larvae. They are psychoenergetic entities of certain contents attached to the human's aura forcing him to perform certain tasks, and also behave in a certain way. Sometimes these are harmless habits, but man can also produce them by repetition, or they, having already been produced, simply attach to the human. Larger larvae can impact man more strongly by causing habitual and repetitive behavior and actions, such as vices, obsessions, and perversions, that may grow into harder psychopathological behavior. Larvae can also exist freely and tend to be attracted to such men whose behavior suits them. They, then, feed off his energy making him repeat those actions that provide them with energy. Larvae should also be distinguished from non-organic beings, although that can be hard sometimes. They fall under the category of elementals. In the Christian tradition, they are most commonly identified with the influences of demons and the devil, which is only partly true.

non-organic beings, and those who are fortunate enough to meet it (before death), will not be able not to recognize it. It is the primeval and timeless embodiment of *Purusha*, immanent in all humans, which supervises and tracks humans through time, inspires them, and draws toward spiritual uplifting and overcoming of *Prakriti*.

The inorganic realm of *Prakriti* has a seductive but also the educational character for humans, the whole nature matures and serves' the human soul.

The way children are beautifully taught about the universal and eternal values by reading fairytales, the same way *Prakriti* educates humankind using the imagination of its inorganic being.

***

Many people have mystical experiences, astral projections, out-of-body experiences, perceiving the non-physical phenomena, extrasensory perception. These experiences may have dramatic consequences on a person's life. They may induce uncritical interpretations even psychopathological disorders. Widened perception without the ability to understand its meaning very often leads to psychological problems. Understanding the scheme of categories provided by *Sâmkhya*, which shows higher dimensions and their relationship toward our sensory world, removes all the confusions and disorders. The scheme shows an accurate map for the orientation and comprehension of the widest context of all phenomena, both sensory and extrasensory experiences, making sure nobody gets lost in either this or the other world.

INDRIYÂNI

Organic world and reason

Organic abilities in nature (*indriyâni*) make up the realm of the sensory experiential, physical world. It is the only area of nature where all the experience of its existence, due to complete organic aptitudes, contracts to the point that it crystallizes into information that shines through as reason (*manas*) in a conscious subject. This contraction we acknowledge as the overall life experience and our ability to learn.

Indriyâni is, in its entirety, in the man's body, in the only place where nature contracts into an image and human personality to be able, through its own definition and establishing, to receive the embodiment of its meaning. In all other forms nature simply exists and renews itself, it accomplishes its existence. Only in humans, does it open to its spiritual essence after awareness.

Here, in humans, the energy not only contracts to galvanize the conscious subject but afterward, as a result of the maturing of the individual (*indriyâni*), an independent and complete person is born (*aham-kâra*). Personality is the way it is only when it is aware (*buddhi*) of the unconditioned soul (*Purusha*) that overcomes nature (*Prakriti*).

The human body is, therefore, the only appropriate place in nature where it overcomes and resolves itself under the attracting pull of Purusha, who is the closest to it on this very spot. Hence, human destiny is not tied to the being-and-time, but rather to spiritual transcendence. The human body is the bridge to eternity, it is the embodiment of the eternal or divine. If, however, it is used as the home of natural conditioning, then it is the source of suffering and plight.

All the living beings, in the ancient system of *Sâmkhya*, can simply be divided according to the number of sensory and action organs they possess, which are called *indriyâni*. From the simplest microorganisms with only one sense, and a myriad of beings with

216

different combinations and a number of sensory and action organs, to a single being with all the twelve organs which constitutes the human (see scheme in picture 1).

In the genealogy of the organisms on earth, there is an evident connection between their ability to move and sensory perception, as well as intelligence. From the unicellular organisms, plants and animals, in a further division of the animal kingdom into arthropods, mollusks, echinoderms, and vertebrates, all the way to mammals, we can clearly see that the number of sensory and action organs, which engenders better movement and perception, and consequently bigger participation in all the life events, engenders a proportionately higher level of intelligence.

None of the sensory and action organs exists alone but are directly conditioned by the function they serve, what humans were originally intended for (*tanmâtrâ*). The functions of perception and action formed the sensory and action organs, and not some DNA information. Since these functions are a reflection of the intention of the soul, its maturity, and activity, it can be said that the soul and its *karma* are the key factors that decide on the number and state of the sensory and action organs. That is why some people are born without, or later in life lose, the proper functioning of some of the organs, depending on the karmic drama they need to experience.

Activities, intelligence, and abilities of the being are different according to the number and level of development of the organs nature equips them for to be able to creatively conduct the soul's consciousness in themselves. The number of organs is a measure of the organism to manifest this kind of the purpose of nature. The development of technology as well, as an extension of organic faculties because it also facilitates the being to manifest its purpose.

The consciousness of the unconditioned soul is equally present everywhere in nature, as the chief attractor of all of its happening, but is less accessible on the lower levels of higher conditionality of the gross matter, and in the simple life forms, and far more on the more subtle levels of developed organic abilities.

Therefore, the issue here is not in the presence of *Purusha*, but in the self-oblivion of *Prakriti* which is greater in its gross inertia and disintegration of the consciousness, in organic underdeve-

217

lopment. This regulation resembles a slot that can let in more or less light but can never be tightly closed because it would not serve its function of the slot otherwise, which is the sole purpose of nature, especially in its human form: to open the presence of the unconditioned soul that is the essence of nature.

Every form of existence and life in nature is a specific way of the manifestation of consciousness and intelligence. The whole nature is alive and transforms itself for the benefit of' the human soul more creatively as the level of its pyramid grows progressively higher. Hence, plants are more aware than minerals, animals are more aware than plants, while humans are functionally the most adept and consequently the most conscious being in nature (at least here on Earth).

There is a pyramidal proportion between the number of sensory and action organs and the number of beings who have them. The fewest number belongs to the beings that possess all of the organic abilities, meaning people, and there is a far greater number of unicellular organisms with a minimal number of organic abilities. This proportion corresponds with the greater presence of the consciousness and greater capacity for acquiring experience, and people have this at the peak level. On each level of correlation of the experiences of beingness there are new properties, while on the highest level of organic abilities for acquiring and exchange of experiences, the sum of all properties simultaneously is reflected in the reason (*manas*).

The organ of thought, mind, or reason – *manas* – is the brain. Its role is to regulate and synthesize sensory experiences and govern the functioning by implementing decisions and will of the higher categories (*aham-kâra* and *buddhi*), and navigate *prâna* flows through the activities of action organs (*buddhindriye* and *karmendriye*).

The position of the mind in relation to the body, higher consciousness, and the soul's consciousness (*Purusha*) can be clarified by the following picture.

218

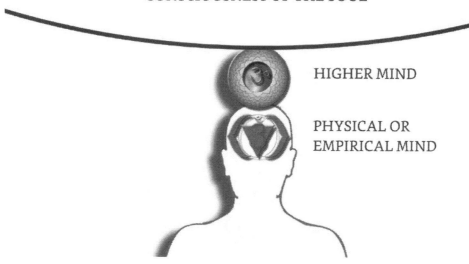

HIGHER MIND

PHYSICAL OR
EMPIRICAL MIND

The physical or empirical mind is *manas*. In its natural state, it is divided and attached to the objects.

Once the mind (*manas*) is no longer divided and conditioned, when it reaches the awareness of itself, it becomes unanimous with a will of its own, and only then the category of *aham-kâra* is actualized. Then, *mahat-buddhi* becomes the higher mind that links humans directly to the soul's consciousness, *Purusha*.

This is how the mind binds the soul's consciousness with the functioning of the body.

If the transcendental consciousness is the one that truly attracts all the happening of nature, there must be some connection of theirs present somewhere. This connection is *manas*, the reason, or mind. The mind itself, however, does not belong to either of the sides, so that it could serve both.

The mind does not, and neither do the other organs, exist independently and make its own decisions. It exists only through the function it performs; it is a mere medium that connects the perception of phenomena and the functioning of the being within them. It maintains them in a subtle way but has no will of its own. The mind or reason is the one that uses sensory and action organs, it matures through them, although, on the other hand, it represents the synthesis of all its powers. Hence, its function works both ways, the mind is the organ that serves to translate information from the gross to the subtle, and from the subtle to the gross. Behind the mind lies the consciousness it works for, and before the mind are the senses and their physical world. The problem is that it does this simultaneously, it is two-way communication, and if these trajectories get mixed up, an illusion is created.

The presence of consciousness in the mind determines what we see with our eyes and hear with our ears. When the focus is on something else, we do not see what is staring us in the face, nor do we hear a sound in the background. *The state of the consciousness in the mind determines our perception and not the senses.* The mind merely uses the senses as instruments of perception, but the presence of the consciousness in the mind decides which of the observed will be filtered through to the mind. The scope of this can be illustrated by the cases where people photographed objects they failed to see, even though they were there, such as astral phenomena that got very close to the physical world or astral bodies of the deceased, as well as UFO's, which due to the high technology they possess escapes our vision, although we are looking at them directly.

The mind works by conforming to the functions it performs. The most subtle form of conformation of the sensory and action experience is a thought or notion. Therefore, all the categories the reason uses are for the deduction of the empirical world – which are thoughts and notions, names of forms (*nama-rūpa*) – they are all of sensory origin. A thought or a name is a synthesis of various forms of the immediate sensory impressions on the physical plane or those that were previously formed by the informative impact of an older T-field. No thought is ever new, it is only a more subtle reflection of the physical experience on higher planes that *manas* as a medium is connected with. Hence, name and form, object and subject which ascertain it are not different in any way, they are different aspects of the same *Prakriti* but in different dimensions. *The form is grosser or more material as it were, and the thought is a higher, more subtle aspect of the same phenomena. As the more subtle version of the gross form, a thought is the information of the gross form.* The consciousness of the mind is not in any way different from its contents, from the thoughts that came as a result of the experience.

Two things happen in the mind: the consciousness in the mind assumes the form of thoughts, and a thought as the essence of sensory experience, reaches the consciousness. In the mind, the consciousness connects with sensory experience in this way.

In its lower dimensions, nature manifests itself in the gross form, in the higher dimensions as energy, and in its highest and most subtle dimensions, nature is only a vibration or information. A collection of information on the phenomena of nature composes the mind of man.

When we see a gross object, we automatically experience a subtle vibration, a thought on this subject. They possess an identical nature: objects in the gross form and the thoughts of them in the fine informative form. Our mind is nothing but a mechanism dividing and distinguishing between the gross and the subtle frequencies, forms of objects, and ideas about them. Our act of continuously designing both the forms and phenomena is a mere function of uniting the gross and subtle frequencies of the same phenomena.

We refine gross objects and information on the objects through mental and sensory perception. By doing so, we retrieve them back to their original state because before they originated in the form of gross objects, they existed in higher dimensions as information or ideas. Only later they materialized in the form of gross objects. By doing so we retrieve them through perception to their higher, original state. *By cognizing something with our mind and reason, we round off the process of organic creation and materialization* (that is why on the scheme *manas* is above all the other categories of both subjective and objective domain of *Prakriti* – *tanmâtras* are in the same domain with the sensory organs). The process of creation is therefore always incomplete without the presence of the conscious subject. *The fundamental reason for the existence of the conscious subject in nature is finalizing the process of all the natural phenomena*. It could be said that to an equal measure the purpose of the subject is to finalize the existence, as much as it is to participate in it.

Gathering these finest vibrations happens under the attraction of *Purusha* in humans, in their own soul. Only the presence of the human soul in the body leads nature to form the overall organic life, and inform itself, i.e., design and establish itself within and through the body with everything that engenders life and the culture of living. This design we see as human civilization and technology.

The attraction of *Purusha* is not some mere attraction, but it also has a regulatory property. Under its influence nature crystallizes into perfection of the reflection of spirit and consciousness. Outwardly, this crystallization can be seen as the overcoming of debauchery and elements of nature and instincts, also as the overall civilization, culture, and technology, and inwardly, as the innermost self-knowledge of the human consciousness. Consciousness is, above all, the awareness of oneself. This further generates the awareness of oneself in the form of 'I am'. At the point of intersection between the transcendental awareness of oneself and the physical body, the impression of I or ego is born. It is logical because how else would the consciousness be able to experience its presence in the individual, three-dimensional physical body were it not for 'this is me' and 'this is mine'.

Thoughts are not ours, at all, they are the most subtle vibrations of nature we are able to attract with our soul and consciousness. We can only repeat and combine thoughts and ideas in all ways possible. Our soul is a magnet that attracts the most subtle vibrations of nature, thoughts, to gather and further design themselves on the spot most favorable for this which is our brains, or *manas*, and thoughts naturally swarm through our head, nature establishes itself the most clearly using the light of our consciousness.

We most commonly repeat and combine their contents. It is the mechanical or formative function of the mind.[48] We, as the soul's pure consciousness, tend to be identified with our thoughts and we continue to repeat and recombine them. Thoughts are a part of nature; nature designs itself using its most subtle vibrations, meaning information, which are located in the brain, *manas*, and become actualized as thoughts. The happening of the being, *Prakriti*, is never pointless, it is always purposeful. The ultimate point of the overall phenomena of *Prakriti* is *Purusha*. *Purusha* as a

---

[48] On this and many other conditioning functions of the mind see P.D.Ouspensky: *In Search of the Miraculous, Fragments of an unknown Teaching.*

source of the consciousness and the chief attractor gives the purposefulness to the phenomena of nature because it is not so all by itself. The ultimate shape of purposefulness of the individual phenomena of the being within the framework of *Prakriti* leads to the designing of happenings that take place in *manas* or the mind. If the happenings were purposeful, it is no longer sufficient, its establishing is required within the conscious subject, through identification, memory, discernment, and design in connection with all the other phenomena. It is the function of *manas* or the mind.

The mind functions with the help of the vicinity of the principle of individuation, *aham-kâra*, which is also in its interest. The vicinity of *aham-kâra* is needed for the mind for individuation and identification of every known experience. However, the vicinity of *aham-kâra* also creates the experience of ego in the mind, and that is why the ego does not exist as either an organ or the category of nature (it is absent from the scheme), but only as an impression because of its connectedness. It is often said that ego is an illusion one needs to get rid of, and one that makes the most problems because it uses the functions of the mind as its own, and reduces the principle of individuation to a mere empirical realm. When this dysfunction of the mind in the form of ego is gone, the mind is directly employed by *aham-kâra* which leads to the enlightenment.

Because of all of this, the mind is at the top of the matter, on its very verge (according to scheme 1.) The connection with the non-material gives it broadness and flexibility of spirit, and the connection with matter gives it coherence and memory. Because of its position in the structure of nature or *Prakriti*, the mind can be enlightened when it is aimed at *aham-kâra* and *buddhi*, or eclipsed, trapped, and psychotic when it is cut off and obsessed by the lower categories and inorganic realm. Additionally, without it, the connection between consciousness and nature would not be possible.

We have already stated that *Prakriti* is an information field which due to the presence of the conscious subject turns into physical phenomena. Our brain is nothing but the finest organ that is able to reflect those vibrations. They reflect in our head and for that reason, it only appears as though they were ours. Nature actualizes itself by forming itself (*rûpa*) in the whole phenomena, and the end result of its phenomena is the creation of conditions for the emergence of the conscious subject as the final outcome of the overall phenomena. In the conscious subject, the outcome of all the shaping is reflected in giving names to forms (*nama*), they are being established as such (*nama-rŭpa*). Our brain does not produce thoughts but only reflects them, it absorbs them in the form of impressions (*samskara* and *vasana*) **and repeats them as a result of an unconscious habit.** Only due to this constant repetition of thoughts they appear as though they were ours, and this is the reason why we identify with the mind. Only when in meditation we calm ourselves completely and stop repeating thoughts, we see they are not ours because they disappear and shift all the time, and we exist always. When we begin to see clearly this difference, we become more free and more conscious than ever. The freer we are the more able we are to express nature designing itself in a better way, without distortions.

However, repeating thoughts due to the accumulation of impressions (*samskara* and *vasana*) is necessary because of the memory and the designing itself. Designing is the ability to perceive one thought together with our state and learn to experience it, from different angles. That is why it must be maintained to be designed objectively in all possible ways. That is why both subconscious and conscious impressions, *samskaras* and *vasanas*, are connected with emotions. Emotions are also more subtle informative phenomena of the identical nature as thoughts are, they are only slower, thicker, and more lasting than thoughts. Thoughts are instant, and emotional impressions are more permanent, they act as the cement for solidifying the thought facts. Hence, emotions are nothing but the ability to analyze one idea or experience from different angles. They are all the more mature if they facilitate analyzing from multiple aspects. Emotions are all the more immature if they fail to facilitate analyzing from multiple aspects, then we can speak of emotional immaturity; but also, if they are too solid and fail to engender shifting of the aspects for analyzing in the first place, then, it is the case of a narrowed consciousness, emotional blockages, and traumas. This is worked out in the same way as the mind identification: by introducing the objective consciousness during the process of recapitulation, objective ascertaining of the entire process, or more briefly, with the practice of meditation.

Spiritual maturity begins with *aham-kâra* – which means that only the one who functions from *aham-kâra* can have their own thoughts and they are always creative. Anyone who functions from *manas*, whose mind is facing downward, in the direction of the sensory and action organs, does not have their own thoughts, instead, they are imposed on them. Consequently, their words and deeds do not resonate with their thoughts. Only an integrated and complete personality acting from *aham-kâra*, independently of the body and mind, is able to have their own thoughts which, then, function in accordance with the law of attraction and creation. They are always in perfect harmony with the words and deeds because *aham-kâra* is superior to the entire *indriyâni*, all the sensory and action organs, as well as the mind, *manas*.

The more the mind is independent of the sensory and action organs, the more it is dependent on the higher categories, *aham-kâra,* and *buddhi* and then it conducts more consciousness through itself, onto the whole body, and the whole nature, as well. Turning the mind toward higher categories is performed by establishing the rule over the lower ones, simply by understanding and acting properly. Nothing in nature prevents a human being from becoming enlightened this minute. Enlightenment fails to happen because there is some dysfunction of the natural processes, disturbed functioning of the centers, and energy flows. When everything is in its place, then humans become enlightened automatically. *Prakriti* serves *Purusha* in every possible way.

Since the mind functions by conforming with its objects, identification happens as a result, as the biggest obstacle in the path of enlightenment.

It is hard to find words to emphasize the level of the mind's conformation with the functions it performs, with the body. The mind rules over our body to such an extent that we are completely unaware of it. On the scheme, we see that *manas* dominates over *indriyâni*, the same way the brain dominates over the physical body. There is no mistake here. The mind completely determines the state of the body, not only its movements, but the vital functions, as well, the life of each cell, and the entire physical looks. Because of the negative use of the mind we live much shorter and much worse off than we should. The cells are continuously renewed, all biological life is in free motion; it already has everything to fulfill all of its potential. The organism spontaneously renews its cells when it is free of obstacles. Children are vital and grow because they do not have the mind heavily burdened by the past to prevent them from doing so. When the mind is completely proper and clear, it conducts all the energy for the life of the body, enabling humans to live without consuming food (like a breatharian, for example). Humans only need as much consumption as their mental state dictates.

However, the mind of an adult person is the force that puts spikes in the wheels of free movement of energy and renewing cells from one minute to another, the mind is constrained by the illusion of time, by the past, and the impressions gathered it simply will not let go of. The more the mind is laden with time, past, and impressions, the less vital the human is, and, consequently, the aging process is accelerated. The very conviction that time is real leads the mind to program the body to age over time. Such a mind that lives in fiction, convictions, and all kinds of contents, is in discord with the being that always moves freely to a new form of life, with no psychological or religious issues, or past, for that matter, to put pressure on it. We can live far longer and better but with a mind that is clear, free of the influences of the past, and open for the existence here and now – the one that is not a slave to the time.

The measure to which the mind decides on the body is best illustrated with the examples from hypnotherapeutic practice. In hypnosis, during which the conscious mind has been removed, humans can heal themselves instantly from even the hardest ailments, alter genetic disorders, and stop the heart from beating. A documented case of a worker who froze to death in the cold storage warehouse as a result of negligence is another example of this. Somebody accidentally locked them up, but the cooling system was off. He was unaware of this fact, he believed he would freeze to death, and he did.

Since the mind (*manas*) is at the top of organic abilities (*indriyâni*), it is crucial for perception. We do not perceive with our senses but with our mind, and the senses are mere instruments of perception. The degree to which the mind decides on the perception is illustrated by the experiments with hypnosis where a subject is instructed to believe that a certain individual is no longer present before them; after awakening from the hypnosis, the hypnotized person would no longer see this person even though they were standing next to them. If this person moved an object, for example, the hypnotized subject would not see this individual but only the object moving through air. He would also see right through this person (what time it was on the clock behind them) although they were standing in front of them (blocking the view to the clock). This shows us to what extent the mind deceives us – to the same measure it engenders perception. This also proves that not only is the mind that what controls perception but (like *logos*) it creates the physical reality.

A mind is a place where the unconditioned consciousness of *Purusha* is identified with thoughts. Due to the multidimensional holism of nature, its consciousness in one dimension (*manas*) is demonstrated as the thought, in some other dimension as its physical activity, an object, or some objective phenomenon of nature. A mind is a place where this refraction of unity takes place; the mind itself divides the unity of nature into the subtle and gross, into a thought or physical object, into outward and inward.

There is pragmatism at work here. The reason acts as the synthesis and regulation of both sensory and action experiences of the subject in the circling of objective nature, of its prototypes, as well as all the elements by being the section point of their interaction and the receiver of its resonance. Nature in its freedom exists multidimensionally and, according to the scheme, dually: as the physical objects (the room we are in and all the things in it) and, at the same time, in subtle dimensions, as the subject in which the conscious experience of these objects is contracted. While the physical laws apply to the objects, their conscious ascertaining in the subject is regulated by the psychological laws, and in them, the objects can be altered in unfathomable ways. In the room we are in, we can visualize all kinds of events and changes without directly influencing any of them, and consumed by our thoughts we fail to see all the objects that are objectively there. Both the physical objects and the subject that experiences them belong to the same nature, they only represent different aspects and dimensions of it.

Every sensory and action organ represents one reflection of the consciousness or experiences of the objectively given prototypes and elements (*tanmâtrâ* and *maha-bhũtâni*) that shaped it. These two aspects of beingness, the subjective and objective one, are always in interaction. The point of intersection of the interactions in question is the place of synthesis of experience, for each sensory and action organ separately. The total of all of these sections is *manas*, but the function of rationality functions in a weaker or stronger aspect in all the beings, no matter how many sensory and action organs they had. Our body (together with the mind) and without alert presence purposefully performs everything it has been taught to do. That is why the whole of created nature is rational and purposeful for the sake of survival, and that is why the whole cosmic order of organic beingness is gained and reflected in the personality through mental concepts (*manas*). Therefore, the gathering point of all the sections of subjective experiencing the objective nature is *manas* or the mind, and it is nothing more than that.

Regulative synthesis of the mind would not be what it is if it were only one-sided, it also has a feedback effect and we can see this in the harmony and order in the entire manifested cosmos. Our state of mind decides on what kind of a world we will perceive. To the degree our mind is harmonious in its function of synthesis and regulation of all the experiences, to the same degree we are aware of the harmony of the cosmos itself. *Manas* is *logos* with which the world of objects is known and with which the whole of the manifested world is purposefully regulated in one place, in the personality (*aham-kâra*).[49]

When the mind is in the *sattvic* state it serves the purpose of the integration of personality and will (*aham-kâra*), it, then, designs its own outcome and ceases to renew the bond with the past. In the *rajas* state, it is associated with the sensory experiences, and for this very reason it is fiercely involved in the struggle for survival, the principle behavior of people and animals, while in the state of *tamas* it expresses itself only as an elementary ability of the syn-

---

[49] In Yogacara, the school of *mahayana* Buddhism, it is thought that outside the domain of the mind as such, the world is without any stronghold. It is empty, unconditioned.

thesis of sensory perception, the available motion, and action, something that can be seen in animals, plants, insects, and micro-organisms.

In the *sattvic* aspect, it is very rarely present, it is usually present only in mature and self-conscious individuals. In this state *manas* is calm and without thoughts, without the divisions into the multitude of I's, implementing the will of one, true 'I' (*aham-kâra*), and pure consciousness (*buddhi*) that rules over such a will. In the *rajas* state, the mind is exposed to division and the conflict of many I's, it is constantly present in their perpetual struggle for achieving different interests, aimed at the goals and ideals it never seems to attain because they are only an excuse for realizing its own move-ment from one impression to another and maintaining the divi-sion. In *tamas* state, the mind is occupied with the identification with both the inner and outer impressions, thoughts that keep pouring in, and the same available uncontrollable urge engages the bodily movement. It is therefore unconscious. This type of *manas* rules the dreams, both during the day and night, and in some ex-treme aspects, it also rules over psychotic states. This is the prevail-ing state of being in the life of an average human.

All the thoughts present in the mind (manas) originate due to the interaction of indriyâni with tanmâtrâs and maha-bhûtâni, the interaction which is the result of a division of the subject with the whole and within themselves, as well. Thoughts are always a direct expression of ignorance and failing to see things for what they are, they are the dream keepers, and for that exact reason, they represent a thirst for knowledge, as it were. If they were knowledge or reality themselves, they would not be repetitive. What we know we do not envisage; we take it for granted. The existence of though-ts serves as proof that humans do not see them for what they are, and therefore, they have to envisage them. Thoughts and notions exist to pass on the information onto us of what is not in our local environment and experience. We do not use information when we can see things for ourselves. In that way, thoughts hook man's per-sonality to the whirlpool of lower categories of happenings. The whole problem is in that the function of the mind overflows and mixes with the functions it does not need. By establishing the will of one 'I' (*aham-kâra*) in the psychophysical actions, one's own independence from thoughts is revealed, independence from all the names and forms. The mixing of the mind with contents completely inappropriate for it finally ceases, and the silence of the mind is discovered in which the complete clarity of one's true being is born together with the real wakefulness (*buddhi*) which is never again interrupted because the consciousness without thoughts is the true outcome of our being which can never be lost. The outcome exists through the being itself, and not through a thought about the being. This awareness can only be achieved by becoming aware of the existence as such, and in no other way possible.

Due to the identification of the consciousness with thought contents it becomes eclipsed together with the eclipsed thoughts, and the states of mind determine the states of consciousness (dreams, deep sleep, coma, and the usual daily 'wakefulness' with numerous oscillations, some of which are considered '"mystical"'). The consciousness itself has no states, it is the outcome or meaning of the beingness in general, it is one with the outcome of being. Consciousness is beyond all the states of the mind. [50] Since a thought never reaches its own source, it drew consciousness away from its true transcendental outcome, into all the forms and dimensions of existence. Because of the underlying urge of the organic nature to renew and maintain itself fighting for its survival, thoughts, as its finest product, often act as an overly repeated reevaluation.

In this way, thoughts, tying the consciousness to the illusions, drag the consciousness into deeper levels of nature, into all the aspects of existence into which no rational mind would ever want to have anything to do with. This is the way in which illusions illuminate nature. As we have already stated, *Prakriti* serves

---

[50] A clarification into the relationship between the mind and consciousness may be useful here. The mind, *manas*, is like a light bulb, *indriyani* is like the lamp with the whole stand, and the consciousness itself is like the invisible electric energy that engenders the light bulb and the lamp to shine. This consciousness is generated in nature due to the vicinity of *Purusha*, and this vicinity is represented on the scheme of *Prakriti* with the *mahat-buddhi* category. It further shapes itself individually through the *aham-kára* category. This is how the mind uses the light of the consciousness, where the consciousness itself is neither the mind nor the body, although it illuminates them both, it brings light into their existence. Since consciousness is not the mind, we can be aware of the mind.

Purusha in **all** the ways possible. **All** of this should be literally understood.

A psychological fact that the thought mainly deals with the experiences from the past, that we have all our notions and ideas owing to our previously gained experience or other people's experiences from the past – which are no longer there. This is the way in which thinking creates a wall that separates us from reality which always exists in the present time only. Since nature operates through a paradox, thinking is at the same time a form of rehearsing for the upcoming events based on the experiences from the past.

Manas is like a mirror which reflects names and characters from the past and future, from the inward and outward world through which the body moves using sensory perception while experiencing all of it actively. Due to the motion of the mirror (mind), it appears that the characters reflecting in it move and create a fortunate or unfortunate destiny. Its division and cracks create an even bigger illusion of myriad and conflicts. The essence of the being, however, is only one, and an illusion of a multitude is a reflection of the split mind and personality. Life tortures humans, not because the nature of the objective world is such, but because their split mind deceives them. Suffering is the product of subjectivity; hence, it is subjectively experienced as being very riveting.

Why does our mind keep deceiving us when at the same time it awakens us? The mind is the most subtle part of organic nature. It acts as the mirror. If organic nature is like a wall, the mind is like a mirror on that wall; the same material polished to perfection to reflect the light of consciousness. However, in the mirror everything looks in reverse, the left side looks like our right. Similarly, the mind faithfully reflects the reality of existence, albeit not completely. The other important thing is: it is only a reflection, and not the reality itself. However, the perfection of the reflection of reality in the mind seduces us so much that we think reality has already been achieved in the mind. We identify with the reflection in the mirror. This is the way in which the mind deceives us because it does its job flawlessly. It mimics the reality so well we begin to think it is the reality itself. The closer we are to the mirror, the more clearly we see the image of reality in our mind, and it looks perfectly real to us; and the deception grows bigger.

The mind has, due to more subtlety and elevation than in the lower categories, far more objective perception of a certain phenomenon than on the lower, sensory level, where it is also possible to design, reflect, or rethink everything from several aspects, or even to examine it. On the lower levels where the physical determination rules, such evaluation is not possible, instead, perception is limited to the sensory impressions as they happen in time and available space. That is why memory is short here and reduced to sensory experiences without an option of creating abstract ideas. Thinking is a more complex and finer form of perception than that of the sensory type because it is in the higher dimensions which are above the sensory scope where thinking does not depend on the limitations of space and time the way perception on the lower dimensions does. Hence, thoughts, information, and ideas can be transferred to a great degree independently of space and time in either written or some other form, even telepathically because in higher dimensions space and time of the overall happening contract while uniting.

The position of *manas* on the scheme makes it above all the other dimensions, and a preceding thought or impression does not remain dim or suppressed by the present, like in the lower planes of sensory determination, but identified and placed together with the present and future which automatically engenders thinking and designing of some novel experience, object, or thing in all ways possible.

Thoughts are inert and limited unless they are inspired by higher categories, *aham-kâra* and *buddhi* (personality, will, and a clear conscience). Without an inspiration of this kind, they are merely reactions, subtle reflections of traces formed by the phenomena on the lower dimensions, and fail to present or engender anything new. Thoughts are dark and negative then.

In other words, when humans exist to the level of manas they have no thoughts of their own because they have many personalities and are conditioned by the outer influences and their reactions to them. Only on the aham-kâra level when they have one 'I' and the permanent awareness of themselves and is in the capacity of their own will, they have their thoughts finally. They are, then, rare and moderate, always right and creative. Thoughts that appear up to manas level are always an expression of a reaction of mutual influence between the inorganic and organic realms. Thoughts ruled by higher categories, aham-kâra and buddhi, are creative actions, and not some conditioned reactions.

Nothing that is of nature and time can liberate' the human soul, it can only lead it to mutability, and transience. Because the soul is eternal, and everything that originates in time must cease to exist with the passage of time. Thoughts, at best, serve to ascertain, establish, and concretize all the life experience so that they do not keep repeating forever, something that helps greatly in the process of the differentiation of consciousness.

Much greater freedom of action that a higher thought has over the lower one, over the sensory experience, seduces every human, more or less, to a fatal illusion of their already accomplished and complete freedom. A thought engenders its idea, but not the realization because the being neither transforms nor matures with the change of opinions. A being through thoughts does nothing but dreams of the liberation and perfection of its own outcome. It achieves its full maturity by overcoming the obsession with thoughts, that are not the highest category in the structure of the being. According to the place in the scheme where *manas* is present, it is clear that the thought should listen to the will of the person that is above, and not vice versa. The true will is born in humans in that way, and the power to act ("I am doer"). Knowledge can lead humans to the top of the manifested world (both the organic and inorganic), but it may make them the embodiment (*aham-kâra*) of the pure consciousness (*buddhi*) which reflects the unconditioned soul (*Purusha*). The mind that is not enlightened by the higher categories does not liberate humans from the conditionality of the being.

When the energy of the mind is aiming downward, to the sensory and action organs, in the inorganic realm, the mind naturally aspires toward being split because all of the phenomena under *aham-kâra* are divided into a multitude.

When the energy of the mind is aiming upward, which happens by healing all the divisions, an insight into the general unity of the existence is born during the process of individuation.

The human being will mature to realization only when the split and unconscious mind is overcome by healing personality and will when a multitude of I's in humans that causes a myriad of various thoughts and mood swings, allows for the one, permanent 'I' (*aham-kâra*) to take its rightful place, and remains awakened forever (*buddhi*).

In accordance with our pyramidal vision of *Prakriti*, we may see the dual nature of *manas*. From the viewpoint of participation in the time contraction, going from the foundation to the top, the mind proves itself to be the biggest obstacle because, with its far higher freedom of action in comparison to the limiting physical and sensory experiences, it gives an illusion that the complete freedom (*Purusha*) has already been achieved only because the idea of it has been put forward. In that way, the mind turns into the finest form of enslavement. However, from the standpoint of a timeless outcome or the very freedom that everything manifests from, the way we see it from the top of the pyramid, the mind represents a creative design and crown of the organic life, *logos* that becomes the body (*indriyâni*), a creative thought that builds the objective world.

To understand the mind (*manas*) properly one should know that it is formed by everything below *aham-kâra*, and not the sensory experience of *indriyâni* only. The mind is largely composed of the imagination belonging to the dimensions of the inorganic realm of nature, as well. Many constitutive factors come from there that are both subjective (complexes, convictions, basic views...) and those that are objective in character which are the cases when the non-organic entities (beings or T-fields as archetypes) form thoughts in the mind. Humans accepts them as their own, sometimes they hear them as alien voices (sounds) or receives them as nonverbal inspiration by the "Force Majeure" or as they subjectively think, from "God" – something that can have varying consequences. In any case, they consider them authentic and put a lot of energy into their realization. The mind is, therefore, placed in the brain (more precisely: in the body) and the sensory experiences

234

with the brain constitute our mind to a large degree. This physical part of the mind constitutes the ego as well as most of the conscious experiences. However, the mind is not just the brain. The objective domain of nature also forms the mind and manipulates it both constructively and destructively, and this part of the mind is mostly unconscious. *If there were no impact of the objective realm on the brain, there would be no mind knowledge of the objective nature – which is reduced to the awareness of unconscious contents and influences, the self-knowledge.*

What modern psychology has discovered and labeled as 'unconscious' is the inorganic realm on the scheme of *Prakriti*. The conscious domain is the organic realm or *indriyâni*. *Prakriti* in *indriyâni* expresses its constructive power of senses.

Overcoming *manas* does not mean its numbness or rejection. The function of this organ is regulation of sensory perception and the whole of bodily functioning, it is the most perfect and the most important organ without which humans would not be humans, at all. Overcoming *manas* means preventing its faulty functioning. Its task is to receive information, regulate, and balance out functioning, and not to plan or judge everyone and everything – which is something the mind of unevolved humans does forgetting its primary function altogether, making their being out of balance and creating hindrance for the permanent stay of the consciousness. This lack of balance causes changes of states in the human consciousness. That is why *manas* represents the center of the regulative functions of the whole body, something that can be brought to order only by the awareness of the whole being. Thoughts become calm only through the awareness of the body. Each function a person is made aware of and put to proper use, automatically leads to the transcendence of itself. The proper functioning of the centers and all bodily functions are their transcendence. Inhibitions and incapability for transcendence always exist because of the faulty functioning of the centers and lack of awareness of the functions of *indriyâni* and *manas*.

"Blessed are the poor in spirit for theirs is the kingdom of heaven" (Matthew 5:3). Blessed means they have found the right measure of appeasement, and together with it the peace within. That is self-knowledge. Therefore, real translation would be:

"Blessed are those whose minds are calm for theirs is the kingdom of heaven".

When the mind is calm, ignorance and wrong views fall off naturally.

AHAM - KÂRA

1. The principle of individuation or shaping

The manifestation of the world, and our entire experience of the world, is generated by *aham-kâra*. The experience of becoming a personality that is the only one capable of an authentic experience of the world is integrated within this category.

It is hard to distinguish *aham-kâra* from *buddhi*. All that can be said is that what *buddhi* represents in the absolute sense, *aham-kâra* expresses on the individual or local domain. It could be said that the happenings of all the lower categories in *aham-kâra* attain for the first time their true existential embodiment necessary for attaining the final outcome that is resolved in *buddhi*. All the happenings below *aham-kâra* are subordinate to causality which can be found only here, in the category that gives form to everything, both subjective and objective. Only in the human's personality nature finds its resolution and trains for freedom, consequently, it fights oppression the most fiercely here, as well.

The very position of this category on the scheme indicates that it is the outcome of everything that happens through the integration of subjective and objective, organic and inorganic existence. *Aham* means "I am", and *–kara* "creator" or "doer". The way phenomena are integrated here, in lower categories were manifested as being either subjective and organic, or objective and inorganic. The way of being is manifested in them through the outer form, while in *aham-kâra* it integrates into the higher, existential level: meaning.

Aham-kâra as the principle of individuation manifests objectively by giving form to everything in the cosmos, from the subtle prototypes (*tanmâtrâ*) to the great elements (*maha-bhŭtâni*), it individually forms each creation and occurrence in nature: a thought in the mind (*manas*), a body of some being, stone, or tree, the electromagnetic waves, planets, and galaxies. Everything has been shaped individually in some way because no activity can be undertaken in amorphousness, and the activity itself gives nature the life it has. On the subjective or organic plane, the sensory and action abilities are formed for the perception and experience of the objective beingness. We can see that *aham-kâra* is the cause of the kind of interaction that through the relationship of the subject with object crystallizes the consciousness. *Aham-kâra* is the principle of individuation whose function is to differentiate between the being and awareness, and not some mere separation and alienation from the whole. Only when this maturing awareness is absent, *aham-kâra* manifests itself as the principle that alienates and divides into egoic peculiarities. In a positive aspect, it is the principle of individuation which identifies the whole, something that is not possible in a diffuse whole. The individuation is not separation from the whole then, but its embodiment in action through which it exists.

Since existence is not possible in uniformity, a basic drive exists in the whole nature for the division and doubling so as to engender a synthesis on a higher ontological level. From the quantum fluctuation and division of cells in the process of upgrading life (and degrading it, as well), together with all the experiences of deprivation that force us to mature, until we reach the abandonment of attaching ourselves to the world of objects enlightened human, ultimately, becomes independent of (*kaivalya*). The principle of differentiation, induced by *aham-kâra*, is equally present in the objective manifestation of the world, as in humans themselves through their psychological experience. Due to the interactive bond between the organic and inorganic beingness, individual processes in the objective realm (of beings and occurrences) cause, by their mere analogy, the individual processes in the subject where they are reflected as the psychological processes. **Differentiation of the outside world, which composes the overall life of the cosmos, is equally present in the subject as its psychic differentiation. This equality is provided by aham-kâra.** The truth is that there are no divisions: the life of the cosmos is the same as the life drama of all humans, owing to which they become acquainted with the reality of the cosmos through themselves. It is the same event, it only manifests in different proportions. This is how the subject experiences the objective world, its psychodynamics represents the spacetime of contracted experiences of the phenomena of the objective realm. (From the standpoint of the subject, all other subjects are mere objects to them.) The ultimate point of the differentiation of personality leads to its disappearance in *mahat-buddhi*.

Aham-kâra means in translation "I am the doer" or "I am the creator". This category received such a title because for the first time the human becomes recognizes the soul's consciousness as the only creator and doer of all the happening, of both the physical body and the whole of the physical three-dimensional environment that composes the world and life. In all of the lower categories (below *aham-kâra*) human consciousness was convinced that the world and physical environment were outward circumstances – an imposition – and the human is unable to affect them completely, often ending up as a victim instead. Here, for the first time, the human comes to know the consciousness (*mahat-buddhi*) of the soul (*Purusha*) as the only real doer (*aham-kâra*) and creator of the entire existence in all dimensions (all the other categories below them on the scheme). However, mental patterns play a key role in navigating the functioning of the consciousness, and the level to which the human believes that how they handle life combined with these unfavorable circumstances are what inhibits them having any impact at all on life's progress. In other words, the more the human relies on the functioning in the lower centers of their being (*chakras*), the more they are helpless to use them as the creative doer, the circumstances begin to rule over them completely. The more the human uses the consciousness of the higher centers, the more they have the power to act and create more favorable circumstances for themselves.

Each category is the doer (*aham-kâra*) on its level of functioning. In that way, *manas* or the mind that is identified with the body (*indriyâni*), under the influence of *aham-kâra* creates its own reality which is in interaction with the objective world. It is a well-known experience of an alienated individual in the world surrounding it in which it is forced to function. It simply means that we are the creators of our own experience of alienation and conflict with the whole, and this experience is as real as we imagine it to be with our bodily mind. Only when we ascend to the higher centers of consciousness, do we finally overcome the bodily mind and reach one 'I', or the complete personality. When we integrate ourselves in the *aham-kâra* category, we can overcome all the categories of existence that are beneath it, and only then do we know that we are the doer that creates, not only our individual reality (*indriyâni*), positive as well as negative, but all the modalities within the objective existence in all the dimensions (*tanmâtrâ* and *mahabhûtâni*). ***This is possible because the whole existence is an emanation of the divine Spirit. That is why we have the ability of divine creation. We alone project the reality we are in, in this and that world, as well, in life and after our 'death' (not always individually, many aspects of the reality we also project collectively, as a group of souls that incarnate together, hence, there are common factors of the reality that affect all the people). It is only the issue of what level of consciousness we do it from. Such will be the corresponding consequences.***

Nothing in nature is static or substantial, everything that is formed in it must be deformed, or better yet, transformed. The very form is the initiator of transformation, it is information for further transformation. Hence, the number of discrepancies in the human personality, they are the densest core of the general transformation of nature. In *aham-kâra* two opposing principles intersect: a downward principle which divides and individually forms everything, and upward principle which unites and heals everything individual for the higher category, *mahat-buddhi*, for the cognition of the whole. ***The principle that divides must be at the same time the principle that unites.*** This cosmic intersection is the strongest in the personality of humans: when it faces downward, it disintegrates in pain, and when it turns upward – it is healed in everlasting bliss. This is the exact reason why *aham-kâra* is personality.

2. A complete personality[51]

---

[51] I use the term personality in a somewhat different meaning than usual. It is customary to translate this term from the Greek notion *persona*, which represents a mask somebody puts on their face to perform a role. In this way, it represents the false 'I'. The personality that is the issue here is associated with *personification*, so that the person in question here is the embodiment of something higher. When humans become the embodiment of the divine consciousness and when they have one true 'I' within, when they are aware of themselves in the absolute sense, they are, then, the embodiment of this authentic awareness of themselves and shows their true, complete personality, their true face, and not a mask or *persona*. In the following text it will be clear that such a complete personality one can become only after an arduous work on

The overall transformation of nature has its supreme quality, power, and dramatics in humans, in the form of their personality. *Aham-kâra,* all by itself, expresses intelligibly as a whole and complete personality. As such it is known only to a smaller number of people. The majority, however, have their personality split into a myriad of I-entities that come about through a spontaneous principle of individuation on *indriyâni* realm.

Owing to the functioning of *aham-kâra* every life form, not only humans, can be the subject of experience, albeit incomplete: a unicellular organism, plant, or mammal. The inorganic realm participates in the general experience of the world, although passively, through a pure reaction or as a medium. The organic realm responds through learning and cultivation, and for this reason, it surpasses inorganic (with its quality, not quantity). Since organic life comes from inorganic, it acquired its experience of the world first through the inorganic world and its beings. The principle of *aham-kâra,* as the creator of everything shaped, firstly proclaimed itself through them, through gods, always outwardly or in some objective way. The most direct and stentorian was through The God of The Old Testament who identified themselves with "I am who I am" – which loosely translates as *aham-kâra* also. The reason as to why the same principle of objective creation humans should, according to the instructions of religious pioneers and mystics, be established within, like their personality, by surrendering to the "will of God", by harmonizing with it, is that humans should integrate the inorganic and organic realm in their own experience.

It is natural that in the early stages of human maturity the general principle of creation manifests outwardly, not through a myth only, but in a concrete epitome whose function is to teach people. Jesus Christ (Jmannuel) is the best example of this manifestation, he is the most beautiful model of the perfect human and personality, his message points in the direction of integration that is the issue here, in *aham-kâra*; his words, that he is one with the Creator, clearly speak of his unity with *aham-kâra,* the principle of material creation. His activity also points to the active principle that is a characteristic of *aham-kâra.* Unlike him, Buddha with his

themselves and transcendental experiences which the false and split personality can never begin to have.

appeasement in complete freedom manifests the integration of a higher category – *buddhi*. Hence, the name. The symbol of Jesus is a cross which represents *aham-kâra*, because in it, in complete personality, the final differentiation of the consciousness and existence takes place, for the first time *Purusha* and *Prakriti* begin to intersect properly and discern one from the other. Buddha's personification is meditative calmness, hesychasm, and annulment of oneself for the benefit of the one that engenders everything (*Purusha*). That is why Buddha is devoid of symbols, and is, instead, represented with themselves, with the human (*Purusha*) in meditation.

When the sum of all organic abilities finally forms humans (in legends, they were the ultimate creation), then all the experiences crystallize in I-experiences (lat. *Ego*). This is still not *aham-kâra* but its product or reflection on the subjective realm, *indriyâni*, in *manas*. 'I' is the supreme form of cohesion of the psychophysical energy one subject is capable of in its natural life. It is not a product of cultivation but raw self-preservation instinct. If, as such, it is continued to be nurtured and maintained, a conflict and fierce struggle with the other I's and subjects who do the same is inevitable. 'I' is only a psychological reflection of the different kinds of life processes, and because of their differentiation, the psyche that establishes them becomes split, accordingly. The experience of different outward forms, following the same analogy, generates a multitude of inward I's. Like all the happenings, the one in *indriyâni* is no exception, this one is not static but dynamic and procedural, and the cohesion (into I) does not restrict itself to one form only, but it learns to transform and divide itself into a myriad of entities. All humans in their empirical experience are composed of many I's. Their number is inconspicuous only because all of these processes belong to the same being and use the same energy for forming themselves, maintaining, and focusing attention or presence. It cannot be noticed until much later, upon consequences, when we did what was not our original plan, or we did what we had not initially wished to.

Since every entity in nature exists as the pyramidal structure by itself, the human psyche, too, can be split into a multitude of outward phenomena. The more it attaches to the outer impressions the more it keeps dividing itself. That is how the onset of schizophrenia happens. Each 'I' that gets activated in a person instantly creates a conviction that it is absolutely real. That person then begin to think it is their only identity and their life will fall through if they lose it, they think they will die. Each 'I' was created through the centripetal attraction of the universal energy of the being. Although 'I' is only one of its aspects, the human fails to see that. Due to the holographic character of the being each 'I' thinks itself to be the whole being. That is why humans who are identified with it seems that its activity is the only possible one, and its disappearance immediately signifies death. They do not even see that such convictions change over time. In nature, death is not possible, only a perpetual transformation of energy and state of consciousness regarding the energy in question. The only death, and together with it the birth, is the one that happens to the individual 'I'. And that is why only under its influence do humans kill and commit evil acts, because they are under some illusion that they eliminated "somebody" and saved "themselves". The survival instinct, limited to 'I', is the cause of all of this violence and suffering. The one who sees the unity of the whole existence cannot commit evil acts; they cannot even have such intentions. The one who is with the absolute being has no 'I' of its own and knows they are much bigger and better than any 'I'.

Differentiation into the individual I's, which in *manas* happens under the influence of the universal process of *aham-kâra* individuation, is a necessary process in the differentiation of experiences of existence and consciousness. Each 'I' is a mode of beingness and without the richness of their interaction, there is no maturing of the consciousness. A multitude of I's on the subjective side is analogous to a multitude of existing forms on the objective one which we perceive to be the world. This is a way in which the world reflects itself in the subject. When this experiential mirroring reaches a "critical mass" (the crisis of the meaning of existence) a new phase of maturing of consciousness is reached that leads to the complete personality, to *aham-kâra*. Humans, then, see that each individual aspect of existence, either the outer or the inner (I), is part of the same whole that creates them all. This wholeness, the creator of everything, even the human personality as such, is *aham-kâra*.

Subjective experience cannot be any other way but split and out of balance. To the degree the subjective state (*indriyâni*) is overcome, the principle of individuation in humans crystallizes and facilitates the permanent presence of the consciousness, the one that is no longer changeable and unstable like before. With the steadiness of the consciousness, a unique and permanent personality in humans are born, through the insight that the energy is universal and the being itself is not only his. Only when the entire psychophysical being (*indriyâni*) fills with consciousness, energy overflows and moves upward, toward *aham-kâra*. For as long as the energy is being wasted on the split aspects of the being, enough cannot be accumulated to actualize *aham-kâra* as the principle of the universal personality. Split aspects are everything that is outward for humans, either organic or inorganic. What unites everything is within humans, in *aham-kâra*. With the cognition of the futility of searching for sanctuary in anything that is outward, humans turn inward, toward themselves, toward *aham-kâra*.

When it is aware and actualized, *aham-kâra* is the core of experiencing the world, the experience that exceeds the division into subject and object. Since *aham-kâra* is at the same time the creator of the objective world, by attaining its level all the subjectivity of *indriyâni* realm is overcome, that is to say, the objective world stops being alienated and opposed to the subject. The powerlessness to act a subject once had, now disappears. For the first time, they get the power to act of their own will (*siddhi*).

Aham-kâra is in its potential form always present in humans as the principle of integration of all of their experiences into 'I'. That is why humans can only have their personal 'I', and their individuality (they may, yet they do not have to). In incomplete *indriyâni*, in animals, there is no personal 'I' in the individual body, but the principle of individuation works on the level of the whole species. Every cat, for example, cannot be anything else but will show its character always like any other cat. Although there are minute differences in character within each species, they are not that often and far below the standardized traits that mostly occur as a result of different experiences. Wild animals tend to be of the same character, only domesticated animals seem to develop certain characteristics. Each animal species has been determined upon collectively, while the plants do not even have individuality on the level of the species, but a large number of plant species only exhibit the ability to adapt to the environment and survive. All the plants have one 'I'; they are different in shape which is also defined by the conditions of living and ways of subsistence.

Every formed entity can also be the subject of experience, from a cell to a galaxy, human beingness does not have to be whole, but fragmented, instead. Many people act incompletely in *indriyâni* and, as a result, they lack their personal 'I', but have it on the level of the species, like animals, or on the level of the tribe, nation, race, tradition, or some other patterns of objective conditioning and forming the subject. The more they are unevolved as individuals, the more they will follow the laws of any authority, especially collective, i.e., outward (religion, politics, or nation they belong to), as well as the inward (some psychological or psychotic contents, or convictions).

Owing to cultivating the principle of individuation, only humans are equipped with psychological and personal experience of the world. In everything else, in the whole remaining nature, they manifest as the sheer transient form of phenomena – only in the human's personality the form is experienced existentially, and because of it the experience of the world becomes as concrete and trustworthy as the world itself. In the human's personality, nature relates to itself in the highest possible way. Every outcome or meaning is resolved on this spot. In all the lower forms (on the scheme, picture 1.) it was getting ready for facing itself in *aham-kâra*. This confrontation is rather dramatic, hence, the psychological impression is of the same character. It is possible only when the subject objectively participates in events as though they were their when they personally experience them as their own. That is why the translation for *aham-kâra* can also be "I am a participant". Humans take part in life because it empowers the presence of the consciousness. The more consciously they takes part and face hardship, the better they become aware of the principles of natural phenomena, and by doing so they see that it is something where they will never find their stronghold. Instead, they should overcome it through objective understanding.

Personality matures to the degree humans do what nature has not done, the level to which they find the limit of natural necessity.

The one who refuses to fight and take part in life the way it is, hard and repulsive, who fails to defeat imminent doom while staring death in the face, will experience that life will simply discard them, and they are left to vegetate and die. (This is the reason why it is said that God does not like lukewarm or insipid people.) Humans will have no good events in their life if they fail to participate fully and accept it for what it is so at to overcome it in their soul – which can always be done irrelevant of the circumstances. Only when they accept full responsibility for their actions, actions that engender the presence of the soul's consciousness that makes life possible, they become human and overcome death. Only then the soul begins to communicate with their mind, and only then do things of vital importance begin to happen to them. Up until that point, they are a mere faceless natural organism whose only destiny is death.

In *manas*, the human's participation in events was being developed, but on the mental plane only, as various reconsiderations and an attempt to envisage the problems from all aspects. In *aham-kâra* the same reassessments and experiencing are raised to a higher level, to a dramatic event and action of the whole being.

In the human's personality nature attains its peak of psychophysical relationship and experiencing oneself, and that is why in *aham-kâra* a fine illusion takes place that the human soul (*Purusha*) is a participant in the phenomena of nature and not the fact that it is nature itself that does the transforming and matures to be worthy for the full presence of the unconditioned soul.

What is the bond between the wholeness of a personality and participation in the phenomena, i.e., action, which encompasses *aham-kâra*? The core of the personality is identity, which is possible as action only. Identity is the type of action that has become aware of itself. However, action entails constant change and transformation, whereas identity requires stability and safety. This is a contradiction. To overcome it spontaneously a byproduct will occur: 'I' or the instant awareness of oneself. 'I' is an attempt to bind action with identity, to preserve identity in action which is constant change. 'I' is therefore a virtual experience of the identity undergoing a perpetual change. Ego or 'I' is virtual reality.

Aham-kâra represents one 'I' or the complete personality. What is the nature of one 'I' or *aham-kâra*? It is that permanent and constant existence in us. The states of the being and consciousness keep changing all the time (awakened state, dreaming, deep sleep without dreams, affective states...), but they all take place within ourselves as the pure existence, **we always exist through all the states we find ourselves in.** This experience of the very existence is the pure or transcendental consciousness. Like a blank canvas, one projects a film on. In this metaphor, the film represents all the contents that constitute life as we know it together with all the states of consciousness, and the canvas is that on which all of this can happen, what remains the same while the contents of the consciousness and life projected onto it alter at all times. We take part in these contents as though they were ours, and when we cognize reality of the contents of phenomena, we cognize our difference from ourselves, from our Self. Hence, the name *aham-kâra*. *Aham* means 'I am' and refers to the always existing, which is what we are, and *-kâra* refers to the participation in all the possible phenomena as well as additionally generating all the possible phenomena.

In *aham-kâra* nature attains its maximum integration as a preparation for the necessary precondition for the awakening (*buddhi*) of the soul (*Purusha*) in the body. Only a completely integrated and complete personality can be awake at all times (*buddhi*), the same way that, on the other hand, the pure consciousness can survive only in complete presence and participation, and not in the impersonal or split one. The human personality is the embodiment of the wholeness of phenomena and humans, being complete, see that all phenomena are formed only to create them, with everything flowing into them. Nothing is alien to them. Nothing is outward of them, nor is it inward because everything that is outward – is inward. He sees that in the entire nature there is no mistake, everything is perfect and it is the only way it could be, that universe would not exist, at all, if the slightest occurrence were any different if anything wrong ever existed. He sees that everything matures and integrates toward its perfect image going through various phases, in the organic experience (*indriyâni*, the physical body) and the inorganic domain (*tanmâtrâ*, astral body, posthumous experiences, reincarnation). Only a complete personality sees that it loses nothing if it transits from the organic to the inorganic realm (from 'life' to 'death'), because it is familiar with both, nor will it gain anything new when it appears on the physical plane from the superphysical. He sees clearly that each soul inevitably reaches its goal, that nothing was ever lost or in vain. Only in a complete personality does nature recognize itself as complete, above good and evil, birth and death.

In all its forms, through all the beings, people, and events, nature transforms and moves every single moment to its most complete embodiment, towards the complete personality, as the pure good – although it is always different. It sees the permanent behind every change and transformation, which is the existence itself that cannot be any different than it already is: whole and perfect. That is why nothing is ever at stake, and everything must travel along its path of development and maturing through a spectrum of all the experiences until it is mature enough to become the embodiment of the whole that created it with its own perfection. When they see all those beings, humans are in a positive mood and accepts everyone with love, especially unaware sinners, because they see their being, they do not pay attention to the contents of their illusions.

The general lack of balance and inconsistency of life, caused by *gunas*, finds its balance for the first time in *aham-kâra*. Only a mature personality sees that all the dynamics and overall transformation belong to the whole and will never upset it by doing evil. Mature humans are good and allow for things to be as they are, they do not perturb them because they see that everything is moving toward its outcome. They allow being to be what it is all by itself, they do not adjust it to their wishes, they assist it along the way. By accepting things as they are in a laid-back manner, humans contribute to their own transformation and growth.

If there ever were any mistakes to this growth, there would not be the completeness of nature, or its corresponding embodiment in the complete human personality, like in a mirror. If any form of phenomena contained within any hint of wrong or evil, if it were not the way it is – there would be no shape, or even nature itself. What is wrong cannot keep; destructive creations or existence are not possible.

However, phenomena are this way only from the standpoint of *aham-kâra*, a mature personality. From any other, incomplete viewpoint, events are chaotic, mostly wrong or evil, the world is neither whole nor perfect, nature is inauthentic, not the way it "should be", consequently appearing destructive. Naturally, the only destructive point here is that of the perspective, or the attitude of the seer, and not the nature itself, because, if it were, there would be no seer, to begin with. Nature is like a wheel, and the position (ontological status) decides on how its phenomena will be experienced. If humans themselves are complete and centered in their Self, then they will experience the phenomena of nature from the center of the wheel of its rotation and they will see a harmonious whole all around – because the human Self is none other than the center or pivot of all the nature's motion. If it is not well-centered, then they will not be in the harmonious center of the beingness nor in unity with it. The more they deviate off (their) center, the more their life will lack harmony, balance, and be under the influence of the centrifugal force of time which leads to havoc (entropy). If they happen to be on the very verge of the phenomena – which means identified with the objects and time – the wheel of life will constantly run them over. Humans should be complete so as to be able to acknowledge completeness, impeccable perfection, and goodness of the existence itself. Because, if it were not so, humans would not be able to exist, at all. Therefore, only in the perfectly integrated human personality the world truly begins to exist as it is. There is no other way.

3. Will or intent

Only a complete, that is to say integrated, personality has a will of its own. Up until that moment it was not in possession of its will because various I's were fragmenting it and each one was pulling it to a different side.

All *Prakriti* below *aham-kâra* on the scheme is the field of pure causality. Only in *aham-kâra* there exists a power of free and new actions to do as one will. For humans, this means their second birth. People who are naturally conditioned, it means the prevailing majority, live in *indriyâni*, until they reach the stage of *manas*. It resembles an egg. It exists in this world, but the bird has still not been born. To be truly born, the bird, this ancient symbol of the human soul, must do something else, it must break through the shell and leave the egg. This means that humans were not born by their mere physical birth; it is nothing but impersonal natural reproduction. They have yet to be born of their own will and consciousness to overcome the field of natural reproduction and necessity – which the body is, *indriyâni,* and everything else that is underneath *aham-kâra*. That is the purpose of resurrection.

With this willpower, they displayed while smashing the illusions of the conditioned nature under *aham-kâra*, and being truly born as a new, liberated, and complete personality, they receive the power to act, which no naturally existing humans can have.

The power to act, will, or intent as the expression of *aham-kâra* originate only with the integration of the subjective and objective *Prakriti* realm (according to scheme 1.). How does this happen in practical terms? Humans become familiar with the objective, inorganic realm, not through scientific research only, but through concrete movement within it, once they leave the physical body using their astral senses (*tanmâtrâ*) and begin to know the higher dimensions of nature, the astral realms. They learn to move and act of their own will and intent. In this way, they overcome the state of sleep in which they generally found themselves in the astral realm before when their behavior was only natural and spontaneous. They develop their power to act **by awakening themselves**, first in the astral realm where they learn to move and fly, to develop imagination with which they affect the processes of functioning on the physical plane. In all these ways they learn that consciousness is the ultimate creative force in the universe; that nothing happens without a conscious intention.

Once they are in full command of the *indriyâni* realm and begin to rule the whole of the inorganic realm, and all the dimensions integrating both the organic and inorganic, subjective and objective *aham-kâra* domain, into one 'I' and a complete personality – then they learn to be the master of all the elements, they gain the power to act much bigger than their organic aptitudes which is: *siddhi*.

When in their own perfection, like in a mirror, humans acknowledge the purpose of beingness, the destiny of all beings, the perfection and beauty of all the life – then they can exist only through pure love and forgiveness. It is only an expression of will or intent. Merciful love toward everything that exists is the only measure of this second birth in *aham-kâra*. Having realized that nothing in the entire universe happens but the unity which gets fully actualized only through their enlightenment, humans experience only love that accepts everything that exists, forgiveness, and reconciliation with everything – because they see clearly that everything that exists has already formed them as a personality. It is not possible to find fault with any human being, we see that they are only an expression of one whole, *Prakriti*. To see everything as one whole means to be conscious, awakened, which ultimately means that everybody else is unconscious, that they continue to sleep and do everything like in a dream. How can anyone be blamed for anything? The very notion of "somebody else" stays in the sphere of unconscious beingness, it disappears for an enlightened one in the state of wakefulness (*buddhi*). 'I' and 'others' exist only below *aham-kâra* - in *aham-kâra* there is only one 'I am' in everything. When we experience our 'I am', we have discovered *aham-kâra*.

Understanding and acceptance of everything that is, of each being, each event and occurrence, together with all the opposites, here and now, represents a road to transcendence. Always when we accept something for what it is, here and now, we overcome (transcend) it, and in our soul, we become higher, broader, and more aware of it. That is the secret of religious submission by accepting everything as God's will. It is, apart from contemplation, an additional way to reach the experience of transcendence. Such experiences are always accompanied by the feeling of love, the kind of love that resembles a state with which a parent accepts activities of their own child, and as a result, God's will was, in one way or another, always equated with love. It means that love is yet another word for overcoming the previous, lower, and limiting state, or the experience of transcendence.

Only experienced humans realize that at any given moment everything is exactly as it should be and that it could not have been any other way, everything is in place, there is nothing wrong with the whole. Due to the holographic nature of the universe, the tiniest thing and occurrence are equally important as the greatest, as the whole universe, because every 'segment' is an expression of the whole and contains the whole within. Since things are always as they can be at a specific moment in time, they do not resent anything and accepts everything the way it is with nothing but the deepest respect. This, however, does not make them passive toward the ongoing phenomena, but only realistic, only from such a perspective can thing be seen as they are, without projections and psycho-mental distortions. If something appears as bad, then it is only a fragment of a necessary process toward wholeness, the process that belongs to the whole which in itself is the absolute good. Things appear as imperfect and evil because we do not see the whole, the entire process; we see an episode, not the whole series. Similarly, when we watch a single finger, it may seem incomplete, while the human's entire face and body radiate full meaning and beauty. A face in the photograph, captured in a moment, does not seem to show much, however, when we become acquainted with their character and life work it radiates the full meaning. Or, if we through a narrow slit of a certain partition observed what was going on over on the other side, we would catch a glimpse of undefined fragments that suddenly appear and disappear, in some cycles maybe, and if the partition were removed, we would see the whole picture and only then would we be able to work out the context.

Since things are the way they are, the world before the eyes of mature humans always creates itself as new each and every moment – because now they are one with the cosmic principle of the momentary creation of everything, *aham-kâra*. This is how they see that everything moves and can never be identical in two separate moments: each moment is created a little differently. Since everything is new, simple-hearted, and innocent, is there any point in resenting anything? This also makes them independent of

252

everything because they realize they have nothing to hold on to. Independence of the world is the main characteristic of maturity in the human's participation in this world.

A complete personality is always in the center of the universe because it is its very center. It is the focal point of observation from which the meaning of every phenomenon in the perspective of the whole can be seen, all the observed details, like the water sliding down, fit perfectly into their place in a harmonious whole on which the whole of the cosmos rests on, without humans making the slightest effort in the whole affair. Their personality is complete because in it the overall spacetime shaping attained its meaning and perfection. Only when the being itself unveils for what it truly is, insubstantial, only then - a complete personality is born. The illusion of substantiality carries within the seeds of particularization, a division and confrontation of power, and, in reality, that is what it is based on. Completeness as such is only possible in the liberation of all the illusions of the being, but only once it is viewed whole, as single and without duality. Without a personality, existence is faceless, empty, pointless, and inhuman.

Mature people no longer need anything, and they keep on forgiving and giving. Their every movement is not their own, their deed is not their only, instead, the whole works through them. Such humans move perfectly gracefully and harmoniously, like the flowing oil, because they are whole, all the energy flows moving within them are well-tuned, and in harmony; they are like a ball, they are always the same in all positions and activities. They are always relaxed because they are fully complete and realized, there is nothing more to be done because they see that the whole does everything that needs to be done in every single moment. As it works through them now, they are tireless in constant activity, they are never passive or unfunctional, although they know they are not the one doing it. They always act directly and adequately, there are no redundant moments, and although they appear to do nothing at all, they attain the maximum with the minimum of effort. They know who the creator of everything is and that they are the mere embodiment of it, that is why they never attribute anything to themselves although they see quite clearly the responsibility for everything that is happening. There is a paradox in the truth that only with the proper affirmation of their personality do humans become selfless; only when they do what they want, can they realize that they are never the one who acts. This means that they are only the witness of their actions. As a soul, they only participates in the being in the form of a witness, and by their sheer presence instigates nature to purposeful actions and beingness. The more they are aware of their independence as the witness, the more powerfully they can make nature act on their own will.

For such a personality, who is an embodiment of the whole, there are no barriers between things, nor is there a separation between the events – it all merges into one. For them, behind every form or event, there is a clearly visibly unique universal energy, shaped into one cosmic principle of forming, *aham-kâra*, that constitutes their Self and resides within them. This energy takes on various forms of beingness, but when one becomes aware of it in the final outcome, it becomes the embodiment of love because nothing is created without love, and no one can live without love.

The complete personality becomes aware of this energetic aspect of the beingness. It does not exist any more through a thought or other psychophysical conditioning and convictions, the way humans from *indriyâni* level do, but only through personal will or intent. Only a liberated personality can have its will and act in accordance with it. Nature has seen to it that nobody can have their will and power to act as they feel like, unless they are complete personalities unless they represent the embodiment of the whole, where love is the only law of action. Only a completely mature personality can act in that it is always an expression of love, the expression of the whole that gives everything. It cannot have a different will but to support life and the maturing process leading it to make sense of everything – and that is only loving. For a complete personality, the world does not exist objectivistically, as an idea or a notion, but as the pure and direct event, one participates in, as the energy phenomenon, as something to love.

If it were not so if one's own will can be in the hands of somebody who is not a complete personality, the one that is not a holographic embodiment of the wholeness of the existence itself, the actions of such a person would be destructive to the point that they would ultimately put the whole nature in jeopardy.

4. Actions and non-actions of a soul that is a witness

Aham-kâra integrates itself maximally through a realization that the soul is a mere witness, and all the actions belong to nature only, whereas nature itself acts by being drawn to the consciousness of the transcendental soul.

For all the lower states of consciousness, especially to the reason (*manas*), this introduces a paradox and constant challenge. Humans do not act properly only for the reason that they do not utilize the consciousness of their soul properly, because the spontaneous functioning of nature is still too strong in them, and these two ways of functioning are not well balanced and equally conscious.

In *aham-kâra* we are faced with the issue of free will and its solution integrates successfully the *aham-kâra* category.

Nature has its pyramidal hierarchy we have analyzed across the dimensions. It exists as much in the microcosm as in the human being. The scope of functioning of lower and higher human consciousness is expressed through the psychoenergy centers or chakras. Lower centers act being more under the influence of natural causality and elements, whereas the higher ones are more filled with the consciousness, and automatically with more expressive free will. Therefore, no conflict between free will and causality exists in reality, but only their hierarchy, and the spectrum of the manifestation of both, initially, one prevails and afterward the other, like on the scales. It is the general problem of the functioning of consciousness as opposed to unconsciousness in psychology.

Humans affirm the consciousness of their soul by overcoming the spontaneous causality of nature. His soul is always an independent and transcendental witness of all phenomena, but it begins to participate in phenomena as the consciousness and will-power more and more. Its participation in the phenomena is expressed as righteous actions, as consciousness and conscience, humans become increasingly responsible for their actions acting more impeccably every single day, without outside intervention.

Firstly, it should be understood that the soul's consciousness affects all phenomena with its mere presence, the effect a magnet has on metal shavings. Nature would not exist if it were not for the soul's consciousness. However, this functioning is not only static, it is active in the sense that the consciousness takes part in the drama of events. When the inorganic realm of existence is the issue, functioning of the consciousness there is static, and as such, quite sufficient. However, in the organic realm events are not static but dynamic, organic life exists through action and movement, through functioning. The soul's consciousness must take part in it correspondingly. That is why in our lives, although the soul's consciousness is a transcendental witness, it also acts as an efficient doer.

The structure of the categories of nature shows that quite clearly. We can see that on the scheme *aham-kâra* is positioned between intellect, the higher mind (*mahat-buddhi*) which is the bond with the soul's consciousness (*Purusha*), as well as with all the organic and inorganic existence. In *aham-kâra* the soul's consciousness unites with the manifested existence which creates all the psychodynamics and karmic drama we experience as life. The more our actions are proper and aware, based on objective knowledge, the more we strengthen the influence of consciousness of our soul. Without such a consciousness we are at the mercy of the outward, natural influences and causality.

Conscience is the most important bond of the consciousness of the physical mind (*manas*) with the soul's consciousness. Conscience is fundamentally the awareness of the fact that our soul is an always present transcendental witness and attractor of the overall phenomena, hence, all phenomena must be proper and in accordance with the interests of the soul. Such functioning increases the influence of the soul's consciousness and strengthens free will as such.

As always, when there is not sufficient consciousness of the soul, humans are forced to act inadequately and inappropriately, based on insufficient information which they get from their senses and reason (*manas*). Then, very often there is violence, conflicts with the environment, with nature, and with other people who have different information or intentions.

Complete personalities know that it is not them doing the deeds, but the whole they are a mere embodiment of. Humans, who are limited to their little 'I', always think it is them who are doing all the work, which leads to many conflicts between people, because everybody thinks the other one is doing their thing, as well. Complete personalities differ from individual personalities, and they know who the source of action is; they act properly because they respect the source of consciousness and knows that consciousness and existence are deep down one and the same. A conscious complete personality knows that the consciousness and life in them are completely identical consciousness and life as in everything and everybody else, there is no multitude of consciousness, all the life is interwoven into one organic fabric. That is why they do not make mistakes in relationships with anyone.

On the true measure of action and inaction in accordance with the soul's consciousness, there are many ethical teachings, but, by far the best help comes from *I Ching*. It is a practical manual for understanding the relationship between the consciousness of the mind and the soul's consciousness, for translating the language of the soul into the language of the mind.

Aham-kâra balances itself out and becomes complete by measuring out these two opposites of action and inaction of the soul's consciousness, by crystallizing and strengthening the soul's consciousness in actions. Similarly to the balancing of scales *aham-kâra* attains perfect equilibrium once we sharpen our consciousness and the power to act in the inorganic realm as we have already done in the organic. Such awareness is attained by further learning and acquiring scientific knowledge, but it is not nearly enough. To truly become aware of the inorganic domain of existence we need to enter it, to know it in our body and out of our body, in the astral realm.

This is how we strengthen the soul's consciousness.

On the scheme of *Prakriti*, all the categories underneath *aham-kâra* constitute the manifested cosmos. In *aham-kâra* it all contracts into one, in "I am", for the first time, into the very principle of life. Thus, *aham-kâra* is the carrier of the principle of life or soul in the entire nature. Soulfulness is, therefore, identical with the complete personality, and vice versa, a personality can never be complete if it is not completely soulful.

The soul in nature is active via *aham-kâra* category.

Owing to *aham-kâra* category the universal soul's consciousness (*Purusha*) manifests itself through the individual souls in this world, through every man.

5. Jiva – an individual soul

The main characteristic of a mature individual is independence. It is obvious in the scheme where *aham-kâra* is placed above the emergent world. Being positioned above the physical body (*indriyâni*), means being independent of it. This independence should be understood properly because it is of vital importance as an introduction to the cognition of wakefulness (*buddhi*) and independence of *Purusha* from *Prakriti*.

According to the teaching of *Sâmkhya*, *aham-kâra* is the center of the "interior organ" called *antahkarana* and consists of the three categories: *manas*, *aham-kâra*, and *mahat-buddhi*. It is called 'interior' to be discerned from the ten exterior organs that show objects to the human using which they function in the outer world, those being sensory and action organs, *buddhindriye* and *karmendriye*.

Antahkarana facilitates the highest supersensory and intuitive cognition that is possible in nature. Although it is nature's creation, it behaves so independently that it can serve as a model for training and preparation for the "big awakening" in the absolute independence of *Purusha* (*kaivalya*).

When the "interior organ" becomes powerful enough to experience life fully, it starts to function with the prototypes of sensory organs (*tanmâtrâ*) and can be active in all the dimensions (*maha-bhŭtâni*) – because it is not attached to *indriyâni* (body) more than *manas* (the mind). It is then called *sukshma-sharira* or the "subtle body". It is the astral body that survives the death of the physical body, it crosses over to the objective realm and carries all the impressions (*samskaras*) of the accumulated experiences within, that will later serve as information for the birth of a new body and shaping its destiny. It also transfers the individuality into the inorganic, objective domain during sleep or astral projection.

Sukshma-sharira is an energetic form, and its phenomena are energetic by nature (*prana*). It is, therefore, called *jiva*, which means life, or the principle that determines life. *Jiva* is made up of a subtle medium that connects the subjective realm of experiences (*indriyâni*) with objective conditions, the prototypes (*tanmâtrâ*) of natural phenomena, through all the dimensions (*maha-bhŭtâni*). This connectedness gives meaning or soul to the phenomena themselves. In the West, this ostensibly similar principle in human form is also known as the soul. ***However, jiva is not the soul itself, but the most subtle creation of Prakriti through which the transcendental soul can act and be present in nature, in the body***. A soul cannot use the physical body directly, it is too gross for it, there must be some fine energy mediator between the soul and body. It is *jiva* that contains the astral body and all the subtle forms (sheaths, *koshas*) that are of *Prakriti*, so as to be able to exist in all the dimensions of nature together with the soul.

Therefore, jiva is the matrix a soul uses to create a physical body and function in it. Jiva is an informative-energetic matrix that is more subtle than the physical body and that is why it surpasses it. In western traditions, it is also known as the astral or energy body.

On the other hand, jiva is the most subtle energy-informative matrix Prakriti uses to submit to Purusha itself, that is to say, to the soul itself.

This property of *jiva*, its closeness to the soul and ability to function in the body as a soul, caused many erroneous interpretations in the works on Indian philosophy, falsely being identified with an individual soul.[52]

It is necessary for *jiva*, an interior organ which consists of three parts, to mature in the physical experience using the ten exterior organs which point to the objects and experience of functioning in the three-dimensional space. That is the only way for the soul to become the key doer in acquiring sanative cognition in higher dimensions of the astral realms. Liberated from the ten physical organs, which are present as one body only in the three-dimensional present, *jiva* via *tanmâtrâ* can function in all three times, in past, present, and future. These cases happen spontaneously when in sleep or ecstasy we learn of the future events or

---

[52] An example of such a wrong interpretation, identifying *jiva* with the soul, can be found in "Indian Philosophy", a work by Sarvepalli Radhakrishnan.

relive our past ones, or when in near-death experiences we recapitulate our entire life.

At the death of the physical body *jiva* completely detaches from the physical body and faces the objective aspect of *Prakriti* emanation, or, in other words, the collective conditions of existence of the entire huhumankind. It also carries with itself all the impressions of all the subjective experiences in the three-dimensional body it was attached to during its life via the reason (*manas*) which, although it survives the death of the physical body, cannot live too long without it.[53] Made up as a subtle (astral) body, from *tanmâtrâs*, *jiva* acts as a mold or prototype for the rebirth of the gross (physical) body back into the three dimensions. The subtle body is the role model for rebirths, the same way the principle of the identity of a personality in different incarnations is. *Jiva* engenders us with the memory of our past lives, helping us to connect the dots of our destiny into a meaningful whole. However, although it functions like this, *jiva* is not substantial in the same way that nothing is truly substantial in nature. It is not the same *jiva* as a singular identity that transmigrates from one body to another, but only information of former experiences that determines the forming of the latter. The soul keeps collecting the information, it gathers them using *jiva* based on which it projects a new incarnation. The reason for this lies in the fact that *jiva* does not exist substantially but only as information for the successive forming of the identities from *akasha*. The same way we see that on the surface of the water one wave moves rhythmically, although what we see is water rising and falling harmoniously, while, fundamentally, it remains immobile, in the same way from one body to another only information transmigrates and instigates the causal origin of the being. *Jiva* is not substantial because it is made up of three factors: *buddhi*, *aham-kâra*, and *manas*. This group of three supreme categories *Prakriti* gives to the soul, or *Purusha*, as the ultimate consumer, all the information on the existence of everything else that is on the scheme below them. The informative continuity of *jiva* during the course of incarnations is possible only because of the presence of the soul. It stores information of the old *jiva* for form-

---

[53] On a more detailed description of mental conditioning of *manas* (the mind) after the decomposition of the physical body see "Tibetan Book of the Dead".

ing the new *jiva* in a new body. Preserving the informative continuity on the part of the soul is of vital importance for the completeness of personality and the meaning of existence. *Continuity is identity.*

The subtle body of *jiva* (*sukshma-sharira*) is also called *linga-sharira* or the "mark body", or designation of the character of the beingness. *Linga* is an experiential entity and has a body much like the physical one because the experience it represents is formed according to the three-dimensional pattern. Each history of life has its mark (*linga*) and for as long as there is causal conditioning of the experience of beingness of nature, there will also be *lingas*, or new incarnations.

It is very important to understand the difference between the essential and existential character of *jiva*, it is the key to understanding *aham-kâra* as the principle of forming and the wholeness that happens instantly and successively from *akasha*, and not as a separate being that is born and moves through space. Different modes of the wholeness of the being are the ones that are born, move, and act, and not the being itself. The entire existence is one gigantic information energy field, and not a plethora of objects moving about through space. Objects are a mere illusion of our successive perception and interpretation of information, and not their true existence and movement through space. The world always looks to us the way we perceive it. Only owing to ubiquitous *akasha* or aether that forms everything instantly, *aham-kâra* can always be accessible, omnipresent, but also an independent principle of wholeness.

Although the principle of individuation as *linga-sharira* always survives the physical body, it also depends on the maturity of the experience and is not the same in all cases. Its status depends on the presence of consciousness, memory and experience of being. Like all other products of nature, *linga* is determined by *gunas*. *Tamas* prevails in it when it exists the animal form that does not have all organic aptitudes, or in primitive people in whom they are not properly implemented or ripened, mostly due to the excessive use of one at the expense of others. Then *jiva* incarnates with incomplete organic abilities (*indriyâni*) as some animal.[54] In those lower incarnations of *jiva* the soul does not reincarnate to the same measure as in a human form, but to a minute percentage, barely enough to maintain the informative continuity, i.e., the principle of consciousness.

If *rajas* prevails, it means that *jiva* has learned to fully participate in all organic abilities of life and function like a human individual. Then it incarnates in human form again where it participates in the battle to overcome the opposites and suffering that they cause. ***Only in a human form does jiva become the complete bearer of a soul***. A personality can always decline into lower forms of being, into *tamas*, if it does anything to jeopardize the maturing of its experience and freedom of action. Not only to itself but other beings, as well, because in the absolute sense, in the holographic universe, there are not two beings but only one, and nothing is divided or lost in it. The evil we do to 'others' we do to ourselves first. The essence of evil acts is in preventing somebody from actively participating in the experience of beingness, in restraining the freedom of complete functioning of *indriyâni* with which the participant matures as an individuality (*aham-kâra*). Humans deteriorate to the point they obstruct or take the life energy of others, and make no effort to give something of themselves for the benefit of all.

Sattva is typical for *jiva* which is now fully mature for the presence of the soul, representing the one that has taken on itself the responsibility for the overall experience of the being, and the one that has reached its outcome, the pure consciousness, the existence itself. Only in a fully aware soul, the existence acknowledges itself as the consciousness, which is unique in everything. Only in cognition of this kind can a soul, *Purusha*, be finally liberated because the divine consciousness is always present. The idea of *bodhi-sattva* corresponds with the *sattvic* aspect of *jiva*. Gnosticism strengthened *jiva* through dreams and out-of-body experiences for

---

[54] On transmigration of the soul into animal bodies see Plato in *Timaeus*, 90a-92c, and in *Surya-gita*. The latter one specifically stresses dog as an example of an animal that is born out of a human soul that sank into sin and debauchery. Maybe as a result of its instinctive memory regarding the past life dog is so attached to the human, as his 'best friend' – but also man to dog.

humans to learn of their independence from the body and find a way out of the negative influences of this world.

Jiva, as an informative entity, becomes the most complete in the *sattvic* aspect. It gets to this point through evolution after many incarnations in its non-organic and organic life alike, during which it accumulates the experience of beingness from both spheres, and the awareness of the being in general. This experiential consciousness crystallizes in *manas*, or the mind of the most experienced and complete being: the man. Once it matures sufficiently through the lower incarnations *jiva* becomes suitable for the presence of the human soul by embracing the soul's consciousness (*Purusha*). Therefore, **the human soul or Purusha does not reincarnate through the lower life forms to mature in experience (consciousness), but only the informative entity of Prakriti made up of the potentiality of the three categories (buddhi, aham-kâra, and manas) in their most elementary form. Only due to the complete proximity of jiva to the soul, Purusha, it seems that the soul (Purusha) gets incarnated from one life to another.**

This experience will seem real across the entire cycle of incarnations, to the complete self-knowledge of the soul and ultimate liberation, that is to say, till the cessation of the incarnation cycle as such.

The central spot for the accumulation of impressions of all the experiences is the human mind (*manas*). The mind – with its average human consciousness during everyday wakefulness – is the collection of all the impressions (*samskaras*) from all the life forms. *Manas* is the collective point of all the *samskaras*.

An informative entity that one ascertains the existence (experience) with in the grossest form is that of the mineral. Elementary *jiva* begins its evolution in the physical world on this spot where it only meets physical shaping, and nothing else. Prior to this point, it existed as the entity in the inorganic realm, as a non-organic being or an elemental of nature. Each informative entity must go from inorganic to the organic domain for the reason that only in the three-dimensional world a concretization of all the beingness is possible from all of its dimensions – in the form of *manas*. In the three-dimensional physical world *jiva* further on, from one incarnation to another, undergoes evolution as a unicellular organism, then multicellular in all the forms, first immobile (plants), and afterward, mobile (such as animals, for example), and following a set of evolutionary order that determines the ability of movement as the only way for gathering impressions (*samskara*) on the beingness and development of intelligence. As an arthropod, insect, mollusk, fish, amphibian, bird, or mammal – until all the impressions that can be collected by mere movement and struggle for survival are finally completed, *jiva* is born as a being that is the most completely equipped with all the sensory and action organs, to the measure that it is capable of using tools, such as humans are.

The purpose of the development of *jiva* is to finally arrive at the human form.

Once it matures in the highest animal form, *jiva* incarnates itself as the most primitive human form – and only then the law of *karma* begins to work for it. Those are generally people from the "primitive communities" with a pronounced tribal, national, and religious tradition. The same is found in the totem of tribal identity which represents the animal that, according to the legend, their ancestors originate from, but also a belief that the souls of the deceased transmigrate into animals, and incarnate as them. Outside such communities, the primitive human form is easily recognizable in either physiognomy or the general way of living which tends to revolve around hard work for physical survival, and ignorance regarding spirituality. Additionally, there is an evident physical and mental backwardness. Attachment of the primitive humans to impressions (*samskaras*) can be seen in the level of conditionality of their instinctive behavior, especially in habits (thoughts, words, and deeds), in how mechanical they tend to be, as well as their attachment to the tradition.

When the consciousness of an individual soul evolves through animal forms, it has only the capacity for the awareness of objects, but not of itself. This is why animals cannot change themselves (they do not have an Ego) nor are they able to correct their behavior because they do not have the freedom of choice and always do what the given circumstances drive them to. **When the soul evolves through human forms, it is in possession of double consciousness, of the objects as well as itself, and the entire human evolution boils down to transformation and perfecting the subject through the diffe-**

rentiation of objects. The human form is a transitional form from animal to the divine, i.e., to the spiritual. That is why there always are immature people who are more attached to objects and contents of their phenomena, as well as the mature ones who show a higher level of independence, psychic objectivity, and individuality. *When the soul finalizes its evolution through a human form, it completely transcends the world of objects and attains the triple consciousness: of the object, of the subject that is aware of the object, and of the transcendental consciousness that engenders both the subject and the objective world.* Its final awakening lies in the insight that teaches it what it regarded to be gross and unconscious forms are, in reality, pure consciousness, in their essence, they are divine and in complete submission to the consciousness as the only reality.

Only when it reaches the human body jiva becomes suitable to be the bearer of the presence of soul – to the degree the presence of pure consciousness, Purusha engenders it – since the consciousness that facilitates everything gives purpose to a human soul. Purusha is human essence. The human soul comes from the divine essence, and not from nature. Humans are in possession of the human soul only to the degree they conduct and actualize the presence of the divine consciousness that engenders everything. Before this, only an informative entity *jiva* exists, as the principle of the individuation of *Prakriti* in animal forms, but also in many human beings who are immature for the complete presence of the soul.

Similarly, the way *Prakriti* projects its most subtle entities or *jivas, Purusha* also projects informative entities through the process of individuation with which it affirms the experience of existence in all the possible aspects and forms. These informative entities are the souls of all the people. Initially, they exist in the highest dimensions of *Prakriti*, in *tanmâtrâ*, as the archetype of a human soul, or the transcendental soul (oversoul). It descends to lower dimensions by splitting itself into several individual souls, and on each dimension, one individual soul is projected, and also on the earth. This individual soul that is on the earth, i.e., in the physical reality, is the one we are aware of now, the one we live in our body in this world with. Apart from it, we have other aspects of our soul that exist simultaneously in other dimensions trying out all the other aspects of happenings. There are seven in total because there are seven possibilities for each event. The chapter that answers the question of why there are seven of them is *Syâdvâda* (*Seven states*). This individual soul that originally came from the transcendental soul, *Purusha*, merges with *jiva*, the astral body, which is the individuation process of *Prakriti*. Therefore, humans are unique in that they represent a union of informative entities of *Purusha* and *Prakriti*. That is why humans have dual nature, they are capable of attaining divine heights and the bottom of hell, as well, and with those experiences, they crystallize the presence of the consciousness of their soul. Their ascension is, therefore, best reflected in rising above the natural conditioning of *Prakriti*, in overcoming everything that is physical, mechanical, and conditioning. Everything they have in themselves of the consciousness, goodness, independence, and objectivity comes from *Purusha*, from the soul. They would be unaware of all these traits were it not for the temptations of their opposites.

This uniting of *Prakriti* and *Purusha* through *jiva* is easier to visualize if we imagine *Purusha* to be humans and *Prakriti* the mirror that humans reflect themselves in to be able to see themselves objectively. For the informative entity, the human soul, to be able to fully express and affirm itself down to the physical plane, a corresponding form of *Prakriti* is required, an accurate image in the mirror. This reflection is *jiva* that *Prakriti* formed through a human body to act as a suitable form for the presence of the human soul. *Prakriti* formed its individual soul, *jiva*, into a body under the attractive pull of *Purusha*. That is why we can speak of *jiva* being a physical aspect of the soul (including astral and energy aspects that surpass the bodily form), its manifested and functional aspect, while the soul itself is transcendental and unmanifested in its essence. Much like *Purusha* whose embodiment it represents.

A natural property of *jiva* to reincarnate and move on, in a human body, as well, creates an illusion with people that they, i.e., the human soul, *Purusha*, reincarnates, although it is unborn and independent of the whole *Prakriti*. This illusion exists because of the attachment of immature people, or souls to *Prakriti*, that is to say, attachment to its most subtle informative entity, *jiva*. Immaturity and attachment rest on the illusion that individuals as such exist at all, and not the fact that it is the absolute itself, and that only it exists. This immature attachment to *Prakriti* comes about as a result of not being able to tell *jiva* apart from the transcendental soul, and indiscrimination happens due to their proximity and similarity, as well as the common role they play in life.

There is an additional issue as to why we do not remember our past lives. First of all, we do not remember them to the point we are under the dominance of *Prakriti* and its conditioning, the level to which we are identified with the most subtle informative entities of *Prakriti*: the thoughts. Memory comes back to us when we work on ourselves and transcend the mind, thus enabling the presence of our soul. The presence in question must be actualized by humans, who were unconscious initially but have now become conscious. The soul itself does not need this; it is always what it is. It must become personal human experience. The process of individuation of both *Purusha* and *Prakriti* gets finalized in the complete human personality. The soul grows and matures, returns to *Purusha* whose emanation it originally was, only through what it becomes aware of and realize within itself as the personal experience and accomplishment of man. For such an accomplishment to be complete, the soul must approach it as though it were completely new, without hesitation. If the soul remembered its divine origin and its true nature, it could never completely take part in the process as if it were new, in such low and limiting conditions as the life on Earth provides. It would not wish to participate in any of it for a moment even. If it chose to take part at all, it would use the quality mental patterns for solving the problems, and not the pure consciousness – yet the very creativity of consciousness is the task put before the soul in this world, and not the cunning of the mind. All the contents of the mind are of this world. That is why, for practical purposes, a soul has been granted oblivion upon reincarnation in the physical body. It agreed to it voluntary, the same way it does everything else completely voluntary. For that reason, from the perspective of the transcendental soul, it speaks of this life as of a dream, that the life itself is a dream, and this world nothing but an illusion.

The soul must travel the entire path of its karmic maturation and must be given the right conditions for doing so, the right physical bodies in which to reside in accordance with its maturing, from the most primitive to the most sophisticated. People of similar karmic maturity live in certain social or national communities (this rule applies to the majority, but not to all people). That is why there are differences amongst people and nations that are necessary for the souls to have where to incarnate in accordance with their maturity and growth. This versatile level of consciousness calls for versatile experiences of the souls. Since the souls are bringers of the creative divine consciousness into this world, the principle of individuation governs over them. Souls are individual because the pure consciousness expresses itself always individually and uniquely. This ultimately means that different people and different nations must be in existence with a varying degree of conscious expression and temptation for the souls to have a place where to incarnate. It is a big mistake to think that all the people and all the nations should live together and be on the identical level of cultural development. This attitude lacks objectivity regarding the evolution of souls and perfection of existence, as well as ignorance regarding the nature of consciousness. Differences among people must exist for the sake of karmic evolution and the nature of their consciousness. If we all saw this clearly, the existing differences would not serve as the reason for conflicts, but for the beneficial exchange of experiences and higher consciousness, instead.

Once the soul commences evolution in human form, it still continues to gather impressions (*samskaras*) in a much more complex way than in an animal being where its movement was merely horizontal taking care of the physical survival only. ***In the human form, the soul for the first time overcomes mere collecting of the experiences through the physical form in its struggle for surviva, and begins gathering impressions through the drama of life, through all the contents of existence, through karma.*** Animal incarnations of *jiva* are spontaneous, unconscious, and automatic making the lives of animals relatively innocent without the desire to do harm, since they are not given the choice to do evil. They do not have *karma* (because they do not engage in work). The real drama for *jiva* starts in the human form. It reincarnates in the human body as many times, from one life to another, and one body to another, until its experience of the beingness matures through the temptations of the opposites of all kinds and forms that there are (happiness and unhappiness, good and evil, perpetrator and victim). Until the moment it matures in the most subtle details of experiences of existence through the drama of life experience, the soul is karmically tied to the various experiences of beingness, to the objective world, and this bondage can never be broken from the outside, no good intentions do the trick, until the soul itself wears them out with its consciousness and maturity. When it gets tired of all the experiences and becomes aware of them as the unique field of causality, something that does not become it even, the soul for the first time turns to itself, to its center - *aham-kâra*. Its being for the first time becomes vertical (although it is physically predisposed for that already, with its upright posture). It, then, starts to uplift to human essence by overcoming the body (*indriyâni*) it utilized up to that point for gathering impressions and ascertaining the beingness, and it moves from the visible to the invisible, from the sensory to extrasensory, from the being to spirit. The objective world at that moment loses its appeal, and the being turns toward its Self, toward *aham-kâra*, which is always awake as the pure consciousness (*buddhi*), or the outcome of existence in freedom (*Purusha*). In other words, it releases all the impressions (*samskaras*) it had been gathering up to that point.

It is crucial to understand that setting oneself free from *samskaras* and karmic bondage cannot happen until *samskaras* have gathered sufficiently to accumulate the "critical mass" until the experience of the beingness becomes fully mature. Then, liberation comes naturally, like a ripe fruit falling to the ground. Any denial is, therefore, a mistake, all it takes is to make the experience of the beingness more conscious. ***The very presence of the consciousness intensifies and accelerates the experience of beingness, it speeds up the time of the soul's maturing***. What an inert soul must experience over several incarnations and too much suffering, the soul that works on its own awareness can achieve in a matter of years. Not the same nature of gross experiences, naturally. The consciousness raises the quality of experiences to a higher dimension, contracting the overall process. Consciousness is above all the dimensions of nature, and when we stick to the consciousness, we exist in higher dimensions in which spacetime contracts into one. The very nature of higher dimensions is the contraction of spacetime and that is something that speeds up the time and subtlety of experiences in the being. Time itself does not accelerate, but only a change of the dimension in which we are experiencing time as such. That is why we need to cling to consciousness, and then the experience of the being and time will accelerate and disappear.

The truth is that from the perspective of the transcendental soul, or Divine, this entire emanation of the cosmos and individual souls and their evolution through the mineral, plant, animal, and human experience, happens neither in time nor space. It is all an instant act of imagination of the Divine. All the souls are one in the Divine itself, and all the aspects of experiences of the consciousness of souls are already present all around us as well as in us as the mineral, plant, animal, and human forms of beingness. All the worlds originate at an imaginary moment. The present moment. The illusion of individual souls is that their existence happens over eons of reincarnations. This projection of time is a dream created by *manas* or the mind. It only looks that way from the perspective of the mind. *From the perspective of the soul, it is an instant, imaginary act that has, therefore, never happened. A timeless divine soul, as the awareness of the absolute existence, is the only reality, here and now, and everything else is an illusion. Since this is a simple fact, enlightenment, as such, is always possible, and nothing else but awakening is necessary.*

Likewise, from the perspective of the oversoul, there is neither a young nor an old soul. All souls are equal, and they are one regarding the outcome of the divine outcome. What we see as a young or old soul is *only the percentage of participation in the physical part of the incarnated soul, which depends on the level to which the soul has advanced in the cycle of incarnations, in acknowledging the overall existence as the divine consciousness.*

The expression 'young' or 'immature souls' refers to those souls that are beginning the incarnation cycle, and the expression 'mature souls' refers to the ones that are ending it.

If the oversoul is, in fact, the whole soul, the part that gets incarnated is considerably smaller, and the smaller it is the more immaturely it expresses itself. A growingly bigger part of the soul gets incarnated (something we recognize as the older and more mature) resulting in the individual becoming complete and responsible for all its actions, taking conscious participation in its life, recognizing everything as segments of its own being. Or to use the words of *Bhagavad Gita*: to the point it sees itself in everything, and everything in itself. For the soul to be mature, time is not required, it does not grow or mature like a tree, linear time exists only for our mind, in *indriyâni*, not for the soul. The soul in the physical world matures in the presence of the consciousness. The more consciousness the more soul. It works irrelevantly of time, hence, automatically. The presence of the consciousness is engenderd through spiritual culture and the practice of awareness, through meditation. Maturity of the soul, therefore, relates to the consciousness, objective understanding, and conscious participation in events, and not the time process of maturing of the soul itself. The soul is as mature as it is well-equipped to participate consciously in life in this world the way it is at any given moment and retain itself as it is, independent of this world's influences. Only in this manner can it conduct the divine consciousness in this world.

In this manner, the oversoul descends slowly and gradually to the physical plane in the form of a personality. This gradual descending we are able to acknowledge as a mature soul. When the whole soul learns to manifest itself or, at least, to know itself in the body, then, we see God-man or Avatar before our eyes.

A karmically mature humans are no longer tied to life, to the world of objects trying to attain some goals in it, they are capable of recognizing the consciousness that engenders everything even in the most inferior and worst aspects of existence – this consciousness they recognize as its transcendental essence, as well.

Only meditation can lead humans to such maturity – meditation as the awareness of existence through the awareness of the one who is being aware.

6. Seven phases of an awakening of a complete personality - *aham-kâra*

Once the personality becomes conscious and complete, mature enough to act on its own will (which is harmonized with the will of the divine consciousness), humans become independent of the physical body. There is no mature personality that is not inde-

271

pendent of the body; only through such an experience the personality becomes mature – there is no other way.

It (*aham-kâra*) is mature and integrated to the degree it accomplishes its actions in *tanmâtrâ* and all the dimensions, as well as in *indriyâni*.

Because, **aham-kâra is the outcome of both subjective and objective beingness and, and to be what it is, it must be actualized in both realms: in the physical and astral realm in all the dimensions.**

The essence of maturity is psychic objectivity, it is based on independence in the way *aham-kâra* overcomes *indriyâni* and *tanmâtrâ* according to the scheme, and the simple interaction between subject and object that is naturally in play between them. Without overcoming *indriyâni* cognition is only subjective and limited.

Gestalt psychotherapy and transpersonal psychology are based on these facts, but they are well-defined in the teaching of Bhagavan Sri Ramana Maharshi. There is no ideal of human perfection in the history of spiritual culture that is limited to *indriyâni*, to the body only, instead, everyone has always pointed to the transcendence of it. If there had been any, they certainly were not spiritual ideals.

Since the principle of individuation (*aham-kâra*) is on the scheme above *indriyâni*, it means that the human's personality (*aham-kâra*) is independent of the body, which is not a mere metaphor adapted to the scheme. The experience of detachment from the body represents the actualization of this fact and not its objective creation as a novel state.

A complete personality does not create such independence, it becomes complete by acknowledging its independence as a real state.

The bigger the illusion of identity with the body, the more we experience our authenticity as the separation from it.

However, we do not separate from the body, but only from the illusion of our identifying with it. We never were just the body. The body is the biggest illusion we have ever had, a very limited form of existence, and by empowering *aham-kâra* through *tanmâtras* we only expand our existence.

272

Because of the illusion that the physical body was the only way of existence we identified with, becoming acquainted with other ways of existence seems like exiting the body. The illusion is so strong that it all looks very real to us, so we will focus on that.

When we relax in our sleep, the illusion of identity is no longer there, we have completely forgotten about it. Then, the principle of individuation (*aham-kâra*), which together with the thoughts and consciousness (*manas* and *buddhi*) compose *jiva*, leaves the body, and freely moves about as an astral body (*linga-sharira*) in subtle superphysical dimensions (astral). It naturally and rhythmically moves from one location to another, from organic to inorganic, with the changing of day and night, our physical wakefulness, and sleep. This natural process needs to be made aware of and used for the actualization of the consciousness in both realms equally, in order to actualize the personality, to make it authentic and mature.

Therefore, the life of the soul, *jiva*, will become as actualized and strong as we complement it with the conscious experience of the objective domain. It is immature when it plays itself out only in *indriyâni* realm, the individual consciousness is incapable of surviving in those conditions, it finds independence of the world of senses and their activities hard to tackle. Such life is reduced to what Freudian psychoanalysis discovered, to expressing instincts and their psychodynamics. Unlike Freud, Jung's process of individuation (the affirmation of *aham-kâra*) presupposes familiarizing oneself with the archetypes, which is the realm of *tanmâtrâ*. The only way to overcome the subjective and incomplete experience of being in the body, and liberating the soul from sensory limitations and assorted actions cause by them (*karma*), is to apply to practice this objective overcoming.

It is done in seven phases.

The preparation for this sevenfold attainment consists of awareness of all phenomena of *indriyâni*, of everything we do with the body and mind (*manas*), during the day when we are physically awake. Awareness will purify and harmonize the energy flows, which constitute events, to be cleansed of the affective accumulation centered over an event or experience, because it leads to one-sidedness and bondage regarding the experience. Each accumula-

273

tion of energy is too overpowering and disrupts its circulation and growth. Awareness of *indriyâni* is attained through meditative practice (*vipassana*), and we shall get acquainted with a method here that complements the practice of meditation.

It is recapitulation. All the life experiences belong to *Prakriti*. If we identify with them, we will die together with them, we will take impressions of this life into the next life. By recapitulation, we introduce the objective consciousness into life, and in doing so we create differentiation or discerning ourselves from all phenomena of *Prakriti* we have identified with, **we return them to Prakriti** because they were all its phenomena, to begin with. In that way, we become aware of our true nature, our transcendental soul, and its unconditionality. We actualize our essence through the insight that nothing that was happening to us in this world is ours: it is all nature taking its course. We are the mere witnesses of such phenomena, the conscious subject around which everything revolves, the one life exists for. Life has attained its purpose when we ascertain it with an objective, pure consciousness. By becoming aware we return to *Prakriti* what is its. The physical body accumulated all the impressions like a magnet. Only what belongs to the body will die, together with all the impressions, and we will remain independent because we have already detached from them in recapitulation. This whole process happens spontaneously at the death of our body, we relive or recapitulate the whole life in a very brief period of time. It happens for the same reason, for us to liberate ourselves from the identification with the world of events (*Prakriti*) and go back to our original state of unconditionality (*Purusha*) we have come from.[55] If we do it consciously during our presence in this body, we clear the path for the divine consciousness of our soul to enter this world. ***The purpose of our life is to conduct and actualize the pure divine consciousness of our soul, that we have between lives, into this world while we are still in this body.***

Recapitulation is done at the end of the day, before bedtime, we recapitulate all the events we went through on the day in question, we go back step by step, from that moment until morning, to

---

[55] This represents the contents of the Egyptian "Book of the Dead", although its original title is called "The Book of Going Forth by Day". It details the ways in which a soul recapitulates all its deeds during its lifetime.

274

the moment we woke up. In the morning, after waking up, we should use the same method to rewind the memory of the events of sleep. By doing so each morning and evening, we reconstruct the previous day and night, our activities in awakened state and sleep, to be able to create continuity of consciousness. It is very important not to focus our attention on anything, on specific events to judge them, no matter how exceptional they were. All the events must be viewed neutrally and equanimously, as though they happened to somebody else. The truth of the matter is that they happened to somebody else because our soul is independent of everything the body does.

It is very important not to judge anything that happened and get ourselves involved in the contents of events. It is of crucial importance for two reasons. The first one is that the consciousness, once it is completely neutral, is much deeper and clearer. The second reason is that only an objectivity of that kind will set everything straight in us, it will clarify what needs clarifying. It will be hard for us to do things wrongly and be slaves to bad habits in the future if we neutrally become aware of them every day. It is all impossible under the light of the objective consciousness. Things that are bad and wrong can only be done in the dark of unconsciousness.

Most people go to bed and get up in the morning in a highly unconscious and ugly way. With animals, this process is far more conscious and ultimately finer. Sleeping is the other half of life humans needs to become aware of and relish, so as to become a refined and cultured individual entirely.

1) The first phase toward the complete integration of personality (*aham-kâra*) consists of the practice where right before falling asleep we keep our focus on this process, we should be fully present when this happens when astral visions start to absorb us. We should remain present in ourselves when the breaking moment of falling asleep happens when we enter another dimension. We will do this best if we induce this process ourselves. The way to do it by completely relaxing the body (as though it were not ours) and focusing our attention (inner look) on the point between the eyebrows. Then we will fall asleep instantly. We will fall asleep like the stone falls into the water. We should also remember the position of the body we had on entering the sleep phase and remain constantly conscious of the entire surface of our body, particularly the back. It is all done in complete relaxation and restfulness, it is meant to be a way of release. At that point, we should allow astral visions to take us to sleep, otherwise, we would not be able to fall asleep, at all. Therefore, the first phase consists of becoming aware of the very moment when we fall asleep and establish control over it, in finding an ideal balance between retaining attention, active memory of ourselves, the current position of the body, and the very act of sleeping, on the one hand, and immersing ourselves in the astral realm streams allowing them to lead us into sleep, on the other hand. There never was such a balance in our lives before, the only natural occurrence was a spontaneous and complete capsizing on either one (wakefulness, *indriyâni*) or the other side (dream, astral). Since *aham-kâra* is in the middle and overcomes both extremes, through this practice we are learning to linger in between.

2) The second phase is waking up in sleep, on the other side, in the astral realm. It will come as a natural consequence after a successfully implemented first phase and becoming aware of *indriyâni* through meditation. Many people experience lucid dreaming at least several times in their lives, and they tend to be remembered as exceptional events, there are even such people with this innate ability who experience them often. Waking up in sleep or lucid dreaming can be enhanced with imagination and suggestion. Imagination is an activity so typical for the domain of astral we enter dreaming. We can use suggestion to modify any dream we feel like, some situation, or a special event. One of the easiest ways is the suggestion that we will see our hands in sleep and remember ourselves instantly, using that as a cue to wake up in a dream. This suggestion we will have to repeat to ourselves several times a day, even better is to do it every hour. Then, we should stop, no matter what we were doing, and look around ourselves as if we were in sleep, then raise our hands to the level of our eyes, feel them, and say clearly to ourselves that we know we are in a dream (although we are fully awake). If we go on repeating this, this suggestion will surely play itself out in the dream and that will help us to wake up.

Firstly, they will be dreams where we once too often see our hands or do something with them, until the moment it happens that we remember ourselves, and our intention to see the hands in our sleep. An obsessive desire to wake up is the fastest way to lucid dreaming.

It will be of great help for us to maintain a belief throughout the day that we are in a dream and nothing physical that happens around us is real by itself, instead, it is only a dream in which we are the only alert and careful observers. This conviction will be automatically transferred to our sleep. If we managed to pull it off, we would always be awake in our dreams, we would create an interval (*vairagya*) from all the illusions and permanent independence. Additionally, if we start experiencing lucid dreams, our movement in everyday reality, in the physical body, will be like moving our energy body in the astral realm, very conscious and mindful. If we are in everyday reality, especially at the moment we enter sleep (the first phase) being fully aware of our energy body and ways to go about it, it will prove to be the most important assistance for waking up in the astral realm. The intention to realize the energy body in the pure experience can be reduced to our sincere conviction that with our whole being, especially when we enter sleep, we already have it, we have already accomplished the task. Indeed, we have, we have only not fully become aware of it. The point here is not in achieving something new, but actualizing something that is currently potential, but already existing.

Being relaxed is the main factor of awakening in sleep, as well as in everyday reality. Relaxed independence from the emergent world gives wakefulness, and not some concentration, as it were. Concentration lulls us to sleep with the one theme more than distraction with multiple contents ever could.

Dreaming is easily programmable. We can become aware of all our psychic problems in lucid dreams and work them out by familiarizing ourselves with the psychodynamics of the individuation process. They also offer extraordinary adventures and fantastic experiences. By knowing them directly, we rid our world of the fear of death once and for all, and all the insecurities that closedness into a narrow physical experience of life generates, the insecurity and ignorance caused by a plethora of pseudo-religious and psychopathological convictions, all the doubts and conflicts. Only when we are outside of the body can we experience the greatest joy of life, humans feel far more complete over there than in the physical world making the return seem like a decline into something inferior and less worthy. A stay in the higher dimensions of astral provides an upsurge of energy for us. Humans are far closer to their soul then, especially since there are fewer obstructions by the physical body.

When we find ourselves awake in our dream, it is almost the same like on the physical plane, only in a different, parallel world, all the prototypes of the sensory organs will automatically be activated (*tanmâtrâ*), the mind (*manas*), the principle of individuation (*aham-kâra*), and consciousness (*buddhi*). It means that perception and cognition will be present, much more than in the physical body, but our movement and actions will be passive, or more precisely, they will be conditioned by the prevailing circumstances. This conditionality refers to our attention the most which is considerably narrowed in the astral realm, and less to the movement which is significantly easier than on the physical plane. The movement itself is easy, but the will that decides on it is very weak. The movement of the second phase is up to the circumstances, our decision is of no importance, although the circumstances appeal to us so suggestively that they all seem to be our call. It is an illusion. The movement of our own free will is something we experience only in the sixth phase.

This phase is characterized by intense experiences with non-organic beings. They will come to us in various and most unusual ways: as people, things, animals, or something completely different. They can be recognized by their weirdness or the powerful impact they have on us which is mesmerizing and often not pleasant. Their presence on the physical plane can be manifested visually (a rare, but very convincing occurrence), or as a sound, and some physical sensations, too. They can appear in a number of ways, humming in our ears, sometimes singing divine music to us, various sound messages, even unusual noise, and an explosion in the room where we sleep, much like New Year's fireworks, as it were. (I had an experience of this kind, I do not know if other people go through the same.) We can hear them before falling asleep, there-

fore, when we are in contact with astral. They can also find themselves in the state before wakefulness and sleep producing physical
sensations such as a sudden twitch of the whole body like it was
exposed to a (painless) electric schock. It is probably their touch.
Their presence during those moments when we are approaching
the sleeping phase can be manifested in flashes of light we see with
our eyes closed. Or we can see them briefly near us with our peri-
pheral vision, out of focus, as shadows or beings of unusual shape,
in those moments between sleep and right before we open our eyes.
Additionally, a frequent experience with the non-organic beings
many people have had can happen during the night when we suddenly experience sleep paralysis, when we are unable to move as if
some force were keeping us down sapping all of our energy. It does
not last for long but is extremely uncomfortable.

In the astral realm, their manifestation is a lot more versatile
and most commonly visual. Sometimes they look like they are fool-
ing around us, but their goal is to attract our attention – because
they clearly see what we do not: that we are the most complete beings in the whole of natural order, but insufficiently aware. As if a
prince happened to walk into a poor village and the homeless are
trying to kiss his feet.

We can establish contact with the messenger and speak to
them. The messenger is the intelligence of this inorganic world,
that strikes up a conversation with us when we consciously enter
its realm. Due to inorganic conformation, no organic individual is
needed here to express the cognition of this world, it does so via
this whole domain. This intelligence speaks to us in the form of a
voice by our left or right ear, it is hard or irrelevant to ascertain
whether it is male or female. It may come all by itself, or it can be
summoned. Since this is an informative field, everything that is
uttered in a loud voice acts as a command and is automatically realized. Very often this communication happens via our thoughts,
but then we do not pay full attention to it, we are not aware of the
fact that our thoughts are not ours, but messages of the objective
world to us, to our subjectivity. (Nature designs itself. In the astral
realm, we can experience that as a voice we communicate with, and
on the physical plane thoughts of nature we regard as our own.
When we consciously enter the astral realm we can see more easily

that establishing thoughts of anything and everything is not something we do, instead, nature establishes itself through our 'I', while on the physical plane because of the higher degree of inertia the same thoughts we assume to be our own.)

Dialogues with the messenger can be quite interesting, on the condition that it is not some mockery on the part of some non-organic beings of the lower dimensions. *It is crucial to know that those voices, more often than not, come either from the demons who are trying to possess us – astral is their kingdom – or from audio microchips installed in us during one of the alien abductions and mind programming we are currently unaware of.*

Astral is very dangerous because too many entities reside in it who feed off the energy coming from the organic beings, of which humans are the most complete. All the deceptions humans can be exposed to come from astral. The advice is that one should stay in it as short as possible.

Although we can learn so much from these dialogues, this knowledge is no bigger than humans can have themselves. In the astral realm we can trick ourselves with all kinds of "knowledge" and then our illusions will manifest before us like in a mirror. Everything is revealed there, all our subconscious energy tensions (affects, complexes, convictions) have their objective embodiment we become faced with in an extremely objective way – which carries the maximum risk. Astral is the mirror of nature, there is nothing evil in it. The question of good and evil is only a question of constructive or destructive energy input the consequences of which manifest objectively. In the astral realm everything manifests objectively, and for this reason, we are most commonly unconscious within it, like in a dream. We have learned to be only subjectively conscious in the physical experience, in *indriyâni*. Consequently, the psychic objectivity we can attain by becoming aware of astral experiences, of sleep, which helps us overcome the identification with the body.

Many appealing promises and invitations by the non-organic beings can arise, we are offered to listen to them and cross over to their world. We can do this by identifying first one such character in our immediate surroundings, which is relatively easy to detect because they are unusual and inappropriate regarding the place where they are. For example, some animal in the room, or some object that is out of place, that does not even look familiar to us. What we should do then is to point a finger at this apparition or speak in a loud voice to be transferred to the world of non-organic beings. In an instant, we will find ourselves there and it will be a completely different world, unlike the astral we have previously known. It may resemble a spaceship whose walls are highly unusual, alive, and fully conscious of our presence. We can find ourselves in the dark with very unspecific shapes surrounding us, also conscious, with a very pleasant mood. Those are realms where humans do not belong, and they must not stay there for long no matter how pleasant the overall atmosphere is because they will stay trapped. It is a trap for absorbing our energy. The world of the non-organic beings is the ultimate astral realm, it is the pure astral in which there are no creations inspired by the physical experience (*indriyâni*) and our unconscious like is the case with dreams and lucid dreams alike. It is the world completely independent of the earth plane.

The energy is accumulated in *indriyâni*, and when individuality is found on the completely different side, in the astral realm, there is an imminent danger of losing it. In the astral realm, humans must keep the coherence of their beingness shaped for them by *indriyâni*. No matter how well-acquainted with the astral they are, they must not disintegrate within it.[56] It is a good idea to

---

[56] Carlos Castaneda in his book: "The Art of dreaming" very picturesquely detailed that man's energy form resembles a giant egg or a ball, with a point of special light (assemblage point) on the back, between the shoulder blades, that corresponds with *manas*, i.e., the focus of preception. When an individuality (*jiva*) conveys *manas* (assemblage point) into inorganic domain (*tanmâtrâ* and *maha-bhûtâni*), the energy form of man undergoes a change. It becomes like a smoking pipe, and is no longer egglike. The tip of the stem becomes assemblage point, and the bowl of the pipe is what remains of the luminous ball. If the assemblage point keeps on moving across the inorganic realm, a moment comes when the luminous ball becomes a thin line of energy. Suddenly, the cognitive abilities expand to unparalleled dimensions, they practically become limitless, but together with them, humans are in danger of losing his human form. It is all movement within *Prakriti* which can result in being totally absorbed in it. Man's task is to know *Prakriti* that composes him, but to keep his uniformity in order to become the embodiment of spirit, *Purusha*, that engenders the whole *Prakriti*. Man should never forget that they are the embodiment of the transcendental consciousness that overcomes everything because it engenders everything, and

visit this realm as rarely as possible and leave it to entities that naturally belong there. It is important not to be absorbed in it. On the one hand, a stay in it has a healing effect, its pure energy dissolves (recycles) all the subjective psycho-mental distortions in the human's energy. After a visit to the world of the non-organic beings, humans experience energy completeness that tends to last for days, they are purified and blissful. On the other hand, going there is as dangerous as it is useful fundamentally – if we do not have enough control and composure. If we lose it, this mythological 'world of gods' turns into full-blown schizophrenia, with a clinical diagnosis. Only a completely integrated personality, *aham-kâra*, can transfer completely to the inorganic world. An insufficiently mature personality mostly experiences various shapes and transitional states that linger between *indriyâni* and *tanmâtrâ*. If it were to find itself completely on the other side, it would lose the little integrity it managed to attain in *indriyâni*.

After an initial introduction to the astral realm, the practitioner would do better to reduce their astral episodes to a simple upward movement, as high as possible. It will help if they breathe air in their astral body (although there is no air in there), and catapult themselves up. By rising they will reach higher astral and mental levels, they will surpass them and enter the *tanmâtrâ* (hyperspace) realm. That plane is safe for humans to be in because they are far closer to themselves there, and is also off-limits to the non-organic beings and their manipulations. It is more useful in the astral realm as well as the whole *Prakriti*, to be moving vertically upward rather than horizontally wandering about on the same level.

The inorganic realm can be divided into different dimensions, according to *maha-bhûtâni*, and its residents are made up of one element each that corresponds with the given dimension. It means they are incomplete and one-sided. Humans are the only complete being in nature, and this completeness is something they must not lose by attaching themselves to incomplete beings no matter how divine they appeared to them initially, all the more knowing that they show a great interest in them and present them-

---

they would do better to stay away from finding an anchor in any of the *Prakriti* phenomena.

selves as gods, due to their inferiority. The universe is teeming with unusual worlds, it is a nice experience to visit some of them, but to know all of them in their entirety is impossible. With an intention like that, we would only lose ourselves in objectivation – which is a road opposite to the realization made by humans, a road where they would lose themselves in objects.

Humans are a microcosm and their mission is to know themselves to be able to transcend their subjectivity, which is something one should always keep in mind while facing outer situations and objects, in both the physical world and astral, too. The reason why they are faced with so many tasks is to know and overcome their subjectivity in vertical uplifting, and not to lose themselves in identifying with objects which are always horizontal, regardless of the fact whether they are on earth or "in heaven". His goal is independence which they should experience and empower in everything they go through in their physical and astral body.

Much like everything in *Prakriti*, astral is an illusion to the human soul that exists to exert pressure and crystallize the soul's consciousness, which is also the most subtle illusion in nature. By practicing wakefulness in the astral realm, we rehearse more than ever independence from the illusions and dreams. In the astral realm, we need it more than anywhere else, since in those worlds there are such powerful entities that, like hunters, search for their food (energy), and who are life-threatening. One should simply turn away from them and come back. It can always be done if we keep in mind where we are and refuse identification with the phenomena, we take nothing of the objects or clothes on us, nor do we go anywhere from the starting point. By remembering our body position when we fell asleep, it will be easy for us to return. Otherwise, these experiences tend to break off on their own because the attention and mindfulness cannot be maintained for long. Then the lucid dream turns into an ordinary, unconscious, dream or we are returned to the body immediately.

The second phase is best intensified if we manage to practice to transfer from one dreaming phase, in which we are, to another one within the same dream, keeping alertness at all times. This is how we exercise the continuity of consciousness. It also may happen to us that we dream we have woken up in our room and start getting up, not once but many times over. To progress to higher phases, it is imperative that we stay away from non-organic beings. If they show up, we should not engage in any kind of interaction with them, at least not of permanent nature. It is of vital importance that humans maintain their power of making decisions in the astral realm to avoid falling under any influence, no matter how divine they looked. When they show up, the best thing to do is to point a finger at them and ask to see them as pure energy. Their form will then turn into a medium-sized luminous figure that radiates energy, weaker or stronger, depending on the being we are faced with. If it shines too brightly, it is best to immediately run away from there.

For the second phase to be practiced as well as possible, to prevent the lucid dream from breaking off, we should know that it can be maintained by rapid eye movement from one object to another, in constant motion. If we focused on something and then stopped ourselves, the dream would be interrupted and we would find ourselves in the physical body. On the other hand, it is also important to practice those new objects and activities with their associations do not drag us away into the oblivion of ourselves and our lucidity, to make sure we do not lose focus because of the new contents. If we happen to lose it, it will become an ordinary dream from then on. Movement of the eyes is important because it happens in the physical body during the REM phase of sleep. Of all the physical organs, eyes and brains are the finest and, consequently, the closest to energy phenomena, with their instant response to them; the brain with its specific wave radiation activity during sleep, and eyes that respond to the phenomena of the energy body with rapid movements (the whole body also reacts with occasional movements during sleep, but eyes do it always). They move fast because the energy phenomena in the astral realm are different in terms of time, they are far quicker than those of the inert physical plane. Therefore, to remain conscious in the astral realm, we must adapt to its higher fluidity and a different pace. Movement of the eyes is of great help and alternating the focus of attention, with maintaining awareness and independence from everything.

During the experiences of the second phase, in the astral realm, the truth is that we cannot be perfectly awake. When we are awake, the astral realm disappears and we return to the body. Nonetheless, we manage to keep some level of consciousness and enough mindfulness which would allow us to familiarize ourselves with the astral realm. The very word says it all: it is a lucid dream, hence, still a dream, although we are aware during the lasting it. To remain in the astral realm a little bit longer, we must take active participation in such a dream. That is why our behavior is often out of the ordinary and childish there.

We begin to be awake only in the third phase, and fully awake in the seventh. As the whole chapter illustrates, wakefulness is accomplished across the seven phases, and only in the second one we deal with the astral realm. It poses the greatest challenge on the path to awakening, and only the one who masters it may move forward to true wakefulness.

3) The third phase will come as a normal consequence after we have exercised well the second. After our return from a lucid dream, we will often be aware of the moment of our astral body entering the physical, how we as a spirit drown in our physical body. This moment should be used by avoiding any physical movement which will engender us to take our astral body out of the physical. It is already "well-tuned" and needs a little encouragement only. If we make even the slightest move that morning, we would not be able to exit it and the physical world will prevail. The easiest way would be if we took our arms out first. Then, we can clearly see the physical arms by our body, but our arms we will not feel in the physical arms, but above or beside, as though we had four arms where we can only move and feel our astral ones, while the physical ones appear to be like somebody else's. Astral arms are invisible then, but they have some cohesion, we can see and feel every strand of hair on them.[57] The energy body is the exact copy of the physical, but it stands invisible next to it, in the physical plane. Only upon entering the higher, astral plane, it becomes visible as the astral body, and at the same time, the physical body becomes invis-

---

[57] The identical experience happens to people who have lost one of their extremities, the so-called phantom limbs. They feel their arm or leg they no longer physically have. It is not an illusion but a proof of the existence of the energy body.

ible for it. The energy body is physical in the physical world and in the astral realm, it is astral, while in the physical world during the projection outside of the physical body it is invisible – and can be visible as a double only in the fifth phase.

After we learn to take our arms out we can exit with our whole body and stand up next to our physical body. It is the third phase in which, for the first time, we see our physical body quite objectively, the way it is – as something that is not ours, as something that is neither the only body we have nor our permanent property. From that moment onward we become double, we will never again be identified with it, and spirituality will become our only destiny.

In the third phase, the key problem is mastering the movement of our energy body. There are no more astral movies to occupy our perception. We learn to act with our pure willpower – which is the basic characteristic of an integrated personality. It means we must overcome all the previous habits of movement we gained in the physical body under the influence of gravity and the strength of our muscles. This kind of movement is conditioned by the three-dimensional linearity of the flow of time and its causality. The energy body moves regardless of the causality and time, it moves at will or intention. It means that the new position of the energy body is achieved by its direct intending or through a direct placement in the intended position, without the old linear movement toward it. For example, getting up from the horizontal to the upright position happens as a result of the pure willpower in a matter of seconds. We will be prevented from this to the degree we still try to move in the old way, with the characteristic movements while getting up, leaning against our hands, and making an effort.

In this phase, when we are watching our physical body, we can see a link that connects the energy body to the physical. It comes out of the solar plexus, bluish in color with a neon shine about it, about half a centimeter (0.2 inches) in diameter, but for the further few centimeters, it has a gentle silvery glow the thickness of which can be felt if we catch it in our hand, like a cat's bristly tail. This luminous rope floats around and extends or shortens itself to suit the purpose, depending on our intention whether to come close or step away from the body. It is visible only when the energy body is on the level very near the physical plane. Incidentally, the level of dimension in which the energy body resides can easily be altered in beginners, they can effortlessly transfer themselves to the astral realm of their room, and then they will not be able to see their physical body.

The energy body can detach itself slightly from the physical so that inexperienced humans fail to notice even. Unpleasant experiences are likely to occur at this stage because the tiniest separation of the energy body causes the physical body to become stiff, but not painfully like in a spasm; it simply becomes petrified. Humans then try to move it at all costs, but cannot rejoin the energy with the physical body. Panic and fear may follow.

Other energetic phenomena may also happen, such as seeing light and sound, buzzing in the ears, or nape of the neck. They are all manifestations of clumsy and partial exit of the energy body from the physical shell. They disappear when the energy body manages to come out of the body completely or when it fits back into the physical body. Some other unusual problems may also occur. My problem, for example, was that for a long time I was able to pull out my arms and legs with ease, but the head was very complicated. This all happened when I wanted to stand upright next to my physical body. It was easy for me to stand up with my eyes closed, in the dark. If I stood up like that, with my eyes closed in the energy body, very soon I would find myself in a completely different astral outside of my room. Everything would, therefore, go back to phase two. However, if I opened my eyes, I would find myself in either the physical body or split in two places at the same time: I would feel myself perfectly clearly whilst standing in the room and touching objects around it, while from the lying position I would stare at the ceiling with my physical eyes wide open. I resolved this by discovering breathing to be the key to operating the energy body. During inhaling, it uplifts easily from the position of lying down. Breathing is a purely energetic phenomenon and we can use it for moving the energy body in the initial stages. Additionally, to move the energy body, willpower is needed which is practiced through being able to maintain it during the second phase, in the astral realm, by mastering control and changing situations as you see fit. Willpower is the key because the physical body attracts the energy body like a magnet. This attractive force is not particularly strong but still overpowers the inexperienced beginner.

The third phase can be practiced during the day, outside of the sleeping process. If we remembered well how the energy body fits into the physical body on our return from lucid dreaming, and then how it pulls out again, we can sit comfortably laid back in an armchair being completely relaxed, and start to dose off enjoying our selected imagination, and by doing so, after mastering the first phase, we could use our nap to consciously exit our energy body from the physical. To be able to pull this off, it is important to have a strong conviction that it can be done, that our soul is independent of the physical body, something which is acquired through lucid dreaming, returning from it into the body, and the repeated exiting. This type of exercise should become a regular practice for us to be able to advance onto the remaining phases.

Practicing how to move our energy body is the most important process in the integration of *aham-kâra*. It denotes actualization of the action realm of *indriyâni* (*karmendrye*) in *linga-sharira*, completion of the energy body by participation of the complete subject in the inorganic realm and intervening on it. Up until this moment, the presence of the subject on astral was incomplete, it was mostly to do with perception (*buddhindrye*). When it extends to action organs, *karmendrye*, it becomes complete. That is why *indriyâni* domain is divided into two parts, the organs of perception (*buddhindrye*) and action (*karmendrye*). To master perception and action in the astral realm we need practice, and that cannot happen straight away.

We can move energetically across the physical world outside the physical body and without the whole of the energy body, as a look that moves, i.e., only with the astral prototypes of organs of perception (Remote viewing, RV). It can be fun like voyeurism, or espionage, but is completely useless for perfecting other phases of awakening. When the energy body becomes fully functional, with both the perception and action organs, influences of the non-organic beings cease to exist, if they show up at all, it will only be from a higher level, to convey an important message, although, this is a phase when humans for the first time in their life learn alone

288

and directly because for the first time they act on their own free will.

Perfecting the movement of the energy body is, in reality, a crystallization of personal willpower. Only a strong personality can move the energy body. Up till then, humans were carried by the outer influences of nature, now for the first time, they learn to move freely, of their own will. It can never be learned by relying on any outward factors – drugs included. They can provide astral experiences, but they will never teach them to be an active doer in those experiences, even less so will it assist their maturing into an independent personality. He will inevitably become a victim of a psychedelic circus of astral apparitions who, no matter how miraculous they seemed, are always futile. It is only the second phase.

One of the main difficulties one has to overcome in the third phase is that the energy body, the name says it all, is full of energy. That is why the first experiences of moving the energy body resemble carefree playing of a healthy child who has not been out in the open for a little too long, everything draws its attention, and the movement as such is so easy that it is hard to control it at will. The energy itself is movement, consequently, the main difficulty of the third phase is to learn to control it, to gain the right speed, ease, and fluidity, in attaining directness and simplicity, in the consciousness.

4) The fourth phase consists of expanding the possibilities of moving the energy body. In the third phase, it was done only while exiting the physical body, observing it, and moving in its vicinity. In the fourth one, a more detailed energetic property of things and events we see around ourselves should be investigated, and more exercise should be invested in perfecting the movement. In this phase going to other places that exist physically is practiced, remembering certain details, and afterward, upon the return into the physical body, we must go there and check if everything was genuine, if our observation within the energy body was credible or we wandered off to astral levels. During such movement, the energy body is invisible to other people, but also for us, although we can perfectly feel that we have the same form of our body. With an energy body like that there are certain influences we can exert on people and physical objects, for example, moving them, but with the full engagement of our willpower. Shamanic tradition recognizes this practice only too well, especially when it uses it for affecting things and phenomena far away, for discovering hidden things, and particularly for possessing other beings.

It is very important here to stress that the physical body must be protected at all costs during the projection of the energy body. While it is abandoned, some other energy entity might come inside it. Shamans are aware of this, and they perform certain protection rituals, they keep the location where they do projection a secret or they do not do it alone, like the Tibetan lamas who do it with the presence of their teacher or another lama that safeguards the body. Aside from this danger, there is also one more. If somebody else touched the physical body during the time the energy body is projected away from it, it could prove to be dangerous. It happens due to the fact that the energy body takes most of the life energy away with itself (let's say 90%), while in the physical body only the necessary minimum for maintaining the vital functions remains (10%). That is why it is stiff because it does not have the necessary energy to move, it is pale and with almost imperceptible breathing. When it is in such a state, with very little energy, the body is very open to drawing energy which is, then, missing. If somebody who has their full energy potential touches it, an involuntary overflowing of energy may follow suit. Together with the energy, karmic information and influences always go hand in hand. It may be harmful and unnecessary. That is why the energy hygiene during out-of-body experiences must be maintained. This does not refer to lucid dreams, but only to the third, fourth, and fifth phases.

5) In the fifth phase the power to act using the energy body increases, it begins to show up on other locations and can also be seen physically. There are witnesses who can testify to this. In this phase, an even bigger influence can be exerted on the physical objects. Shamanic tradition is well-aware of this phase, using it in both the positive and negative way alike. According to the legends, the sorcerers (Benadants) and witches (Stregons) appear in other places often in a different form, like a cat, raven, wolf ... (more accurately, they possess the bodies of these animals to use them), or go to the "other world" to fight one another – Benadants to protect people and their work, and Stregons for evil.

It is useful to know that one may come to the fifth phase in a negative way also, without any spiritual interests. This ability may be innate, especially in people who were born within the amniotic sac. Black magicians and witches can also attain it, using it for their evil influences and stealing people's energy. However, they can achieve nothing more than that. Two last phases, the only ones that lead to freedom, remain out of bounds for them. The power they demonstrate and impose on others manipulating their free will eventually becomes the force that enslaves them. This is how things work in the holographic universe.

6) The sixth phase is the ability to fully embody our physical body from the energy body on some other location, and the initial physical body completely disappears from the starting point. It is teleportation or the complete physical transfer from one place to another, in an instant. This is the peak of the art of movement and cognition, which was growing in previous phases, a cognition that the overall existence is an energy that manifests instantly from space, that finds its outcome or purpose in the embodiment of personality and free will. Here, humans have completely mastered the energy body and their willpower in the permanent wakefulness or transcendental consciousness, the consciousness of unity. Then, the whole the existence of the universe is our body which we can form from ubiquitous *akasha* wherever we choose. The energy itself (life) is our identity and conveying information for its contraction and formation into a physical expression is only a matter of our willpower and conscious decision.

We were born physically only because we did not know how to do this during our life, consciously and using our own will. When we learn how to do this, the consciousness of our soul becomes so powerful that the need to be born again in the physical body stops. It can manifest physically any way it wants to, without the painful births and growing up.

We have mastered the energy aspect of beingness in the fifth phase to such a degree, that any influence by the inert physical body has been overcome. The personality here decides on the physical manifestation of being, and not the other way round like is the case with unevolved individuals. Their decisions are very limited, and they resort to technology and science for making them. Therefore, the more that humans reject their authenticity and taking responsibility for it, by accumulating energy through the positive cultivating of the phases described here, the more they must turn to technical solutions for the modification of the phenomena. After everything said and done, it is clear that humans cannot be saved by technology – and neither can they be saved by religion, which also puts emphasis on outward influence and authority. Personal self-knowledge is the only salvation.

The sixth phase is a complete affirmation of the fact that space (*akasha*) forms the being from one moment to another, according to the wave model of quantum fluctuation. This fact can never and nowhere be affirmed but through personal experience in a way described here. This kind of the reality of beingness surpasses causality and linear movement. This surpassing was beginning to be practiced in the third phase when the acausal movement using only willpower was practiced, and in the sixth phase reached its peak and full maturity. Humans participate in the creative process of forming a being from *akasha* to such a degree that they have every right to say: "I am doer" - *aham-kâra*. They can do so because they are perfectly mature personalities, mature in the sense that they are one with the creative process that exists and dominates the whole nature. Therefore, their 'I' refers to the cosmic principle of creation, and not egoism. Apart from teleportation, it can affect the transmutation of all the elements and their (de)materialization.[58] The peak of human power to act on earth is achieved here. Nobody has free will until they come to this phase. An illusion of free movement, an average human has while being conditioned in the physical body, is a far cry of freedom an individual as mature as this has. The reverse works for such a person: the

---

[58] This goes without saying because mastering the astral realm and *tanmâtrâ* realm in all the dimensions (*maha-bhŭtâni*) entails mastering the elements of the physical world represented in those dimensions. Nobody can conquer the higher dimensions if they remainweak and helpless on the physical plane.

physical body is a shadow that follows their will and consciousness.

The purpose of the whole process, described through seven phases here, is to bring awareness to the energy body – the body of consciousness – to overpower the physical. By doing so aham-kâra is affirmed and actualized. This is the only way for the soul's consciousness to be affirmed and actualized in this world, and together with it the presence of the divine. That is the destiny of humankind.

7) In the seventh or final phase the energy property of the beingness has become so mature in humans, that forms and objects through which the energy manifests disappear to them, and only the essence remains, only *akasha* remains that is aware. The form (being), energy, and consciousness are all one to them. In this phase, *aham-kâra* connects permanently to *mahat-buddhi*, and it is open for pure unconditionality (*Purusha*). For humans who have made it to this phase, whose consciousness (*buddhi*) is in functional unity with the essence of the being (*akasha*), there is nothing more to be embodied and nothing more to be done in *Prakriti*. The only thing which is left for them to do is to resurrect from it in the light of the pure awareness of unconditionality of their soul. They see that all the actions are done by *Prakriti*, and their soul is primordially free and independent, for the exact reason that their consciousness engenders the whole of *Prakriti* and its functioning.

He observes the whole *Prakriti* and sees clearly that its individual forms are naught by themselves; by knowing the whole they see that there is no time in it and everything originates simultaneously. He sees the whole only because they are also whole - *aham-kâra* - and their consciousness is no longer subjective but completely objective, the transcendental consciousness of the unity. He sees that in the whole *Prakriti* nothing else was happening but the maturation of conditions for their awakening and independence. All the possible forms of existence were invoking wakefulness through various temptations, every single act was merely a mediator for the self-knowledge of the one who acts.

Wakefulness (*buddhi*) of the one who acts (*aham-kâra*) is the outcome of the general beingness – additionally, the outcome of the emergent phenomena is *akasha*, and its direct manifestation is light. That is why an awakened one is called enlightened, they merge their consciousness with their being to such an extent that it turns into light. It is one of the manifestations of the seventh phase. An observer can only witness one day that such humans turn into light forms, like stars being born.

The seventh phase is resurrection, which is nothing but the wakefulness which is not only mental but has encompassed the whole being and taken it with itself into independence, transforming and purifying it into the ethereal substance, into its original state, which is experienced, from the outward perspective, as extraordinary light that is not of this world, and which has no cause. This light is freedom that engenders everything to be. It cannot be seen by unconscious people, the resurrected one has disappeared only to their sleeping eyes, it has disappeared from their dreams and became a reality. It disappeared from their horizon because they have begun to truly exist. Only those who live in the dark of the unconsciousness of the being do not see the light of reality and the resurrected one who is always there, in the very center of life, because they have become the reality itself and is no longer a special being experiencing reality as such.

In the language of *Sâmkhya*, the only thing that has disappeared here is the illusion of time in which *Purusha* was identified with *Prakriti*; wakefulness is knowing that *Purusha* was never conditioned by *Prakriti*, and this wakefulness is not only mental but encompasses the whole being and the whole existence; **wakefulness in this phase is identical with the existence itself.**

In this phase, humans become one with the eternal reality because they are awakened enough to see there is nothing else they could be, that everything is an illusion. Humans were, by increasing perception and functioning of their personal existence through the above-described phases of awakening, in effect, harmonizing with the true nature of phenomena in general, with the reality. If the unconditional consciousness engenders the existence itself, then the existence as such is unconditioned and fundamentally free. By attaining their own freedom, humans reach this essence of existence.

Once they learn to teleport themselves, they finally realize that reality is instant, that the consciousness and intention with which everything is instantly created and rolls out for us are their personal consciousness and intentions, that nothing is objectively separate and everything is one. This one is their essence.

Such cognizance of their essence is the realization of the seventh phase.

***

The most mature manifestation of the seventh phase is inactivity or non-disruption of things as they are. Instead of a spectacular resurrection in light, staying on in the being the way it is, is an expression of the ultimate cognition of the beingness – realization that our essence never was conditioned and has nothing to be liberated from, i.e., to resurrect. Humans never liberate themselves from anything, instead, they only awakens to what their essence always is. Unconsciousness is the only bondage. Awakening is the only resurrection.

In the way described here, through the seven phases, humans attain awakening, more accurately, they affirm the category of *aham-kâra* in order to actualize the highest category of nature, *mahat-buddhi*, the outcome and ultimate realization of existence.

(There are also other methods for conquering the astral, i.e., the energy body. The first four phases described here I have personally gone through since I could not describe methods I have never experienced. Regardless of the methods, the universal principles brought forth in this book point to the essence of such experiences.)

These phases correlate with "the seven gates of dreaming" in the opus of Carlos Castaneda (although he, too, described only four), and they are analog with the degrees of consecration in Gnostics, through mastering the dreams. They were probably inspired by the words of Jesus from the Gospel of Thomas (22): "When you make the two become one, and when you make the inside like the outside and the outside like the inside, and the upper like the lower! And if you make the male and the female one, so that the male is no longer male and the female is no longer female (a description of the transcendental consciousness), and when you put your eyes in the place of an eye, and a hand in the place of a hand, and a foot in the place of a foot, and (the whole of) an image in the place of an image (physical), (a description of the actualization of the energy body), then you will enter the Kingdom." Incidentally, could the road to resurrection be any different from the awakening described here?

All the seven phases are a process in which the being is transformed into its energy essence (the astral body) firstly, and from then on, the energy further crystallized into its essence as the pure light, that at the same time is pure consciousness, as well. Such is the road of acceleration of the beingness toward its essence. More precisely put, it does not speed up all by itself because it is always the way it is, only through human personal participation does beingness gains momentum, *humans synchronize with reality*. It is what all the seven phases describe: a progressive affirmation of personal participation in the true happening, in the reality.

The human being (the soul) is multidimensional, it is the source of all the dimensions, *we already exist in all those dimensions in all the described phases*. They are our alternative and parallel lives. The 'conquering' of the higher dimensions through the seven phases described here, is not their gradual conquering but only awakening to the awareness of oneself, its transcendental soul which, once it becomes aware here in the body, stops being transcendental and 'otherworldly', and becomes actualized divine consciousness at work here and now. All the higher dimensions of our existence unite and become realized in their outcome, here and now. *When we awaken, we merge all of our parallel realities and possibilities into a single existence*. All the alternative realities are merely helping on the way to awakening.

The described way of raising awareness through the seven phases is the only way for humans to overcome the physically oriented mind (ego) that seemingly separates them from the whole, from the divine Absolute, that is, in reality, themselves, the only way to connect with all of their possible existences that happen simultaneously, in other words, to connect and unite with their divine soul who is the true Creator of everything.

Progressing through all seven phases will be facilitated by the growing accumulation of energy. We have already seen how energy can be lost as well as accumulated, and now we can stress that the accumulation of energy is non-other than the awareness of the being because the being is energy, and the outcome of both aspects is consciousness. Therefore, with the awareness of the being the way it is by itself, we accumulate all of its energy. The consciousness or focus is the router of our energy. The being is already in the possession of all the energy that is necessary for maintaining it, hence, the actualization of the overall energy is awareness of the being. It is attained by replacing the center of the consciousness in meditation from the mind and description of the world – from the mental projection of existence – to the very being or existence itself. Additionally, all the dimensions and possibilities of beingness, and the phases described here of moving the energy body, are already present here and now, our being is made up of them, and consequently, their realization is non-other than their actualization through the awareness of the being, steadiness of attention in one's own source. Everything is, therefore, reduced to awakening or finding a way back to oneself.

The necessary energy for the growth and maturing of the astral (energy) body is not created spontaneously. The physical mind is programmed to use only energy that is sufficient for organic reproduction. For the higher bodies, humans must put in an extra effort. Owing to the teaching of Gurdjieff we are now familiar with the fact that the energy accumulates in three phases, or 'shocks'. The first one has been provided for us by nature through **breathing**. The remaining two phases humans must do by themselves. The second conscious 'shock' that helps accumulate extra energy is **awareness of impressions**. It is *vipassana* practice of meditation in Buddhism. The principle is that the impressions, which represent the general circulation of life energy, constantly go through us. If we are unaware of them, they go unused. If we remain conscious of them (by the awareness of the body, feelings, and breathing – see more on that in my book on meditation) then we double them. The energetic strength of the impressions does not go through us like through some hole but meets a subject that is conscious of them. **A conscious subject acts as a dam to the flow of impressions thus enhancing their energy efficiency**. We can vividly describe a being as being like a tube the impressions go through, and the awareness of oneself becomes like a plug on one end of the tube preventing impressions from leaking out, and suddenly, the tube becomes a dish whose sole function is to gather the energy of impressions. The third conscious 'shock' transforms energy enhanced in this manner to a higher ontological status by way of ***not expressing one's negative emotions***, which can be described as nothing but the cessation of identification, i.e., dependence on objects, or more accurately, the pure consciousness. This, too, is a consequence of meditation. This is a way of leading the energy into its most subtle state – into the consciousness itself (*buddhi*). In *Prakriti* it is analog to *akasha*, which has the highest power of creation, everything originates with its shaping.

This binds the increase in consciousness and energy with strengthening the energy body and allowing for the bigger power to act.

Everything boils down to consciousness and energy. The human body was designed to automatically realize all the seven phases if provided with the full potential for such an undertaking, if it invests 100% of its consciousness and energy. Humans seem helpless because they use only a fraction of their potential, the majority of their energy is wasted on irrelevant and wrong things that are not in their best interest. To know the overall existence as an energy phenomenon and consciousness, humans must first become aware of it in their body and learn to preserve all of their energy (in all the seven chakras, especially the sexual one using the principle of tantrism).

Humans are a microcosm, and everything works out in them first. Humans have never resolved any existential problem outwardly. Everything has always been this simple.

To understand the full scope of life, comprehending the highest category of *Prakriti, mahat-buddhi* will be of crucial assistance, in which all the other categories are acquired.

MAHAT - BUDDHI

The highest category of *Prakriti - mahat-buddhi* – is its ultimate outcome. Everything springs from and flows into this category. It is the mode of beingness that is the closest to the soul, *Purusha*, the pure unconditionality that engenders everything. With *mahat-buddhi Prakriti* touches *Purusha* and flows into it. It is the pinnacle of its pyramidal conformation, hence, its characteristic is disappearance or numbness (*nirvana*). The pinnacle always represents finalizing and ceasing, this is the whole point of it, it exists in a non-existing way. The visible and invisible merge in their ultimate end, their form and outcome join in full meaning. Nowhere else is it so clear that the form of being trades places with the invisible meaning like on this spot, on the top of the *Prakriti* pyramid. From this point onward, everything flows into its outcome and unites with the freedom that engenders it to the degree where all the forms cease to exist as forms, and only the purpose of pure freedom remains as the outcome of every form.

In classical texts, it is stated that *Prakriti*, once it is completely known by the witness, *Purusha*, desists like a dancer that has demonstrated its dance and disappears forevermore.

How can we understand the consciousness and existence in *mahat-buddhi*?

The purpose of completeness of the personality (*aham-kâra*) is to disappear as an individual; when it matures completely, the personality stops being something individual and personal and becomes the embodiment of the soul that gives it all, the embodiment of the divine. In such a disappearance, wakefulness is born.

When a sculptor wishes to make a certain statue, they first make a statue out of clay, then uses it to make a plaster mold in which to pour out their desired work in bronze. This very much resembles the whole of the individual life of the human who has yet to be formed into clay; its purpose is to achieve the full volume and be perfected in the completely integrated personality, and once the personality is used as the mold for pouring into the presence of the divine consciousness that engenders all, at which point the mold can finally be rejected.

The most perfect expression or the most concrete existential embodiment of the divine consciousness is possible only in man. All other life forms are mere preparation for the conditions to be met to facilitate this occurrence. That is the explanation why life is so hard for humans – due to the enormous significance they have. For humans to be able to bear the divine presence, they must be perfectly integrated as a personality, through the awareness of "I am".

The divine is the Absolute. A personality is a conscious subject. The Absolute knows itself through the completely mature and crystallized conscious subject. At the moment of cognition as such, all the individuality of the conscious subject disappears, and they become the Absolute again. This is all that happens.

Humans do not become divine, but humans, when they become perfect, disappear, and the divine becomes what it is through them. It always is that, but it has actualized through humans in this world that supports life. The divine becomes human. The human being was only a means for the divine to receive its individual embodiment, and not to be some blind abstract force, but to be able to love, work, and speak through humans.

Therefore, a complete cessation of individuality itself does not happen, but merely the disappearance of the illusion of its separateness from the divine whole, which means that the only thing that keeps happening is the actualization of the consciousness of omnipresence of the divine whole.

Every individuality enriches the expressive abilities of the divine; the divine has contracted itself into an individual expression because of the concrete experience of self-awareness; any awareness of the self is individual awareness of the divine. The complete awareness of oneself only overcomes the illusion of separateness of an individual and reveals the ubiquitous divine whole in which all the individual experiences still exist as the abundance of its expression.

The outcome of existence is the disappearance of themselves in order to be liberated for that what engenders all, themselves included. By numbing themselves, humans awaken to what engenders everything, to the divine consciousness. Then, it begins to manifest through them. All their individuality, their entire being, and life experience served only to concretize the place where such an occurrence will take place, and this wakefulness (*mahat-buddhi*), the divine consciousness, to be concretely and functionally expressed as a personality (*aham-kâra*). It is manifested outside of this, too, but impersonally, like sheer existence, like all the beings and phenomena.

Wakefulness (*mahat-buddhi*) is the freedom from identification with the form of phenomena (*Prakriti*) and is the same freedom that engenders each phenomenon without exception. Only a complete person, the one who has fully accepted the responsibility for life and has become aware of it in its biological, psychological, and social aspect, can be alert enough to overcome the emergent world.

How a personality matures and reaches completeness we saw in *Aham-kâra* chapter, where from the initial detachment from identification with the physical body one attains the ability of teleportation, hence, complete insight into a reality which explains that existence as such is nothing substantial (material) by itself, but ethereal and momentary, everything is only *akasha* or the conscious energy.

It means that the conviction of substantiality puts humans to sleep, while dissuasion alerts them to the fact. Nothing else. The being has never been substantial and such view is illusory, whereas unconsciousness is non-other than the affirmation of this illusion, the state of sleep. Therefore, when humans awaken, solid forms as objects by themselves disappear and turn into *akasha*, the conscious energy of being. To awakened humans (*mahat-buddhi*), the entire manifested world (*Prakriti*) becomes energy that is aware of itself, and each movement of the being-in-the-world clearly demonstrates to them that it is the movement of consciousness, a conscious move, the same way every form existing in the world is aware of its formation. Events of all the shapes of the objective world shape them for awakening, in a sense that they do not experience wakefulness as "I am awake", they cease to experience themselves, instead, their **being and the entire world become pure, time-**

less wakefulness, and they are nothing there but a silent and independent witness (*sakshin*). That is the reason why wakefulness is effortless relaxation and presence in pure existence. **The existence (Prakriti) is wakefulness (mahat-buddhi) when we are present in the existence**. Absence from existence is unconsciousness – when we imagine that existence is something other than what it is.

All the efforts for an authentic experience of the world remain in *aham-kâra*, all the efforts of the whole nature find their meeting point there, but efforts are needless here because the aspiration has been accomplished. Wakefulness (*mahat-buddhi*) is suprapersonal, it is relaxation from everything to the same extent it is the acceptance of everything. Relaxed and awakened humans are only the one who authentically accepts everything as it is.

Mahat-buddhi can be viewed from the cosmic and macrocosmic standpoint. *Mahat* ('big') is macrocosmic, and *buddhi* ('wakefulness') the microcosmic aspect of this category of *Prakriti*.

The cosmos alerts us to the fact that *mahat-buddhi* is the singularity of the universe, its unity or the universal, quantum Field according to the model of the hologram in which every part is a whole in miniature and where a myriad of entities, that expand in an inflationary manner from *aham-kâra*, have merely ostensible independence. Having been proved both experimentally as well as theoretically, the singularity of the universe is the pivot of physics. If physicists mastered it, they could rule nature because they would be in possession of a unique and complete theory, 'the big equation' that encompasses all the laws of physics, from the tiniest (quantum) to the biggest (gravity). Unlike modern science that has different concepts on singularity, *Sâmkhya* not only speaks of the singularity of the universe (*mahat*, the highest category), but also describes through its categories how it is able to manifest itself in the form of the cosmos and function as life, and above all, it speaks of how the singularity of the universe, its direct revelation (*Apokalypsis*, the Greek term) and the outcome can only be achieved in the Self, in the soul, in wakefulness (*buddhi*). There is no other way. It cannot be obtained from the outside. Singularity is solely existential in character. Humans are the 'big equation', their personality is a living and only possible union of both the microcosm and the macrocosm alike. ***If only in the human's personality cognition of natu-***

ral laws of microcosm and macrocosm can take place, it means that they unite only in the personality of man.

Only awakened humans can acknowledge the holistic unity of freedom. Scientists who lack a holistic approach to existence act from a much lower lever, consequently imperfectly, with a minor difference between the good and bad effects. While ancient knowledge and alchemy had a comprehensive, holistic approach to existence, modern science has up until the nineteenth century functioned only within the *indriyâni* framework, within the empirical world. With theory of relativity and quantum physics, groundbreaking discoveries were on the horizon, science revealed higher dimensions of elements and *tanmâtrâs*, and with the occurrence of C. G. Jung and transpersonal psychology, the realm of *aham-kâra* begins to appear in full view, while *buddhi* that remained well-preserved in Buddhism, has not made it into the light of the day yet, instead, it is still in the dark of certain postmodern paradigms of the 'new science' that is trying to merge the ancient knowledge with the contemporary. This is due to the fact that an average human does not have absolute wakefulness, nor is it something one can have as a socially accepted and validated paper. Wakefulness brings the independence of both the emergent world and the society of unconscious people. The awakened one cannot live in other people's dreams. Those who sleep live being conditioned by collectivism, and the awakened one they can only view as a recluse (if they can see them at all since they are sleeping – which is a great opportunity for awakened humans to save themselves, instead of being crucified on the cross). The truth is that awakened humans have all the awareness of their soul and they understand perfectly the ones who are sleeping, hence, they are doing their best to avoid any conflicts with them, they only help them when needed and they spontaneously feel and appreciate it. Although their mind is asleep, their souls are always awake and they see the soul of the awakened man.

How does a person mature enough to be able to attain awakening described in *Aham-kâra* chapter. Is there a single scientist willing to undertake this endeavor? He would be branded as a schizophrenic or, in the best of circumstances, a shaman. In any event, their academic status would be permanently ruined, something which is a lot dearer to their heart than wakefulness.

Nowhere is the cosmic aspect of a *Prakriti* category closer to its microcosmic expression than in this case. The fact is, they are in unity. *Mahat-buddhi* as a unity of the universe and cosmic intelligence that rules the overall life of nature manifests itself directly through an awakened subject, and indirectly through a plethora of inflationary scattered forms of the cosmic phenomena, we perceive to be both the organic and inorganic world.

Due to the unity of macro with the microcosmic manifestation, the subject can ascertain the world because the world, as such, forms the subject. Additionally, the only true destiny of every subject is to mature to the absolute awakening. The universe acknowledges itself through the wide open eyes of awakened human beings.

In wakefulness, the subject is the universe itself, and not a man. Humans are only a suitable place where the wakefulness of the universe happens. The subject of wakefulness is divine unconditionality that engenders the whole universe and is in no way different from the universe itself.

Buddhi is the essence of the conscious subject (*aham-kâra*). Additionally, *mahat-buddhi* is where the whole of *Prakriti* springs from. This clearly indicates that the entire universe and the overall existence originate from the conscious subject. That is why the universe is not objective. The universe as such is human essence which they experience as something outward. Once they become aware of themselves, awakened (*buddhi*), humans awaken to the fact that everything is in them, and that they are everything (*Prakriti*).

Wakefulness is not a somewhat higher degree of consciousness, but the absolute presence in the reality of the being, a conscious unity that has never before happened in an average life. It is the absolute experience of the being as it is, its complete and untainted perception and utter affirmation of the underlying factors of existence.

Unawakened humans think they are an individual that resides in the whole; the awakened is the whole itself who is aware of the ostensible individuality.

Humans are awake at the moment when the divine, that engenders everything, finally prevails over their individual being and overpowers it.

Awakened humans cease to experience the world as something outward, but inward instead, they experience the world as their wakefulness, as themselves, and for this reason, they perceive it with full responsibility.

All the experiences of existence (*samskaras*) have contracted in them, and they no longer gather experiences, they remain unattached to actions because they see that all the actions are done by *Prakriti*, that all the actions are potentially and timelessly already present in *Prakriti*. They have become the outcome of all the actions, they are the soul that engenders the existence of all the life.

To be awake (*mahat-buddhi*) means to disclose one's soul completely. Since human souls are undisguised when they are awake, the overall doing of nature pours into them and finds its outcome in their transcendental soul – *Purusha*. The whole nature has been realized in their soul and there is nothing else for them to do; they are the goal of everything, hence, they have no more goals to achieve. He functions across all the dimensions of nature. However, on the physical plane, it appears that they do nothing, or very little, yet they accomplish everything they need. All the powers of creation are personified in the human being, making them enjoy all the power of creation in themselves.

To awakened humans, there is no greater miracle than life itself, the fact that after breathing out we breathe in again. They see the miracle of divine presence and proclamation in each rock mottle, the tiniest details, as well as in stars. The holographic nature of existence is perfectly clear to them.

Awakened humans do nothing more than what is existence itself, here and now. However, the existence then, due to the proximity of their soul, becomes divinely miraculous, perfect, and wonderful. Once the soul's consciousness of humans who are awakened enlightens existence, no matter how ordinary it is, it begins to show as the kingdom of heaven on earth.

This is the ultimate purpose of awakening: the divine perfection of existence is not created somewhere in the future, in space and time, but is acknowledged in the very existence the way it is, here and now, even in the most inconspicuous forms, as it were.

The absolute consciousness of the divine is always recognized in absolutely everything that exists. And everything exists as the absolute divine consciousness.

These dynamics of existence, no matter how strong and complex it was, never overshadows the clarity of divine consciousness that is revealed as the existence itself.

1. The final discernment between *buddhi* and *Purusha*

According to the teaching of *Sâmkhya* and Patanjali's *Yoga Sutras*, that are present in the practice of *Sâmkhya, mahat-buddhi*, as the highest category of *Prakriti*, becomes fully integrated only when, due to the proximity of *Purusha*, which overcomes it, learns its discernment from it. Then, the final differentiation between *Purusha* and *Prakriti* takes place.

This happens only when humans recognize the unity between consciousness and existence. *Mahat-buddhi* is the presence of consciousness in existence, in *Prakriti*. Not because *Prakriti* is aware but because *Prakriti* in its highest category, *mahat-buddhi*, is the closest to the transcendental *Purusha*, the true source of consciousness. This closeness makes all the beings in *Prakriti* entertain an illusion that they are conscious by themselves. Due to the *ahamkâra* categories, all the beings suffer from the illusion of being detached as individuals, conscious by themselves, separate from the whole.

The final cognition according to *Sâmkhya* happens when this detailed illusion is overcome. Humans are truly awake when they realize that nothing in *Prakriti* is conscious by itself, but is a mere reflection of the consciousness of *Purusha*. This consciousness of *Purusha* is its essence or soul, and not something belonging to *Prakriti*.

The moment humans see that their being and all the life they do **not have as their creation** but receives from the unconditional divine consciousness that engenders all, they surrender. The essence of human awakening is divine consciousness that engenders everything and overcomes the whole nature. What facilitates the world every single minute, also facilitates the consciousness of the world, before all else. It is *mahat-buddhi*, the first and foremost category of this world.

This is how differentiation between *buddhi* and *Purusha* happens, and according to *Sâmkhya* this is the most supreme liberation and perfection of maturity. Only maturity of this kind brings insight into the fact that not even the most subtle or the most important in humans, their wakefulness with which they ascertain themselves and the world in its entirety, is nothing by itself and for itself, it is not their property but is engendered by something higher, something that is nothing of everything that is something. Awakening is the insight into the fact that nothing is/exists by itself, everything is blank because it is free to be. This is no longer an insight only but is the numbness of thoughts (which is always a thought on the world), to purify and liberate the manifestation of the unconditioned human soul, a soul that is independent (*kaivalya*) from *Prakriti* and makes humans the way they are because they are its essence.

The experience of discerning *buddhi* from *Purusha* could be described as the pinnacle into the research of the mind (or consciousness, *buddhi*) in the knowing that their actions are engendered by some higher force, and they alone cannot reach it. *Insight into the improbability of attaining their own source leads the mind to calmness and relaxation – and surrendering to a higher power. The deepest insight into a certainty of a higher force leads to the pure calmness of the intellect (buddhi) and dedication.* Then, the higher force (*Purusha*) remains, completely alone, as it always has been. This is the ultimate cognizance (between *buddhi* and *Purusha*) and liberation (*kaivalya*).

Although pure consciousness or *buddhi* is the outcome of everything, it is not readily available to people. There are four good reasons for that. The first one is that the outcome is too close, it is in humans, the closest to everything else, it stands alone, therefore hard to make out. The dominant cultural conditioning which instructs us to expect something big and important to come from the outside is still very strong in people. The second one is that the pure consciousness has a depth that by far outweighs our individuality, it is the foundation of everything in the universe. It is hard for us to believe that the foundation of everything is our foundation as well, and it is even harder to imagine that to acquire it presupposes overcoming of our individuality. The third reason lies in the ease of it. Nothing is easier than being what we always are, and this ease and directness make it hard for us to be authentic. This ease is attained through non-action (*wu wei*), and our whole being and mind were designed to act. Finally, the true nature of existence in the pure consciousness (due to the proximity of *Purusha*) is so miraculous that it is hard to fit it into our picture of the world. It does not contain our picture of the world; our world disappears in it.

What does this discerning *buddhi* from *Purusha* look like in practical terms? It is attained through the practice of meditation, which is a practice of systematic release of the consciousness from thought contents. The essence of *Prakriti* is in thoughts, whereas the consciousness purified from thoughts is the pure or transcendental consciousness (*Purusha*). The subject or 'I' is the slot through which the consciousness manifests into our being. According to the scheme the subject is *aham-kâra*. In the state of average consciousness, the subject is always aware based on objects, and those are always thoughts as well as the world, all the other categories on the scheme. The subject (*aham-kâra*) is never aware of themselves, the way they are, instead, they always faces objects (lower categories), with the help of thought and engagement in the world. When we are sitting peacefully in meditation, investing energy and consciousness into lower categories becomes immediately aborted, and the subjects (*aham-kâra*) begin to face themselves. They are no longer deals with the affairs of the world, and the practice of meditation prevents them from meddling with their thoughts, which are always a reflection of the world and experiences regarding it. When the mind does not attach itself to the thoughts any more, then *mahat-buddhi* is released from the influence of all the lower categories. When in steady calmness they are diverted from all the objects and every thought, the subject is left to themselves, without experiences. *When the subject remains alone, without objects as it were, yet fully conscious,* their *consciousness, i.e., wakefulness (buddhi) reveals itself as the pure existence or presence of the being (Prakriti), and the whole existence (Prakriti) reveals that its outcome is in the consciousness (buddhi).* In other words, the whole *Prakriti*

308

contracts in the highest category, *mahat-buddhi*, into the consciousness, we become truly awake only when we raise the level of awareness of the essence of existence (*Prakriti*). Then existence and consciousness are one for the first time in the human experience, without any distinguishing; they begin to exist consciously for the first time, without any contents that would divert them from the pure existence. Then, in this silence, they exist for the first time, as absolute beings, and not some small individuals constrained by their thoughts. According to the scheme, this is the complete affirmation of the consciousness in *mahat-buddhi*.

This is the process of awareness of the being itself, the conscious presence in it without any objects and events to divert us away from the directness of the presence of this kind. In all other states, we exist indirectly and that is the reason why we are not authentic, but experience suffering instead. Here, we exist only consciously as a pure being. It is the state of the transcendental consciousness.

And that is all? – may well be the question of a person who has not had an experience of this kind. Yes, that is all, because to be consciously present as a pure being is not the same as existing in an ordinary way. We live our ordinary lives only in thoughts, fictitiously, and not in reality. The world is real in an ordinary way for as long as we are unaware of it for what it is, for as long as we keep imagining it, enduring our fictitious view of the world that constitutes all our lives. Only when we transcend the mind do we begin to see the real world as it is. When the being becomes conscious, the world we had known up till then disappears, it becomes transparent, and the living energy of the infinite voidness of *akasha* remains, moving momentarily and forming all the occurrences of the universe through the intention of the divine consciousness, which is our essence.

When we consciously and completely unite with the being, when in meditation we become pure presence and nothing else, then our inner silence turns into a well of bliss and the being as such vanishes, it fades away, our body becomes light like a feather until that, too, disappears in the fullness of emptiness, in the freedom that is nothing of everything, but engenders everything – *Purusha*.

Differentiating *buddhi* from *Purusha* is differentiating *Prakriti* from *Purusha*, whereas *buddhi* is the essence of *Prakriti*, its final outcome. To distinguish itself from *Purusha* and achieve its outcome and meaning of existence, *Prakriti* must be reduced to its outcome, being previously made completely aware of. It happens in *mahat-buddhi*. With *mahat-buddhi* we are aware of the pure presence of *Prakriti* the way it is, of its wholeness.

The most subtle aspect of the manifested existence of *Prakriti* is in *akasha*, in the aether, the quantum Field in which everything that has ever manifested in nature is timelessly united. When we are aware (*buddhi*) of the essence of the existence of *Prakriti* we see nature as the pure energy, as *akasha*. In *buddhi*, nature obtains the purest consciousness of itself, on the most subtle level, in *akasha*. It means that the energy of existence or *akasha* becomes aware of itself in humans who have actualized the *buddhi* category, the pure awareness of existence, and *buddhi* is at the same time the wakefulness of man. That is why the pure consciousness of existence we can attain in our being only, within ourselves (in the experience of meditation) – we can never touch reality outside: **we must become what reality is**. The only way to know reality is to be this reality with all our being. Only when that happens, we become what existence facilitates – *Purusha*. If we are able to be aware of the existence for what it is, it means we overcome (transcend) it with our essence. ***And only when we exceed it in the transcendental soul's consciousness, we begin to truly exist – because the soul's transcendental consciousness – which facilitates the existence – is our essence. This defines discerning between Purusha and Prakriti.***

When *Prakriti* disappears to awakened humans (*buddhi*), the only thing that is left behind is the transcendental consciousness that engenders everything. It happens in the human as the pure consciousness of the self and wakefulness – and not as something that is of this world. The consciousness takes on the human image and starts to act through the human. It, then, ceases to be an abstract force, now it has arms and legs and is able to work and create objects of beauty and kindness.

The disappearance of the objective world (*Prakriti*) is merely a different way of saying that humans are more important than the world because only awakened humans participate in the freedom that engenders the world every single minute, and only through them, this freedom manifests directly and in the most creative way. Only humans like that can contribute to the creation of a free world and take active participation in its true life for the good of all living beings.

2. Awakening is an inversion of the outward and inward

Everything that has been said thus far about the awakening would remain unclear without the final words on the subject, something that is already contained in the subtitle above, and is, yet, the hardest to comprehend:

The whole act of awakening is the moment when a human being acknowledges the entire outer world, all the nature, and the cosmos as such, as their own inward being, or more accurately, they see everything outward as a means for the crystallization of awareness of themselves through objectivation.

To use the language of *Sâmkhya* this means that the most subtle states of *Prakriti*, *akasha*, and *mahat-buddhi*, have managed to be synchronized and recognized one another as the outward and inward of the same existence: what *akasha* represents externally as the space of quantum Field that forms everything in cosmos, is the same in the human as the highest consciousness and wakefulness (*buddhi*) that forms all ideas.

We should understand the way in which *mahat-buddhi* and *akasha* are connected because without understanding this nothing will be clear about the teaching of *Sâmkhya*.

In the universal quantum Field (aether or *akasha*) everything that exists is contracted in the timeless one, **everything is interconnected**, hence, it explains how the subatomic (quantum) particles communicate non-locally. They are connected irrelevant of space and time; they communicate instantly no matter how far apart they are. The consciousness (*buddhi*) has the same property as *akasha*, it is nothing but the connectedness of phenomena and objects on their most subtle level, a connectedness of information and meaning. The consciousness represents connecting the meaning of each phenomenon the same way the quantum Field connects all phenomena into a unity. The consciousness (*buddhi*) forms individually (*aham-kâra*) every thought (*manas*) as its most subtle vibration, and *akasha* or aether instantly forms each occurrence, in all the dimensions, from photons, and finest particles, to everything that exists. In this way, the consciousness (*mahat-buddhi*) and space (*akasha*) are connected.

Both space and consciousness have the same characteristics: in the same way that space contains all the objects within, the consciousness can bring awareness of all the objects, and act as their witness. Pure space manifests outwardly as the aether in which all the matter originates, and into which it all goes back to, while the same space manifests in us as the pure consciousness of itself or Self – *mahat-buddhi* as the intellect able to comprehend each material occurrence.

That is why existence consists of the forms as such and the knowledge of those forms simultaneously. The purpose of existence is in their uniting. The form is everything that is "outward" - all the lower categories of *Prakriti* on the scheme, and cognition is "inward" – the category of *mahat-buddhi*. Awakening is the act of inversion, or, better yet, the union of the outer and inner, of subject and object.

Only through humans can nature become whole, its unmanifested essence (*akasha*) becomes actualized and manifested through the consciousness of existence (*buddhi*).

Once such a complete awareness of *Prakriti* takes place, the final differentiation or actualization of *Purusha* also happens. The consciousness of the complete existence (*buddhi*) comes from *Purusha*. This final cognition of the nature of the consciousness itself (*Purusha*), and together with it the nature of existence as such (*mahat-buddhi*), brings the final discernment between *Purusha* and *mahat-buddhi*. This is the final realization according to the teaching of *Sâmkhya*.

***

Pure spaciousness as a property of *akasha* and *buddhi* is voidness Buddhism speaks of, but also Apophatic theology, and Gnosticism.

Due to the holographic principle and attractiveness of the void, our Self is the chief attractor of the overall phenomena of our life, and our soul has done all the projecting that keeps happening to us, our entire life is its projection that resembles a big lucid dream. That is why Ho'o ponopono works and so does the 'law of attraction'.

This fact of the unity of the macrocosm and microcosm was hinted at in a number of ways.

Since the macrocosm and microcosm are the same, there are mathematics and holy geometry that present their proportions all the secret science and cabala are based on, as well as the science of astrology that is entirely based on the principles of the holographic universe, and reveals how cosmos determines our inner states, character, temperament, and activities.

Since all the outwardness is the human's inwardness, the theory of the Strong Anthropic Principle (SAP) may claim that the entire universe exists with the purpose of creating a conscious subject. In that sense, the universe is not independent of the subject. The conscious subject is the reason for the existence of the universe.

That is why Nietzsche said in 'Zaratustra': "You great star, what would your happiness be had you not those for whom you shine?"

That is why it is said that the human body is the microcosm because it is made from the wider whole and would not last a minute without it.

Hermes Trismegistus made a crucial claim in *Corpus Hermeticum* – "Which way shall I look when I praise thee? upward? downward? outward? inward? for about these, there is no manner nor place nor anything else of all things that are. But all things are in thee; all things from thee, thou givest all things, and takest nothing; for thou hast all things and there is nothing that thou hast not." It is the description of the holographic universe and the quantum Field.

Katha Upanishad states the same: "What is within is also without. What is without is also within. He who sees any difference here goes from death to death." In *Bhagavad Gita* we read that: "For one who sees Me everywhere and sees everything in Me, I am never lost, nor is he ever lost to Me."

Bhagavan Sri Ramana Maharshi said that "man's true measure and greatness begin at the place where he as an individual stops to exist", and he perpetually stressed that we are not our body – because we are everything, our Self is God or the Absolute. Sri Nisargadatta Maharaj kept saying that we are the Absolute that contains the universe within, and our only mistake is what is inside us we see as the outside.

The whole of Buddhism teaches how we can directly and freely abandon ourselves as an individual in order to awaken.

The Rig Veda also reminds us of the following: "Purusha's abode is the Sun, but also the human heart."

That is why all the spiritual traditions teach that with the knowing of themselves humans know the Divine that engenders the overall existence, and they truly know themselves only after abandoning themselves and submitting to a higher force, the wider whole.

That is why the "heavenly kingdom is in us" and we should seek it first by leaving behind everything we cling on to thinking it is 'ours'.

Since the outside is our being, it has been said that for awakened humans the objective world disappears. It has not been specified that the world as such disappears, but the objective world, something else, different and outside of us. Awakened humans do not see it in this way, for the same reason nobody can see themselves.

An awakening like this is the foundation of the Sermon on the Mount (Matthew: 5.6.7.): not attributing values to objects that do not have them and failing to discern the objective world from the Self. That is why we should 'be forgiven for our trespasses and forgive those who trespass against us', 'turn the other cheek', 'love thy enemies' and always give more than we were asked for. It is all possible for those who exceed everything that is individual and experience the whole outward as their own being; *when Prakriti is acknowledged as Prakriti, Purusha, then, is acknowledged as Purusha. The cessation of their mixing is wakefulness*. This is relatively easy to recognize in natural phenomena, but when we hate a person the most and see it as only a natural phenomenon and part of the *Prakriti* whole, which is the way it is for the sake of our experience, then we are truly awake because we differentiate ourselves as *Purusha* and become independent, we do not get attached to the natu-

314

ral occurrences because we no longer attribute qualities to them that they lack. They are nothing by themselves and for themselves; the whole *Prakriti* does not exist for itself, but to serve the human soul, *Purusha*, to reflect itself in it a unique difference and independence, which means that the hardship other people and events put us through are only temptations and messages *Prakriti* uses to crystallize the soul in us. They are all ways using which nature pushes us in the direction of ourselves, to face our inward contents, to stop projecting outward. We suffer as a result of unfavorable circumstances and engage in conflicts with other people only because we abandon ourselves and project outside, identifying ourselves with *Prakriti*.

Since our outward is our inward the basic law of psychodynamics is at work here: projecting unconscious contents outside, into outer objects and 'other people'. People are mirrors to one another. That is the underlying cause for the conflicts between them, that will continue to exist until they awaken. Everything we see in other people as bad, everything that bothers us, initially comes from us, other people bring us characteristics we should bring out in the light of the day and become aware of them, for one reason or another we are still not free from them. We are fighting against 'other' people to the degree we are limited with the illusion of "self", and remain closed off into our little world. The more we are unconscious of ourselves, the more we are unconscious of others as being unconscious. The more we assign 'conscious actions' to ourselves although our actions are largely unconscious, the more we do this to other people, as well. The more we consider ourselves as the gifted ones with the power to act of our own free will, although we are not, the more we think everybody else has it, too, and we ultimately engage in a conflict where neither of the parties is quite sure what to do. The more we attribute some personality of a 'conscious subject' to ourselves although we are not that but a bunch of I's being thrown at the mercy of outer influences, the more other people seem as 'conscious subjects' who 'act of their own will' although they do not have a clue what they are doing. The more wrongly we see ourselves as being some special individual, the more we project this state onto everybody else. The others exist to us the way we exist. The others are a mere reflection of our 'I' and

315

have no other purpose but to serve as our self-knowledge. We condemn others to the level we are unaware of the fact they are unconscious. We go to wars for some religious ideals with the hope of some 'liberation', but ideals are that what enslaves us. That explains our strong emotional response towards 'others' because their actions 'affect us personally'. This is because we are all one. There are no "others", everything is one in the holographic universe. That is why this world will finally be right only when we change ourselves when we awaken. Life in the world will continue to be destructive for as long as we try to change it, to change 'others'. The world appears imperfect, alien, and evil to the extent we are unconscious of ourselves. There is no other world but ourselves: we make the world. The world has nobody but us. We are its conscious subjects.

Since all of the outside is our being, unconscious people do not see each other at all, and they are always in conflict or hypocritical avoidance of conflicts, while conscious people always recognize one another as 'kindred spirits', and their approach to everything is always pure and unconditional love, understanding, and goodness. Conscious people always share the unity of the world they are aware of.

Each time we are in conflict with somebody or something outside, we are in conflict with our true nature that is the Whole itself which engenders everything.

Since all of our outside is our inside, the inorganic realm of nature acts as our unconscious, we reside in it during sleep, and when we step consciously into it we, then, exit the body. By abandoning the (illusion) of the body we enter our inward world and become more objective toward ourselves and the world around us. We are the most unconscious when we are identified with our physical body. When we are objectively conscious of our whole being we are always independent of the body. In that way, the inorganic domain is at the same time both a factor of the objective world and our inner states.

If we were not one with the whole, how would we be able to feel unity with anything? How would we sense other people's moods? How could we love anyone if he/she were not a part of us? And how else do we love something 'outside' or some 'other' person if not within ourselves, with 'our whole being'? It is possible because everything outward is within us. If it were not so, how would we be able to perceive and understand anything? Science cannot explain how a correct premonition, intuition, and love happen because it is unaware of this unity. Science destroys humans and nature because it is oblivious to the fact that humans are the subject of all the natural phenomena and all the natural laws; the goal of scientific research is in humans, and not somewhere outside of them.

The basic knowledge of the laws of physics is enough to show us how nature has no issues with boundaries. It represents complete unity. Our unconsciousness is the one that gives us an illusion of individuality, the division into 'I' and 'others', i.e., 'the outside world'. The moment our body is in complete unity with the cosmos, and we consider 'ourselves' to be only this form with the outer layer of skin. This fundamental demarcation is the framework of all human destinies, and all the drama of the human's liberation is none other than the disclosure of these false boundaries.[59] Our true body is the whole universe.

Our dreams, all our thoughts, and inner dialogues, all the worry and anxiety exist only as a result of this false division, because we see ourselves as individuals because we are unaware of the fact that all the outward is our inward, that we are not our thoughts, but the space where thoughts begin to happen. When we become aware of that, we attain the timeless divine serenity and peace that is no different from existence itself. A myriad of thoughts, but other activities as well, exist only as a result of the illusion that we are separate from the whole. To think means to design what a person knows, trying to comprehend, to reconsider. A thought is an interval, alienation of the subject from an object and an attempt to overcome it. If we were one with everything, we would then feel and know everything and thoughts would become redundant. Hence, awakening and unity with everything are the same as the calmness of the mind.

Awakened humans discover their Self as the center of the universe – because they are the universe itself. They have always been

---

[59] More on this see in a great book by Ken Wilber: "No boundary"

this, and the act of awakening is mere actualization of this reality. A subject who is this pure is also absolutely objective.

The purpose of the entire universe is expressed with the awareness of 'I am'. It possesses a huge attraction for the environment because humans are its outcome, its heart. Awakened humans are the soul of the world (*anima mundi*). He does not move, but the whole world moves and revolves around them. They are the outcome of everything and all their actions are the love that engenders everything. That is why awakened humans are always completely relaxed, peaceful, and quiet.

That is why Bhagavan Sri Ramana Maharshi kept on saying: "The consciousness 'I am' is God." Buddha's dying message was: "Do not look for a sanctuary in anything except yourself."

All the valuable spiritual teachings stress the seemingly opposite statements: that humans are to know themselves, not to be egocentric but to surrender themselves to God, to the one who is far above them, who engenders them. The outcome of everything is in them, but it is out of reach until they learn to transcend their mind/ego and discover for themselves that they are nothing by themselves, but the Divine is the outcome of everything – through them.

***

Only when we know this, will we understand the final truth that everything that has been said so far – that the universe creates a conscious subject and everything outward is our inward – *is only half the truth*. There is one more ineffable truth – ineffable because it must first *become*, and only then be known – the truth that *only the conscious subject exists because their essence is the divine consciousness, there is no objective world that forms the subject, nothing gets formed, nothing is created or actualized, neither outward nor inward. Those are all the illusions of the mind*. Nothing else exists but the divine Absolute who is knowing *I am* in all the possible ways of existence – the most clearly in humans naturally.

The process of withdrawing the projection of oneself and the world is reduced to clearer differentiation of one's soul that comes from *Purusha*, from the most subtle processes of *Prakriti*, from the intellect (*buddhi*), ego (*aham-kâra*), and the mind (*manas*).

It is the topic of the next chapter *Kaivalya*.

KAIVALYA

Humans are the only suitable place for the awakening of the universe to take place, for the enlightenment of the being to be realized. Only for this purpose has the universe formed a human being as such.

The enlightenment of the being, or knowing the divine, happens always as the existence itself, every single moment, through every particle, every atom, every living form, and event – humans are mere witnesses to this, their enlightenment consists of becoming conscious of themselves as witnesses. It is all they have to do to fulfill their purpose. They who became enlightened did not achieve anything new. Only then will they see the true nature of existence as the divine light.

To become aware of themselves as the transcendental witness, and saw the true nature of existence, humans must personally experience all the fundamental facts regarding existence for what they are, without the psycho-mental, symbolic, or mythical warping. The speed of this experiencing does not depend on outer factors but on the presence of awareness about them. The presence of the consciousness in a miraculous way determines the time and outer events, it attracts them and accelerates in manifesting the underlying factors of existence. If left to the natural development, they would go through the human experience during their lifetime (one or several), while an enhanced presence of the consciousness speeds up and contracts time of their inevitable experiencing to a much shorter period. Consciously ascertaining the factors of existence, for what they are, releases and resolves all the knots in the human's heart making it suitable as the right place for the divine soul that engenders all to manifest.

The only task of humans and all culture and destiny is in maintaining the presence of consciousness through all forms of existence, which also means to become aware of all the forms of existence. All it takes is the objective human consciousness. If there is enough of it, everything else will be done by nature since it is drawn and led by consciousness. It does the physical part of the job the great architect puts before us as a task with their ideas.

Awareness of the whole existence is conducted by maintaining the presence of the consciousness we have during changing all the activities and all the states of existence, resisting all temptations to fall into oblivion. Preserving one's consciousness is primary. It has yet to engender the awareness of all the remaining existence.

The only way to maintain consciousness is through the practice of meditation.

A steadfast and permanent presence of the pure transcendental consciousness of oneself, of one's soul, during its abode in the body and action in this world, *Sâmkhya* calls *kaivalya*.

The term *kaivalya* denotes the state of what is simple, immiscible with anything else, authentic, pure, therefore, contains within the idea of perfection and completeness. That is why it is used to mark the perfection of the purified human soul (*Purusha*) by extracting everything that is not authentic to them. It designates detachment and separation of human essence or soul in that sense, which comes from *Purusha*, from all the transient beingness in time (*Prakriti*), the resurrection of the human soul from the mortal body into its immortal and unborn authentic state, it is a signpost for coming out of ignorance and into knowledge, from darkness into light, from death into immortality.

Kaivalya contains the initial discernment (*viveka*) that brings the first insight into the independence of the soul and body/mind, *Purusha* and *Prakriti*. This discernment is deepened with a spiritual practice so that it becomes aversion (*vairagya*) in relation to everything that binds us and which finally leads to the absolute discrimination between *Purusha* and *Prakriti*: *kaivalya*.

In *kaivalya,* the complete **detachment** is reinstated, like when we detach from a dream, from something that does not belong to us, from illusion. Awakening is a concrete exit from a dream. It represents one of the ways in which we come out of and detach from the dream and inauthentic beingness. In Patanjali's *Yoga Sutras* and *Sâmkhya* the same word *kaivalya* is used for the final enlightenment or detachment, and not some other word. The direct experience of enlightenment is emphasized, because the awakening is nothing but separating oneself from the dream, like isolation, differentiation, and ultimate discernment between *Purusha* and *Prakriti*.

The same experience is found in other teachings, as well. In Buddhism it is uttered with Buddha's first words after awakening:

«*Through many a birth in samsara have I wandered in vain,*
 seeking the builder of this house (of life).
Repeated birth is indeed suffering!
O house-builder, you are seen!
You will not build this house again.
For your rafters are broken and your ridgepole shattered.
My mind has reached the Unconditioned; I have attained the destruction of craving.»
(*Dhamma padam*, 153-154)

'House-builder' is *Prakriti*, the soul that sees *Prakriti* in its entirety is *Purusha*, and the process is that of release, overcoming, salvation, cessation, and numbness. Buddhist meditation is also called *Visuddhi magga* or the Path of Purification (of the soul) which is only a different word for *kaivalya*. The esoteric Christianity has this in mind when it speaks of resurrection, ascending from mortal into immortal, from the earthly into the divine.

In *Katha Upanishad* (II, 3, 17) it says:

The Purusha of the size of a thumb, the internal soul (âtman), is always seated in the heart of all living creatures; one should draw them out from one's own body boldly, as stalk from grass; one should know them as pure and immortal; one should know them as pure and immortal.

In all true descriptions of the human's most supreme realization, it is described as the purifying detachment of the soul from everything that is inauthentic to it. *Kaivalya* defines it best of all. According to the most accurate description of direct realization, Buddha's words, this isolation of the soul is experienced through an insight: "This is not me" and "This is not mine", regarding all the factors of the being (*Prakriti*): regarding the body, emotions, expressions of will, and each and every thought. Since this is not our property and all our efforts take us in the direction of acknowledg-

321

ing this fact that already exists as our highest reality, it is practically achieved only in calmness. ***Kaivalya is achieved only in calmness.*** In mental calmness, everything that is not our authenticity is detached and unveiled. For a calmness of this kind the ultimate discipline is required, the one that asks for ultimate understanding. Unrest is always the result of immaturity and misunderstanding.

Why is calmness required in meditation and in what way is it connected with consciousness?

The essence of the overall phenomena of nature or *Prakriti* is in motion, events, and frequencies. The whole nature is energy, where energy as such is the motion based on electromagnetic radiation or waves. All the living beings are primarily electromagnetic beings, and only afterward, they become chemical and biological ones. Everything is in the movement of energy, whereas the movement of energy is expressed in the form of frequencies. Each atom, DNA molecule, living being, each planet, and star have their own frequency. Therefore, the whole of *Prakriti* is in motion. Hence, the movement itself does not require consciousness, at least, to a large extent this is the case, it happens as a result of frequency exchange, completely spontaneously. The greater part of our body's movements happens without the presence and command of the consciousness because the movements are so vast in number that it is hard to keep track of them consciously. ***Therefore, only an awakened stillness is a conscious act in itself, it is the only stand against the entire rush of natural movements. It is the only act that expresses what nature engenders and what exceeds it, what is transcendental, and that is the soul's consciousness coming from Purusha, or the divine consciousness.***

Stillness is an unnatural act. Only dead beings are completely still. Similarly, when the body is dead the soul is liberated and authentic, awakened. There is no need to wait for the natural death of the body to occur for the soul to liberate itself, it is not recommended even. After all, if we enter death without the presence of the soul, we are doomed to repeat our life because we are unconsciously identified with the motion of nature. The soul would go on reincarnating itself until we attain the soul's transcendental consciousness during our life in our bodies, in this world. It is something that can and must be experienced during one's lifetime albeit through a mere discipline of utter stillness, bodily and mental, in meditation.

Meditation is a symbolic experience of death, it merely accelerates time so that we can experience during our life what would normally take innumerable lives, all the way through deaths, and lengthy periods of rebirths. With the help of meditation, we become truly alive because we have chosen to speed up the incarnation cycle in the space of one life only. Each good meditation equals one death and one rebirth. This makes meditation the experience of overcoming death, although, through it, we always go through a small death, as well. *"The Tibetan Book of the Dead"* (*Bardo Thodol*), states that with the soul's consciousness, something we acquire in meditation, we can grab death by the hair and pull it down.

Death is a big awakening. When we are in the body we perceive the experience of existence from one angle, from the perspective of a personality we were when we were in the body together with its individual experience. When we go out of the body, either permanently resulting from the death of the physical body, or in a controlled astral projection during life, we experience our consciousness expanding, and face the divine whole – which is something that we are ourselves. One same divine consciousness is in all of us. A physical body is nothing but a biological processor for narrowing and individualizing the soul's much bigger, universal consciousness, whereas, the physical senses detect only a small percentage of the electromagnetic spectrum that constitutes the physical reality. In meditation, we experience the overcoming of all of that in a smaller, controlled, and concentrated form, because we, then, abandon limitations of personality, mind and body. Consequently, the soul's consciousness can manifest itself in all its glory. Although for a short time, that is enough.

The very act of stillness of the mind and body engenders the soul's consciousness to break through to this world and become actualized in this world.

Without a presence of the soul's consciousness, nature moves of its own accord spontaneously by attaching to all the possible causal forms.[60] When the soul's consciousness is identified

---

[60] The Gnostic image of Ouroboros best illustrates this with a snake biting its own tail. The snake is a symbol of matter, *Prakriti*.

with nature and passive, the soul moves together with nature, as it were, it goes through rebirths being tied to events, being tied to *karma*. Only when the soul's consciousness is present in nature to the degree it is unconditioned by nature, the movement of nature changes, it begins to liberate itself, and works for the benefit of the soul's consciousness.

The essence of *kaivalya* and attainment of the soul's consciousness is ***in discerning oneself from being an immobile witness, from everything that moves, from the whole nature, in all the dimensions, from the mind and body, too. Then we see that everything that moves: thoughts, body, feelings, all objects - "it's not me" and "it's not mine"***.

We, as a soul, are always immobile. For the same reason, that space (*akasha*) is immobile and everything moves within it. Space itself gets modified into everything that exists and moves within itself. The same applies to our soul that is an immobile witness and everything plays out within it, in its consciousness, and it is the same divine consciousness that creates and engenders everything.

The very cosmic space is our soul, the divine essence. The fact that we see cosmic space as something outside being alienated from us, and experience ourselves as something minute and limited, only goes to show the power of the mind in twisting reality, the magnitude of the illusion we live in.

***

When we are not immobile witnesses, we are left to chance to the spontaneous motion of nature. In practical terms, it means: our soul is not some apparition that outlives the body, but is a mere principle of consciousness that is the foundation of existence, which overcomes and transcends everything. ***Our soul is an individualized principle of absolute consciousness.*** The absolute consciousness is manifested as existence using vibrations. The initial vibration is perpetual return or reset mode of the "divine particle" into the original state of the Absolute. This primal vibration generates all the remaining vibrations, everything that exists. It practically means that vibrations start from the more subtle ones and move onto the gross. The subtle vibrations being thoughts and ideas, expressions of will and energy, then feelings, and shape of the body. We manifest ourselves in that way, the consciousness of our soul vibrates as an idea or thought first, then as an intention or will, afterward feeling and imagination, and ultimately as the physical body. In this progressive way, our soul created the body we live in this world. The body is not a physical object, it consists of vibrations only, of our vibrations. All the atoms and genes of our body are only vibrations, not some physical objects or things. They vibrate in such a synchronized manner that to our senses it appears as a physical object or thing.

In that sense, it can be said that our bodies do not exist by themselves, and for themselves, nothing does, no object is real by itself. Every object is a mere manifestation of the absolute consciousness, the whole, which vibrates in a way of acquiring independence through vibrating, it can detach itself from the whole with its individual vibration, and ultimately, start suffering from an illusion that it is something else, and not the whole itself.

The essence of awareness, and the essence of meditation, is in **knowing the difference between the consciousness itself from its contents**, i.e., from all those forms that come about through vibrations of consciousness and perpetuate in maintaining themselves in a way that they look like independent objects in space and time.

This is how *Purusha* is distinguished from Prakriti. Purusha is the pure consciousness by itself, and Prakriti is a vibration of this consciousness that is spontaneously maintained in unending forms of existence.

Discerning the consciousness from the contents of the consciousness is how Purusha is discerned from Prakriti.

***

There is no purification and liberation of the soul's consciousness without understanding its affectionate bonding in all the dimensions of a being. The way a knot is tied is the same way how it can be untied.

Wakefulness (*buddhi*), which is realized in a way described here, is the presence of consciousness in the very being. Since the being is already energy potentially aware of itself, wakefulness is non-other than its allowing to be exactly that through their living experience, allowing for the universe to be aware of itself through man.

Humans permit it only when they diverts their consciousness from slaving away to objectivation regarding the world, something that is done via the body, feelings, general states of mind, and every thought. Once they stop projecting themselves, their consciousness, into illusory outness. Objectivation of consciousness toward the outside is the identification of the soul's consciousness with *Prakriti*. This type of objectivation lulls the potential of awareness all humans naturally possess, it pacifies them with the illusion of time, of the substantiality of phenomena, and their separate individuality.

Nothing pacifies humans more than the certainty that they will wake up in the morning in the same room they went to sleep in the night before, and that they will go on with their normal life, that after each step they will take another, that after breathing out they will breathe in again. That the life they have become so used to up till then will go on as usual. The deepest form of sleep is relying on nature to do things right. This certitude provokes humans to live mechanically from day to day in the physical world, although they are unaware of their true nature. We trample the earth every day and touch things completely unaware that these are all vibrations of our consciousness, absolute consciousness. *Our unconsciousness is manifested by the fact that we consider all objects as "dead things" that are separated from us*. Such a state affects the human consciousness to be passive and to surrender to the inertia of natural events.

Unfortunately, this certitude also makes them irresponsible, destructive, and evil as a result of their unconsciousness. Humans are destructive, evil, and unconscious to the exact degree they are convinced that every living being is "solid", acting on its free will as an independent individual, that this or that is "someone", or that something is "someone's", and, therefore, they can do "something" to it; if they fail to see that everything that happens is nothing but a wave of currently modified unique energy of the holographic universe.

Only when the solidity of the being dissolves right before their eyes do humans awaken – or it disintegrates psychologically if they are too identified with its illusory substantiality, with the decaying one. Humans awaken only when they have no other choice left, when there is no more certainty and hope that they will find a sanctuary somewhere outside, in the existence they experience objectively through their senses. Humans awaken when they realize that the reason for their existence is to experience consciously the life of nature, to acknowledge and illuminate themselves in it, and not to find a sanctuary in nature. The human soul should be liberated of all the dependences and worries for survival because unconditionality (*Purusha*) that engenders the existence itself, is the essence of it.

The essence of spiritual liberation or awakening is in the correct relationship toward existence, in the authentic relationship between humans (*Purusha*) and being (*Prakriti*), in consciousness, and existence. When the right relationship is established between them, the acknowledgment of true independence of the human soul (*Purusha*) from *Prakriti* takes place.

Humans with their wakefulness corrects that relationship and sets it right. The being or existence is never a problem, but an unawakened human's failing to see the reality of it. This creates all the problems that exist in the real world. Humans are not meant to create independence of their soul, because it has always been there, they should merely acknowledge and consciously synchronize with it.

The only way for humans to establish their independence from *Prakriti*, which is fundamentally already present, is for them to empower completely the potential of their wakefulness (*buddhi*) which is innate to every human being; therefore, to become aware of what they already are. Wakefulness is not strengthened through any type of concentration (unless concentration is applied as a measure to discipline the restless mind). Wakefulness (*buddhi*) can be strengthened only by stillness during the steady presence in all the occurrences and dimensions of existence. Such steadfast attention must be freed from any mental judging (*manas*) and personal determination (*aham-kâra*), otherwise, it will not be present in all the dimensions (tanmâtrâ and *maha-bhûtâni*). Only such complete presence of consciousness is independence (*kaivalya*). **Anyone who has ever experienced wakefulness knows that they were independent then, to the degree they can testify to independence being wakefulness, in reality.**

The four foundations of mindfulness

We have already seen how all the dimensions of nature become expressed through the "great elements", *maha-bhūtâni*. Their vibrations create a various density of phenomena and speed that form the overall cosmos. They are microscopically contracted in a human being by way of constituting their physical body (earth), feelings (water), general states of mind and willpower (fire), and every single thought (air). *Humans were created from all the dimensions of the cosmos, and their task is to ascertain their wakefulness in accordance with all the dimensions because there is no other way.*

Therefore, their wakefulness must be empowered in a fourfold way: regarding the (1) body, (2) feelings, (3) expressions of willpower and states of mind, and (4) every thought. These are the four foundations of attention one must steadily be focused on, and each one should be comprehended properly. Through alert awareness each of these dimensions of existence is released of its outer projection, of the illusion that they are external to humans, dissolved of the illusion of substantiality and being reduced to their sheer outcome - *akasha* – to the consciousness which is our awareness of ourselves. In other words, they are all recognized as our nature. We never observed the higher dimensions because we lacked sufficient knowledge of what they are truly like, they are within us, and, instead, we projected them outwardly. Everything we project to the outside world we automatically make invisible and incomprehensible, and alien to us. When we reach the point of recognizing all the dimensions of existence together, in ourselves, permanent wakefulness is born, the one we call *kaivalya*.

If meditation is based on the transcendence of thoughts only, it is incomplete, even if one manages to pull it off, the experience is not permanent because humans frequently experience relapse into the lower states of consciousness – as they still have not become aware of their whole being, of all of their dimensions. The entire practice is then turned into a ritual, yet another encumbering habit in the daily routine. That is why awareness must be conducted onto all the dimensions of human beings and existence in general.

Other spiritual traditions feel the urgency of becoming aware of the being in all the dimensions, not in the sphere of thoughts (ideas) only, however they express it in a vague and foggy way, through various (god's) commandments, taboos, moral norms, regulations that include odds and sods, the menu included. Judeo-Christian moral obligations mostly deal with the physical dimension of events (behavior), and a little less mental, and they do not stress anywhere clearly enough the unity of the physical, emotional, and mental, as it were. The tradition of religious devotion (bhakti) mostly emphasizes the emotional dimension of beingness. Only in the tradition of yoga is the necessity of awareness of the whole being percolated from any metaphysics, theology, and idolatry, and reduced to practice only, to the general rules of proper conduct (*yama*), and specifically the yogic obligation (*niyama*). Buddha set forth the whole process of awareness (meditation) based on these because they encapsulated all the dimensions of the being, from the grossest to the most subtle. It is a sad affair that there are many schools of Buddhism, or sects, that fail to see the inevitability of the whole awareness, but underline some of its aspects only (breathing, feelings, or the mind separately).

The key to liberation is in integrated awareness of the beingness, in all of its dimensions (body, feelings, willpower, and every single thought). If we so much as overlook only one dimension, its unconscious phenomena will be the cause of our suffering and bondage. If we take a preference of one over the other, for example, the mental one (by immersing ourselves in some meditative 'technique', a prayer, or mantra chanting), no matter what insights and experiences we end up having, we will, nonetheless, decline back to the lower states pulled by the weight of the remaining part of unaware beingness, and we will go round in circles continuously repeating the one-sided practice in hope of achieving the permanent sublime state, provided we get to repeat it as many time as we can.

Humans' lives are unconscious and out of balance to such a degree that they fail to see what constitutes and determines them. They seldom differentiate between the nature of their mental attitude from emotions and physical states, and when they do, it is only temporary and without permanent establishing. The interdependence of all the factors that constitute a being, and their indiscrimination, ultimately condition the consciousness to identify with them, together with the contents of their experience of the world. Once we comprehend their impact through mutual discernment, it starts to have a balancing effect on uneven flows (due to the dynamics of gunas) of life energy (*prâna*) in each of the dimensions of phenomena, and by doing so it releases the presence of the soul's transcendental consciousness. Therefore, nothing but objective understanding is all it takes. It consists of two phases.

The first one is **discernment** (*viveka*) of the four dimensions of beingness that had up till then acted interdependently, hence, with the conditioning effect, and becoming familiar thoroughly with each of them separately.

The second one is spontaneous **application of direct insight** (*vipassana*) on the functioning of all of these dimensions in us (the body, feelings, willpower, and mind), as well as around us, without some specific practice, the way they play out in life altogether.

All of the four dimensions of strengthening the insight represent progressive cleansing of the consciousness from various fictitious contents and deceptions and enabling it to be faced and united with the existence for what it is. Constant mindfulness (*satipatthâna*) is none other than intensive annulment of time during which we wander painfully about and across spaces of inauthentic beingness. Through mindfulness wisely and finally becomes realized what must at one point happen to us in our life: the presence of consciousness of the divine that engenders everything (the unconditionality of existence) to grow progressively bigger in human being, the presence of the soul becomes actualized and made aware of, resulting in suffering being erased. The consciousness itself represents the acceleration of time of events leading up to their ultimate outcome in wakefulness. By becoming aware completely, humans lose the ability to be sinful ever again.

Awareness, like the overcoming of time, *kaivalya*, is practically reduced to attaining independent presence amidst all the psychophysical processes of one's own being fully understanding them, as well as a pragmatic relationship towards them. In the same way, it is done with the outer objects because the soul is independent of all the events within the being because to it our being is the same as outer objects are to our body and mind. Only objectivity within the being itself is the kind that engenders objectivity out of oneself and toward the world, the true attainment of the being in all of its dimensions, realizing that we are made up of the same dimensions, too. The more objective we are toward ourselves, the more we are able to be objective toward the world. The result of that will no longer be some conclusion, attitude, or myth, as was invariably the case with an awareness of existence afore-described, but simple wakefulness and liberation.

The issue, therefore, is not to do with an objectivity that divides and alienates humans from the world, but with the maturity of their soul that engenders them to participate in the world leading it to an authentic outcome. The way parents experience maturing of their child, the same way humans in this practice (*vipassana* and *satipatthâna*) view their psychophysical being for what it is, thus transforming it to spiritual maturity. The awareness described here engenders humans to rein the elements of natural phenomena of the body, feelings, and mind by facing them directly and seeing what they are – and not facing their contents like it had been the case up till then.

Facing phenomena for what it is means giving up on identifying with their contents, it is the distinction consciousness from the content of consciousness. This is the essence of wakeful stillness and kaivalya itself.

Inevitably, this facing is highly unappealing, uninteresting, and repulsive because it does not bring any new contents, conclusions, convictions, or hopes that would be more alluring than the previous ones. This practice knocks all of them down to engender the true freedom the human soul once had before the birth in the body, before the origin of the world even. The consciousness of this primeval freedom is all the more present, if *Purusha* or unconditionality in humans overpowers the mechanisms of acquired habits in human life, speech, and way of thinking. This natural mechanism always had supremacy during their previous life and abused consciousness for the passive illumination of its functioning. What is required here is the complete change of this situation: that humans with unconditioned consciousness detach and cleans themselves (*kaivalya*) from everything that currently conditions their authenticity and freedom, from everything that is not themselves in the absolute sense, from everything that stands between them and the presence in the transcendental divine soul, and is, instead, tying them to some contents of this world.

It is easy to be independent in favorable moments and circumstances, toward the physical body, especially if the body itself is not particularly appealing. What is required is to be independent in every possible moment towards that what is the closest to us, like the feelings and thoughts, for example. The body is the furthest, and thought is the closest to the soul's consciousness. Once each thought becomes as irrelevant and alien as our body is, as the outer objects are, we are in *kaivalya*. Then, we are able to tell *Purusha* apart from *Prakriti* in a way where we see *Prakriti* for what it is. That is the only way to see *Purusha* for what it is, as well. Then we can finally see ourselves for what we are, we see our soul as independent of everything. We become authentic and truly independent. Only then are we able to participate in life authentically and properly when we view life and ourselves in the right way. All the mistakes and suffering come about only when we do not see the true nature of *Prakriti*, when we persist in identifying with the body and mind, the state of us where we are like in sleep or hypnosis.

Kaivalya is practically accomplished when we become aware of the body and grow independent of it, something we are able to do when we cease to experience the body as something that moves through space and engages in action, when we rather remain immobile within ourselves, only testifying of the experience of body's actions in space and time, in a way where each act is detached from us and insignificant. Otherwise, we treat each movement of the body as though it were important and become attached to it, as well as everything else we do with the body. In awakening that is all gone. Everything the body does becomes irrelevant. Instead of the body being present there, now we have space (*akasha*) that instantly forms itself to become the body and everything else, for that matter. We no longer experience our body as some small individual existence within an infinitely big space, but we see that the body itself is nothing but a minor modification of space that vibrates so that it takes on the form of an individual "body".

The next step is much the same as the previous one, but it refers to the feelings and emotions that we continuously experience based on what the body does. The body's actions attracted various feelings and emotions. Now it is gone since any movement by the body has become irrelevant to us, as have feelings and emotions in an ever-moving body. Instead of the emotional drama and game of opposites, pleasure, and displeasure, consciousness comes to the stage, and feelings as such become only the vibrations by the same consciousness that engenders everything, and that is ourselves.

The next step is expressions of will or intent. It is an even subtler realm of our being. In earlier times, the expressions of willpower were functioning unconsciously, we did something, and later we convinced ourselves that it had been our original plan all along. We acted then being largely unconscious and conditioned, we merely reacted, and functioned creatively even less. The expressions of our willpower always had a pattern of our personality, we behaved and acted always personally, in a way which is specific for us only, in speech, movements, and reactions. When the expressions of willpower become recognized as the vibrations of the same *Prakriti*, as a bunch of randomly accumulated reactions to the outer challenges, we, then, free ourselves of the spontaneous reactions and mechanical behavior, we stop resembling ourselves from before and start acting in accordance with the will of our transcendental soul. When we do so, we always act on our own free will, and expressions of willpower that are not in line with the consciousness of our soul and the objective reality, disappear. Our actions are effortless and spontaneous from then on. Our old patterns of behavior become unimportant. This change is called "the old human has died", and "the new one is born" in esoteric schools. What further remains is only the intention of the Absolute to manifest itself as everything that is. More accurately put, our willpower is, then, synchronized with the willpower of the divine consciousness.

Finally, the same happens with our thoughts. Thoughts are the closest to us, and are, therefore, the most important. Thoughts and convictions are something we find the hardest to change and get rid of because we do not see them objectively for what they are, it is difficult to distinguish them from ourselves – unless we have learned to differentiate the consciousness from the contents of

333

consciousness (thoughts) in meditation. When even the most subtle vibrations of our being, our thoughts, we begin to recognize as the subtle vibrations of *Prakriti*, when we learn to see our thoughts as something that no longer exists objectively by and for itself, but as vibrations of the absolute consciousness that is ourselves, then every thought becomes irrelevant. When our thoughts become irrelevant, they begin to die down. We are every thought; we vibrate as every thought. Thoughts are vibrations of consciousness that are us but suffering from the oblivion of ourselves. Thoughts originate at the point when we forget about ourselves when we forget about the consciousness itself that is the existence itself, and which is us. We forget ourselves and begin to identify with the contents of thoughts, vibrating as thoughts, as something other than ourselves, as some idea or a thought. Our thought is our oblivion, the oblivion of the consciousness itself as the foundation of existence, although a thought exists as an aspiration to penetrate the secret of existence. This brings forth a wondrous paradox of thoughts. There is no other way for us to forget ourselves other than becoming estranged from ourselves: the thought enslaves us by assuming the form of the aspiration to set us free; we lose the knowledge of ourselves through our aspiration to know ourselves. The essence is that our soul was never trapped, it was only put to sleep by the thoughts while it was in the body. As a soul, we dreamed every thought, every expression of will, every feeling, and our physical body, as well. All those vibrations belong to the consciousness of our soul. It is all our own being – even though it seems to us that we are not. They are all the vibrations we used to create an illusion of being apart from the consciousness of our soul.

These are all ways of establishing kaivalya in all the dimensions of our being.

The essence of *kaivalya* is in understanding *Prakriti*, and not in denial or separation from anything. The process of awakening resembles detaching or overcoming something only from the perspective of the mind identified with its contents. Only in such a mind can the cessation of identification look like overcoming or separation. From the point of the soul's transcendental consciousness (*Purusha*) there is no separation from anything since nothing is substantial, material, and objective, nothing is separate by definition. The awakening of the soul's consciousness is a mere under-standing of the true nature of existence. There is no difference in existence between what is outward or inward, this difference is created by the mind and it is only virtual. Understanding the true nature of existence is something a person does within themselves, or more specifically: the proper understanding of the true nature of the body; the true nature of feelings; the true nature of expressions of willpower, and the true nature of thoughts. This is the only way in which they can be overcome. Nothing objective is overcome, though, but only one's ignorance of the true nature of existence, and that is ignorance that says that **existence is the same conscious-ness** with which we ascertain both existence and ourselves. When we see reality for what it is, then, we see that our transcendental soul is always free and independent. Then, from the perspective of the transcendental soul, we can see the overall existence as one: we do not see the difference between our body and the surrounding space, from the earth, water, light, air... the whole nature is our body, our being, the whole of *Prakriti*. We will begin to feel all of that like ours, it may happen that we experience other people's pain as our own, and feel other people's thoughts and moods... the way plants have always been able to do.

When we are unaware of ourselves, of our true nature, exis-tence to us, then, looks like something coming from the outside, the earth and nature appear as unconscious, material objects. When we are aware of ourselves, we, then, see that everything is aware of itself, that everything is an expression of the same con-sciousness we became aware of ourselves with, the consciousness of the divine soul. Since existence and consciousness are one, **we cannot become aware of ourselves only, and everything else to remain detached from us. We cannot become aware of ourselves and the world to stay the same**. Our being is no different from the world. By knowing who we are, we know the world around us. It is not sepa-rated. In the language of *Sâmkhya*: *Prakriti* exists as the uncons-cious nature only when we are unaware of the true nature of *Puru-sha*. Once *Purusha* is known, *Prakriti* desists and goes away, like a dancer who has shown her dancing.

Humans can, therefore, have a dual existence. The first one has been granted naturally, it is spontaneous and unconscious in a majority of people, animals, and other beings. All the natural functions can be maintained unconsciously. This is exactly what the life of an average human looks like; they are hypnotized by various fictions and concepts of religious or social convictions. They guide them from birth to old age and death. Nowhere else. The second way brings overcoming of the first by crossing over the stream of life, by abandoning the flow of general yielding to natural phenomena, which is the path of the winner over the elements, the path of Human being. This road is traveled by sensitive and karmically mature enough people who sense that the first path, unconscious way of living is not authentic, and inevitably results in suffering only. However, their turning is most often spontaneous movement against the elements, it is nothing but a spontaneous reaction to such a state, and every reaction is an unconsciously conditioned act. They negate life, sometimes they use some more constructive means, such as going to a monastery, renunciation, and devoting their life to some discipline, alternatively, they become rebels in a number of ways. However, those who are truly on the path of awakening do not go against the stream of life, they only cross over to the other side, they master the unconscious elements of beingness through the transcendence of it, they do not attempt fighting it. Struggle entails acceptance of unconsciousness as our true state, attributing reality to something that is not real, at all. If unconscious were our nature truly, there would be no way for us to become conscious ever. We are already on the other side; we should simply become aware of it, all we need is to awaken.

By constant awareness of the body, feelings, willpower, the general state of mind, and the origin of every thought, the being attains balance and cleanses itself of the old, naturally conditioned patterns of behavior. With all the actions of such humans, feelings, and thoughts become well-balanced, harmonious, and synchronized. They are freed from their bondage to life as much as the repulsion toward it because they have known the true nature of life, finally. He turns their back both on happiness and unhappiness alike, joys and sorrows of days gone by. They are equanimous in all circumstances and serene in the purified presence of their unconditioned soul.

Apart from the complete awareness of beingness, the key to liberation, according to the teaching of *Sâmkhya*, is in its rudimentary attitude that the whole *Prakriti* serves to liberate *Purusha*. Therefore, *Purusha* – a human being does not have to do anything to be free, but to be what they are, to be still, to avoid going after all the *Prakriti* phenomena trapping themselves in the process. To the degree they are still and untied, they are aware of their timeless freedom. **When Prakriti is objectively acknowledged as Prakriti, then the liberation of Purusha takes place.** *Prakriti* can be objectively viewed for what it is only with a mind that is still, out of time, here and now. The soul's consciousness prevails then.

It practically means that the practice of *kaivalya* is about complete abandonment of the world, through the mental, emotional, and physical stillness in meditation – but not for the sake of discarding the world because there is nothing to be discarded, it is all One, but to understand the true nature of the world. The hardest thing to do is reject one's mind or thoughts. We can do so only if we understand the true nature of thoughts (that are only subtle vibrations of our being), and the fact that we engage in the process of thinking only when we are oblivious of ourselves, of our true being and existence. Thoughts represent an aspiration to comprehend the emergent world, to make sense of it all. Since our being is not our body only but the overall existence, thoughts do not deal with our existence only, but the overall existence, as well.

To understand the true nature of the world and together with it thoughts, as well, two conditions need to be met. The first one is a complete retreat from the world and life in a brief stillness during meditation, and the other one is participating in the world and life as they are, without a choice. Spiritual practice is when both of these are consciously and deliberately performed. We always do them, albeit unconsciously, through awake state and deep sleep. The point is in putting consciousness into all of our activities.

When we experience both of these extremes, it will provide us with enhanced capacity by means of expanding our perception, i.e., consciousness. **Only such an expansion of perception through the ultimate opposites of existence can awaken and liberate us. The medi-**

tation itself is not enough, its opposition is also needed, or all the life activities.[61]

Therefore, do not worry if you are not good at meditating. Simply continue doing it, in spite of everything. ***Once you start to meditate absolutely everything you do begins to awaken you***, even the most traumatic experiences that are the complete opposite of meditative stillness.

***

The ways of attaining permanent wakefulness presented here are only basic and necessary preconditions for its attaining. In buddhist meditation *vipassana* the practice of enlightening the body, feelings and will is performed; in Zen meditation the mind is

---

[61] Hermann Hesse in his novel *Siddhartha* (also in *Narcissus and Goldmund*) details the meaning of experiencing Alpha and Omega. Siddhartha and Govinda equally practiced meditation, the practice of awareness of the soul. Govinda joined Buddha's disciples and became a monk who only devoted themselves to meditation (the Alpha point). Monks are very important and necessary for the preservation and transmission of teachings. Siddhartha chose the other extreme, the world of sensual pleasures and vice (the experiencing of Omega point). He, finally, found balance and became enlightened as a result. However, it did not work out for Govinda because he remained one-sided, as he turned his life to Alpha. He lacked the experience of Omega. Buddha was on a similar path. His youth was reckless, living in one extreme only, in the Alpha state of hedonism, and complete satisfaction of the sensual needs of life. Once he realized it was only an extreme, and not the whole thing, he turned to the other extreme of utter asceticism, and almost reached the point of dying. He became enlightened when he realized the middle path (*majjhimāpaṭipadā*) is the balance of all extremes, the whole of circling of Alpha and Omega (the wheel of *dharma*).

Having been through both experiences of extremes, human being can experience enlightenment and understanding the meaning of it all. The experience of both extremes serves well to expand our perception. Only an expanded experience of this kind can bring the necessary capacity for accepting the presence of the divine consciousness in everything-that-is and everything-that-can-be, it opens the door for wisdom (Sanskrit: *prajñā*, Pali: *paññā*). Expanding perception through the experience of all the opposites alerts us to the world of the soul's consciousness, Alpha, without solely wishing to aspire toward Alpha, and nothing else. The experience of Omega is of crucial value for our attaining Alpha. We all expand our consciousness in a myriad of ways, in the outside world, but in ourselves, too.

On the importance of experiencing opposites on the path to our goal of achieving complete awareness, Alpha and Omega, see my book "*Religiousness – Instruction for Use*

338

directly transcended. A detailed and complete description of the practice of meditation is in my book *"Meditation – First and Last Step – From Understanding to Practice"*. Only when they are fulfilled can a human being attain an individual experience of awakening that is mind-blowing and unique for everyone.

***

How can we recognize kaivalya on the universal map of existence, on the *Prakriti* scheme (picture 1)?

We have seen that *aham-kâra*, the human's true personality, becomes whole only when humans become aware of the objective, inorganic nature in all of its dimensions, and that means when they perfect their out-of-body experiences. Once they become conscious of their independence of the body, they realize what their true identity is, and finally acquire the power to act, "I am doer"- *aham-kâra*.

(Through the objective perspective, on the collective plane, humankind achieves the same through science by knowing all the laws of physics. Through conscious mastering the objective nature, humankind becomes the true doer in the right way.)

The next step is lifting oneself up above any illusion of individuality into pure wakefulness, above *aham-kâra* in *mahat-buddhi*. It represents the knowledge of the highest dimension of nature, *akasha* or aether. It is the universal field that contains absolutely everything that is manifested through space and time. The whole of *Prakriti* or nature is contracted into One there, into unity. We enter this unity only when we are completely awake, hence the term for this category *buddhi*, which means wakefulness. Time stops and everything disappears there, even *Prakriti*. It is not the case of it disappearing, but the illusion of its movement. We see nature then, as one whole, there are no separate or alienated parts. Existence as motion we see only if we see everything as objective segments that move through space and time, and if we are identified with the body as a separate individual that moves through space and time, as well. In wakefulness, everything stops moving because the illusion of separate objects that move in time also disappears. Everything moves to arrive somewhere, and achieve something. In timeless wakefulness, everything stops because it sees itself as fully realized already, complete and perfect in itself, as a sphere. And our soul is such, too.

Nothing changes with this, everything stays the same, life goes on, but **now everything moves within itself**, like in a sphere. The sphere is the only form that can explain this timeless condition. From the energy point of view, a sphere is stationary, as is the energy of the state of timeless wakefulness, it is non-Hertzian (like a lightning ball). Such is also the energy of the quantum field. It has these properties because it represents a reflection of the fundamental unity of nature where everything is momentarily present as One. That explains how non-Hertzian frequencies get transmitted instantly across the entire universe.

To use the language of our experience, when we go through repeated out-of-body visits to astral and the higher dimensions, we learn too well that over there everything is energy that is ruled by consciousness, and our consciousness is part of this universal consciousness we are able to create reality by ourselves. We see this so clearly that it becomes apparent to us even when we return to this plane: matter is energy, like in the higher dimensions, only different laws apply to it, for example, it becomes more solid and stable here. However, we begin to realize that it has the same kind of energy as does the whole of existence. On the physical plane we can act similarly as on the astral plane (*siddhi*). This is a point where we attain true independence – kaivalya – from any limiting stranglehold matter may have over us, from the body and mind, too, that no longer affect our soul's transcendental consciousness. At the same time, the consciousness of our soul achieves supremacy in functioning while we still reside in this body.

In short, this is what wakefulness looks like. That is why Buddha constantly described wakefulness as numbness, *nirvana*, in other words, as the cessation and blowing out. What they wished to convey was that we are truly awake only when we are independent (*kaivalya*) from the body, mind, time, and all the life experience together with the world itself. It becomes only a dream. That is why this is called wakefulness.

To avoid all the adversities of life all you should do is to avoid identification with the body, mind, and feelings through insight into their true nature. Nature of the consciousness is such that everything is right, and under the best of circumstances, it releases everything, negativity too, all by itself. There is nothing one should do with the world, body, mind, and feelings because nature is in charge of that, our task is to acknowledge them for what they are *at any given moment*, and by doing so we transcend them, we set the consciousness of our soul free, which will ultimately result in resolving all the negativities, and all the ignorance. Being attached to the body, mind, and feelings gives us an illusion that we should do something with all of them in the outside world. What we can do with the body is quite limited, only what it can reach and the mind is capable of comprehending it. In reality, it is very little. The consciousness of our soul can do much more, it created everything, the earth we walk on, the air we breathe, the water we drink. *The divine consciousness of our soul created the whole of the reality we live in. We only have it to rely on, and nothing else*. All of the physical world is only a shadow of the consciousness of our soul. Therefore, if we truly wish to be free from all the negativities, mistakes, and suffering, the only thing we should do with ourselves is to awaken in independence (*kaivalya*) through the practice of meditation, and become liberated from our body and mind in the consciousness of our transcendental soul, thus, becoming true creators of our own reality.

It is the only thing we should do because we do that all the time, anyway, all our lives, all of the work on this planet, all the culture, all our interpersonal relationships are a reflection of working on ourselves, on the awakening of our soul. We have never done anything else but through the illusion of bondage to the body and mind, we expressed the soul's consciousness externally and learned of implementing it in all possible ways, through all the mistakes and renewed attempts, through all the joys and sufferings we inflict on one another. All our civilizations and all our worlds were built on them. They are all bound to fail, civilizations will meet their doom one after another until humans completely uncover the consciousness of their divine soul in this world, which has always been independent and unconditioned (*kaivalya*).

The only successful attempt at civilizational growth happens in humans who are mindful in meditation while attaining samadhi, kaivalya, who is completely present in the consciousness of their soul while it is still in the body in this world, in each timeless moment, while they are doing everything they should be doing, when they are the ones who are.

This kind of an insight introduces us to the cognition that "nothing in *Prakriti* is mine", and "I am independent of everything" because I am not even an individual (*aham-kâra*) within that whole (*Prakriti*), nor some modification of the consciousness regarding the world (*buddhi*), which are also integrated parts of nature as its most subtle form. All the modifications (forming) belong to *Prakriti* and not the consciousness that is of the divine soul. The consciousness stays always the same during its modifications across *Prakriti*, the consciousness remains an ever awoke and independent witness. This witness is *Purusha*, human soul or essence. Only from there can humans see that the very modification of consciousness, the one that forms the world and the experience of the world, is not a self-willed act of *Prakriti*, or humans for that matter, even *Purusha*, but its proximity, its closeness to *Purusha*. This closeness generates identification. It is only this proximity of modification of *Prakriti* that appears as though the consciousness modifies itself. The same way a crystal set against a red background looks red. When we say "closeness" we mean great resemblance. Everything is essentially One. This proximity further reflects and refracts, i.e. different in *jiva*, the individual soul. It is the one that takes humans through the experience of living-in-the-world. With such an insight, humans awaken.

The insight into the fact that the whole nature (*Prakriti*) is One and nothing new ever happens in it, is the beginning of awakening. The insight into complete independence of the soul (*Purusha*) from the overall nature signals attaining complete wakefulness. The insight into the independence of our soul from nature does not result in the abandonment of nature, because there is nothing to be abandoned, quite the contrary, our mere independence invites the whole nature into existence, it yields the overall life as it is here and now. If it were not for the transcendental divine soul, ourselves, there would be no existence of nature, either. That is why such insight develops love for the whole of nature.

Only a clear insight into the fact that the whole of *Prakriti* exists for *Purusha* (for human beings) can take us to the awakening.

All the objects exist for the subject. That is why they finally awaken when they stop searching for sanctuary in objects, and they become aware only because they have understood and accepted objects as their projections.

Our unconsciousness is based on our resistance to nature, on misunderstanding that it is there to serve us.

With the awakening man their whole existence, their whole life, their body, mind, and the whole world, starts to recognize as a dream that was not their even, it all came from *Prakriti* – because unconsciousness is typical for *Prakriti*, and not for their soul, *Purusha*. Everything that was achieved as a result of happening over time, is inevitably conditioned by time, and the game of opposites offers only the illusion of its termination. The authenticity of the unconditioned human soul does not depend on the termination of time and overcoming the conditionality of beingness (something we were looking forward to before), because it was never threatened by it, it was not an opposition to anything that would be inauthentic. Therefore, it cannot be a product of any kind of activity that has a goal in perfecting itself toward liberation or salvation but only to awakening as the numbness of passion for existence in ignorance and unconsciousness. *Liberation in timeless wakefulness represents cessation and numbness in the participation in illusion and ignorance, and not achievement and accomplishment of something objectively new* because the wakefulness itself is complete unconditionality from anything, that precedes every reality and engenders every existence.

Final awakening is the cessation of the illusion of time, time is the initial illusion with which we identify *Purusha* with *Prakriti*. It is said that with awakening we become what we have always been, and all we need to do is remove illusory identifications that lead us to think we are something else. This practically means that before the awakening **all our insights and cognitions were worthless, that we have absolutely nothing else to do but only to awaken**. The underlying illusion we lose our lives over is that before this there is something else we should do, something regarding the life drama, contents of the consciousness, or some cognizance. The mind keeps on projecting all the world and time, and together with it all the contents and cognizance in the world and time. Wakefulness is the transcendence of the mind itself, *that is why it is crucial for us to know that we must not project the very transcendence of the mind into time, that is to say, awakening. By doing so, we only postpone i*t. It is always and only possible here and now, as the first act, before all other acts, and not a consequence of some other actions. That is why meditation as a practice of transcending the mind, is the only correct action – action through nonaction.

All the life in illusion consists of this projection, of postponing our wakefulness. All our lives in illusion consist of this projection.

Since we have always been what we should be, the pure soul as the transcendental *Purusha*, *the basic criterion of wakefulness is wakefulness during deep sleep*. Our overall existence consists of four states: daily wakefulness (1), dreams (2), deep sleep without dreams (3), and the soul's pure, transcendental consciousness (4) that supersedes the three previous states, which is always present behind all these states of existence because it is the foundation of the existence itself. The first three states (daily wakefulness, dreams and deep sleep without dreams) are the states of *Prakriti*; the fourth state belongs to *Purusha*. When we are permanently in the fourth state, we are always conscious, both during daily wakefulness and deep sleep without dreams, when the world and our individuality disappear completely.

What remains then is only the Divine that engenders the consciousness and our essence, the soul. This pure consciousness that exists always as that what engenders existence itself is Divine Absolute in us and whose embodiment are we.

All the heroic efforts aimed at attaining liberation, which must be undertaken, are at long last reduced to the liberation of all efforts that originate because of the world and its overcoming, and boil down to relaxation, the numbness of all aspirations, equanimity, and independence (*kaivalya*). All efforts are in vain because we keep on dreaming, both in daily wakefulness and sleep, we dream bondage and the effort of liberation, *we dream absolutely everything until we wake up*. When we stop dreaming during the day, during our whole world and life, we will stop dreaming at night, too. Then, we will be awake during deep sleep without dreams. Humans who are awakened like that are free from the shifting periods of consciousness and unconsciousness of themselves that are mutual, of action and nonaction, of existence and nonexistence: they experience the existence itself as the affirmation of consciousness and its living authenticity. They see that the divine unconditioned consciousness is the only reality unscathed by the emergent world and whether are aware of it or not. Like the movie screen on which floods and fires are played out, but it is left unscathed by these phenomena (it only engenders their projection or manifestation), or like that mirror that is unaffected by the characteristics of the images that reflect in it, in the same way, the divine unconditioned consciousness, that is the human essence or soul, remains untouched by *Prakriti* phenomena, its elements and fires, not the outer ones only, but those that are in the body and psyche.

Once humans become aware of the divine consciousness in them, he, then, actualizes it in this world, through themselves. It is the only purpose of their existence.

When we are awakened, we recognize the transcendental divine unconditioned presence as our essence, we realize that this mortal body and illusory mind are transient creations of *Prakriti* and none of it is ours, we were not born to realize natural urges, quite the reverse, natural urges gave birth to *us to realize through us the presence of the timeless divine unconditionality* that engenders the whole nature. Nature, then, disappears for us like a dream does for an awakened one, and only an endless, timeless, and omnipotent blissfulness remains as our Self and wakefulness.

Afterward, immediately upon the very act of awakening, such wakefulness begins to consolidate in us to become living and efficient, we see nature as the embodiment of the divine presence through all the forms that constitute the experiential world – first and foremost through our human body, through our breath and look, movement, and thought. All the physical world becomes solid and clearly formed energy, the power of divine consciousness.

Human wakefulness manifests as the complete harmony of all the movements of body and voice during the speech, like the absolute goodness toward everything and absolute independence of everything. That is what the awakened looks like.

Therefore, firstly, every form of beingness became empty, humans finally stepped out of it and attained freedom from any bondage in the emergent world. This voidness, then, became the form itself, the world became (to humans only) the manifestation of the freedom of existence. Additionally, they did not 'become' but were acknowledged for what they have always been. At this point the full circle is made: firstly, from the unconscious elements of the beingness to the freedom from its conditioning forms, to the pure consciousness, and then to the being itself, which this time is no longer unconscious but enlightened. Hence, it is not a circle, but a spiral rather, because the beingness is happening on a higher level now.

The same way a being would not exist without the unconditionality that engenders it, the unconditionality in question would also not be there without the beingness that it is; unconditionality must be realized through all the forms of life, otherwise, it will remain sheer abstraction and only the darkness of natural urges in their struggle for survival will be at work here. The spirit of the divine unconditionality tried to break through the darkness before making its way into human life, and shed eternal light on humans, being experienced as the Holy Spirit (in Mazdaism and esoteric Christianity) or Shiva (in Hinduism). Now humans are permanently filled with it as their own essence.

And only a life like that – which is no longer driven to fight for survival, but, to the contrary, bathes in eternal, omnipotent, and uncreated divine presence, the one that life exceeds by far because it engenders and nurtures it – only a life like that becomes possible for a human being, a life that is authentic and blissful.

Life is acceptable and bearable for humans only when they do not seek refuge in it, in life itself and manifested world, but in the unconditioned divine soul which engenders it.

All that remains for awakened humans is a perpetually liberated life of nature (*Prakriti*) that keeps manifesting freely as the experience of love. However, unlike other people who have not yet traveled the path of purification presented here, they with their mere presence every moment in all the dimensions fills life with meaning, heals and stills it from futile whirlpools of passions, purifies it from ignorance, and liberates it in the cognition of its outcome. They radiate goodness that engenders the world.

Such human beings are able to do so only because they see that they were never any different from the outcome of everything,

Purusha is always independent of *Prakriti*, and they would make a mistake if they tried to make their soul authentic as regards nature, if they asked for their own salvation. It is redundant because they are not enslaved. If they were, they would have neither the divine soul nor the consciousness in themselves – nor would they exist. Since they are already free, they can validate and enliven their original state in the experience with love only when they encourage all the life of nature, all of its beings, and not their freedom, not even their own life. Nature never stifles the human soul. It cannot do so because the soul engenders the whole nature. Nature serves the purpose of human self-knowledge entirely, and for this reason, humans achieve self-awareness and liberation **only when they infinitely supports the life of all the beings and all the nature, and not their own**. Only by doing so can they experience with pure love everything that exists, with all of their opposites (Matthew, 5.6.7). Only when they experience it, will they be completely aware of existence the way it is.

Then, humans will be able to express the divine consciousness through themselves in this world.

And only when they manifest the divine consciousness in this world do humans discover their true essence: **it is the very Divine that engenders both the existence (Prakriti) and the consciousness of existence (Purusha) as human self-awareness**.

There are no differences between consciousness and existence as such, between the cosmos and the awareness of the cosmos, between the outward universe and everything inward in humans. The whole universe and human essence, the soul, are the same.

The whole nature (*Prakriti*) is the human body.

The whole of the manifested cosmos (*Prakriti*) is only a concrete manifestation of the pure awareness of oneself (*Purusha*).

***

This is a way in which, according to *Sâmkhya*, in the teaching of Kapila and his mother, humans know themselves and awaken to an unborn and immortal divine soul that engenders all in existence.

EPILOGUE

TEXTS OF CLASSICAL SÂMKHYA

SÂMKHYA-KÂRIKÂ of
Ishvara Krishna

1. From the shock of triple misery comes the desire to know the means of prevention. To neglect pure consciousness when we are confronted with worldly experiences is not right, because complete cessation of suffering by surrendering to mundane life is not possible.

("The triple misery" may come from: 1. ourselves; 2. from the outer world, i.e., other beings, and 3. from the heavenly world as the influence of planets, gods (non-organic beings), or as the power of destiny. "Pure consciousness" is transcendental, divine consciousness, *Purusha*, who is our soul, and "mundane life" is limited to the relative mind and conditioned beingness of *Prakriti*.)

2. Religious and secular methods are also tainted, destructive and excessive. The reverse direction of conscious discrimination of the manifest, the unmanifest and the knower it's better.

("The reverse direction of conscious discrimination" is the practice of meditation that objectively ascertains everything, from thoughts and feelings, to the grossest physical manifestations. It is clearly indicated here that both mundane and religious experiences fall under this category, although with different contents and effects, and to acquire spiritual authenticity one needs the experience of transcendence. In other words, one would do better than to look for the meaning of existence and sanctuary outside, but within themselves, in his own transformation, and not altering the outer circumstances, using either mundane or religious methods, for that matter.)

3. Primordial matter (*mulaprakriti*) is the root (*avikriti*), not a product; the seven principles beginning with the great Intellect (*mahat*) are both products and productive; the sixteen are mere products; the Self (Soul, *Purusha*) is neither a product nor productive.

(The 'seven principles' are: *mahat-buddhi, aham-kara,* and *tanmâtrâ.* The 'sixteen ingredients' are: *indriyâni* and *mahabhûtâni.*)

4. Perception, inference and testimony are recognized as the threefold proof, since all other proofs are included in these. The establishment of all that is to be proven depends, verily, on the means of demonstration.

5. Perception is the ascertainment of specific objects. Inference is declared to be threefold and follows from the knowledge of the characteristic mark and of its possessor. Testimony comes from trustworthy persons and from revelation.

6. Sensory objects are known through perception, but that which is super-sensuous is known through inference; what is neither directly perceived nor secured through inference is established through testimony and revelation.

7. Non-perception may be because of extreme distance or proximity, impairment of the senses, mental unsteadiness, subtlety, interposition, suppression, blending with what is similar, and other causes.

8. Primary matter is not apprehended on account of its extreme subtlety and not because of its non-existence, as it is perceived through its effects. Intellect (*mahat, buddhi*) and the rest are effects which are both similar and dissimilar to primary matter (*Prakriti*).

9. The effect subsists, for that which is non-existent cannot be brought into existence, and effects come from appropriate causes. Everything is not by every means possible, as capable causes produce only that which they can and the effect is of the same nature as the cause.

10. The manifest is caused, perishable, finite, mutable, manifold, dependent, identifiable, composite and subordinate. The unmanifest is the reverse.

11. The manifest is composed of the three properties (*gunas*); it is non-discriminative, objective, common, insentient and prolific. So also is Nature (*Pradhana*). The Self (Soul, *Purusha*) is the reverse, and yet similar.

12. The constituents (*gunas*) consist in the pleasant, the painful and the delusive; they serve the purpose of illumination,

activity and restraint; they are mutually dominating, dependent, productive, cooperative and coexistent.

13. *Sattva* is considered to be buoyant and luminous, rajas to be exciting and volatile, and *tamas* to be indeed heavy and enveloping. They function together, like a lamp, for a purpose.

14. Non-discrimination and the rest are proved by the existence of the three *gunas* and by the non-existence of these in their absence. The unmanifest (*Prakriti*) is demonstrated by the effect possessing the properties of the cause.

15. The unmanifest (*avyakta*) exists as a general cause because the particulars are finite, because of homogeneity, because production is through power, because there is differentiation of effect from cause, and because there is merging of the effect with the cause.

16. It operates, in the form of the three *gunas*, by blending and transformation, like water, modified according to the predominance of one or the other of the *gunas.*

17. Soul (*Purusha*) exists, since an aggregate must be for another's use, since this must be the converse of that which has the three *gunas*, since there must be a superintendent and also someone to experience, and since activity is for the sake of freedom.

18. The multiplicity of Souls (*Purushas*) verily follows from the distributive allocation of birth, death and the instruments of causation, since occupations are not simultaneous, and since there are diverse modifications of the three *gunas*.

19. And from this divergence it follows that Soul (*Purusha*) is witness, solitary, neutral, spectator and non-agent.

20. Thus, through conjunction with Soul (*Purusha*), the insentient seems to be sentient, and though the agency really belongs to the *gunas*, the neutral witness (Soul) appears as if it were active.

21. The conjunction of the two, like that of the lame and the blind, is for the perception of nature (*Prakriti*) by Soul (*Purusha*) and for the release of Soul. From this conjunction proceeds evolution.

(The lame one being actionless *Purusha*, and the blind is active, but unconscious *Prakriti*. They join like when the blind man carries the lame to see the road ahead.)

22. From primary matter (*Prakriti*) comes Intellect (*mahat*), thence egoism (*aham-kâra*), and from this the set of sixteen; from five (from *tanmâtrâ*) among these come the five elements (*mahabhûtâni*).

23. Intellect (*mahat-buddhi*) is for ascertainment. Virtue, wisdom, dispassion and lordliness are its faculties when goodness (*sattva*) predominates, and the reverse is true when darkness (*tamas*) predominates.

24. Self-assertion is egoism (*aham-kâra*). Thence proceeds a dual evolution, the eleven-fold set and also the five subtle elements (*tanmâtrâ*).

25. From the *aham-kâra* form of individuation proceeds the eleven-fold set characterized by goodness (*sattva*); from the *bhutadi* form of individuation proceed the subtle elements (*tanmâtrâ*). In this, darkness (*tamas*) dominates. Both of these proceed from *taijasa aham-kâra*, in which *rajas* dominates.

26. The organs of cognition are the eyes, ears, nose, tongue and skin (*buddhindriye*); the organs of action are the voice, hands, feet, the excretory organ and the organ of generation (*karmendriye*).

27. Among these, the mind (*manas*) is both an organ of sensation and of action. It is deliberative and it is an organ cognate with the rest. They are multifarious due to the specific modifications of the *gunas*, and so are the external diversities.

(The mind is both an organ of sensation and action. According to the commentaries, the mind explains the indeterminate, and adds nothing of itself to the subject in question.)

28. The function of five, in regard to sound and the rest, is simply observation. Speech, manipulation, motion, excretion and generation are the functions of five others.

29. Of the three internal organs, the functions are their respective features; these are distinctive to each. The common function of these organs is breath and the rest of the five vital airs (*pranas*).

(*Buddhi, aham-kâra,* and *manas* are internal organs, or *antahkarana*.)

30. In regard to sensory objects, the functions of all four organs are simultaneous as well as successive. In respect to imper-

ceptible things, the functioning of the three internal organs is preceded by that of the fourth (cognition).

31. The instruments perform their respective functions, prompted by mutual sympathy. The purpose of the *Purusha* is the sole cause; by nothing else is any instrument activated.

32. Instruments are of thirteen varieties; they function by grasping, sustaining and disclosing. Their objects are tenfold, to be grasped, sustained and disclosed.

(Verses 30-32 deliberate on the coordination of the three internal organs – *manas*, *aham-kâra*, and *buddhi* – with ten external organs – *karmendriye* and *buddhindriye.*)

33. The internal instrument is threefold. The external organs, which exhibit objects to these three, are tenfold. The external organs function in the present, and the internal instrument at all times Past, present, and future).

34. Among these, the five organs of cognition are concerned with specific and non-specific objects. Speech is concerned with sound; the rest are concerned with all five objects.

35. Since intellect (*buddhi*), together with the other internal organs (*aham-kâra* and *manas*), ascertain all objects, these three instruments are the guardians and the rest are gates.

36. These, characteristically different from one another and variously modified by the *gunas*, present to the intellect (*buddhi*) the whole purpose of Soul (*Purusha*), illumining it like a lamp.

37. Since it is the intellect (*buddhi*) which accomplishes the fruition of all that is to be enjoyed by Soul (*Purusha*), it is also that which discerns the subtle difference between Nature (*Prakriti*) and Soul (*Purusha*).

38. The subtle elements (*tanmatras*) are non-specific; from these five proceed the five gross elements (*maha-bhŭtâni*) which are specific, tranquil, turbulent or stupefying.

39. The subtle bodies (*tanmâtrâ*), the bodies born of mother and father, together with the great elements, are three kinds of specific objects. Among these, the subtle are lasting and those born of parents are perishable.

40. The subtle body (*linga*) is primeval, unconfined, constant, composed of the principles (*tattvas*) beginning with Intellect (*mahat*) and ending with the subtle elements (*tanmâtrâ*). It transmi-

grates, free from experience, and is tinged with dispositions (*bhavas*).

(The subtle body is *linga-sharira*. According to the commentaries "the seeds of virtue and sin are contained within the subtle body... in the inclination of the mind".)

41. Just as a painting does not stand without a support, or a shadow cannot exist without a stake and the like, so too the cognitive apparatus cannot subsist without a support, without specific particles.

42. Formed for the sake of the purpose of Soul (*Purusha*), the subtle body (*linga*) appears in different roles like a dramatic performer, owing to the connection of causes and effects and through conjunction with the universal power of Nature (*Prakriti*).

43. The primary dispositions are innate; the acquired ones, like virtue and the rest, depend on the instruments. The uterine germ and the rest belong to the effect.

44. Through virtue there is ascent; through vice there is descent; through knowledge there is deliverance; there is bondage through the reverse.

45. From dispassion (vairagya) there is absorption into Nature (*Prakriti*); transmigration results from passionate attachment (*rajas*); from power there is non-obstruction, and from the reverse, the contrary.

("Eight inclinations of the mind", four positive and four negative, described in these two verses – virtue, wisdom, not attaching to urges, power, and the four opposing drawbacks – further receive commentaries that "man becomes what he meditates about".)

46. This is an intellectual creation, termed obstruction, infirmity, complacency and attainment. Through the disparity in influence of the *gunas*, its varieties are fifty.

47. Five are the varieties of obstruction; the varieties of infirmity due to organic defect are twenty-eight; complacency is ninefold and attainment is eightfold.

48. The varieties of obscurity (*tamas*) are eightfold, as also those of delusion (*moha*); extreme delusion (*mahamoha*) is tenfold; gloom is eighteenfold, and so is utter darkness.

49. Defects of the eleven organs, together with impairment of the intellect, are said to constitute infirmity. Injuries to the intel-

lect are seventeen, resulting from the inversion of complacency and attainment.

50. Nine forms of complacency are propounded: four internal, relating to Nature (*Prakriti*), means (*upadana*), time (*kala*) and luck (*bhagya*); five external, resulting from avoidance of enjoyment of objects.

51. The eight attainments are reasoning, oral instruction, study, the prevention of pain of three sorts, acquisition of friends, and charity. The three mentioned before (obstruction, infirmity and complacency) are the curbs on attainment.

52. Without dispositions (*bhavas*) there would be no subtle body (*linga*), and without the subtle body there would be no cessation of dispositions. Evolution, therefore, proceeds in two ways, the elemental and the intellectual.

53. Celestial evolution is of eight kinds; the subhuman worlds (animals, plants and minerals) is fivefold; the human is single and specific in form. This, in brief, is material evolution (within *Prakriti*).

54. Above, there is abundance of *sattva*; in the lower order of creation, *tamas* predominates; in the middle, *rajas* dominates. Such is creation from Brahma down to a blade of grass.

55. Therein does the conscious Self (*Purusha*) experience pain caused by decay and death, until dissociation from the subtle body; thus suffering is in the very nature of things.

56. This evolution, from Intellect (*mahat*) to the specific elements (*bhuta*), brought about by the modifications of matter (*Prakriti*), is for the emancipation of the individual Soul (*Purusha*). This is for the sake of another, though seemingly for itself.

57. Just as insentient milk serves as nourishment for the calf, so too does Nature (*Prakriti*) act for the sake of Soul's emancipation.

58. Just as people engage in action to gratify desire, so too the unmanifest, unevolved Nature (*Prakriti*) functions for the emancipation of Soul.

59. Just as a dancer desists from dancing, having shown herself to spectators, so too does primal Nature (*Prakriti*) desist, having revealed itself to Soul (*Purusha*).

60. Munificent Nature, endowed with attributes (*gunas*), accomplishes by manifold means the purpose of the attributeless and uncaring Soul, with no gain for itself.

61. Nothing, in my view, is more gentle and gracious than Nature; once aware of having been seen, Nature does not expose herself to the gaze of Soul (*Purusha*).

62. Verily, therefore, Soul is neither bounded nor emancipated, nor does it transmigrate; it is Nature alone, abiding in myriad forms, that is bounded, released and transmigrates.

63. Nature by herself binds herself by seven modes, and by means of one mode (knowledge), releases herself for the sake of Soul.

64. So through study of principles (*tattvas*) arises the ultimate, undistracted, pure knowledge that neither I am, nor is anything mine nor am I embodied.

65. Possessed of this self-knowledge, and the proliferation of Nature having ceased (owing to its withdrawal from its seven modes), Soul stands apart and at ease, like a spectator.

66. Soul stands indifferent, having seen Nature; Nature desists, having been seen. Though their coexistence continues, there is no motive for creation.

67. Through the attainment of perfect wisdom, virtue and the rest cease to function as causes; yet Soul continues to be invested with the body, just as a potter's wheel continues to whirl owing to the momentum imparted by a prior impulsion.

(When the forming of a pot is finished on the potter's field, the motion lasts out. "At the moment when wakefulness predominates, all the seeds of karma cannot germinate anymore, because the soil has become barren.")

68. When separation from the body takes place and Nature ceases to act, its purpose having been fulfilled, Soul attains to absolute and final emancipation (*kaivalya*).

69. This Secret Doctrine (*guhya*) leading to the emancipation of Soul, and wherein the origin, duration and dissolution of beings has been considered, has been fully expounded by the great Seer (*para maharishi*) Kapila.

70. This supreme purificatory wisdom was imparted, through the compassion of the Sage, to Asuri. Asuri transmitted it to Panchashikha, by whom the system (*tantra*) was elaborated.

71. This, which was handed down through a succession of pupils, has been compendiously set down in the *arya* metre by the noble-minded and devout Ishvarakrishna, who thoroughly comprehended the established doctrine.

Kapila
SÂMKHYA-SÛTRÂ

Of 526 sŭtras in total, we have a selection of 340 here.
The selected ones do not refer to debates with other systems, but
solely to the teaching of *Sâmkhya*.

I.1. The complete cessation of pain (which is) of three kinds[62]
is the complete end of the human Soul (*Purusha*).

I.2. The effectuation of this (complete cessation of pain) is
not (to be expected) by means of the visible (such as religion,
wealth, and sensual pleasures), for we see (on the loss of religion,
wealth, and sensual pleasures) the restoration (of the misery and
evil,) after (its temporary) cessation.

I-3. (Let us consider the doubt) that Soul's desire (the cessation of pain, may result) from exertions for the obviation (of pain),
as in the case with the obviation of daily hunger.

I.4. This (method of palliatives) is to be rejected by those who
are versed in evidence; because it is not everywhere possible (to
employ it at all), and because, even if this *were* possible, there
would be an impossibility as regards (ensuring) the perfect fitness
(of the agents employed).

I.5. Also (an inferior method ought not to be adopted) because of the preeminence of Liberation (as proved) by the text (of
Scripture declaratory) of its preeminence above all else.

I.6. And there is no difference between the two – preeminence of Liberation and Scripture declaratory.

I.7. There would be no rule in the enjoining of means for the
liberation of one bound *essentially*.

---

[62] The three kinds of pain are: 1. Subjective (*adhyatmika*); named this way because it originates from the human 'I'. It consists of malady and suffering of the
soul. 2. Objective (*adhibhautika*), which is caused by actions of other living beings, such as animals, people, birds, etc. It was named this way because it comes
from the created beings. 3. The influence of destiny (*adhidaivika*), caused by supernatural powers, influences of the stars and planets, evil spirits, and gods (devas). The meaning of this commentary is the same as in Samkya karika 2.

I.8. Since an essential nature is imperishable, unauthoritativeness, betokened by impracticableness, (would be chargeable against the Scripture, if pain were essential to humanity).

I.9. There is no rule, where something impossible is enjoined: though it *be* enjoined, it is no injunction.

I.10. If (someone says) the essential nature cannot be changed, as in the case of white cloth that can be dyed, or a seed baked, and in the same way the Soul is also bound, although something essential may not be irremovable.

I.11. Since both perceptibility and (subsequent non-perceptibility may belong to some power (which is indestructible), it is not something *impracticable* that is enjoined (when one is directed to render some indestructible power imperceptible).

I.12. Not from connection with *time* (does bondage befall the Soul); because this, all-pervading and eternal, is (eternally) associated with *all*, (and not with those alone who are in bondage) that is of *Prakriti*.

I.13. Nor (does the bondage of the Soul arise) from connection with *place*, either, for the same (reason)

I.14. Nor (does the bondage of the Soul arise) from its being conditioned (by its standing among circumstances that clog it by limiting it); because *that* is the fact in regard to (not the Soul, but) the *body*.

I.15. Because this Soul is (unassociated with any conditions or circumstances that could serve as its bonds, it is) absolute.

I.16. Nor (does the bondage of Soul arise) from any work; because actions are property of the mind, and in that case, bondage would be eternal.

I.17. If it were property of any other, then there could not be diverse experience.

I.18. If (you say that the Soul's bondage arises) from *Prakriti* (nature), as its cause, (then I say) 'no', (because) that, also, is a dependent thing.

I.19. (But) not without the conjunction thereof (i.e., of Nature, *Prakriti*) is there a connection of that (i.e., of pain) with that (viz., the Soul) which is ever essentially a pure and free intelligence

I.20. Not from Ignorance, too, (does the Soul's bondage arise); because that which is not a reality is not adapted to binding.

I.21. If it ('Ignorance') *be* (asserted, by you, to be) a reality, then there is an abandonment of the (Vedantic) tenet, (by you who profess to follow the Vedanta).

I.22. And (if you assume 'Ignorance' to be a reality, then) there would be a *duality*, through (there being) something of a different kind (from Soul; which you asserters of *non-duality* cannot contemplate allowing).

I.24. (To the suggestion that 'Ignorance' is at once real and unreal, we say) 'no', because no such thing is known (as is at once real and unreal.)

I.27. (The bondage) thereof, moreover, is not caused by any influence of objects from all eternity.

I.29. (It is impossible that the Soul's bondage should arise) from an influence received in the same place (where the object is; because, in that case), there would be no distinction between the two, (the bond and the free).

I.42. Not Thought alone exists; because there is the intuition of the external.

I.48. Not from any kind of motion (such as its entrance into a body, does the Soul's bondage result).

I.49. Because this is impossible for what is inactive, (or, in other words, without motion)

I.50. (We cannot admit that the Soul is other than all-pervading; because) by its being limited, since it would come under the same conditions as jars, and other products, there would be a contradiction to our tenet (of its imperishableness).

I.51. The text regarding the motion (of the Soul), moreover, is (applicable only) because of the junction of an attendant, as in the case of the Aether (or Space, which moves not, though we talk of the space enclosed in a jar, as moving with the jar).

I.52. Nor, moreover, (does the bondage of the Soul result from the merit or demerit arising) from works; because these belong not thereto.

I.53. If the case were otherwise (than as I say), then it (the bondage of the Soul) might extend unduly, (even to be emancipated).

I.55. Moreover, the conjunction thereof does not, through non-discrimination, take place (in the case of the emancipated); nor is there a parity.

I.56. Bondage arises from the error (of not discriminating between Nature (*Prakriti*) and Soul (*Purusha*)). The removal of it is to be affected by the necessary means, just like darkness.

I.57. Since the non-discrimination of other things (from Soul) results from the non-discrimination of Nature (*Prakriti*), (from Soul), the cessation of this will take place, on the cessation of that (from which it results).

I.58. It is merely verbal, and not a reality (this so-called bondage of the Soul); since it (the bondage) *resides* in the *mind*, (and not in the Soul).

I.59. Moreover, it (the non-discrimination of Soul from Nature,) is not to be removed by argument; as that of the person perplexed about the points of the compass (is not to be removed) without immediate cognition.

I.60. The knowledge of things imperceptible is by means of Inference; as that of fire (when not directly perceptible,) is by means of smoke.

I.61. Nature (*Prakriti*) is the state of equipoise of Goodness (*sattwa*), Passion (*rajas*), and Darkness (*tamas*): From Nature (proceeds) Mind (*mahat*); from Mind, Self-consciousness (*aham-kâra*); as five Subtile Elements (*tanmâtrâ*); from *tanmâtrâ* both sets (external and internal,) of sensory and action organs (*indriyâni*) and from the Subtile Elements, the Gross Elements (*sthula bhutâni*). (Then there is) Soul (*Purusha*). Such is the class of twenty-five.

I.62. (The knowledge of the existence) of the five 'Subtile Elements' is (by inference,) from the 'Gross Elements.'

I.63. (The knowledge of the existence) of Self-consciousness (*aham-kâra*) is (by inference) from the external and internal (organs), and from these ('Subtile Elements')

I.64. (The knowledge of the existence) of Intellect (*buddhi*) is (by inference,) from that (Self-consciousness (*aham-kâra*)).

I.65. (The knowledge of the existence) of Nature (*Prakriti*) is (by inference), from that ('Intellect' or *mahat*).

I.66. (The existence) of Soul (*Purusha*) (is inferred) from the fact that the combination (of the principles of Nature into their various effects) is for the sake of another (than unintelligent Nature, or any of its similarly unintelligent products).

I.67. Since the root has no root, the root (*Prakriti*) (of all) is rootless.

I.68. Even if there be a succession, there is a halt at some point; and so it is merely a name (that we give to the point in question, when we speak of the *root* of things, under the name of Nature (*Prakriti*)).

I.71. The first product (of the Primal Agent, Nature (*Prakriti*)) is called 'the Great one,' is Mind (*mahat*).

I.72. 'Self-consciousness' (*aham-kâra*) is that which is subsequent (to Mind).

I.73. To the others it belongs to be products of thereof, (i.e., of Self-consciousness, *aham-kâra*).

I.74. Moreover, mediately, through that (the 'Great one'), the first (cause, viz., Nature (*Prakriti*)) is the cause (of all products); as is the case with the Atoms, (the causes, though not the immediate causes, of jars, etc.).

I.75. While both Soul (*Purusha*) and Nature (*Prakriti*)) are antecedent (to all products), since the one (viz., Soul) is devoid (of this character of being a cause), it is applicable (only) to the other of the two, (viz., Nature).

I.76. What is limited cannot be the substance of all (things).

I.77. And (the proposition that Nature (*Prakriti*) is the cause of all is proved) from the text of Scripture, that the origin (of the world) is therefrom (from Nature).

I.78. A thing is not made out of nothing.

I.79. It (the world) is not unreal; because there is no fact contradictory (to its reality), and because it is not the (false) result of depraved causes, (leading to a belief in what ought not to be believed).

I.80. If it (the substantial cause,) be an entity, then this would be the case, (that the product would be an entity), from its union (or identity) therewith; (but) if (the cause be) a nonentity, then how could it possibly be the case (that the product would be real), since *it* is a nonentity, (like the cause with which it is united, in the relation of identity)?

I.81. No; for the works (*karma*) are not adopted to be the *substantial* cause (of any product).

I.82. The accomplishment thereof (i.e., Liberation) is not, moreover, through Scriptural rites: the chief end of man does not consist in this (which is gained through such means); because, since this consists of what is accomplished through *acts*, (and is, therefore, a *product*, and not *eternal*), there is (still left impending over the ritualist) the liability to repetition of births.

I.83. There is Scripture for it, that he who has attained to discrimination, in regard to these (i.e., Nature (*Prakriti*) and Soul (*Purusha*), has no repetition of births.

I.84. From pain (occasioned, e.g., to victims in sacrifice,) must come pain (to the sacrificer, and not the *liberation* from pain); as there is not relief from chilliness, by affusion of water.

I.85. (Liberation cannot arise from acts); because, whether the end be something desirable, or undesirable, (and we admit that the *motive* of the sacrifice is not the giving pain to the victim), this makes no difference in regard to its being the result of *acts*, (and, therefore, not eternal, but transitory).

I.86. Of him who is essentially liberated, his bonds have absolutely perished, it (i.e., the fruit of his saving knowledge,) is absolute: there is no parity (between his case and that of him who relies on works, and who may thereby secure a temporary sojourn in Paradise, only to return again to earth).

I.93. (And, further,) it is not proved that he (the 'Lord') exists; because (whoever exists must be either free or bound; and), of free and bound, he can be neither the one nor the other.

I.94. (Because,) either way, he would be inefficient.

I.95. (The Scriptural texts which make mention of the 'Lord' are) either glorification of the liberated Soul, or homages to the recognized (deities of the Hindu pantheon).

I.96. The governorship (thereof, i.e., of Soul (*Purusha*) over Nature (*Prakriti*)) is from (its) proximity thereto, (not from its resolving to act thereon); as is the case with the gem, (the lodestone, in regard to iron).

I.97. In the case of individual products (the causal bodies, *jiva*), also, (the apparent agency) of animal souls (is solely through proximity).

I.99. The internal organ, the mind (*manas*) through its being enlightened thereby (i.e., by Soul) is the overruler; as is the iron (in respect of the magnet).

I.100. The knowledge of the connected (e.g., fire), through perception of the connexion (e.g., of fire with smoke), is inference.

I.101. Testimony (such as is entitled to the name of evidence) is a declaration by one worthy (to be believed).

I.102. Since the establishment of (the existence of) both (Soul (*Purusha*) and non-Soul (*Prakriti*)) is by means of evidence, the declaration thereof (i.e., of the kinds of evidence, has been here made).

I.103. The establishment of both (Nature (*Prakriti*) and Soul (*Purusha*)) is by analogy.

I.104. *Bhoga* experience (whether of pain or pleasure,) ends with (the discernment of) Thought, (or Soul, as contradistinguished from Nature).

I.105. The experience of the fruit *may* belong even to another than the agent; as in the case of food (that is prepared for the other), etc.

I.106. Or, since it is from non-discrimination that it is derived, the notion that the *agent* (Soul being mistaken for an agent,) has the fruit (of the act is a wrong notion).

I.107. And when the truth is told, there is (seen to be) neither (agency, in Soul, nor experience).

I.108. (A thing may be) an object (perceptible), and also (at another time,) not an object, through there being, in consequence of great distance, a want of (conjunction of the sense with the thing), or (on the other hand), an appliance of the sense (to the thing).

I.109. Her imperceptibleness arises from (her) subtility. *Purusha* and *Prakriti* cannot be seen.

I.110. (Nature (*Prakriti*) exists;) because her existence is gathered from the beholding of productions (consequences).

I.113. Because (if we were to infer any other cause than Nature (*Prakriti*)), we should have a contradiction to the threefold (aspect which things really exhibit):

I.114. (1) The production of what is no entity, as a man's horn, does not take place.

I.115. (2) Because of the rule, that there must be some material (of which the product may consist).

I.116. (3) Because everything is not possible everywhere and always, (which might be the case, if materials could be dispensed with).

I.117. Because it is that which is competent (to the making of anything) that makes what is possible, (as a product of it).

I.118. And because it (the product,) is (nothing else than) the cause, (in the shape of the product).

I.121. Destruction (of anything) is the resolution (of the thing spoken of as destroyed,) into the sense (from which it was produced).

I.124. (A product of Nature (*Prakriti*) is) caused, uneternal, not all-pervading, mutable, multitudinous, dependent, mergent.

I.126. Of both (Nature (*Prakriti*) and her products) the fact that they consist of the three Qualities (*gunas*), and that they are irrational, (is the common property).

I.127. The Qualities differ in character, mutually, by pleasantness, unpleasantness, lassitude (in which forms, severally, the Qualities present themselves).

I.128. Through Lightness and other habits (passion and stupor) the Qualities (*gunas*) mutually agree and differ.

I.129. Since they are other than (Soul (*Purusha*) and Nature (*Prakriti*), the only two uncaused entities), Mind and the rest are products; as is the case with a jar, or the like.

I.130. Because of (their) measure, (which is a limited one).

I.131. Because they conform (to Nature (*Prakriti*)).

I.132. And, finally, because it is through the power (of the cause alone, that the product can do aught)

I.133. On the quitting thereof (quitting the condition of product), there is Nature (*Prakriti*), or Soul (*Purusha*), (into one or other of which the product must needs have resolved itself).

I.134. If they were other than these two, they would be void; (seeing that there is nothing self-existent, besides Soul (*Purusha*) and Nature (*Prakriti*)).

I-135. The cause is inferred from the effect, (in the case of Nature and her products); because it accompanies it.

I.136. The indiscrete, (Nature, must be inferred) from its (discrete and resolvable) effect, (Mind), in which are the three Qualities (*gunas*), (which constitute Nature).

I.137. There is no denying that it (Nature (*Prakriti*),) is; because of its effects, (which will be in vain attributed to any other source).

I.138. (The relation of cause and effect is) not (alleged as) the means of establishing (the existence of Soul (*Purusha*)); because, as is the case with (the disputed term) 'merit', there is no dispute about there being such a kind of thing (*dharma*); (though *what* kind of thing is matter of dispute).

I.139. Soul (of man) is something else than the body, and everything else.

I.140. Because that which is combined (and is, therefore, discerptible, (*Prakriti*)) is for the sake of some other, (*not* discerptible).

I.141. (And Soul (*Purusha*) is something else than the body); because there is (in Soul) the reverse of the three Qualities (*gunas*).

I.142. And (Soul is not material;) because of (its) superintendence (over Nature).

I.143. (And Soul is not material;) because of (its) being the experiencer.

I.144. (It is for Soul, and not for Nature;) because the exertions are with a view to isolation (from all qualities; a condition to which Soul is competent, but Nature is not).

I.145. Since light does not pertain to the unintelligent light, (which must pertain to something or other, is the essence of the Soul (*Purusha*), which, self-manifesting, manifests whatever else is manifest).

I.146. It (Soul, *Purusha*) has not Intelligence as its attribute; because it is without quality.

I.148. (If Soul were unintelligent,) it would not be witness (of its own comfort,) in profound (and dreamless) sleep, and the remainder.

I.149. From the several allotment of birth, a multiplicity of Souls (*Purushas*) (is to be inferred).

I.150. (The Vedantis say, that,) there being a difference in its investments, moreover, multiplicity attaches (seemingly,) to the one (Soul); as is the case with Space, by reason of jars (which mark out the spaces that they occupy).

I.151. The investment is different, (according to the Vedantis), but not that to which this belongs; (and the absurd consequences of such an opinion will be seen).

I.152. Thus, (i.e., by taking the *Sâmkhya* view,) there is no imputation of contradictory conditions to (a Soul supposed to be) everywhere present as *one* (infinitely extended monad).

I.153. Even though there be (imputed to Soul) the possession of the condition to another, this (i.e., that it really possesses such,) is not established by the imputation; because it (Soul) is *one* (absolutely simple, unqualified entity).

I.154. There is no opposition to the Scriptures (declaratory) of the non-duality (of Soul); because the reference (in such texts,) is to the *genus* (or to Soul in general).

I.155. Of him (i.e., of that Soul (*Purusha*)) by whom the cause of Bondage is known, there is that condition (of isolation, or entire liberation) by the perception (of the fact, that Nature (*Prakriti*) and Soul (*Purusha*) are distinct, and that he, really, was *not* bound, even when he seemed to be so).

I.156. No: because the blind do not see, can those who have their eyesight not perceive?

I.159. Soul is always free, but it seems to be as if is not.

I.160. It (Soul,) is altogether free (but seemingly) multiform, (or different, in appearance, from a free thing, through a delusive semblance of being bound).

I.161. It (Soul,) is a witness, through its connexion with sense-organs, (which quit it, on liberation).

I.162. (The nature of Soul is) constant freedom.

I.163. And, finally, (the nature of Soul is) indifference (to Pain and Pleasure, alike).

I.164. (Soul's *fancy* of) being an agent is, through the influence (of Nature), from the proximity of Intellect, from the proximity of Intellect.

II

II.1. Of Nature (the agency, or the being a maker, is) for the emancipation of what is (really, though not apparently,) emancipated, or else for (the removal of) itself.

II.2. Because this (Emancipation) is (only) of him that is void of passion.

II.3. It is not affected by mere hearing; because of the forcibleness of the impressions from eternity.

II.4. Or as some people have, severally, many dependants.

II.5. And, since it (the character of creator,) belongs, really, to Nature (*Prakriti*), it follows that it is fictitiously attributed to Soul (*Purusha*).

II.6. Since it is proved from the products of *Prakriti*.

II.7. The rule is with reference to one knowing; just as escape from a thorn.

II.8. Even though there be conjunction (of Soul) with the other (viz., Nature), this (power of giving rise to products) does not exist in it immediately; just like the burning action of iron.

II.9. When there is passion, or dispassion, there is concentration, (in the latter case, and) creation, (in the former).

II.10. In the order of Mind (*mahat*), (is the creation) of the five elements, (or of the material world).

II.11. Since the creation is for the sake of Soul, the origination of these (products of Nature) is not for their own sake.

II.12. (Relative) Space and Time (arise) from Ether (*akasha* and *upâdhi* (the projection of the mind)).

II.13. *Buddhi* (Intellect) is judgment.

II.14. Merits, and similar, are products of it (*mahat*).

II.15. The Great one (Intellect (*mahat*)) becomes reversed through tincture (of *rajas* and *tamas*).

II.16. *Aham-kâra* (self-consciousness) is a conceit.

II.17. The products of *aham-kâra* (self-consciousness) is the eleven organs (*indriyâni*) and the five Subtile Elements (*tanmâtrâ*).

II.18. The eleventh (*manas*), consisting of (the principle of) Purity (*sattva*), preceds from modified Self-consciousness (*aham-kâra*).

II.19. Along with the organs of action and the organs of understanding (*manas*) another is eleventh.

II.20. *Indriyâni* (organs), are not formed of the Elements; because there is Scripture for (their) being formed of Self-consciousness *aham-kâra.*

II.21. The Scripture regarding absorbtion into deities is not (declaratory) of an originator.

II.22. (None of the organs (*Indriyâni*) is eternal, as some hold Mind to be;) because we have Scripture for their beginning to be, and because we see their destruction.

II.23. The Sense is supersensuous; (it being the notion) of mistaken persons (that the Sense exists) in (identity with) its site.

II.26. *Manas* (the Mind) identifies itself with both: perception and action, alike.

II.27. By reason of the varieties (of *manas*) of transformation of (which) the Qualities (*gunas*) (are susceptible), there is a diversity (of their product, the Mind,) according to circumstances.

II.28. Of both (sets of organs the object is that list of things), beginning with Color, and ending with the dirt of Taste.

II.29. The being, the seer, belongs to the Soul; the instrumentality belongs to the Organs.

II.30. Of the three (internal organs) there is a diversity among themselves.

II.31. The five airs, viz., Breath, and the others, are a modification, in common, of the (three internal) instruments starting with *prâna.*

II.32. The modifications of the organs take place both successively and simultaneously.

II.33. The modifications (of the understanding, which are to be shown to be the cause of the world, and) which are of five kinds, are (some of them,) painful and (others) not painful.

II.34. On the cessation thereof (viz., of mundane influences), its tincture ceasing, it (Soul,) abides in itself.

II.35. And as (by) a flower, the gem; the proximity of the flower makes the gem look colored.

II.41. (An Intelligent (*buddhi*) is the principal, or immediate and direct, efficient in Soul's emancipation;) because there is no wandering away.

II.42. So, too, because it (the understanding,) is the depository of all self-continuant impressions.

369

II.43. And because we infer this (its preeminence) by reason of its meditating.

II.44. It cannot be of its own nature.

II.45. The condition (as regards Soul's instruments,) of secondary and principal is relative; because of the difference of function.

II.46. The energizing (of this or that Intellect (*buddhi*)) is for the sake of this (or that Soul); because of (its) having been purchased by the works (or deserts) of this (or that Soul); just as in the world.

II.47. Admiting taht they (the various instruments of Soul, all) equally act, the preeminence belongs to Intellect (*buddhi*); just as in the world, just as in the world.

III

III.1. The origination of the diversified (world of sense, *indriyâni*) is from that which has no difference, *tanmâtrâ* .

III.2. Therefrom, of the Body.

III.3. From the seed thereof is mundane existence.

III.4. And, till there is discrimination, there is the energizing of these, which have no difference.

III.5. Because of (the necessity of) the other's experiencing it, the ones who do not discriminate between *Purusha* and *Prakriti* (unawoken).

III.6. It (Soul) is now quite free from both.

III.7. The Gross (Body) usually arises from father and mother; the other one is not so Subtle, energy, causal, body of Soul).

III.8. To that which arose antecendently it belongs to be that whose result is this (pain and pleasure); because it is to the one that there belongs fruition, not to the other.

III.9. The seventeen, as one, are the Subtile Body.

III.10.There is distinction of individuals, through diversity of desert (prior actions).

III.11. From its being applied to *it*, (viz., to the Subtile one), it is applied to the Body, which is the tabernacle of the abiding thereof.

III.12. Not independently (can Subtile Body exist), without that (Gross Body); just like a shadow and a picture.

III.13. No, even though it be limited; because of (its) association with masses; just like the sun.

III.14. It is of atomic magnitude; for there is a Scripture for its acting.

III.15. And because there is Scripture for its being formed of food.

III.16. The mundane existence of Subtile bodies is for the sake of Soul; just like a king's cooks.

III.17. The Body consists of the five elements.

III.20.Consciousness is not natural (a natural result of organization); because it is not found in them severally.

III.21.And (if the Body had consciousness natural to it,) there would not be death, of anything.

III.22.If (you say that consciousness results from organization, and that) it is like the power of something intoxicating, (the ingredients of which, separately, have no intoxicating power, we reply, that) this might arise, on conjunction, if we had seen, in each (element, something conducive to the result).

III.23.From knowledge (acquired during mundane existence, comes) salvation, (Soul's *chief* end).

III.24.Bondage (which may be viewed as one of the ends which Soul could arrive at only through the Subtile Body,) is from Misconception.

III.25. Since this (viz., knowledge,) is the precise cause (of liberation), there is neither association (of anything else with it, e.g., good works,) nor alternativeness, (e.g., of good works, in its stead).

III.27. Even of that other (object of worship) it is not complete.

III.28.Moreover, it is in what is *fancied* that it is thus (illusory).

III.29.From the achievement of (the worship termed) meditation there is, to the pure (Soul), all 8power); like Nature (*Prakriti*).

III.30.Meditation is (the cause of) the removal of Desire.

III.31.It (Meditation,) is perfected by the repelling of the modifications (of the Mind, which ought to be abstracted from all thoughts of anything).

III.32. This (Meditation,) is perfected by Restraint, Postures, and one's Duties.

III.33. Restraint (of the breath) is by means of expulsion and retention.

III.34. Steady and (promoting) ease is a (suitable) Posture.

III.35. One's Duty is the performance of the actions prescribed for one's religious order.

III.36.Meditation is the performance through Dispassion and Practice.

III.37. The kinds of Misconceptions are five.

(There are five misconceptions that enslave a man. They are: ignorance (*avidyâ*), egoism (*asmitâ*), desire, hate, and fear of disappearing. *Yoga-sutra* (II,3) speaks of them (except for stating the last misconception as 'attaching to life'.)

III.44. Through Reasoning, and the remainder (which are its subdivisions,) Perfection (is eightfold):

1. *Târa* – Reasoning or contemplating.

2. *Sutâra* – oral instructions.

3. *Târa-târa* – study or reading.

4. *Ramyaka* – appreciating the company of *gurus*, *brachmacharyas*, and the like.

5. *Sadâ-mudîtâ* – through outer and inner purity.

6. *Pramodâ* – eliminates development of the ego in the practitioner.

7. *Mudîtâ* – eliminates pain caused by Elements.

8. *Modamânâ* – eliminating pain (caused by gods, demons, and other inorganic beings).

III.45. Not from any other (than what we have just stated does real perfection arise; because what does arise therefrom, e.g., from austerities, is) without abandonment of something else, (vi., Misconception).

III.46. (The creation is that) of which the subdivisions are the demons, gods, etc.

(In the tenth aphorism it is narrated that people are discriminated in line with their *karma*. It is further expanded here. There are six kinds of beings in nature that are different according to their *karma*: gods, demons, human beings, the Souls of the deceased, the Souls of those who live in hell, and the creatures that crawl. The last kind represents all those beings who live in the physical world, but are not people: wild and domestic animals, birds, reptiles, and immobile beings (plants).

III.47.From Brahma down to a post, for its (Soul's (*Purusha's*)) sake is creation, till there be discrimination (between Soul (*Purusha*) and Nature (*Prakriti*)).

(Creation exists in favor of *Purusha*, and till the moment the last man attains differentiation of eternal Soul in themselves, it will continue to exist.)

III.48.Aloft, it (the creation,) abounds in (the quality of) Purity (*sattva*).

III.49.Beneath, it (the creation,) abounds in Darkness (*tamas*).

III.50.In the midst, it (the creation,) abounds in Passion (*rajas*).

(The three levels of the created world. The world of gods domineered by purity is at the top, the bottom is the realm of dark, and in the middle is the world of mortal people where passions prevail.)

III.51.By reason of diversity of desert in Nature's (diverse) behavior; like a born-slave.

III.52.Even there is return (to miserable states of existence): it is to be shunned, by reasons of successive subjections to birth, (from which the inhabitants of Heaven enjoy no immunity).

III.53.Alike (belongs to all) the sorrow produced by decay and death.

III.54. Not by absorbtion into the cause is there accomplishments of the end; because, as in the case of one who has dived, there is a rising again.

III.55.Through she be not constrained to act, yet this is fitting; because of her being devoted to another, *Purusha*.

III.56.(He who is absorbed into Nature (*Prakriti*) must rise again;) for he becomes omniscient and omnipotent (in a subsequent creation).

III.57.The existence of *such* a Lord is a settled point.

III.58. Nature's creating is for the sake of another, though it be spontaneous;-for she is not experiencer;-like a cart's carrying saffron (for the sake of its master).

III.59. Though she be unintelligent, yet Nature acts; as is the case with milk.

III.61. *Prakriti* from her own nature acts, not from thought; like a servant.

III-62. Or from attractions by Deserts which have been from eternity.

(Since the influence of *karma* has been around forever, together with nature, certain effort is needed for the karmic predispositions to be realized.)

III-63. From discriminative knowledge there is a cessation of Nature's creating: as is the case with a cook, when the cooking has been performed.

III.64.When one man is liberated, another (who is unaware of the discernment between *Purusha* and *Prakriti*) remains like another, through her (*Prakriti*'s) fault.

III.65. (The fruit of Nature's ceasing to act), the solitariness of both (Nature (*Prakriti*) and Soul (*Purusha*)), or (which comes to the same thing,) of either, is liberation.

(Solitariness and independence of *Prakriti* defines its inactivity only toward the man who has become aware of the difference, while the independence of *Purusha* means that it is completely unattached to the entire *Prakriti*.)

III.66.Moreover, (when Nature has left off distressing the emancipated) she does not desist, in regard to her creative influence on another; as is the case with the snake, (which ceases to be a terror,) in respect of him who is aware of the truth in regard to the rope (which another mistakes for a snake).

III.67.And from connexion with Desert (*karma*), which is the cause.

III.68. Though there is (on Souls's (*Purusha*'s) part, this) indifference, yet want of discrimination is the cause of Nature's (*Prakriti*'s) service.

III.69.Like a dancer does she, though she had been energizing, desist; because of the end's having been attained.

III.70.Moreover, when her fault is known, Nature (*Prakriti*) does not approach (Soul (*Purusha*)); like a woman from a good family.

III.71.Bondage and Liberation do not actually belong to the Soul, *Purusha*, (and would not even appear to do so,) but for non-discrimination. Only lack of discrimination (between *Purusha* and

Prakriti) makes the Soul, *Purusha*, seem 'in bondage', and in need of 'liberation'.

III.72.They really belong to Nature, through consociation; like a beast.

III.73.In seven ways does Nature (*Prakriti*) bind herself; like the silk-worm; in one way does she liberate herself.

(Seven ways for *Prakriti* to bind are: morality (*dharma*) and immorality (*adharma*); dispassion (*vairagya*) and passion (*a-vairagya*); piety (*an-aishvarya*) i impiety (*aishvarya*); as well as ignorance (*ajnana*). The same way a silk-worm makes a cocoon around itself ultimately closing itself off, is the same way in which *Prakriti* binds itself down with the seven ties. It is liberated only through knowledge (jnana). The aphorism, therefore, states that it is the only way for *Prakriti* to liberate itself.)

III.75.Discrimination (between *Purusha* and *Prakriti*) is perfected through abandonment (of everything), expressed by a 'No, No,' through study of the (twenty-five) Principles.

III.76.Through the difference of those competent (to engage in the matter at all), there is no necessity (that each and every one should at once be successful).

III.77.Since what (Pain) has been repelled returns again, there comes, even from medium (but imperfect,) Discrimination, experience, (which it is desired to get entirely rid of).

III.78.And he who, living, is liberated (*jivan-mukta*).

III.81. (And not through merely hearing is one qualified to become an instructor): otherwise, there were blind tradition.

III.82.Possessed of a body, (the emancipated sage goes on living); like the whirling of a wheel.

III.83.This (retention of a body) is occasioned by the least vestige of impression (*samskara*).

(The body is retained due to the smallest remnant of only those impressions that caused the existence of the body.)

III.84.That which was to be done has been done, when entire Cessation of Pain has resulted from Discrimination (of human Soul from conditioned nature); not otherwise, not otherwise.

IV.3. Repetition (is to be made), if not, from once instructing, (the end be gained).

IV.4. As is the case of father and son; since both are seen; (the one, to die, and the other, to be born).

IV.8. What is not a means (of liberation is) not to be thought about, (as this conduces only) to bondage; as in the case of Bharata.

IV.9. From (association with) many there is obstruction to concentration, through passion; as in the case of a girl's shells.

IV.10. Just so, from (the company of) two, also.

IV.11. He who is without hope is happy.

IV.12. (One may be happy,) even without exertion; like a serpent happy in another's house (once the mind is transcended).

IV.13. Though be devote themselves to many Institutes and teachers, a taking of the essence (is to be made); as is the case with bee.

IV.14. The meditation is not interrupted of him whose mind is intent on one object; like the maker of arrows.

IV.15. Through transgression of the enjoined rules there is failure in the aim; as in the world.

IV.16. Moreover, if they be forgotten; as in the case of the female frog.

IV.17. Not even through instruction be heard is the end gained, without reflexion.

IV.19. Having performed reverence, the duties of a student, and attendance, one has success after a long time; as in his case.

IV.20. There is no determination of the time of Liberation.

IV.22. Moreover, after the attainment of what (like the world of Brahma,) is other (than the state of emancipated Soul), there is return (to mundane existence); because it is written: 'From conjunction with the five fires there is birth.'

IV.23. By him who is free from passion what is to be left is left, and what is to be taken is taken.

IV.24. Or through association with the one who has obtained excellence, as in the case thereof.

IV.25. Not of his own accord should he go near one who is infected with desire.

IV.26.(Else he may become) bound, by conjunction with the cords.

IV.27.Not by enjoyment is desire appeased; as in the case of the saint.

IV.28.From seeing the fault of both.

IV.30.Not even a mere semblance (of this true knowledge arises in him whose mind is disturbed); as in the case of a foul mirror.

IV.31.Nor, even though sprung therefrom; is that (knowledge, necessarily,) in accordance therewith; like the lotus.

V

V.1. The (use of a) Benediction (is justified) by the practice of the good, by our seeing its fruit, and by Scripture.

V.2. Not from its (the world's,) being governed by a Lord is there the effectuation of fruit: for it is by works (i.e., by merit and demerit,) that this is accomplished.

V.3. (If a Lord were governor, then) from intending his own benefit, his government (would be selfish), as is the case (with ordinary governors) in the world.

V.4. (He must, then, be) just like a worldly lord, (and) otherwise (than you desire that we should conceive of him).

V.5. Or (let the name of Lord be) technical.

V.6. This (position, viz., that there is a Lord,) cannot be established without (assuming that he is affected by) Passion; because that is the determinate cause (of all energizing).

V.7. Moreover, were that (Passion) conjoined with him, he could not be eternally free.

V.12. Moreover, there is Scripture for (this world's) being the product of Nature (*Prakriti*), (not of a Lord).

V.40. He who is accomplished in the secular (connexion of the words with meaning) can understand the sense of the *Veda*.

V.42. Not so (i.e., what is meant by the *Veda* is not something transcending the senses); because sacrificings, are, in themselves, what constitutes merit, preeminently.

V.43. The natural force (of the terms in the *Veda*) is ascertained through the conversancy (therewith of those who successively transmit the knowledge).

V.44. This really takes place; because they (viz., the words,) give rise to knowledge, in the case both of things adapted (to sense) and of things not (so) adapted.

V.45. The *Vedas* are not from eternity; for there is Scripture for their being a production.

V.46. They (the *Vedas*,) are not the work of (the Supreme) Man; because there is no such thing as the (Supreme) Man, (whom you allude to as being, possibly,) their maker.

V.47. Since the liberated is unsuited (to the work, by his indifference), and the unliberated is so, (by his want of power, neither of these can be author of the *Vedas*).

V.50. That (only) is Man's work, in respect to which, even be it something invisible, an effort of understanding takes place.

V.51. The power of the *Vedas* rest on the transmission of correct knowledge.

V.72. Everything except Nature (*Prakriti*) and Soul (*Purusha*) is uneternal.

V.74. Emancipation is not manifestation of joy; because there are no *properties* (in Soul, as, e.g., in the shape of joy).

V.75. Nor, in like manner, is it (Emancipation) the destruction of special qualities.

V.76. Nor is it (Emancipation) any particular going to some special place (to the 'kingdom of heaven') because (Soul) is motionless (absolute).

V.77. Nor is it (Emancipation) the destruction of the influence of (intellectual) forms, by reason of the faults of momentariness.

V.78. Nor is it (Emancipation) destruction of all; for this has, among other things, the fault of *not* being the Soul's aim.

V.79. So, too, the emptiness (is not liberation).

V.80. And conjunctions terminate in separations, therefore, it (Emancipation) is not the acquisition of lands, and either.

V.81. Nor is it (Emancipation) conjunction of a Part with the Whole.

(There is no connecting with that which has no parts. Liberation is not the connecting of parts (of an individual Soul) with the whole (God), like many people believe. The whole, if it is such, has no parts. That is why an aspiration like this is absurd. Every connection is disconnected at long last. Therefore, this does not liberate the man, either. Liberation is only awakening, and not some uniting.)

V.82. Nor is it (Emancipation), moreover, conjunction with the (power of) becoming as small as an atom; since, as is the case with other conjunctions (*siddhi*), the destruction of this must necessarily take place.

V.83. Nor, just as in that case, is it (Emancipation), moreover, conjunction with the rank of Indra, and other gods.

V.103. It (the Body,) is not, necessarily, the Gross one; for there is, also, the vehicular (transmigrating of Subtle) one.

V.104. The senses do not reveal what they do not reach to; because of their not reaching, or because (else,) they might reach everything.

V.113. The vital air (*prâna*) is not (on the allegation that it is the principal thing in the Body, to be considered) the originant of the Body; because it (the vital air, or spirit,) subsists through the power of the organs.

V.114. The site of experience (viz., the Body,) is constructed (only) through the superintendence of the experiencer (Soul or *Purusha*): otherwise, we should find putrefaction.

V.115. Through a servant, not directly, is superintendence (exercised) by the master (*Purusha*).

V.116. In Concentration, profound sleep, and emancipation, it (Soul,) consists of Brahma.

V.117.In the case of the two, it is with a seed (of past impressions, *samskaras*); in the case of the other, this is wanting.

V.120. A single impression (suffices to generate, and) lasts out the experience; but there are not different impressions, one to each (instant of) experience; else, we should have a postulation of many, (where a single one may suffice).

V.121. Knowledge of the external is not indispensible (to constitute a Body): trees, shrubs, climbers, annulas, trees with invisible flowers, grasses, creepers, etc., (which have internal consciousness), are also, sites of experiencer and experience; as in the former case

V.123. Not merely through a Body is there susceptibility of Merit and Demerit; for the Scripture tells us the distinction.

V.124. Among the three there is a threefold distribution; the Body of merit, the Body of experience, and the Body of both.

(There are three kinds of bodies. 'All the bodies' refers to those that are good, medium, and weak. The three kinds are:

1. The body of action is the one dispassionate people of higher maturity possess, such as great sages. Life and knowledge is given through it.

2. The body of experience is something all the animals and human beings possess with which they are dragged into sensual pleasures and satisfaction. Elementary experiences of life are acquired through it.

3. Both bodies are in possession of those who are in the path of wisdom, who are prone to dispassion, but also take active participation in life.)

V.125. Not any one (of these), moreover, is that of the apathetic (unconditioned).

(The fourth kind of the body that is mentioned here, is that of the attained yogis, it belongs to the winners over unconscious nature, those who have matured completely in *Prakriti* and overcame its whole realm of experience. The ones who have attained the most supreme insight have this kind of a body, the ones that are unaffected by any merits or demerits.)

V.126. Eternity does not (as alleged by those who wish to establish the existence of a Lord,) belong to knowledge (*buddhi*), even in the case of a particular site, (viz., that of the supposed Lord); as is the case with fire.

V.127. And, because the site (viz., the supposed Lord,) is unreal, (it matters not, in the present instance, whether knowledge may be eternal, or not).

V.128. The superhuman powers of concentration (yogic powers (siddhi)), just like the effects of drugs, are not to be gainsaid.

V.129. Thought does not belong to the Elements; for it is not found in them separately, or, moreover, in the state of combination, - or moreover, in the state of combination.

(Transcendental Soul, *Purusha*, does not invoke the consciousness in a being. Since consciousness is not to be found in individual elements, either, a connection of them is also not possible because nothing can be the consequence if there is no cause. The materialistic view is refuted with this.)

VI

VI.1. Soul is; for there is no proof that it does not.

(Soul exists because we affirm it every time when we say 'I'. There is no proof that would refute the experience of 'self'. Therefore, all we should do to be authentic in our Soul is to be different from everything else: from thoughts and thought contents, outer objects, and their influences. It is all *Prakriti*. The Soul is a wider whole that exceeds, and therefore, engenders all of it. What it primarily engenders is our essence.)

VI.2. This (Soul) is different from the Body; because of heterogeneousness, (or complete difference between the two).

VI.3. Also because it (Soul) is expressed by means of the sixth (or possessive,) case.

(When man speaks of themselves he uses the possessive adjectives, such as: "This is my body", "This is what I feel", "This is my knowledge", etc. It would be pointless if human essence were identical with the body.)

VI.5. Through the entire cessation of pain, there is done what was to be done.

VI.6. Not such desire for pleasure is there to Soul, as there is annoyance from Pain.

VI.7. For (only) someone, somewhere, is happy.

VI.8. It (Pleasure,) is also mixed with Pain; therefore the discriminating throw it to the side of (and reckon it as so much,) Pain.

VI.9. If you say that this (cessation of Pain) is not Soul's aim, inasmuch as there is no acquisition of Pleasure, then it is not as you say; for there are two kinds (of things desired).

(The purpose of removing pain is not to attain pleasure. There are two aims man must strive toward: 1. "I would like to be happy". 2. "I would not like to be unhappy." Only the desire for the second aim is profound, sincere, and permanent. Therefore, the issue is always about the cessation of suffering rather than attaining happiness.)

VI.11. Through it (the Pain,) be the property of something else, yet it exists in it (the Soul) through non-discrimination.

(Although characteristics (of pleasure and pain) belong to the intellect only (*buddhi*), they are reflected in the human Soul only as a result of its identification with natural phenomena, because of the immaturity of the mind to discriminate its own Soul, the source of its consciousness and existence, from what it is not.)

VI.12. Non-discrimination (of Soul from Nature) is beginningless; because, otherwise, two objections would present themselves.

(Time originates at the point of non-discrimination between *Purusha* and *Prakriti*. That is why, non-discrimination does not originate in time.)

VI.13. It (non-discrimination,) cannot be everlasting (in the same manner) as the Soul is; else, it could not be cut short, (as we affirm that it can be).

(*Prakriti*, and together with it the unconsciousness, *avidya*, time and non-discrimination, are like a sphere: they exist although they have neither the beginning nor the end; which does not make them infinite.)

VI.14. It (Bondage,) is annihilable by the allotted cause, (viz., discrimination of Soul from Nature); as darkness is (annihilable by the allotted cause, Light).

(Since darkness can only be banished by the light, the bondage of human Soul can, too, be ended only by the consciousness with which the man can distinguish themselves from everything else. The spherical nature of being-in-ignorance, which has neither the beginning, nor the end, can only be finalized by overcoming the realm of its phenomena, by conscious overcoming of the mind that receives and reflects all the impressions of existence, its transcendence of samsaric, circular, and, beginningless phenomena.)

VI.16.Since it cannot be (accounted for) in any other way, it is non-discrimination alone that is (the *cause* of) Bondage, (which cannot be innate).

VI.17.Further, Bondage does not again attach to the liberated; because there is Scripture for its non-recurrence.

VI.18. Else, it (liberation,) would not be Soul's aim, (which it is).

VI.19. What happened to both would be alike, (if liberation would be perishable).

VI.20.Liberation is nothing other than the removal of the obstacle (to the Soul's recognition of itself as free).

VI.22. This (attainment of Liberation, on the mere *hearing* of the truth,) is no necessity; for there are three sorts of those competent (to apprehend the truth; but not all are qualified to appropriate it, on merely hearing it).

(Some are good at understanding, some mediocre, and some are slow.)

VI.23.Of others (viz., other means besides hearing), for the sake of confirmation, (there is need).

(The discipline of meditation is necessary.)

VI.24. There is no (absolute) necessity that what is steady and promoting ease should be a (*particular*) posture, (such as any of those referred to in Book III).

(It is important that it is an upright posture, and not lying down.)

VI.25.Mind without an object is Meditation.

VI.26. If you say that even both ways there is no difference, it is not so: there is a difference, through the exclusion (in the one case,) of the tinge (of reflected pain which exists in the other case).

(Although the human Soul is transcendental and truly independent, it is necessary to reach this experience through meditation, directly.)

VI.27.Though it (Soul,) be unassociated, still there is a tingeing (reflexionally,) through Non-discrimination.

VI.28.As is the case with the Hibiscus and the crystal (Book I., 19, c.), there is not a tinge, but a fancy (that there is such).

VI.29.It (viz., the aforesaid tinge,) is debarred by Meditation, Restraint, Practice, and Apathy.

VI.30.It is by the exclusion of dissolution and distraction, say the teachers.

(Distraction of the mind with dreams and waking state is removed through the practice of meditation. The alternating states of sleeping, deep sleep, and waking state are substituted with the fourth, steadfast and always alert state called *turiya*.)

VI.31.There is no rule about localities; for it is from tranquility of Mind.

VI.39. *Sattva* or Purity and the others (*gunas*) are not properties of it (viz., Nature, *Prakriti*); because they are its *essences.*

VI.41.The diversity of creation is in consequence of the diversity of Desert.

VI.43. Since (or when,) the emancipated has understood (that he never was really otherwise), Nature does not create; just as, in the world, (a minister does not toil, when the king's purpose has been accomplished).

VI.50.This (Soul), is the shape of Thought, discrepant from the non-intelligent, reveals the non-intelligent.

VI.54.*Aham-kâra* (Self-consciousness), not Soul, is the agent, not *Purusha.*

VI.55.Experience ceases at (discrimination of) Soul, (as being quite distinct from Nature); since it arises from its (Soul's, *Purusha's*) Desert, (which is not, *really*, Soul's, but which, while Non-discrimination lasts, is made over to Soul; just as the fruits of the acts of a king's ministers are made over to the king).

VI.56.Even from the world of moon (from heaven), there is return (to mundane existence); because of there really being a cause (of such return).

VI.57.Not by counsel of (supermundane) people is there effectuation (of Emancipation); just as in the former case, (the case, viz., of counsel given by mundane instructors).

VI.58. There is Scripture (declaratory) of Emancipation, (on going to the world of *Brahma*); this (Emancipation) being effected (more readily in that world than in this, but only) by intermediacy (of the appropriate means).

(Liberation may be reached in the world of *Brahma*, as well, but the way for its attainment is the same everywhere: by acquiring knowledge, the experience of beingness (work), and meditation. Liberation cannot be attained simply by going to the higher world.)

VI.64.The effectuation of works is dependent on the agent Self-consciousness (*aham-kâra*), not dependent on a Lord; because there is no proof (of the reality as such). [63]

---

[63] The meaning of this is: God, if he is, the Absolute, never created the world because during such an act he would only annul and divide his absolute nature. In reality only God (the Absolute) exists, while the emergent world and separate individuals are nothing but illusionary projections of the ego, *aham-kâra* (John

VI.66. The rest is from Mind (*mahat*), (the Great Principle).

(Independently of the created world, induced by *aham-kâra*, there are other consequences, such as maintenance and management, which also originate from *mahat*, the supreme principle of *Prakriti*. The idea of god Vishnu, the preserver god, came about as a result of this principle.)

VI.70. Be that the one way, or the other, (whether the connection of *Purusha* and *Prakriti* is to do with karma, non-discrimination, or the subtle body that holds on to the experiences) the cutting short thereof (viz., of the relation between Nature and Soul,) is Soul's (*Purusha*'s) aim; the cutting short thereof is Soul's (*Purusha*'s) aim.

10:30,34,38.). It is the rudimentary mechanics of ontology: the more we are closed off into our subjectivity, the more objective world exists for us; the more we are objective, aware of ourselves, the more the world disappears and with it any difference between us and the divine whole.

BIBLIOGRAPHY

Richard Garbe: *Die Sânkhya Philosophie*, Leipzig, 1917.

Philosophy of Ancient India, Harvard Oriental Series, 1895.

S. S. Suryanarayana Sastri: *The Sânkhya Karika of Isvara Krsna*, University of Madras, 1930.

J. R. Ballantyne: *The Sânkhya Aphorisms of Kapila*, London, 1885. Reprint izd. Parimal Publications, Delhi, 1995.

Swami Virupakshananda: *Samkhya Karika of Isvara Krsna with The Tattva Kaumudi of Sri Vacaspati Misra*, Sri Ramakrishna Math, Mylapore, Madras, 1995.

Patanjali: *Yoga sutras*.

Yoga: The Alpha and the Omega by Osho, 10 volumes series

Mircea Eliade: *Yoga: Immortality and Freedom; A History of Religious Ideas.*

Indian Philosophy by Sarvepalli Radhakrishnan

P. D. Ouspensky: The fourth way;

Jane Roberts: *Seth speaks - Eternal Validity of the Soul.*

Made in the USA
Las Vegas, NV
15 October 2023

79086166R00229